Hi igies

Ha n

Another World!

11

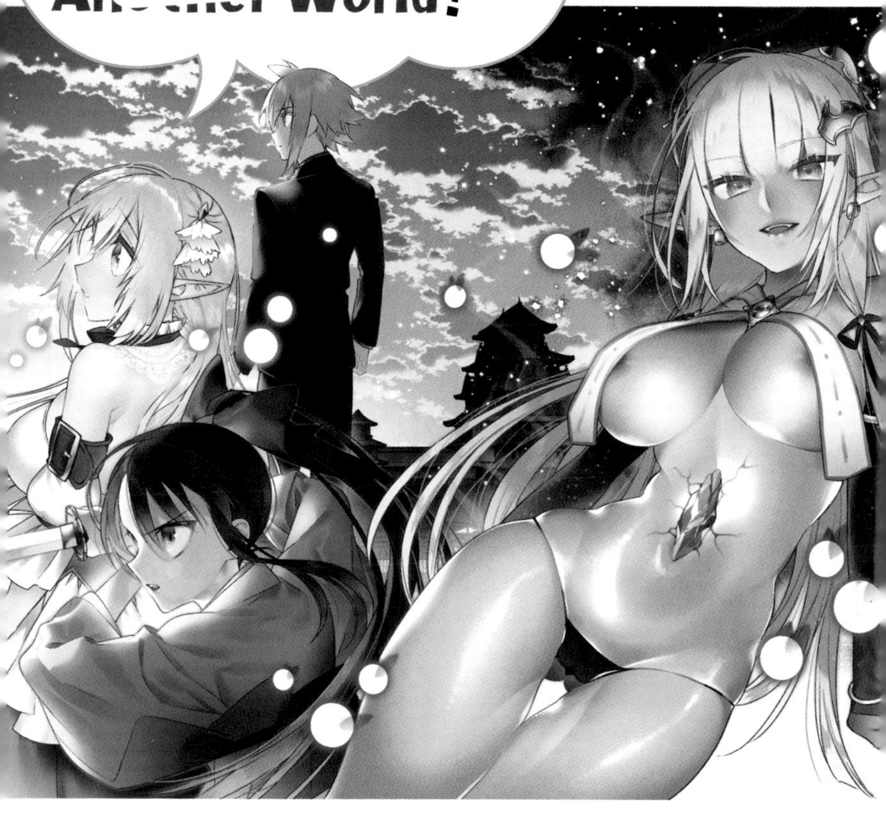

STORY BY

Riku Misora

ART BY

Kotaro Yamada

CHARACTER DESIGN BY

Sacraneco

CONTENTS

HIGH SCHOOL PRODIGIES HAVE IT EASY EVEN IN ANOTHER WORLD!

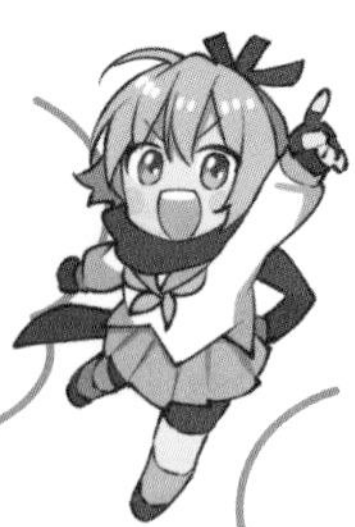

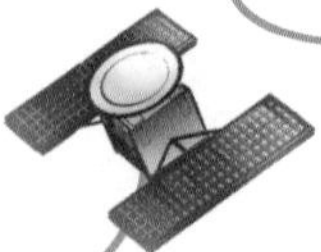

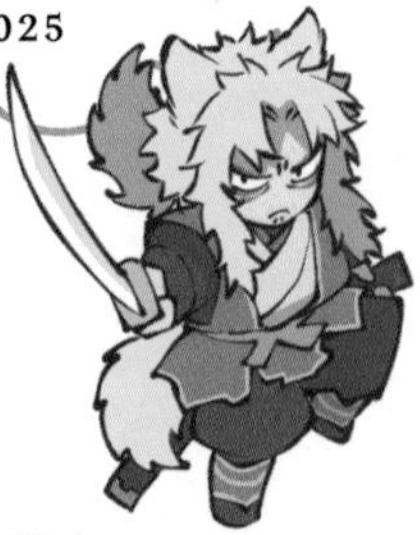

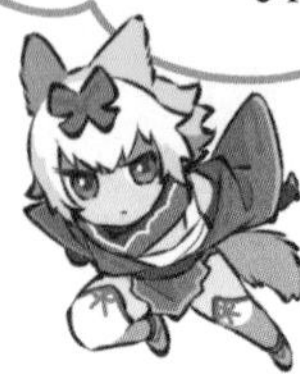

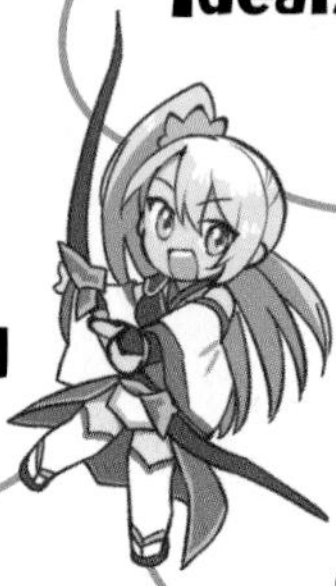

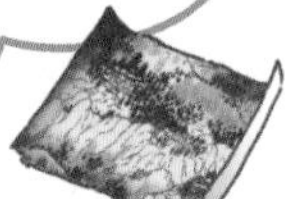

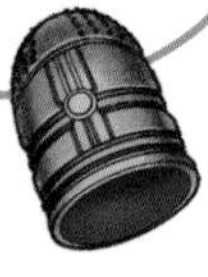

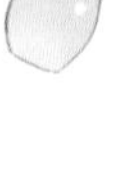

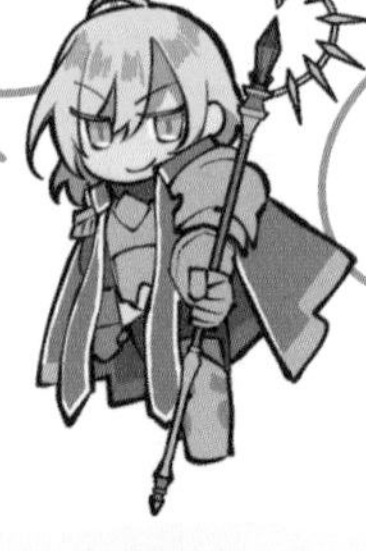

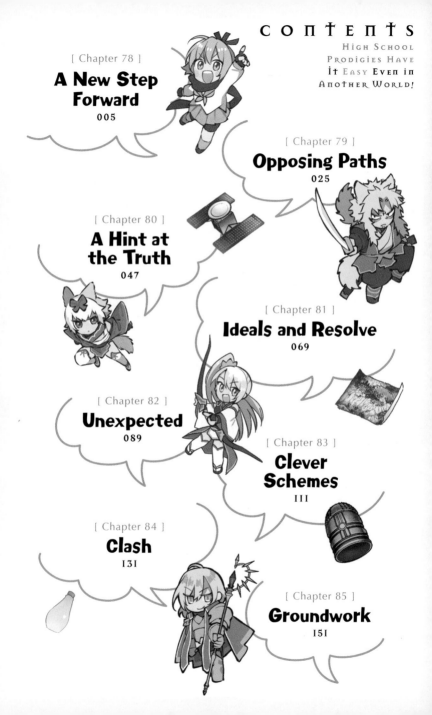

HIGH SCHOOL PRODIGIES HAVE IT EASY EVEN IN ANOTHER WORLD!

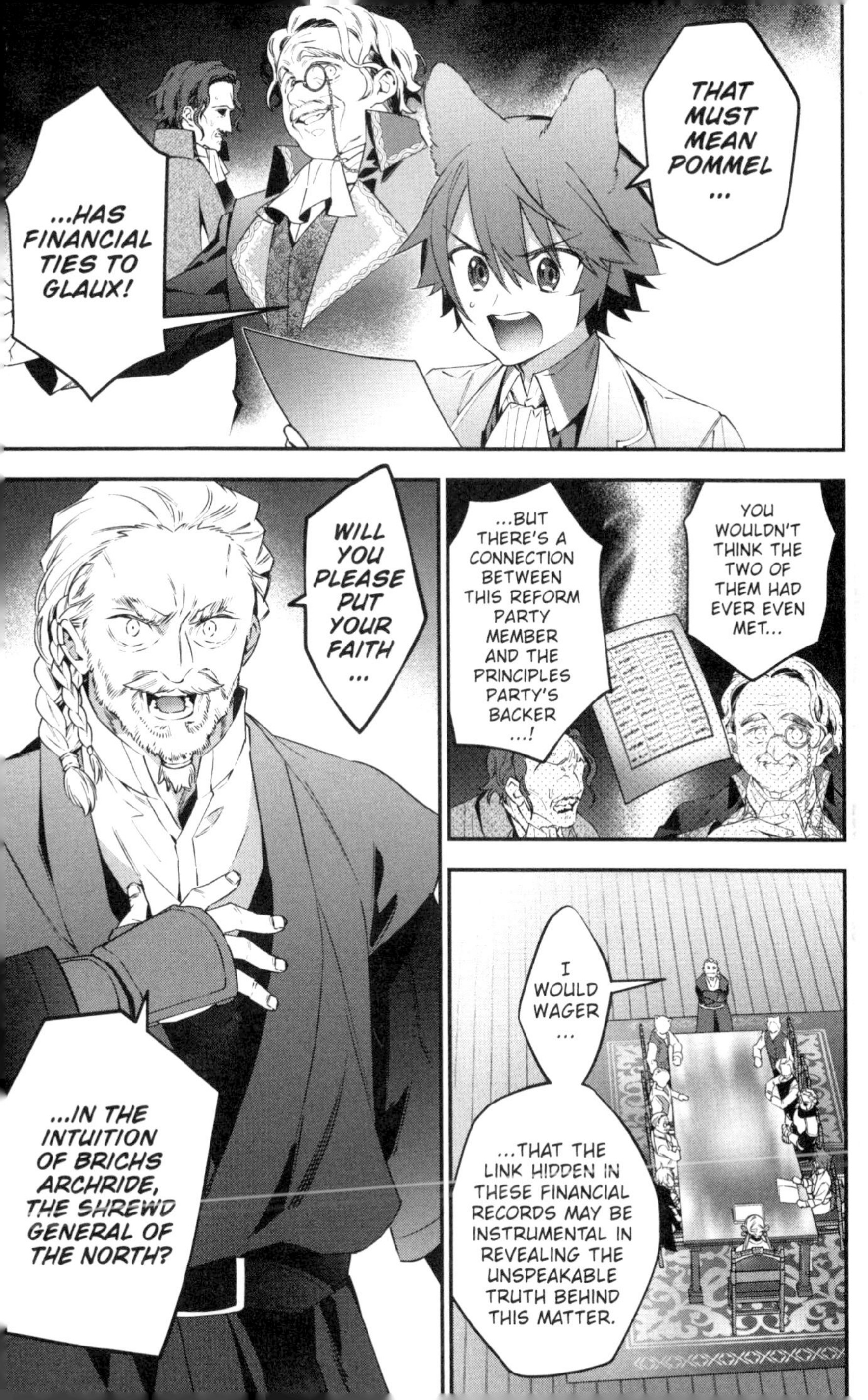
THAT MUST MEAN POMMEL...
...HAS FINANCIAL TIES TO GLAUX!
YOU WOULDN'T THINK THE TWO OF THEM HAD EVER EVEN MET...
...BUT THERE'S A CONNECTION BETWEEN THIS REFORM PARTY MEMBER AND THE PRINCIPLES PARTY'S BACKER...!
I WOULD WAGER...
...THAT THE LINK HIDDEN IN THESE FINANCIAL RECORDS MAY BE INSTRUMENTAL IN REVEALING THE UNSPEAKABLE TRUTH BEHIND THIS MATTER.
WILL YOU PLEASE PUT YOUR FAITH...
...IN THE INTUITION OF BRICHS ARCHRIDE, THE SHREWD GENERAL OF THE NORTH?

CHAPTER 78: A NEW STEP FORWARD

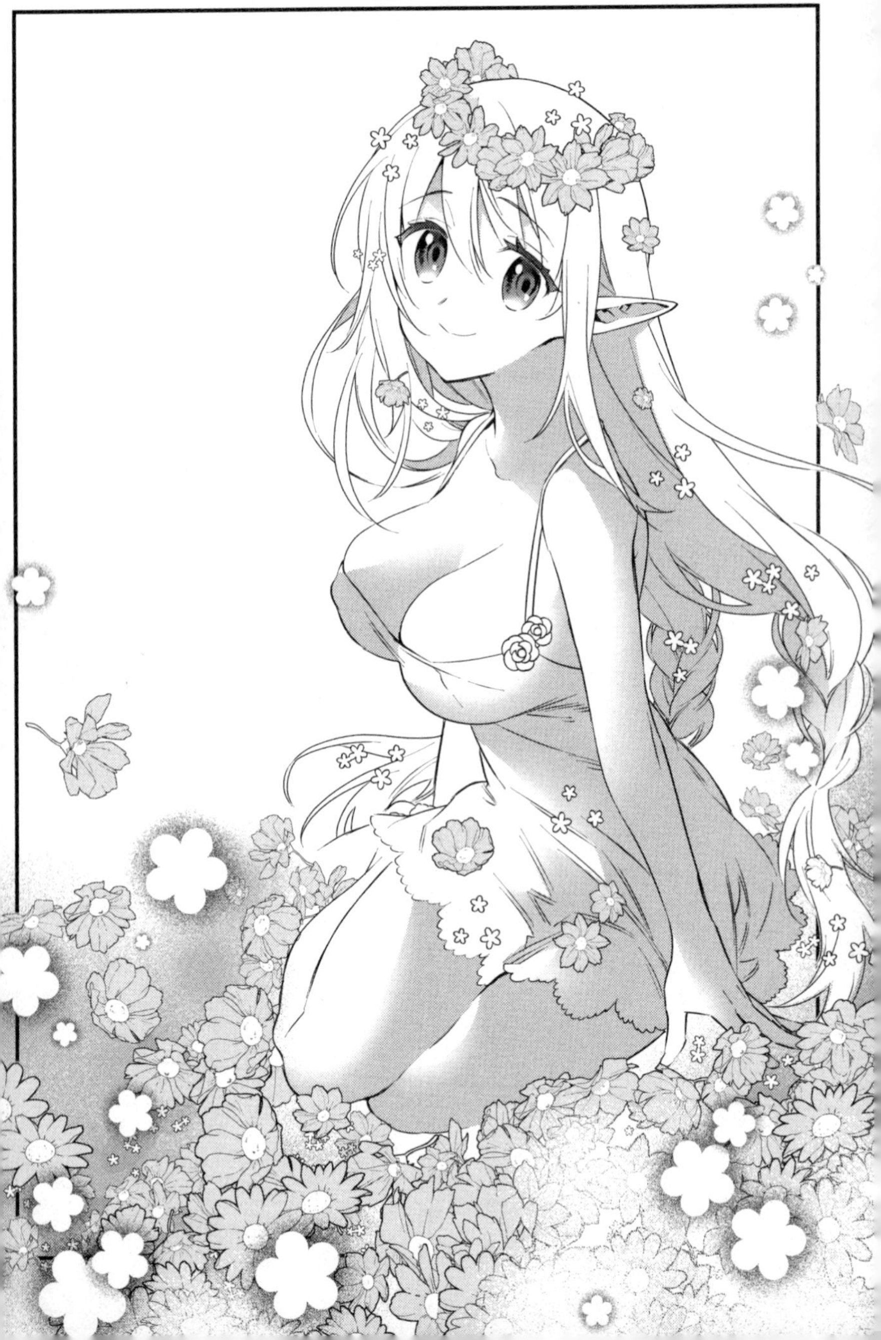

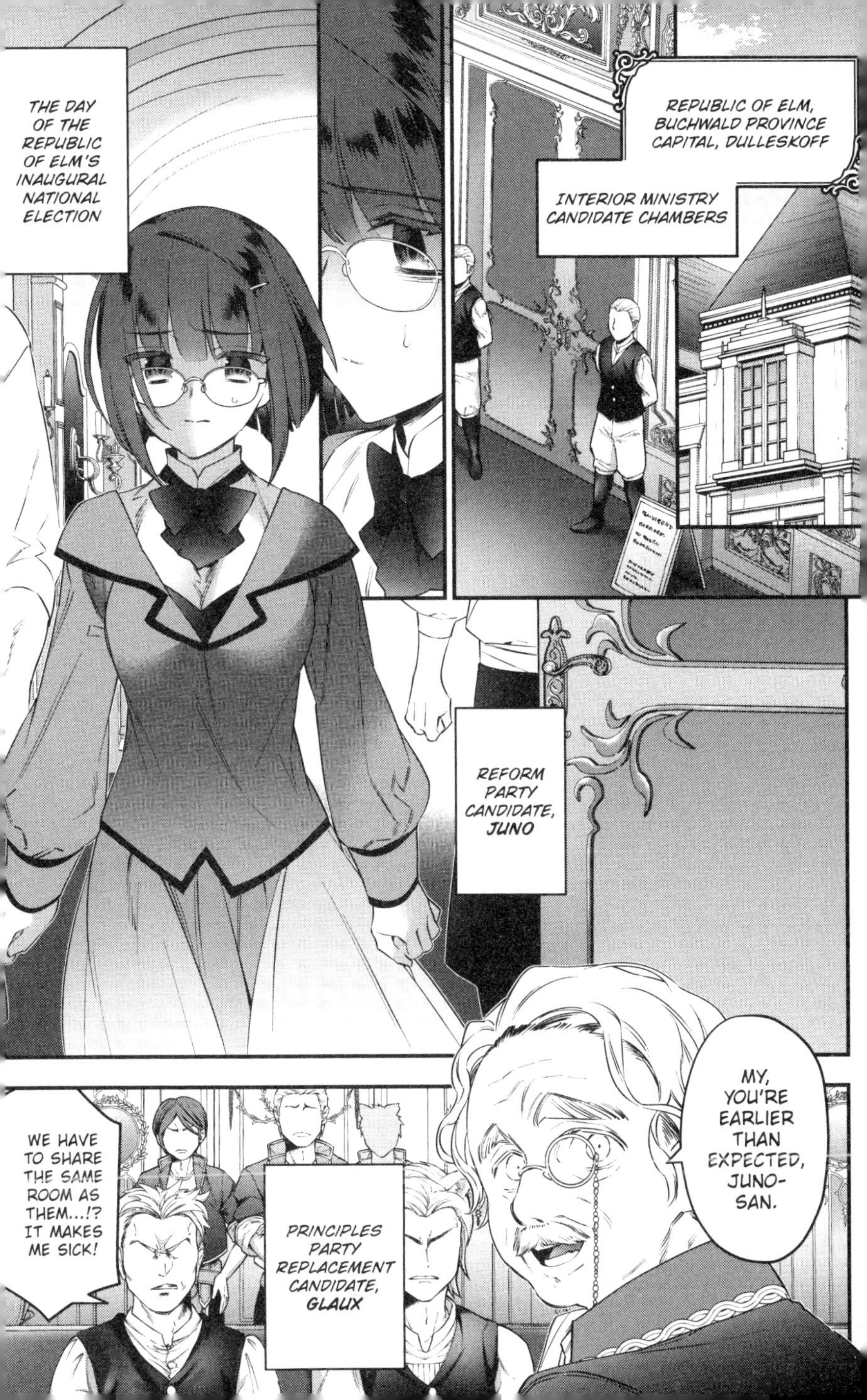
REPUBLIC OF ELM, BUCHWALD PROVINCE CAPITAL, DULLESKOFF
INTERIOR MINISTRY CANDIDATE CHAMBERS
THE DAY OF THE REPUBLIC OF ELM'S INAUGURAL NATIONAL ELECTION
REFORM PARTY CANDIDATE, JUNO
MY, YOU'RE EARLIER THAN EXPECTED, JUNO-SAN.
PRINCIPLES PARTY REPLACEMENT CANDIDATE, GLAUX
WE HAVE TO SHARE THE SAME ROOM AS THEM...!? IT MAKES ME SICK!

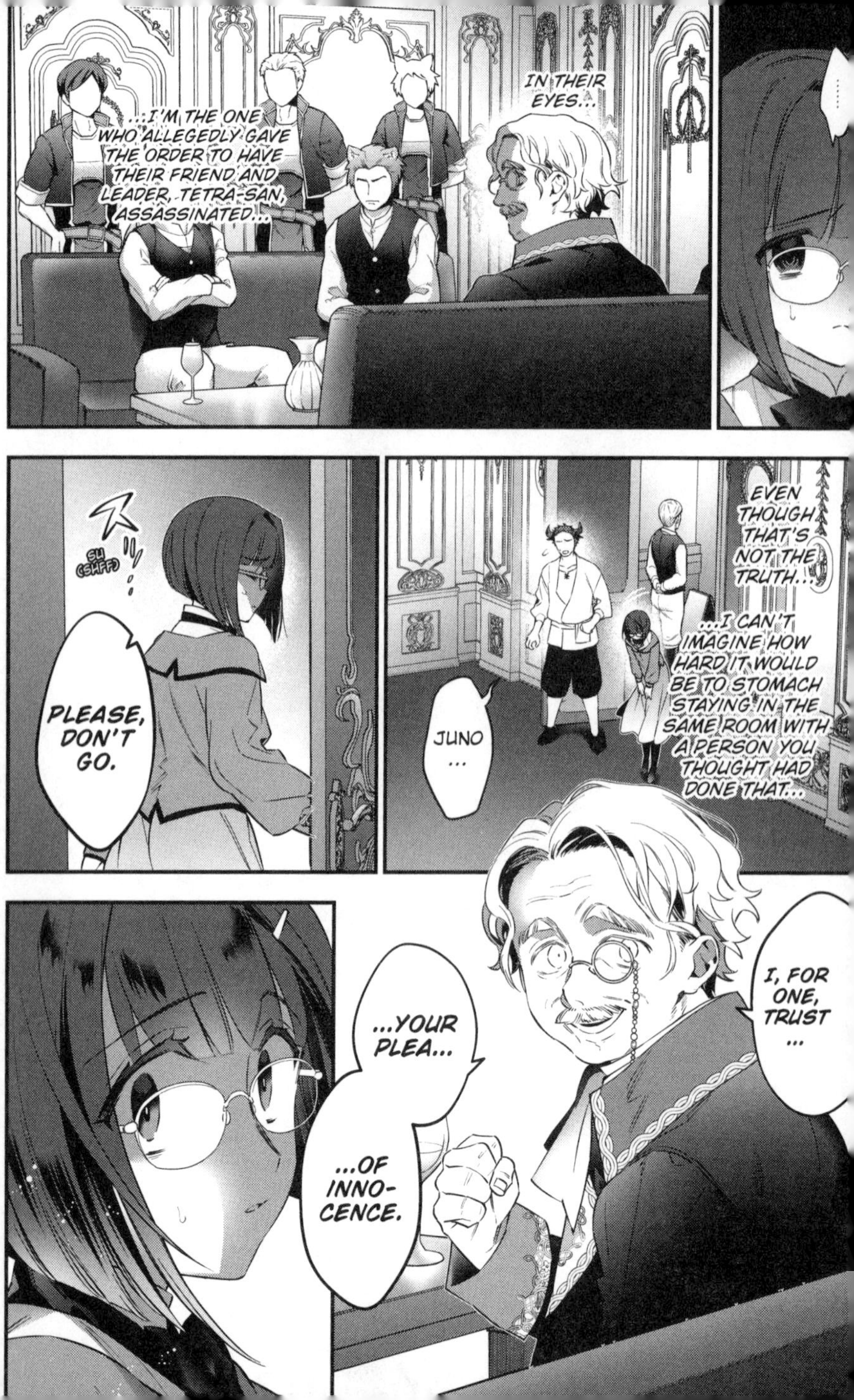
IN THEIR EYES...
...I'M THE ONE WHO ALLEGEDLY GAVE THE ORDER TO HAVE THEIR FRIEND AND LEADER, TETRA-SAN, ASSASSINATED...
EVEN THOUGH THAT'S NOT THE TRUTH...
...I CAN'T IMAGINE HOW HARD IT WOULD BE TO STOMACH STAYING IN THE SAME ROOM WITH A PERSON YOU THOUGHT HAD DONE THAT...
JUNO...
SU (SHFF)
PLEASE, DON'T GO.
I, FOR ONE, TRUST...
...YOUR PLEA...
...OF INNOCENCE.

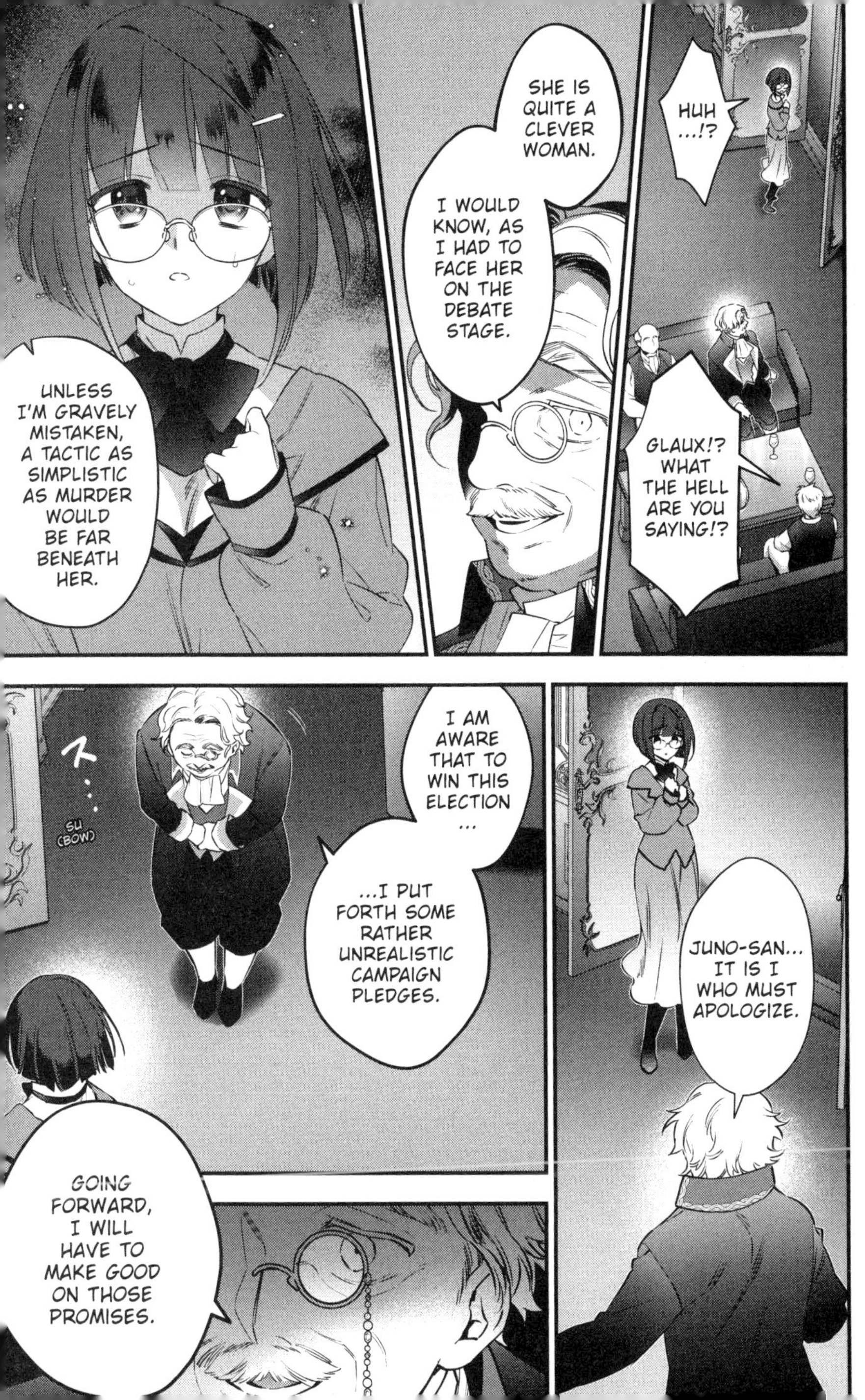
HUH ...!?
GLAUX!? WHAT THE HELL ARE YOU SAYING!?
SHE IS QUITE A CLEVER WOMAN.
I WOULD KNOW, AS I HAD TO FACE HER ON THE DEBATE STAGE.
UNLESS I'M GRAVELY MISTAKEN, A TACTIC AS SIMPLISTIC AS MURDER WOULD BE FAR BENEATH HER.
JUNO-SAN... IT IS I WHO MUST APOLOGIZE.
I AM AWARE THAT TO WIN THIS ELECTION ...
...I PUT FORTH SOME RATHER UNREALISTIC CAMPAIGN PLEDGES.
ス...
SU (BOW)
GOING FORWARD, I WILL HAVE TO MAKE GOOD ON THOSE PROMISES.

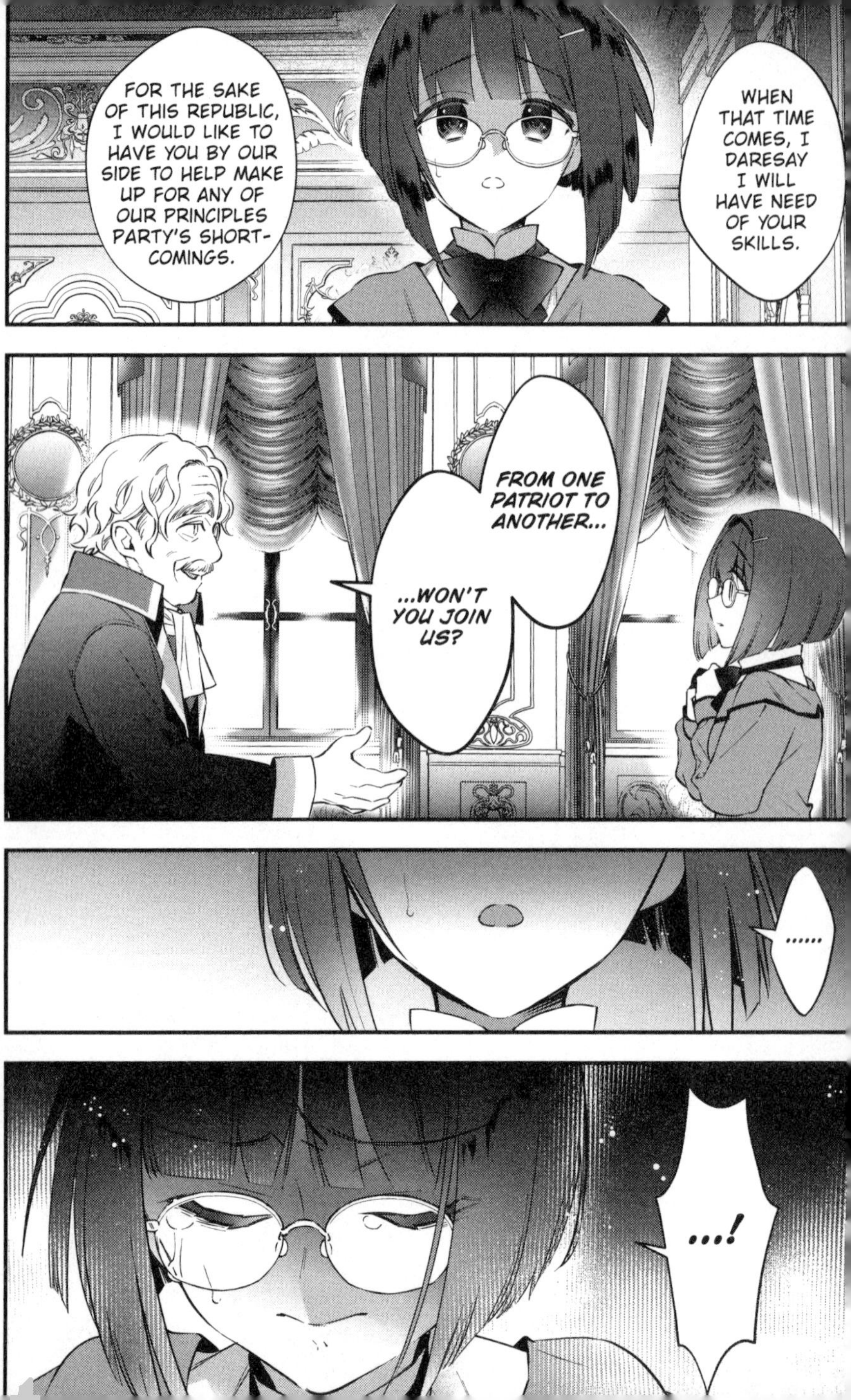
WHEN THAT TIME COMES, I DARESAY I WILL HAVE NEED OF YOUR SKILLS.
FOR THE SAKE OF THIS REPUBLIC, I WOULD LIKE TO HAVE YOU BY OUR SIDE TO HELP MAKE UP FOR ANY OF OUR PRINCIPLES PARTY'S SHORT-COMINGS.
FROM ONE PATRIOT TO ANOTHER...
...WON'T YOU JOIN US?
......
...!

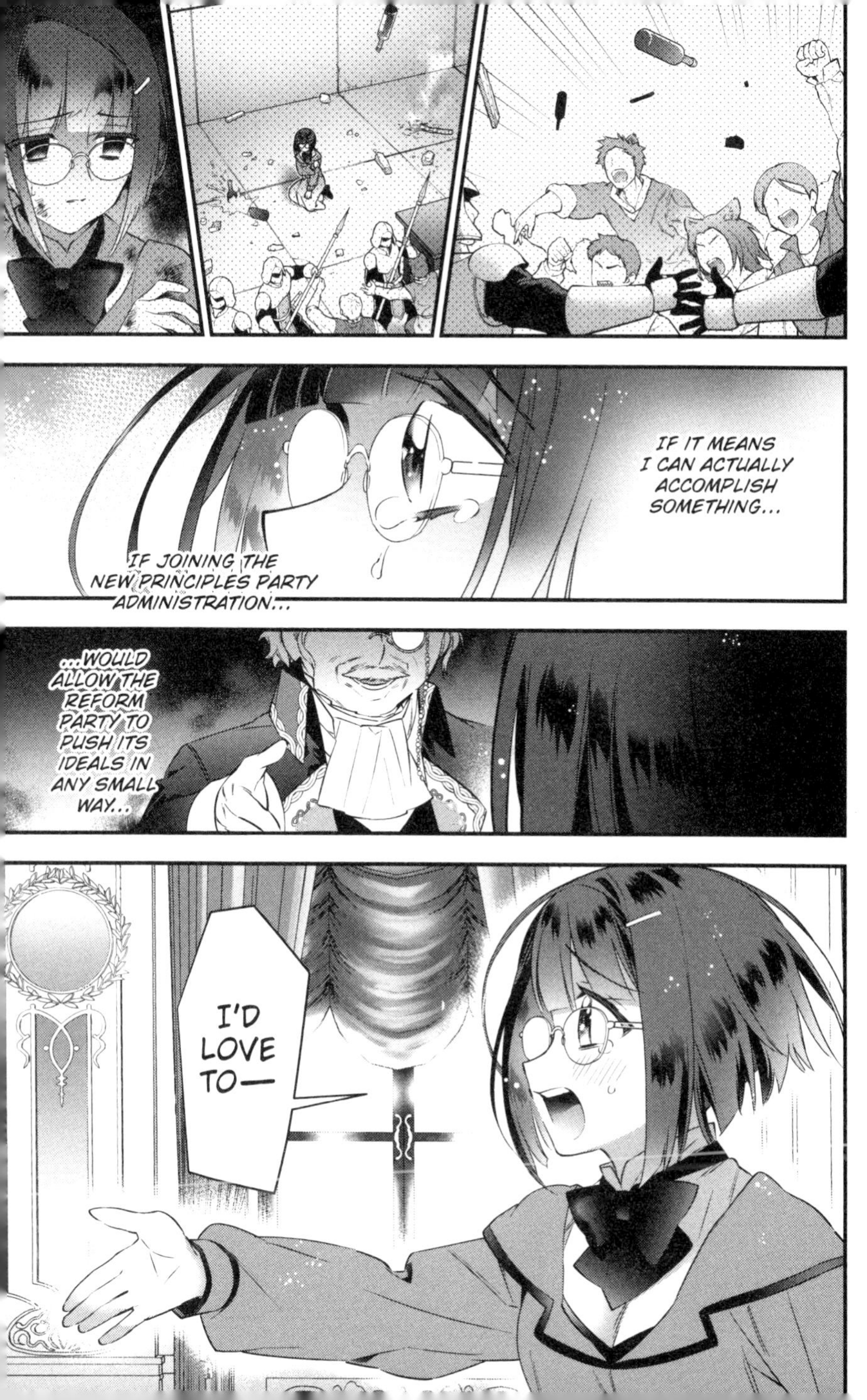
IF IT MEANS I CAN ACTUALLY ACCOMPLISH SOMETHING...
IF JOINING THE NEW PRINCIPLES PARTY ADMINISTRATION...
...WOULD ALLOW THE REFORM PARTY TO PUSH ITS IDEALS IN ANY SMALL WAY...
I'D LOVE TO—

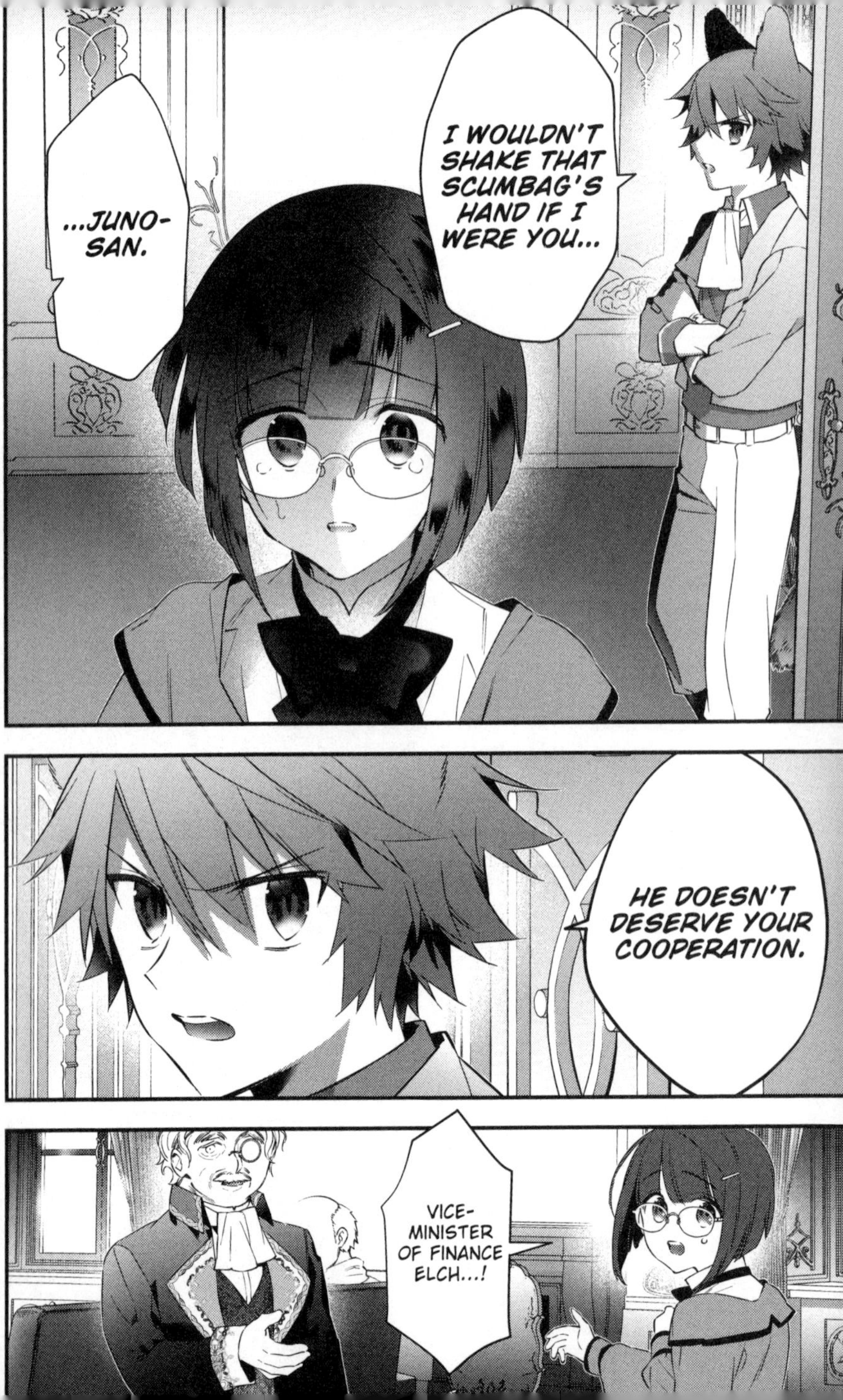
I WOULDN'T SHAKE THAT SCUMBAG'S HAND IF I WERE YOU...
...JUNO-SAN.
HE DOESN'T DESERVE YOUR COOPERATION.
VICE-MINISTER OF FINANCE ELCH...!

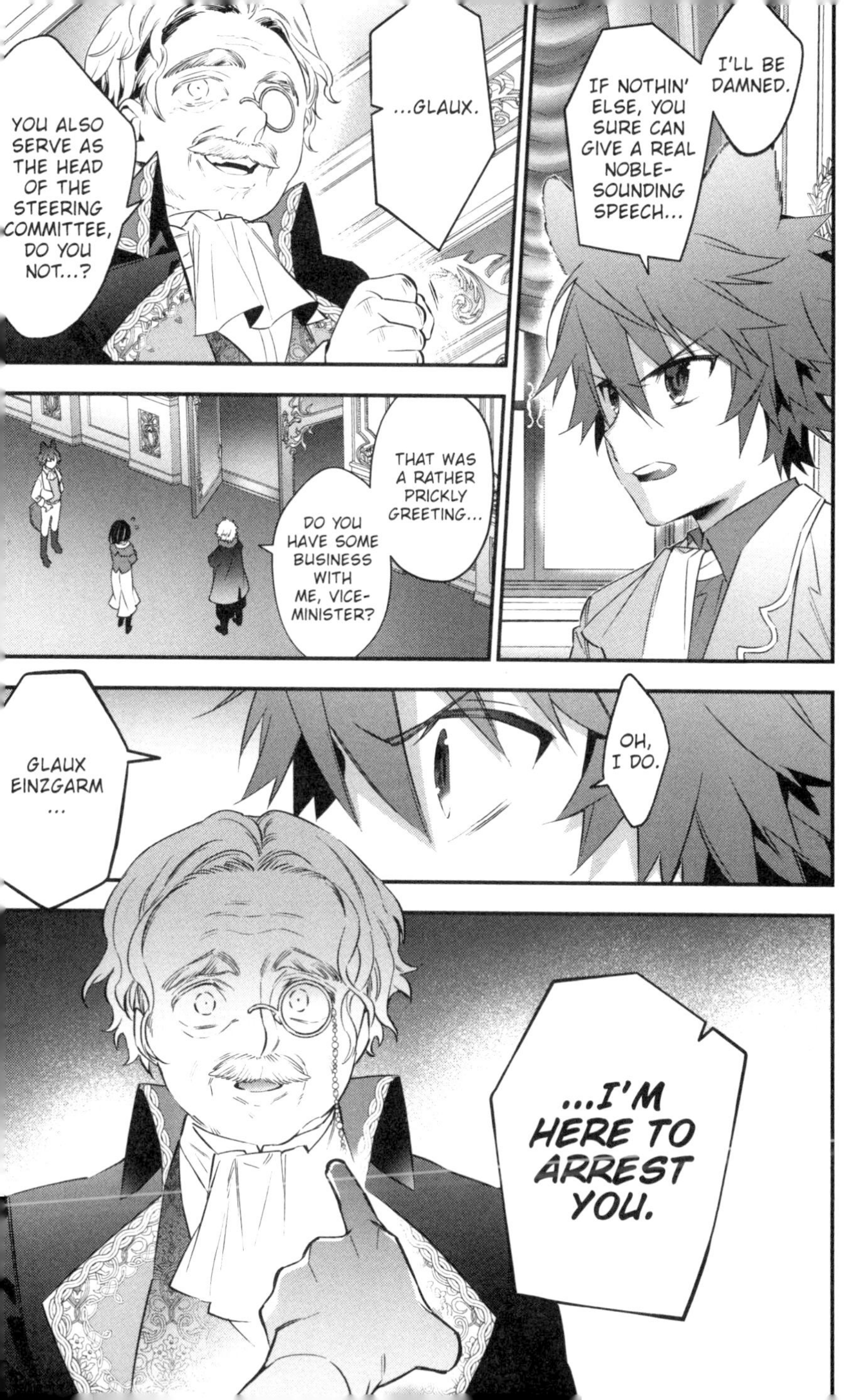

I'LL BE DAMNED.
IF NOTHIN' ELSE, YOU SURE CAN GIVE A REAL NOBLE-SOUNDING SPEECH...
...GLAUX.
YOU ALSO SERVE AS THE HEAD OF THE STEERING COMMITTEE, DO YOU NOT...?
THAT WAS A RATHER PRICKLY GREETING...
DO YOU HAVE SOME BUSINESS WITH ME, VICE-MINISTER?
OH, I DO.
GLAUX EINZGARM...
...I'M HERE TO ARREST YOU.

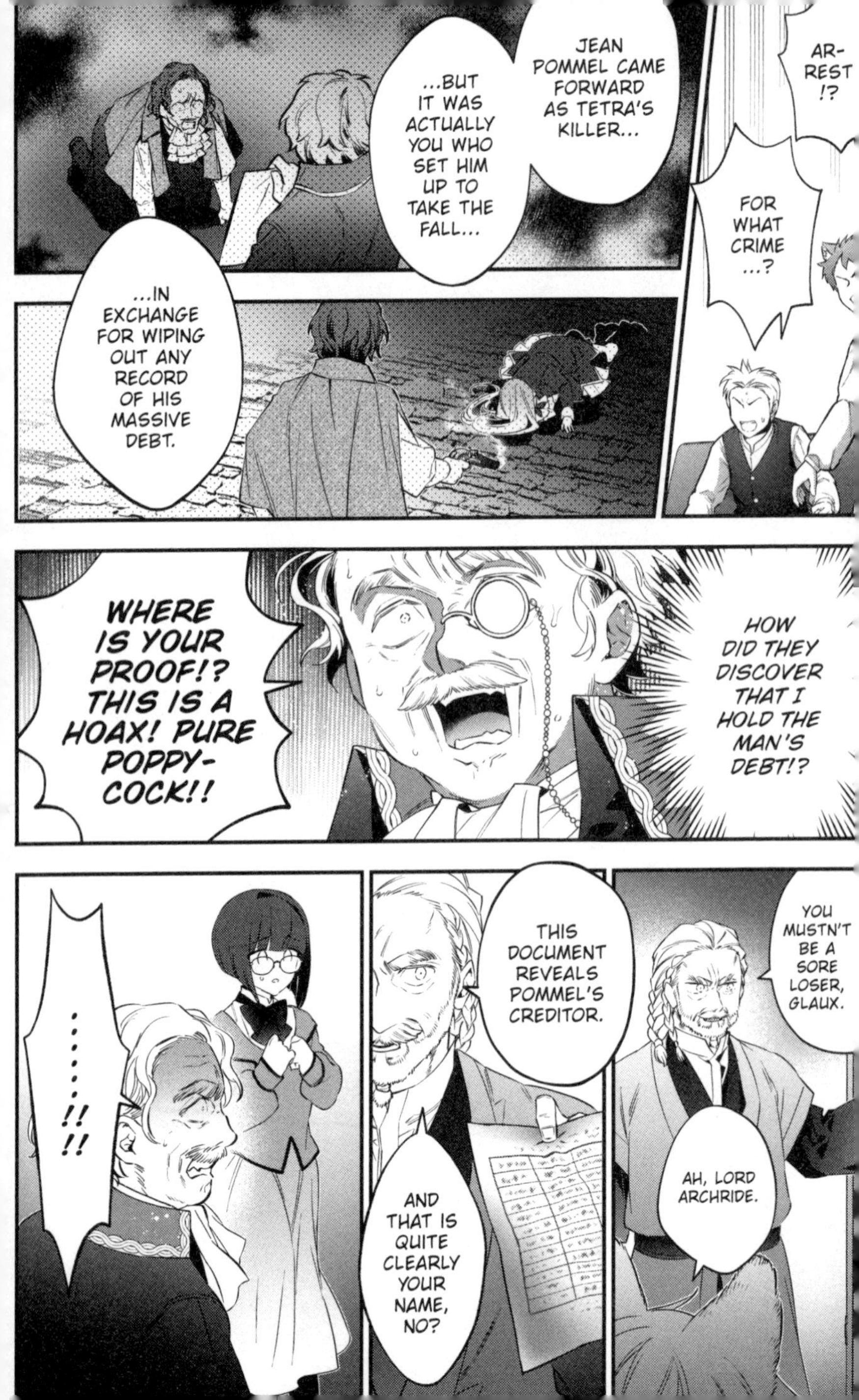
AR-REST!?
FOR WHAT CRIME...?
JEAN POMMEL CAME FORWARD AS TETRA'S KILLER...
...BUT IT WAS ACTUALLY YOU WHO SET HIM UP TO TAKE THE FALL...
...IN EXCHANGE FOR WIPING OUT ANY RECORD OF HIS MASSIVE DEBT.
HOW DID THEY DISCOVER THAT I HOLD THE MAN'S DEBT!?
WHERE IS YOUR PROOF!? THIS IS A HOAX! PURE POPPYCOCK!!
YOU MUSTN'T BE A SORE LOSER, GLAUX.
AH, LORD ARCHRIDE.
THIS DOCUMENT REVEALS POMMEL'S CREDITOR.
AND THAT IS QUITE CLEARLY YOUR NAME, NO?
......!!!!

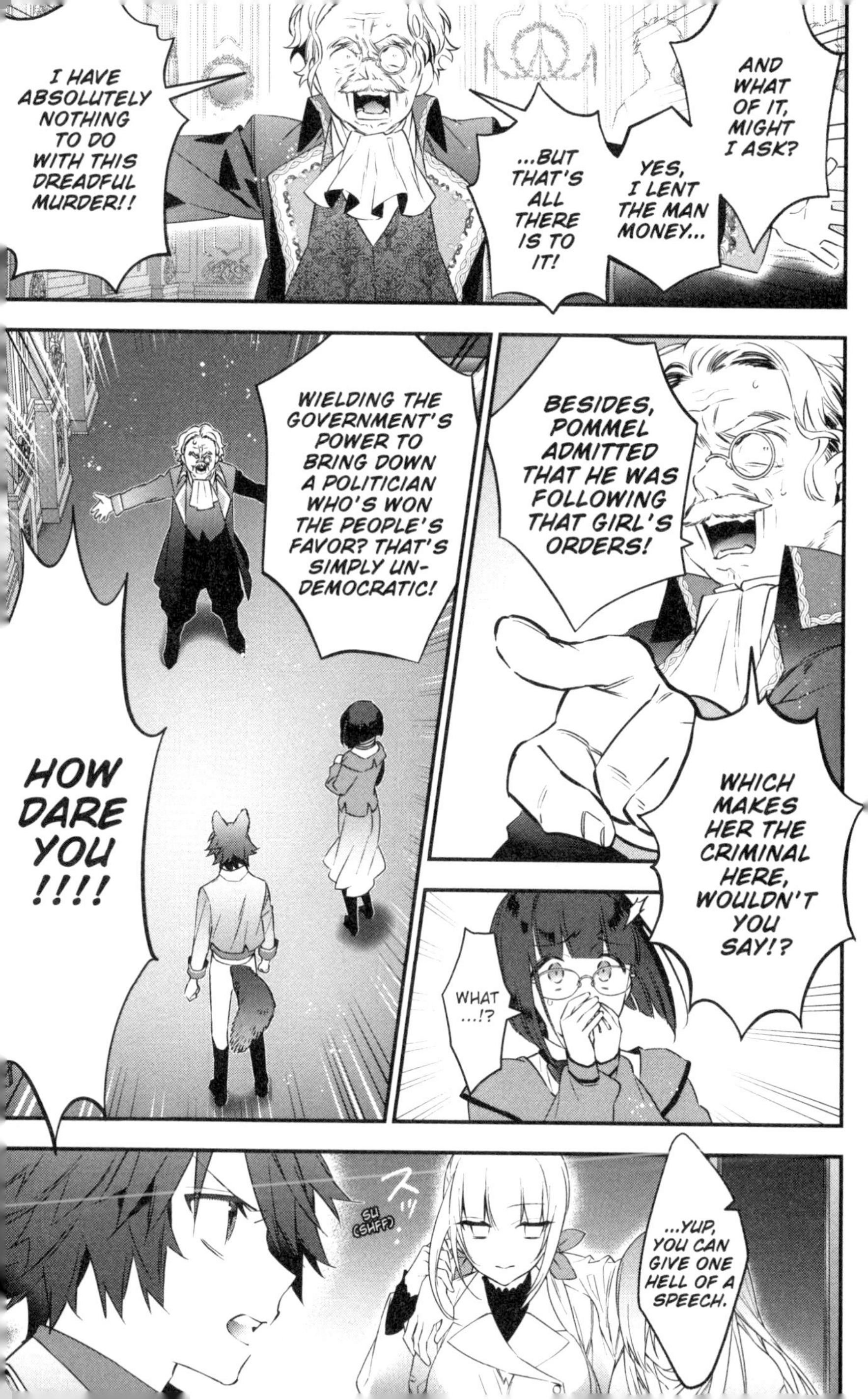
AND WHAT OF IT, MIGHT I ASK?
YES, I LENT THE MAN MONEY...
...BUT THAT'S ALL THERE IS TO IT!
I HAVE ABSOLUTELY NOTHING TO DO WITH THIS DREADFUL MURDER!!
BESIDES, POMMEL ADMITTED THAT HE WAS FOLLOWING THAT GIRL'S ORDERS!
WHICH MAKES HER THE CRIMINAL HERE, WOULDN'T YOU SAY!?
WHAT ...!?
WIELDING THE GOVERNMENT'S POWER TO BRING DOWN A POLITICIAN WHO'S WON THE PEOPLE'S FAVOR? THAT'S SIMPLY UN-DEMOCRATIC!
HOW DARE YOU !!!!
...YUP, YOU CAN GIVE ONE HELL OF A SPEECH.
SU (SHFF)

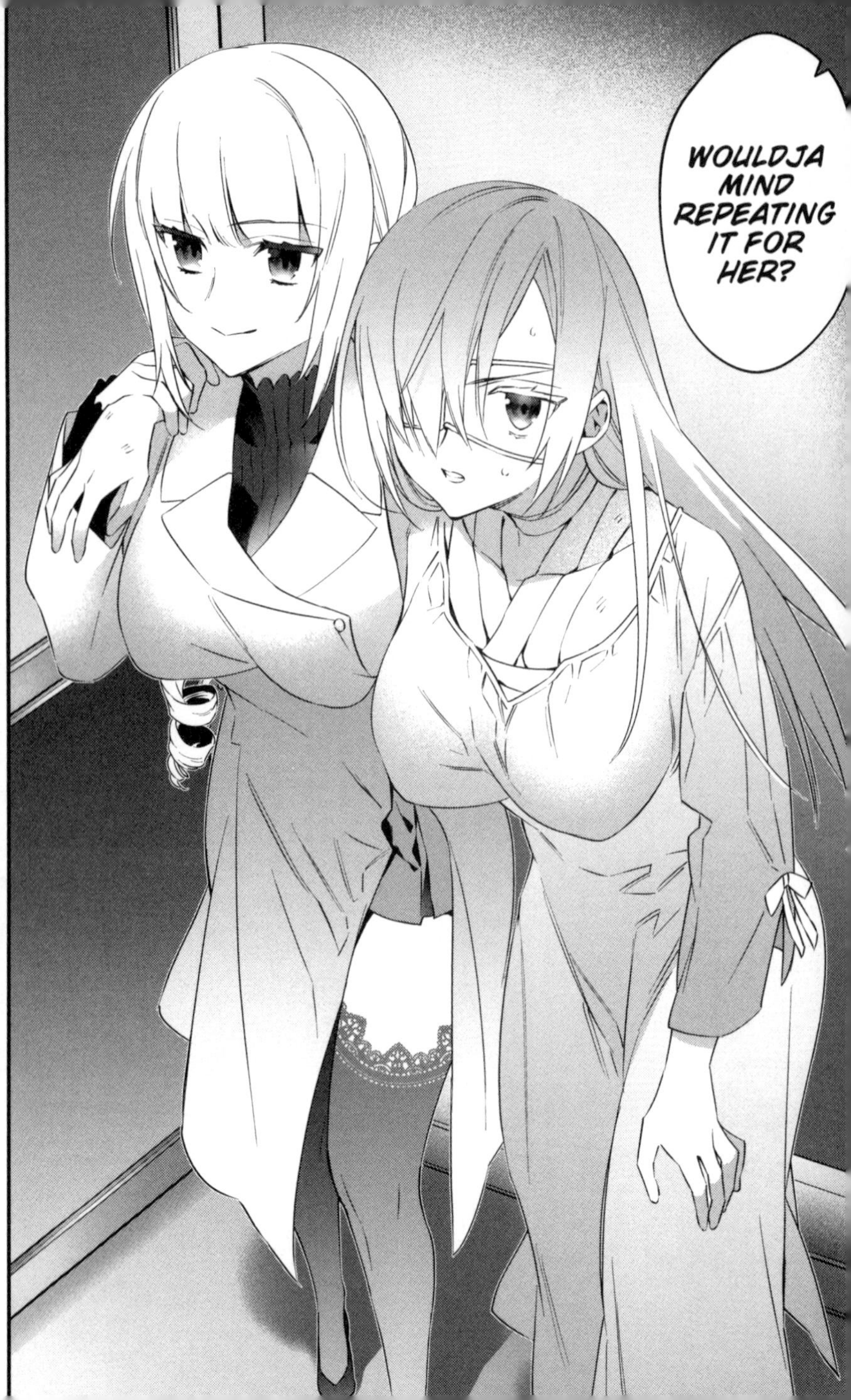
WOULDJA MIND REPEATING IT FOR HER?

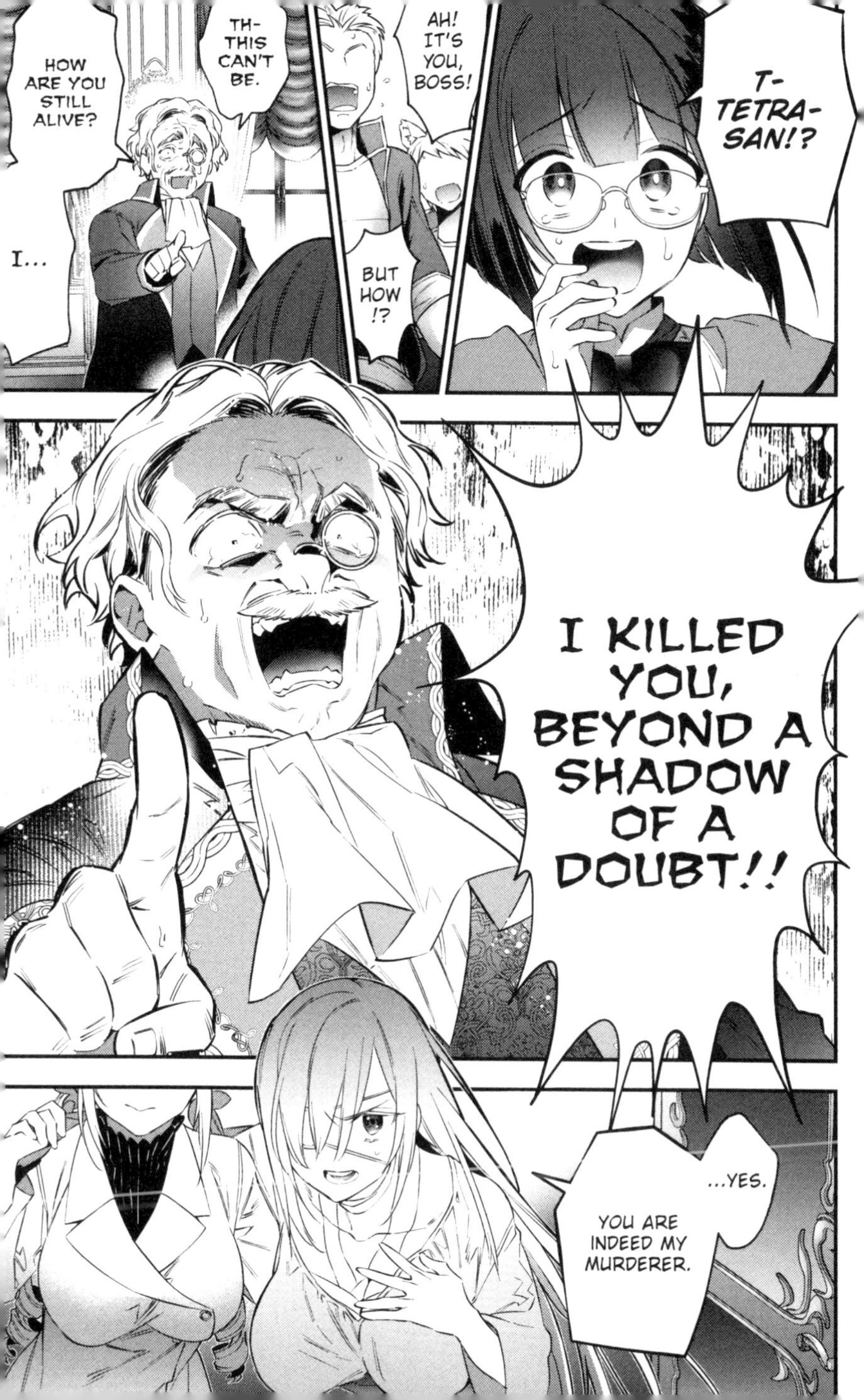
T-TETRA-SAN!?
AH! IT'S YOU, BOSS!
BUT HOW!?
TH-THIS CAN'T BE.
HOW ARE YOU STILL ALIVE?
I...
I KILLED YOU, BEYOND A SHADOW OF A DOUBT!!
...YES.
YOU ARE INDEED MY MURDERER.

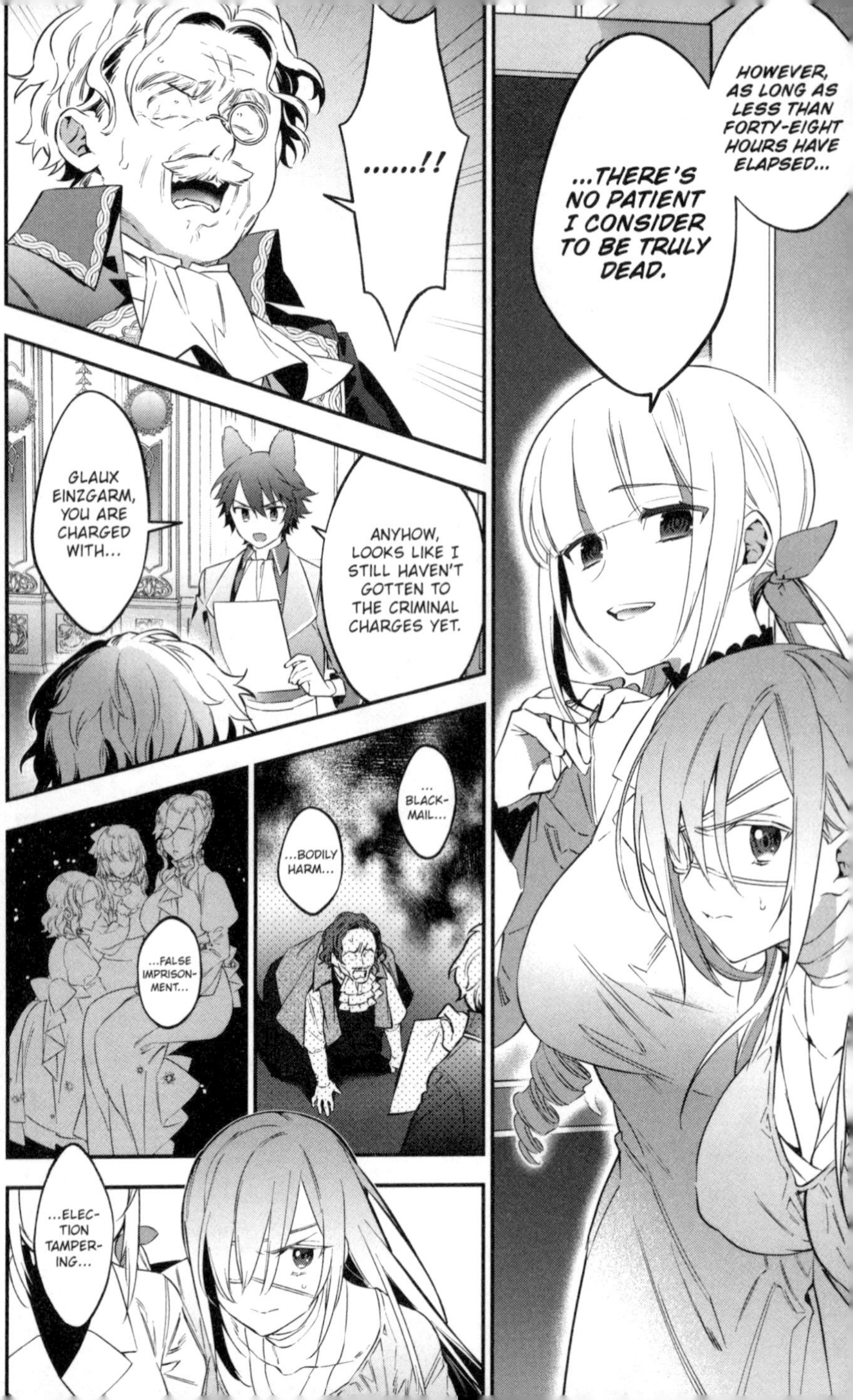
HOWEVER, AS LONG AS LESS THAN FORTY-EIGHT HOURS HAVE ELAPSED...
...THERE'S NO PATIENT I CONSIDER TO BE TRULY DEAD.
......!!
ANYHOW, LOOKS LIKE I STILL HAVEN'T GOTTEN TO THE CRIMINAL CHARGES YET.
GLAUX EINZGARM, YOU ARE CHARGED WITH...
...BLACK-MAIL...
...BODILY HARM...
...FALSE IMPRISON-MENT...
...ELEC-TION TAMPER-ING...

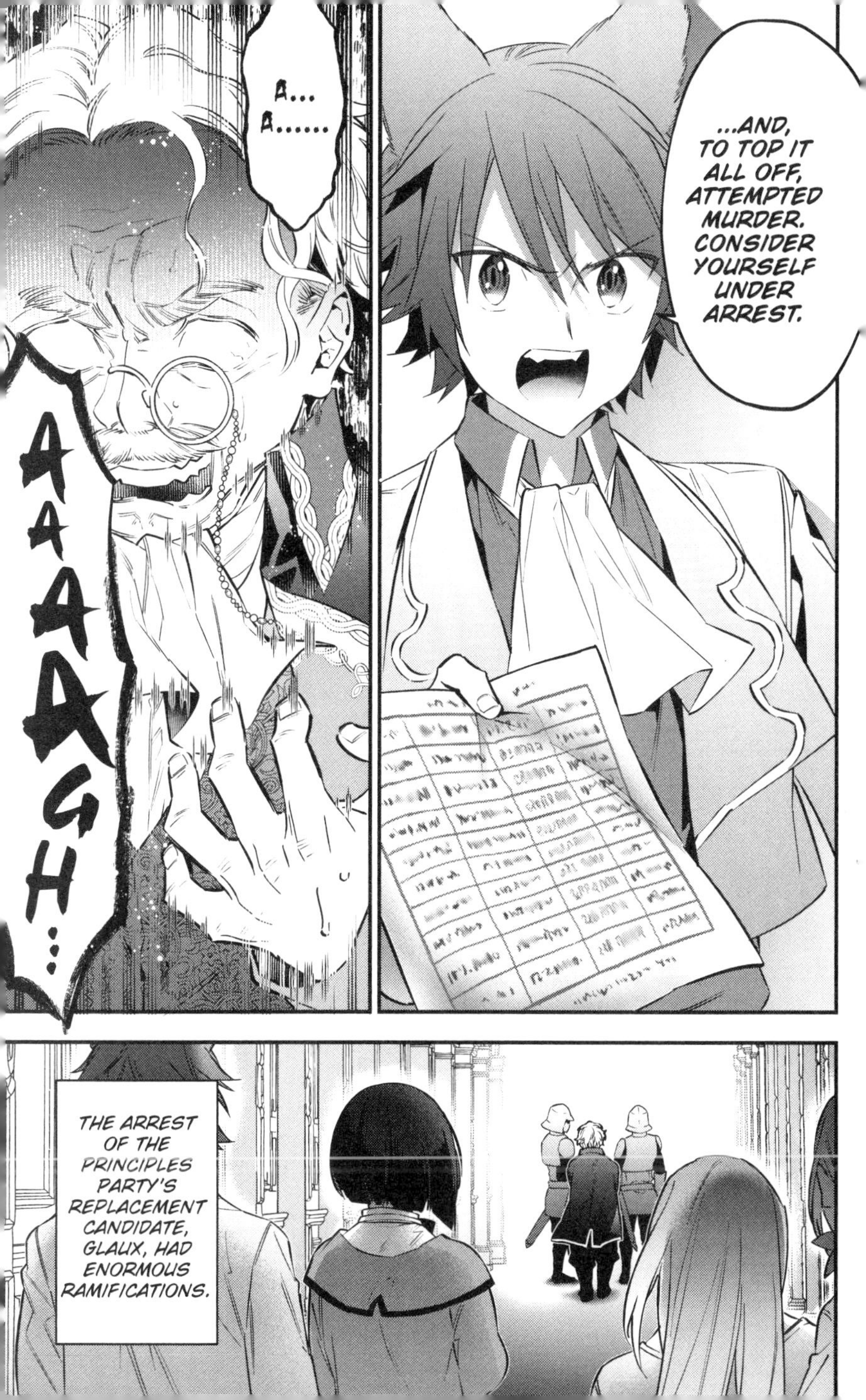
...AND, TO TOP IT ALL OFF, ATTEMPTED MURDER. CONSIDER YOURSELF UNDER ARREST.
A... A......
AAAAAGH...
THE ARREST OF THE PRINCIPLES PARTY'S REPLACEMENT CANDIDATE, GLAUX, HAD ENORMOUS RAMIFICATIONS.

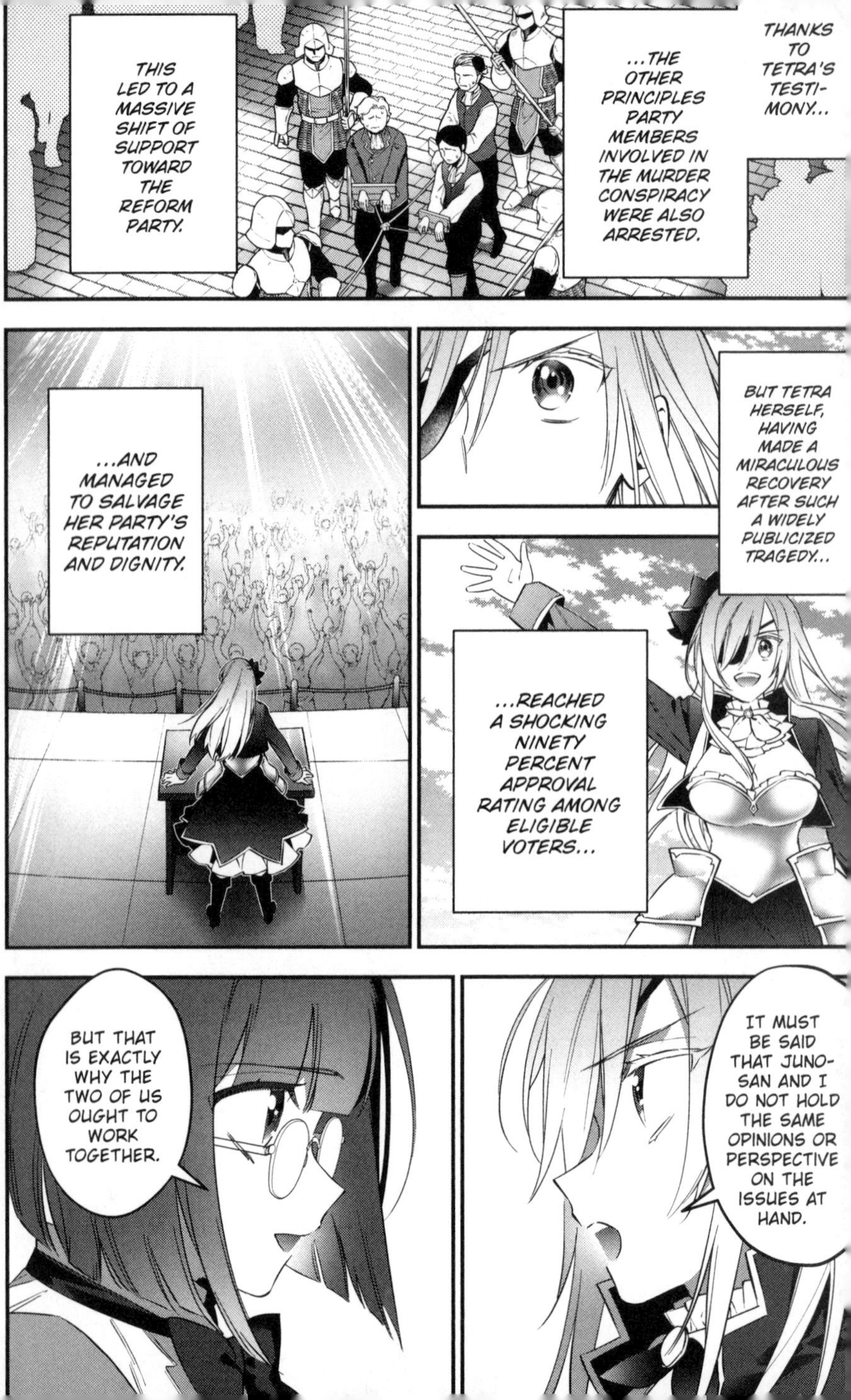
THANKS TO TETRA'S TESTIMONY...
...THE OTHER PRINCIPLES PARTY MEMBERS INVOLVED IN THE MURDER CONSPIRACY WERE ALSO ARRESTED.
THIS LED TO A MASSIVE SHIFT OF SUPPORT TOWARD THE REFORM PARTY.
BUT TETRA HERSELF, HAVING MADE A MIRACULOUS RECOVERY AFTER SUCH A WIDELY PUBLICIZED TRAGEDY...
...REACHED A SHOCKING NINETY PERCENT APPROVAL RATING AMONG ELIGIBLE VOTERS...
...AND MANAGED TO SALVAGE HER PARTY'S REPUTATION AND DIGNITY.
IT MUST BE SAID THAT JUNO-SAN AND I DO NOT HOLD THE SAME OPINIONS OR PERSPECTIVE ON THE ISSUES AT HAND.
BUT THAT IS EXACTLY WHY THE TWO OF US OUGHT TO WORK TOGETHER.

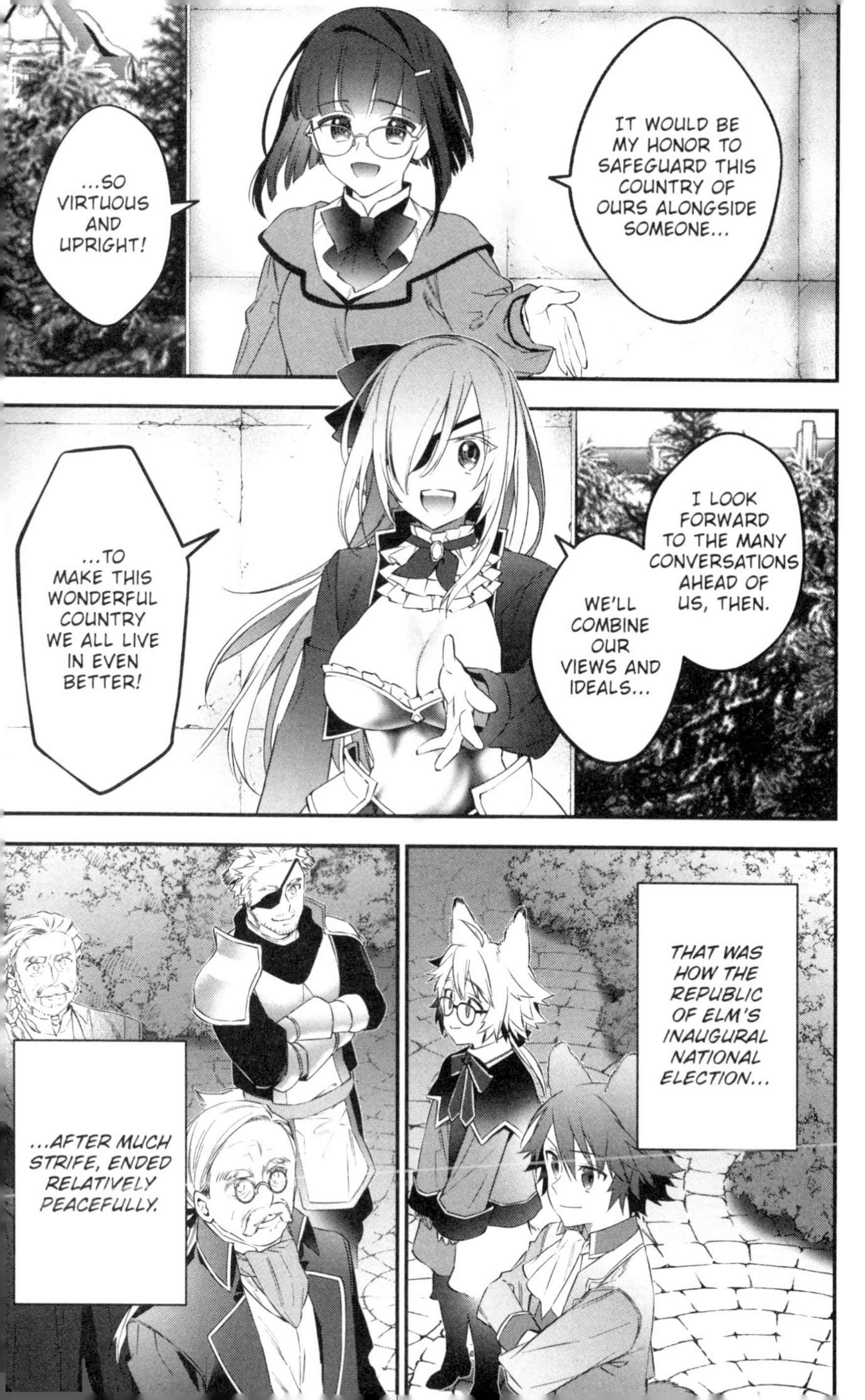
IT WOULD BE MY HONOR TO SAFEGUARD THIS COUNTRY OF OURS ALONGSIDE SOMEONE...
...SO VIRTUOUS AND UPRIGHT!
I LOOK FORWARD TO THE MANY CONVERSATIONS AHEAD OF US, THEN.
WE'LL COMBINE OUR VIEWS AND IDEALS...
...TO MAKE THIS WONDERFUL COUNTRY WE ALL LIVE IN EVEN BETTER!
THAT WAS HOW THE REPUBLIC OF ELM'S INAUGURAL NATIONAL ELECTION...
...AFTER MUCH STRIFE, ENDED RELATIVELY PEACEFULLY.

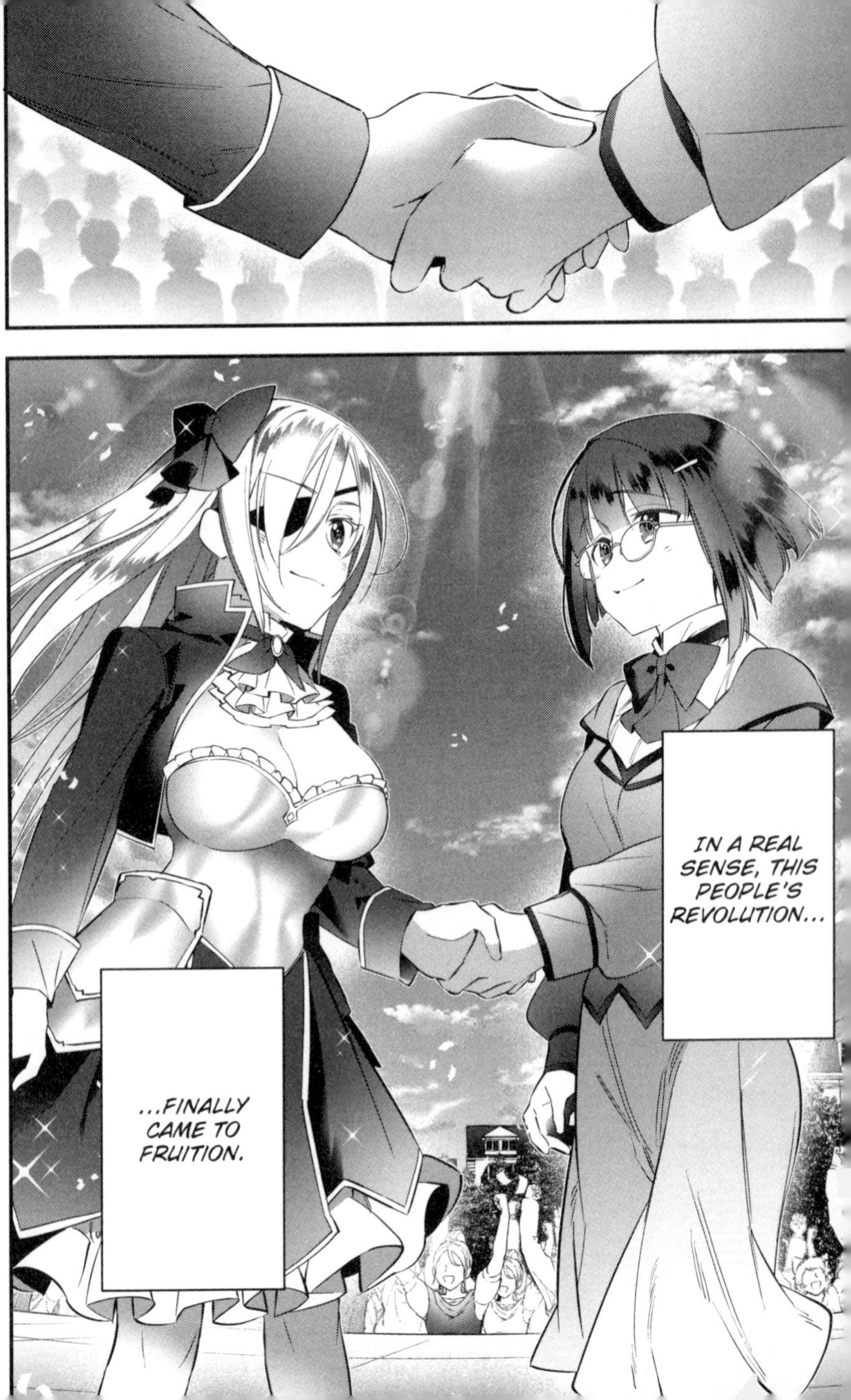
IN A REAL SENSE, THIS PEOPLE'S REVOLUTION...
...FINALLY CAME TO FRUITION.

HIGH SCHOOL
PRODIGIES HAVE
IT EASY EVEN IN
ANOTHER
WORLD!

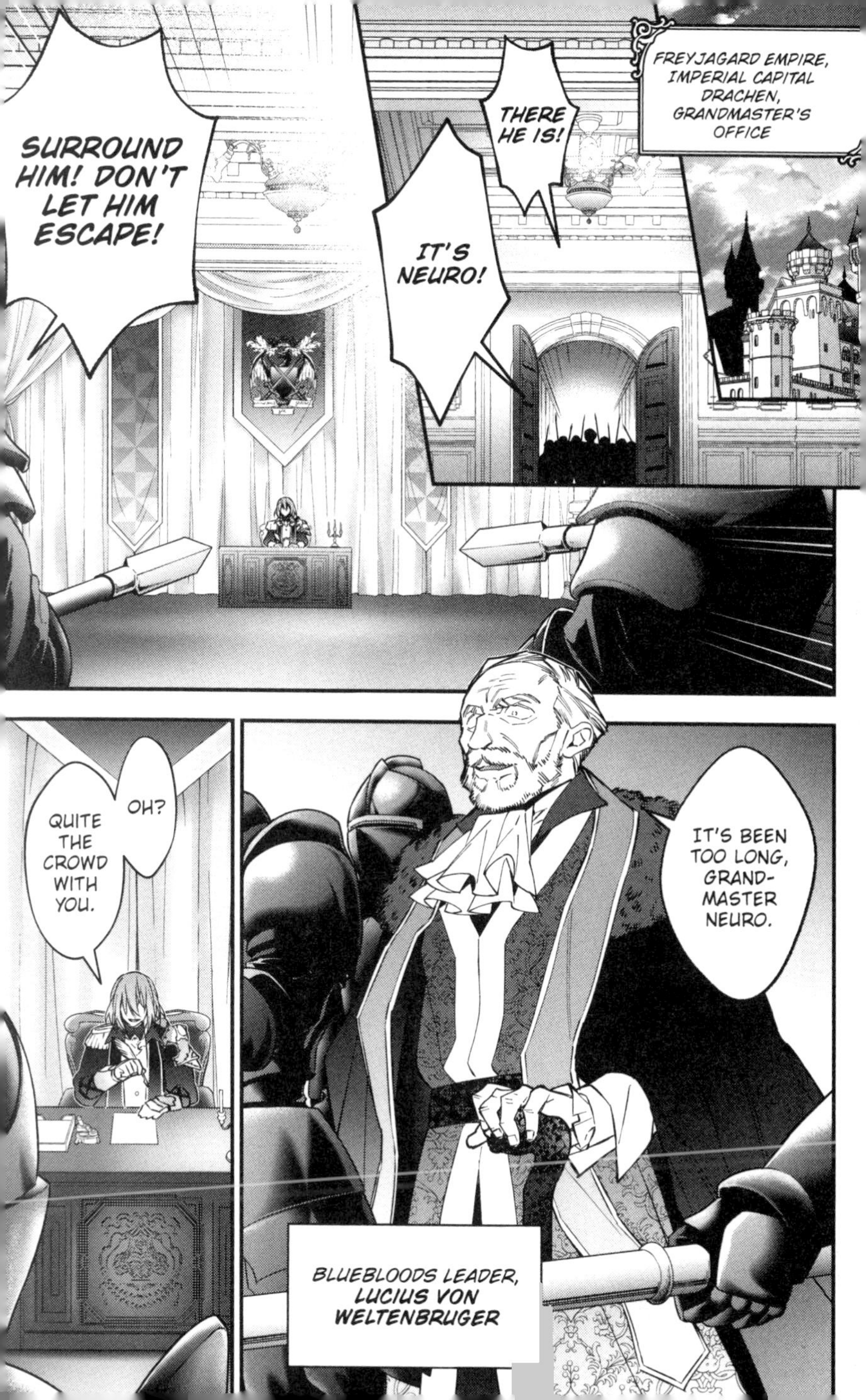
FREYJAGARD EMPIRE, IMPERIAL CAPITAL DRACHEN, GRANDMASTER'S OFFICE
THERE HE IS!
IT'S NEURO!
SURROUND HIM! DON'T LET HIM ESCAPE!
IT'S BEEN TOO LONG, GRAND-MASTER NEURO.
BLUEBLOODS LEADER, LUCIUS VON WELTENBRUGER
OH? QUITE THE CROWD WITH YOU.

CHAPTER 79: OPPOSING PATHS

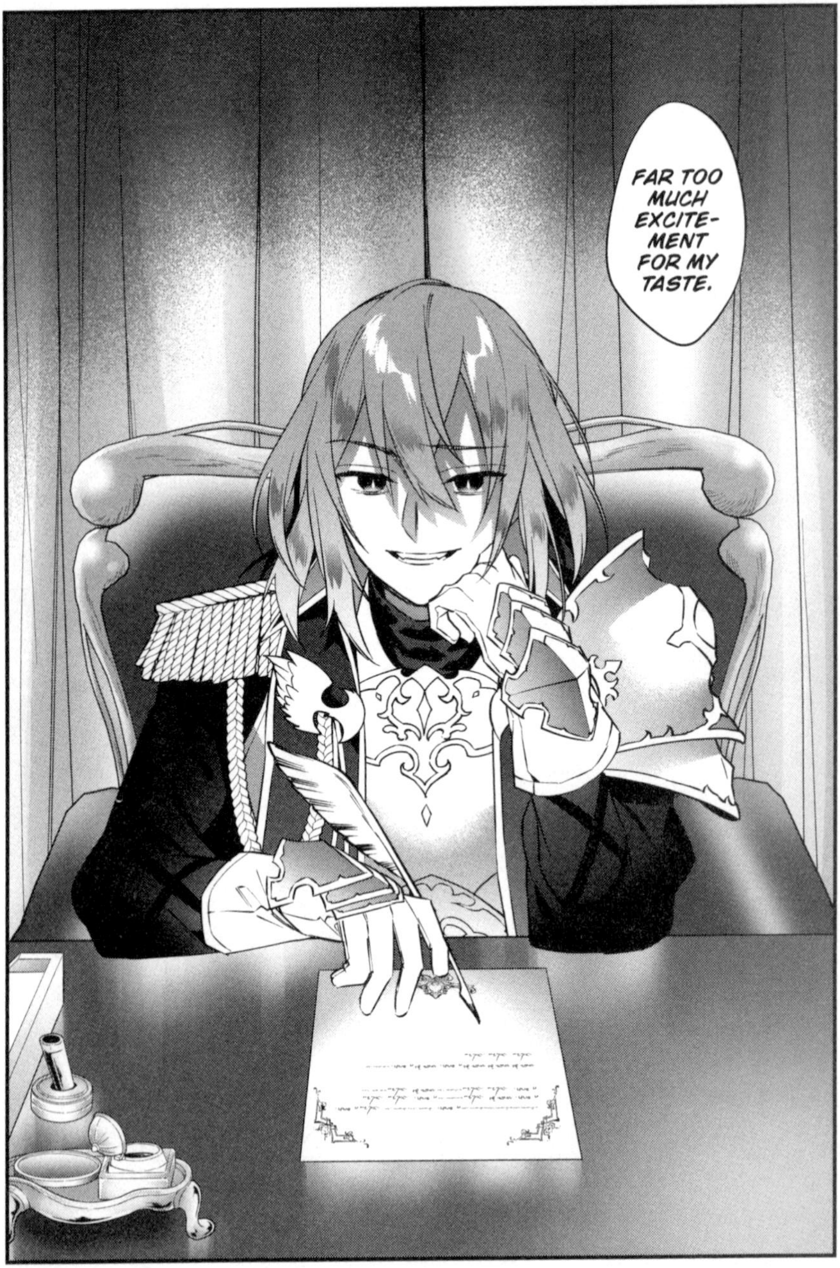
FAR TOO MUCH EXCITE-MENT FOR MY TASTE.

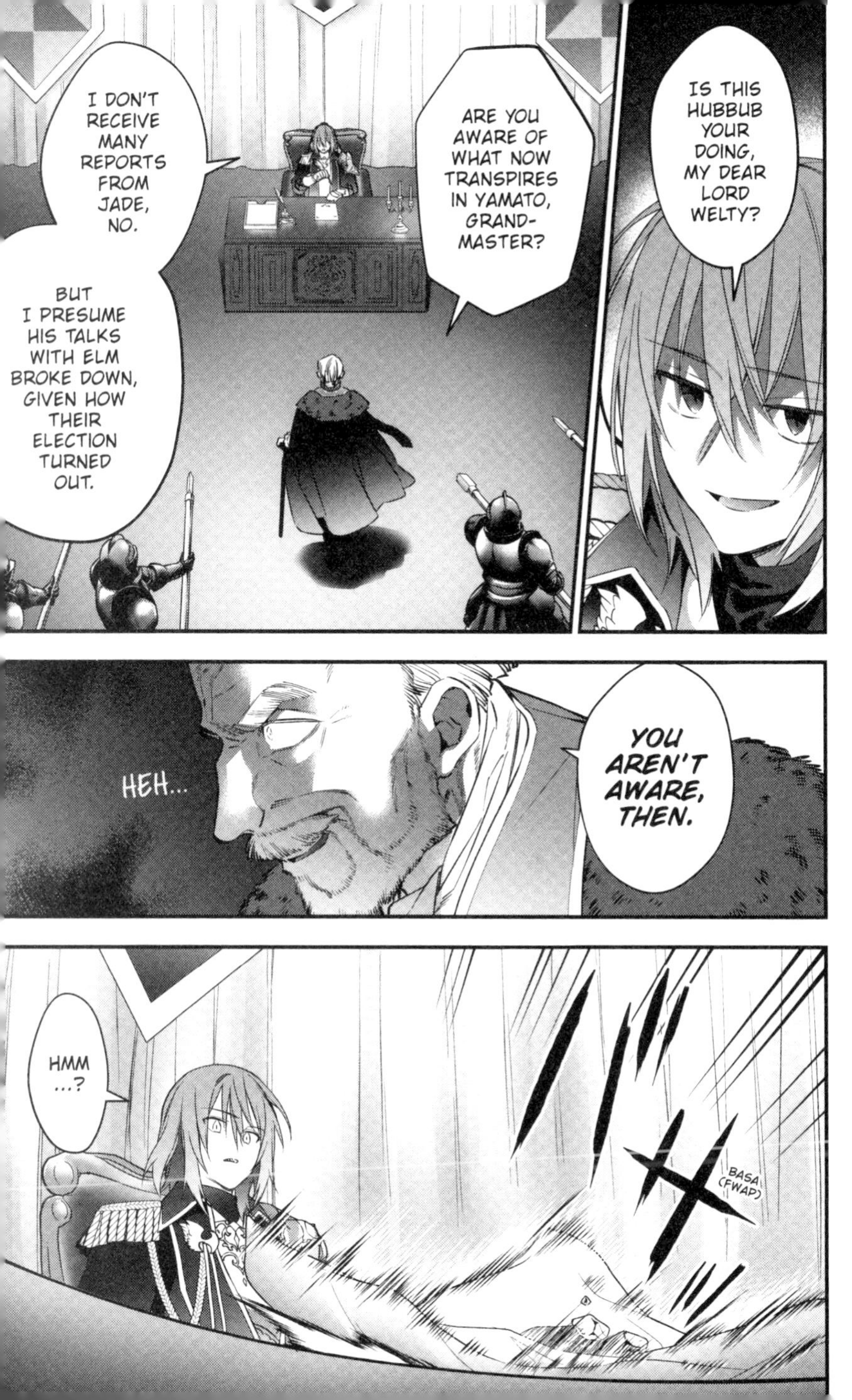
IS THIS HUBBUB YOUR DOING, MY DEAR LORD WELTY?
ARE YOU AWARE OF WHAT NOW TRANSPIRES IN YAMATO, GRAND-MASTER?
I DON'T RECEIVE MANY REPORTS FROM JADE, NO.
BUT I PRESUME HIS TALKS WITH ELM BROKE DOWN, GIVEN HOW THEIR ELECTION TURNED OUT.
YOU AREN'T AWARE, THEN.
HEH...
BASA (FWAP)
HMM ...?

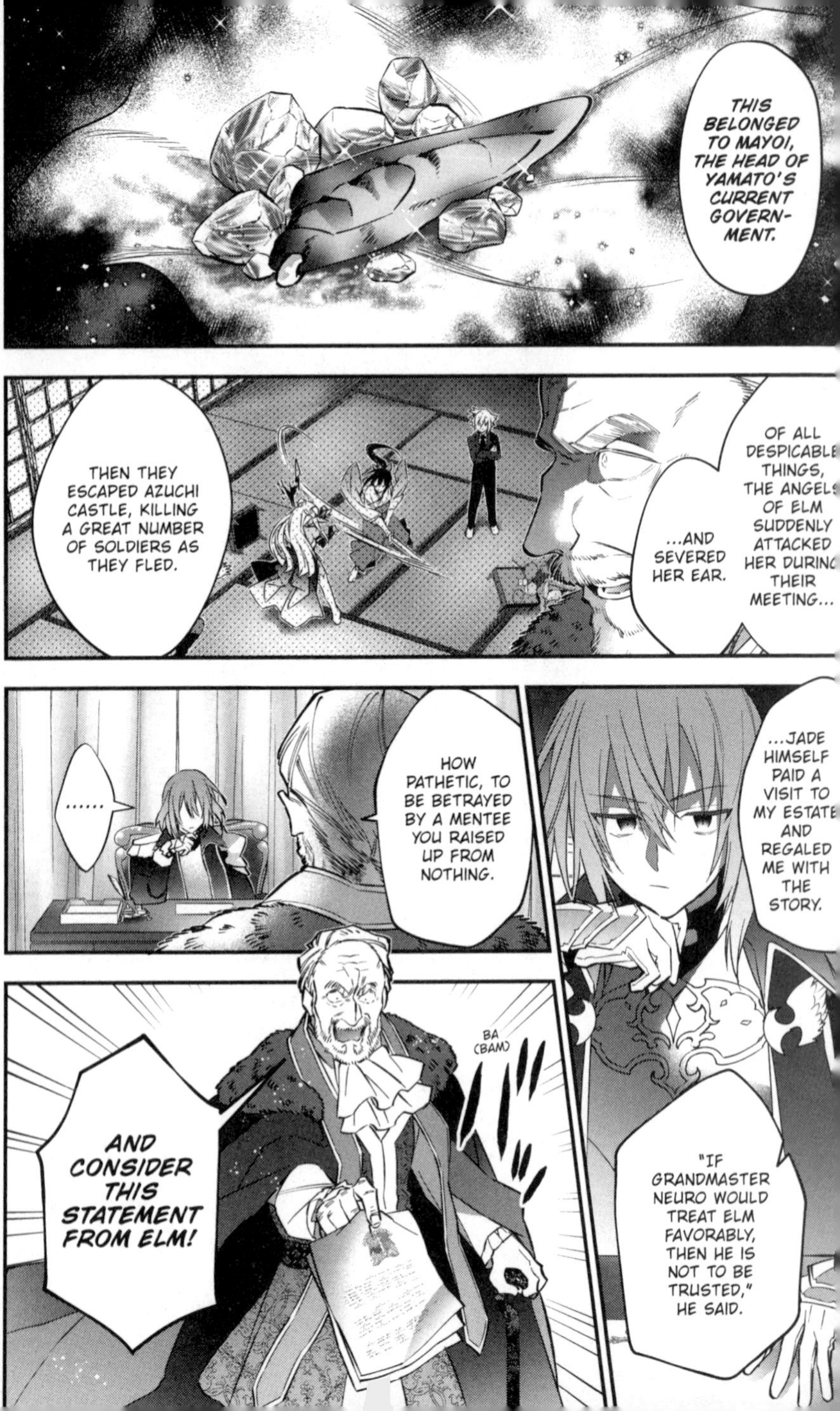
THIS BELONGED TO MAYOI, THE HEAD OF YAMATO'S CURRENT GOVERN-MENT.
OF ALL DESPICABLE THINGS, THE ANGELS OF ELM SUDDENLY ATTACKED HER DURING THEIR MEETING...
...AND SEVERED HER EAR.
THEN THEY ESCAPED AZUCHI CASTLE, KILLING A GREAT NUMBER OF SOLDIERS AS THEY FLED.
...JADE HIMSELF PAID A VISIT TO MY ESTATE AND REGALED ME WITH THE STORY.
"IF GRANDMASTER NEURO WOULD TREAT ELM FAVORABLY, THEN HE IS NOT TO BE TRUSTED," HE SAID.
HOW PATHETIC, TO BE BETRAYED BY A MENTEE YOU RAISED UP FROM NOTHING.
......
BA (BAM)
AND CONSIDER THIS STATEMENT FROM ELM!

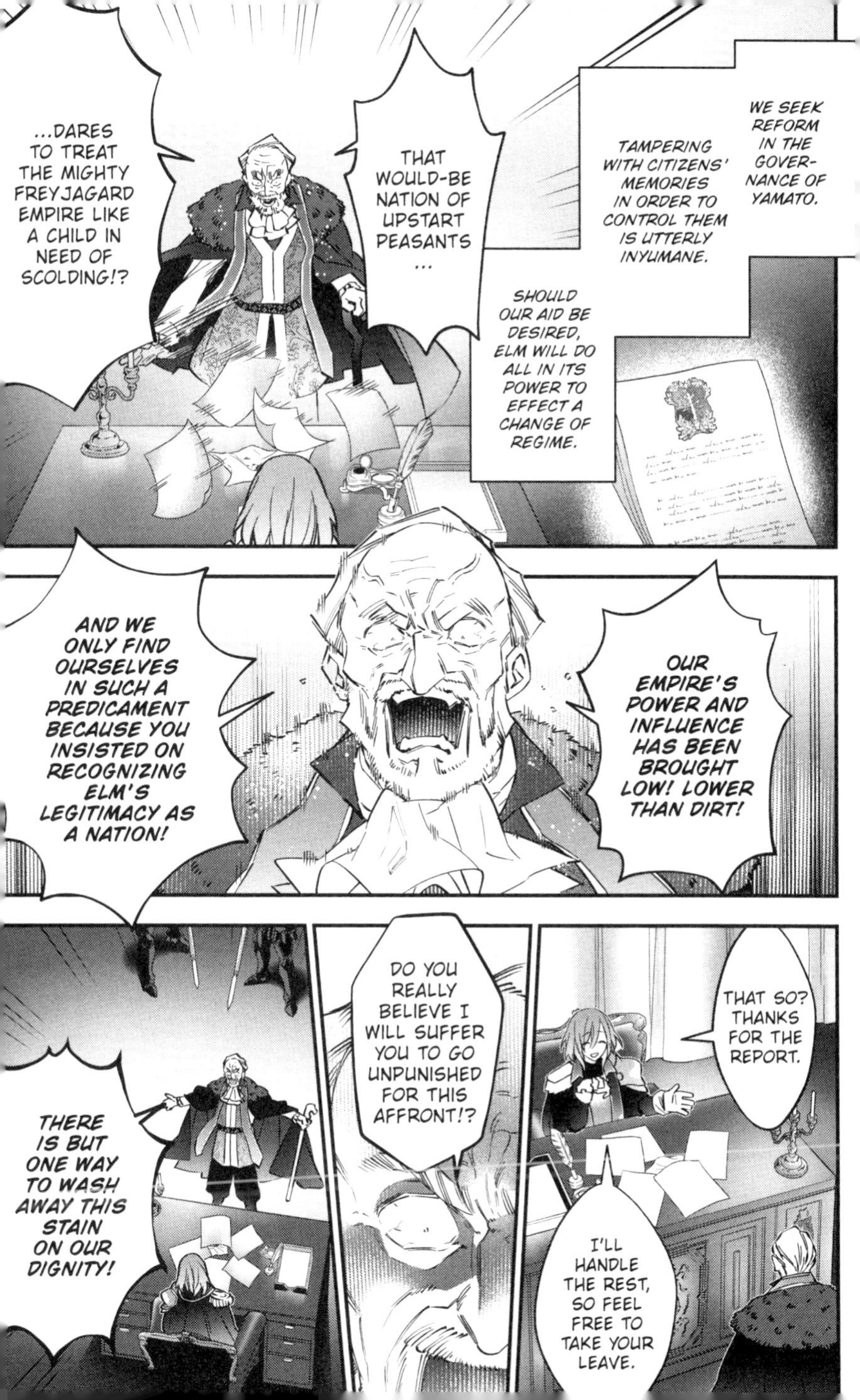
WE SEEK REFORM IN THE GOVERNANCE OF YAMATO.
TAMPERING WITH CITIZENS' MEMORIES IN ORDER TO CONTROL THEM IS UTTERLY INYUMANE.
SHOULD OUR AID BE DESIRED, ELM WILL DO ALL IN ITS POWER TO EFFECT A CHANGE OF REGIME.
THAT WOULD-BE NATION OF UPSTART PEASANTS...
...DARES TO TREAT THE MIGHTY FREYJAGARD EMPIRE LIKE A CHILD IN NEED OF SCOLDING!?
OUR EMPIRE'S POWER AND INFLUENCE HAS BEEN BROUGHT LOW! LOWER THAN DIRT!
AND WE ONLY FIND OURSELVES IN SUCH A PREDICAMENT BECAUSE YOU INSISTED ON RECOGNIZING ELM'S LEGITIMACY AS A NATION!
THAT SO? THANKS FOR THE REPORT.
I'LL HANDLE THE REST, SO FEEL FREE TO TAKE YOUR LEAVE.
DO YOU REALLY BELIEVE I WILL SUFFER YOU TO GO UNPUNISHED FOR THIS AFFRONT!?
THERE IS BUT ONE WAY TO WASH AWAY THIS STAIN ON OUR DIGNITY!

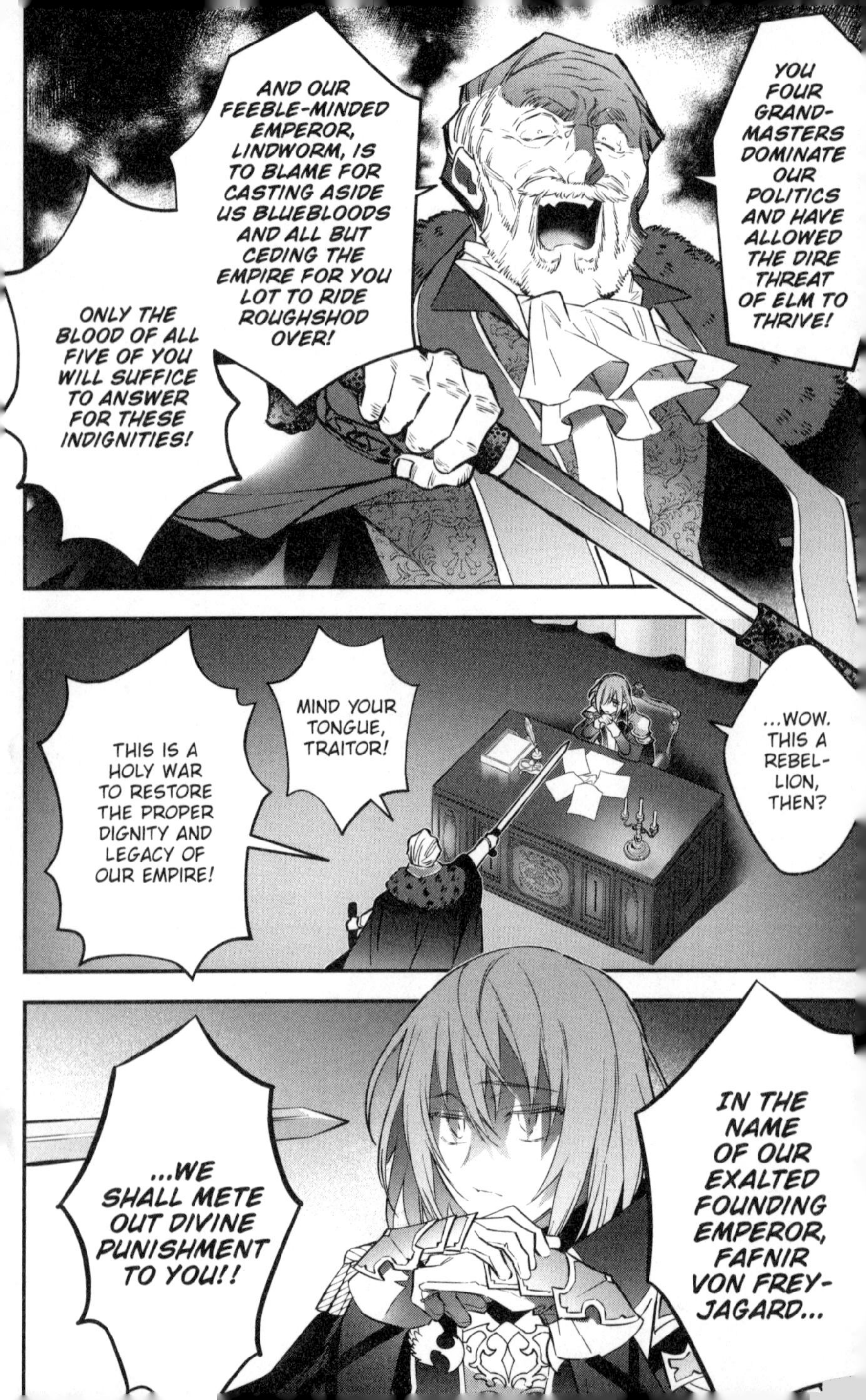
YOU FOUR GRAND-MASTERS DOMINATE OUR POLITICS AND HAVE ALLOWED THE DIRE THREAT OF ELM TO THRIVE!
AND OUR FEEBLE-MINDED EMPEROR, LINDWORM, IS TO BLAME FOR CASTING ASIDE US BLUEBLOODS AND ALL BUT CEDING THE EMPIRE FOR YOU LOT TO RIDE ROUGHSHOD OVER!
ONLY THE BLOOD OF ALL FIVE OF YOU WILL SUFFICE TO ANSWER FOR THESE INDIGNITIES!
...WOW. THIS A REBEL-LION, THEN?
MIND YOUR TONGUE, TRAITOR!
THIS IS A HOLY WAR TO RESTORE THE PROPER DIGNITY AND LEGACY OF OUR EMPIRE!
IN THE NAME OF OUR EXALTED FOUNDING EMPEROR, FAFNIR VON FREY-JAGARD...
...WE SHALL METE OUT DIVINE PUNISHMENT TO YOU!!

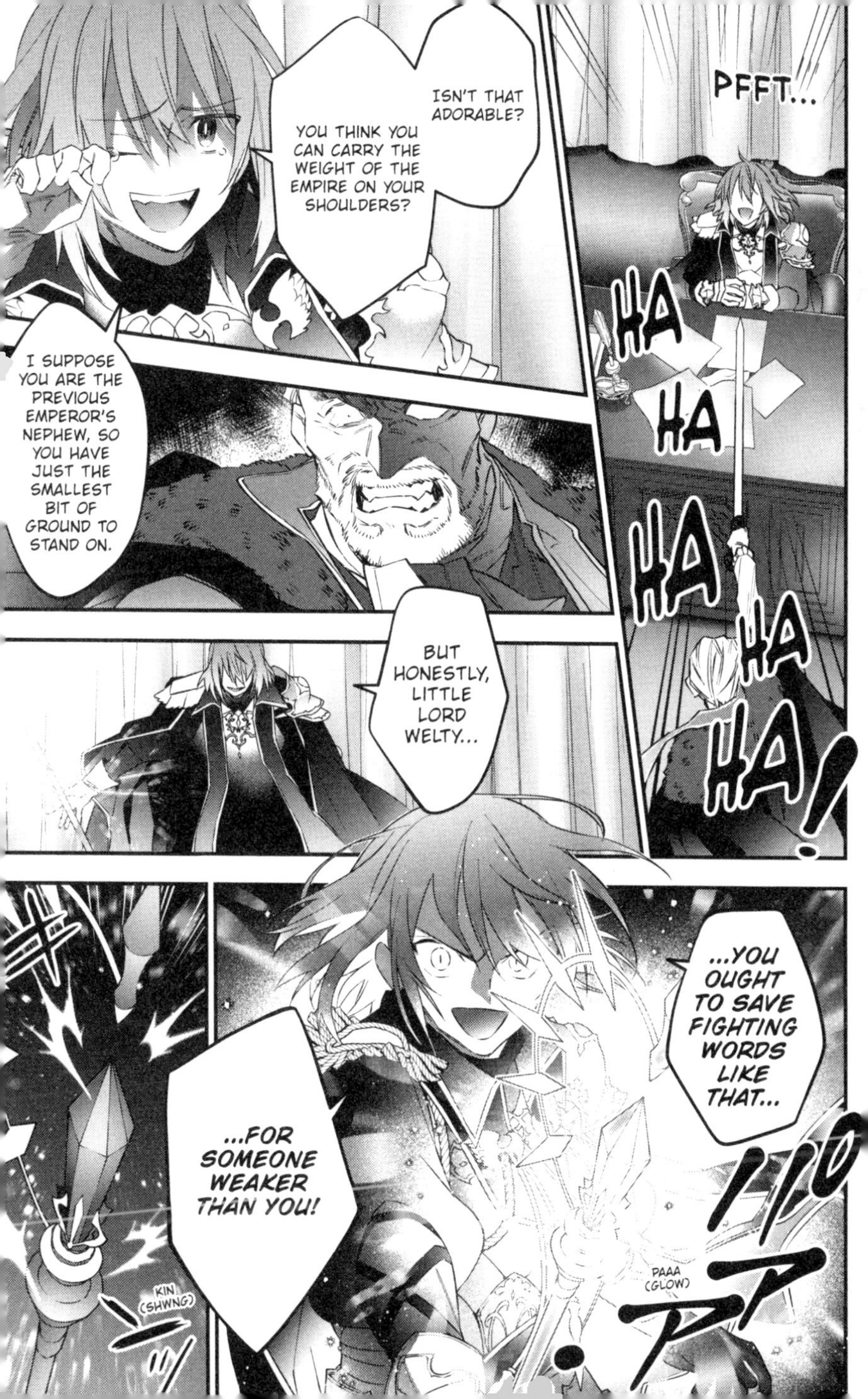
PFFT...
HA HA HA HA HA!
YOU THINK YOU CAN CARRY THE WEIGHT OF THE EMPIRE ON YOUR SHOULDERS? ISN'T THAT ADORABLE?
I SUPPOSE YOU ARE THE PREVIOUS EMPEROR'S NEPHEW, SO YOU HAVE JUST THE SMALLEST BIT OF GROUND TO STAND ON.
BUT HONESTLY, LITTLE LORD WELTY...
...YOU OUGHT TO SAVE FIGHTING WORDS LIKE THAT...
...FOR SOMEONE WEAKER THAN YOU!
PAAA (GLOW)
KIN (SHWNG)

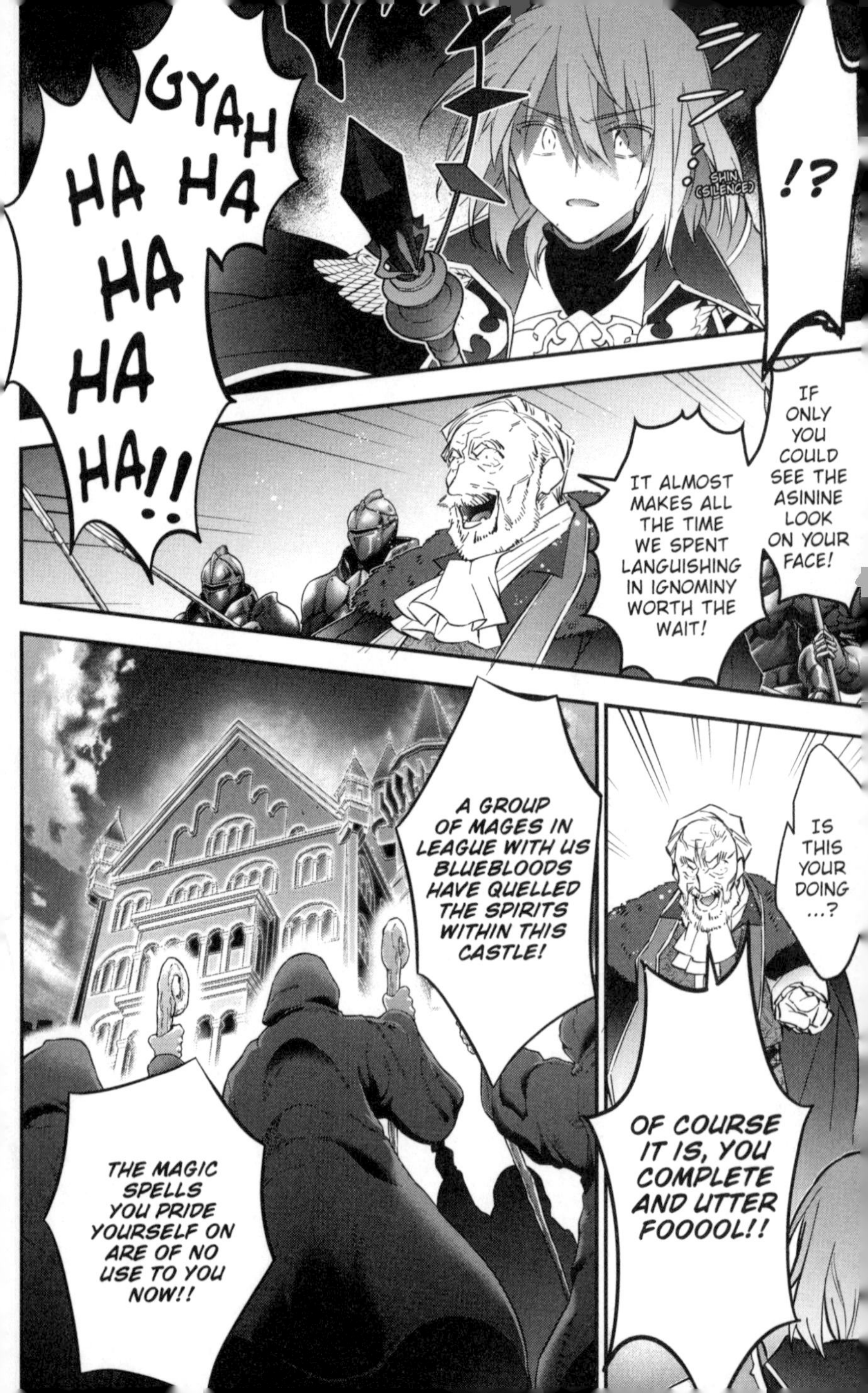
!?
SHIN (SILENCE)
GYAH HA HA HA HA HA!!
IF ONLY YOU COULD SEE THE ASININE LOOK ON YOUR FACE!
IT ALMOST MAKES ALL THE TIME WE SPENT LANGUISHING IN IGNOMINY WORTH THE WAIT!
IS THIS YOUR DOING...?
OF COURSE IT IS, YOU COMPLETE AND UTTER FOOOOL!!
A GROUP OF MAGES IN LEAGUE WITH US BLUEBLOODS HAVE QUELLED THE SPIRITS WITHIN THIS CASTLE!
THE MAGIC SPELLS YOU PRIDE YOURSELF ON ARE OF NO USE TO YOU NOW!!

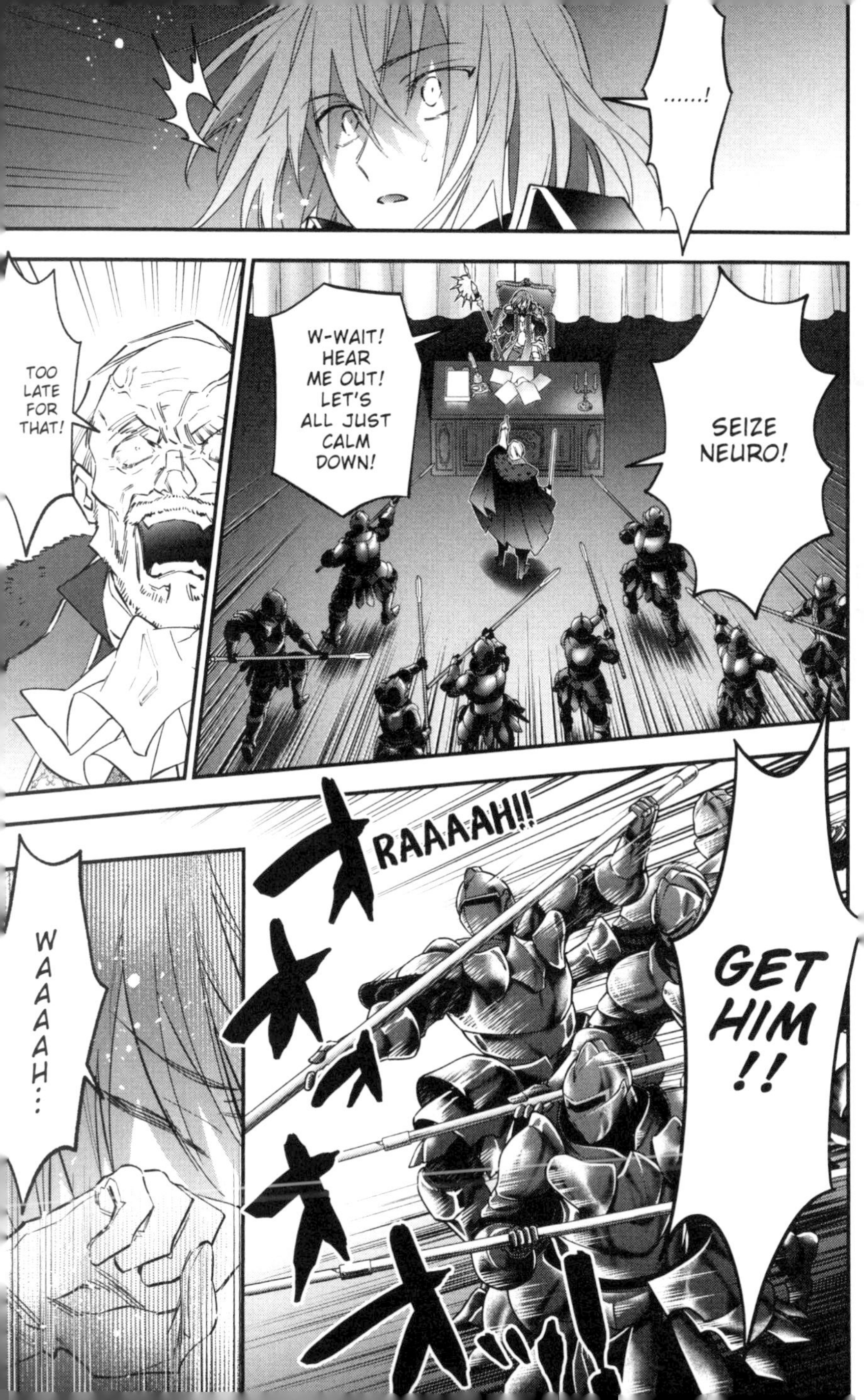
......!
SEIZE NEURO!
W-WAIT! HEAR ME OUT! LET'S ALL JUST CALM DOWN!
TOO LATE FOR THAT!
GET HIM!!
RAAAAH!!
WAAAAAH...

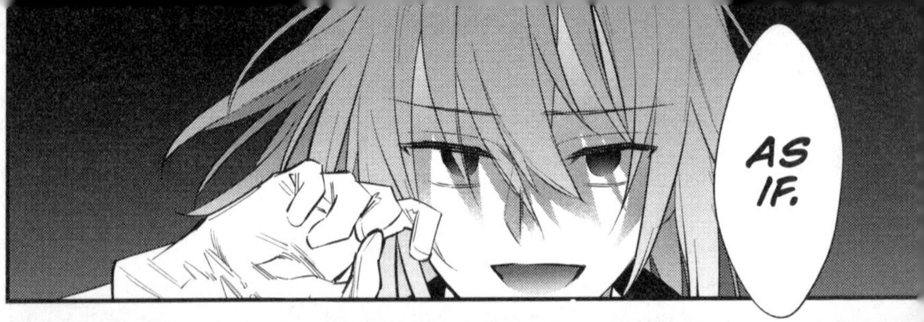
AS IF.
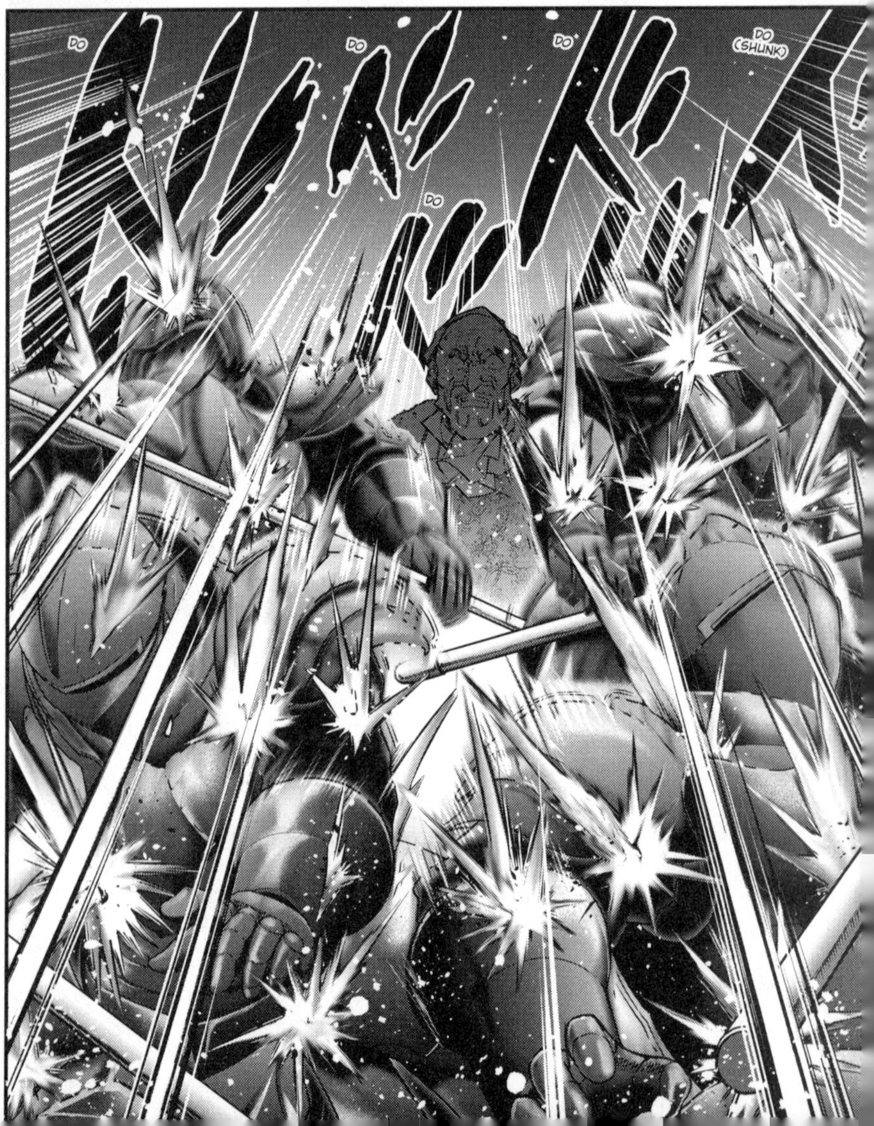
DO
(SHUNK)
DO
DO
DO
DO

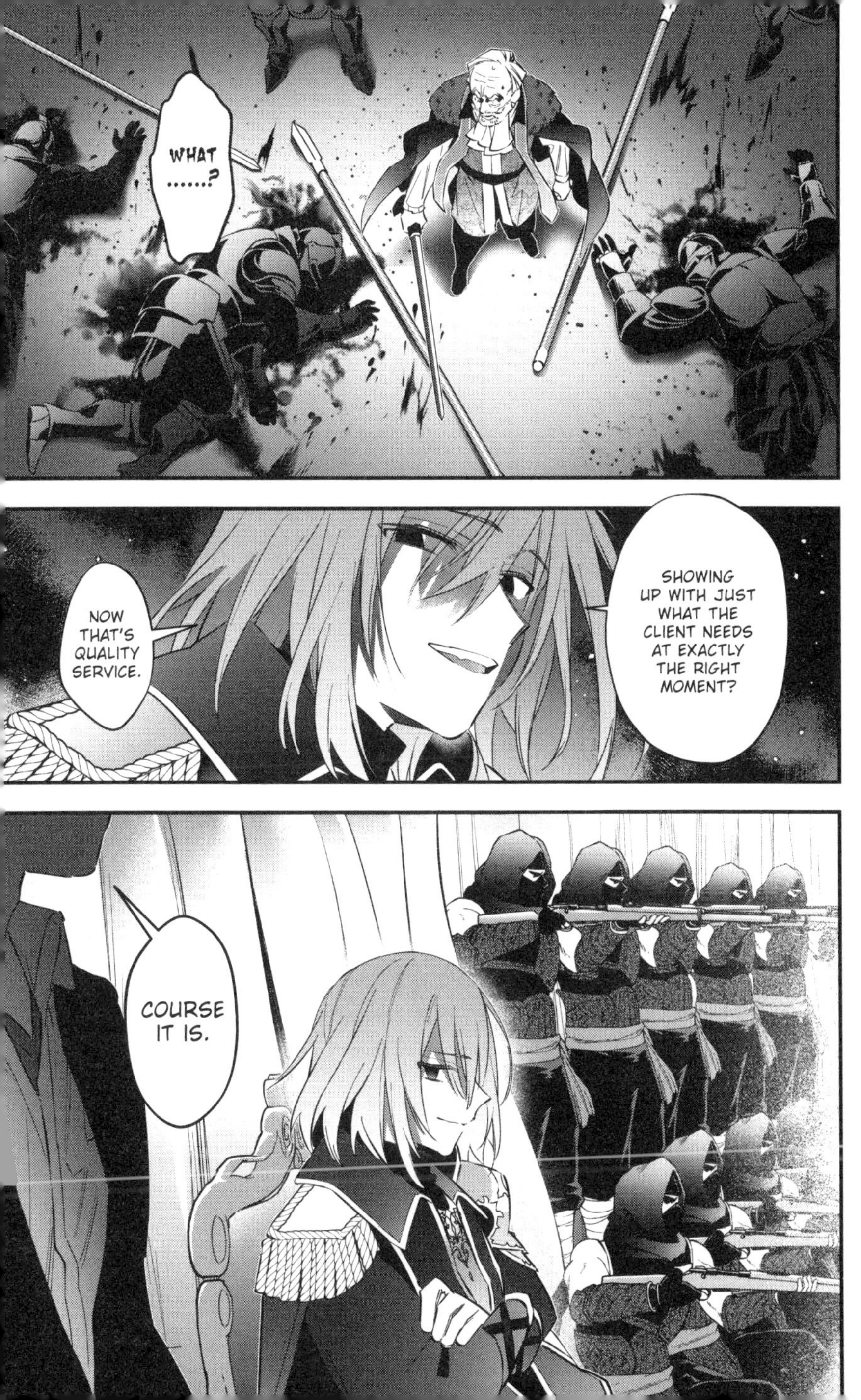
WHAT ......?
SHOWING UP WITH JUST WHAT THE CLIENT NEEDS AT EXACTLY THE RIGHT MOMENT?
NOW THAT'S QUALITY SERVICE.
COURSE IT IS.

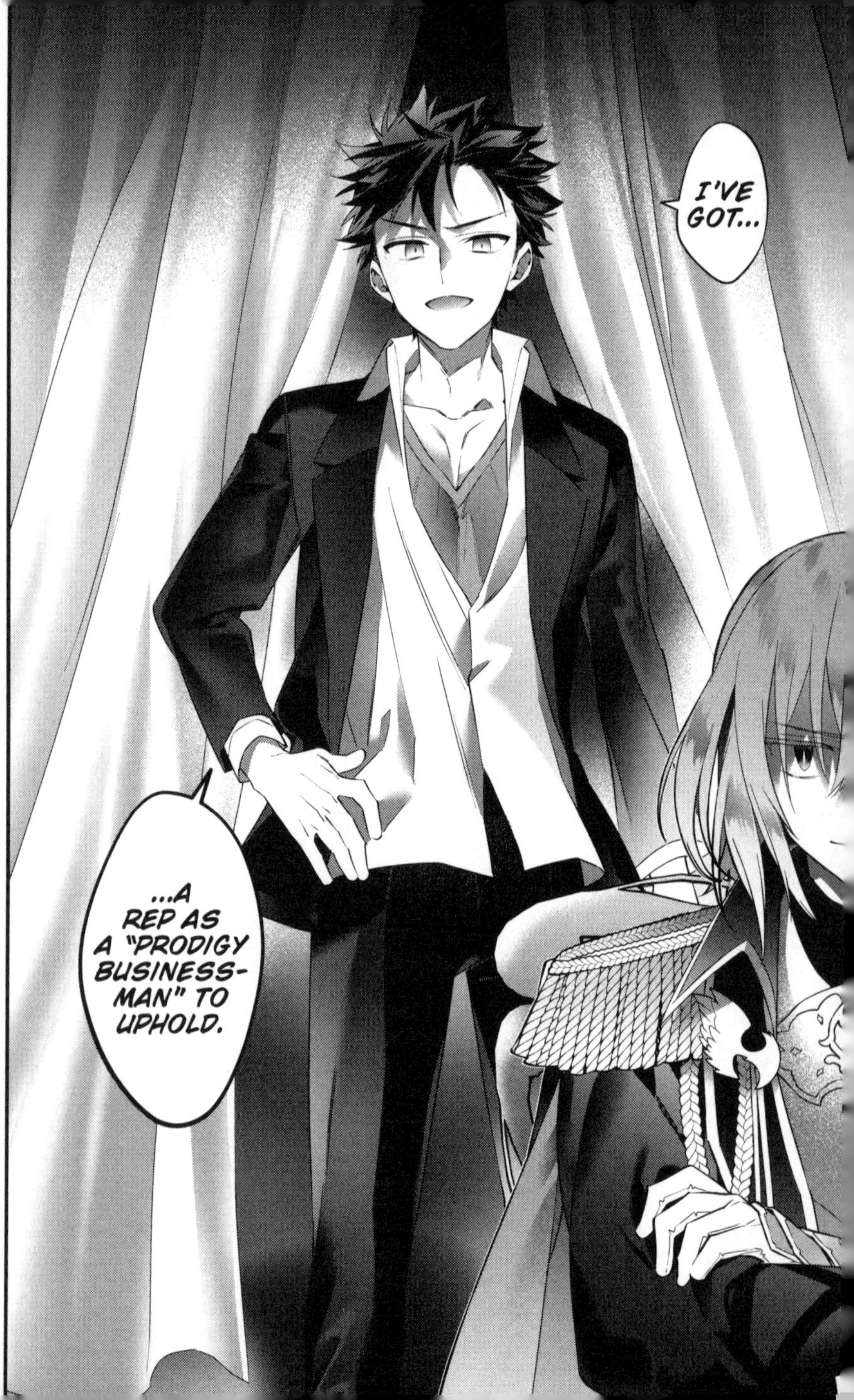
I'VE GOT...
...A REP AS A "PRODIGY BUSINESS-MAN" TO UPHOLD.

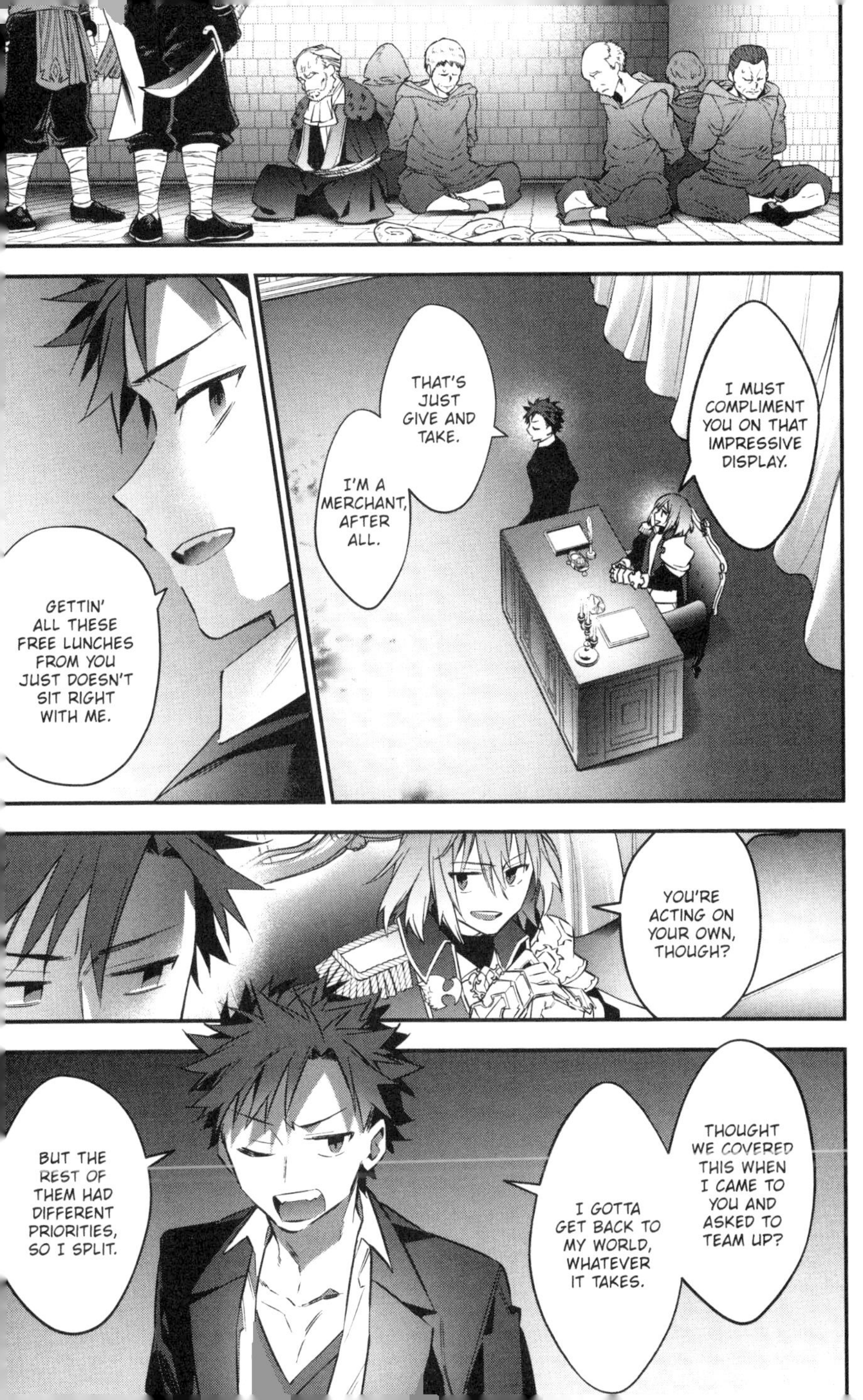
I MUST COMPLIMENT YOU ON THAT IMPRESSIVE DISPLAY.
THAT'S JUST GIVE AND TAKE.
I'M A MERCHANT, AFTER ALL.
GETTIN' ALL THESE FREE LUNCHES FROM YOU JUST DOESN'T SIT RIGHT WITH ME.
YOU'RE ACTING ON YOUR OWN, THOUGH?
THOUGHT WE COVERED THIS WHEN I CAME TO YOU AND ASKED TO TEAM UP?
I GOTTA GET BACK TO MY WORLD, WHATEVER IT TAKES.
BUT THE REST OF THEM HAD DIFFERENT PRIORITIES, SO I SPLIT.

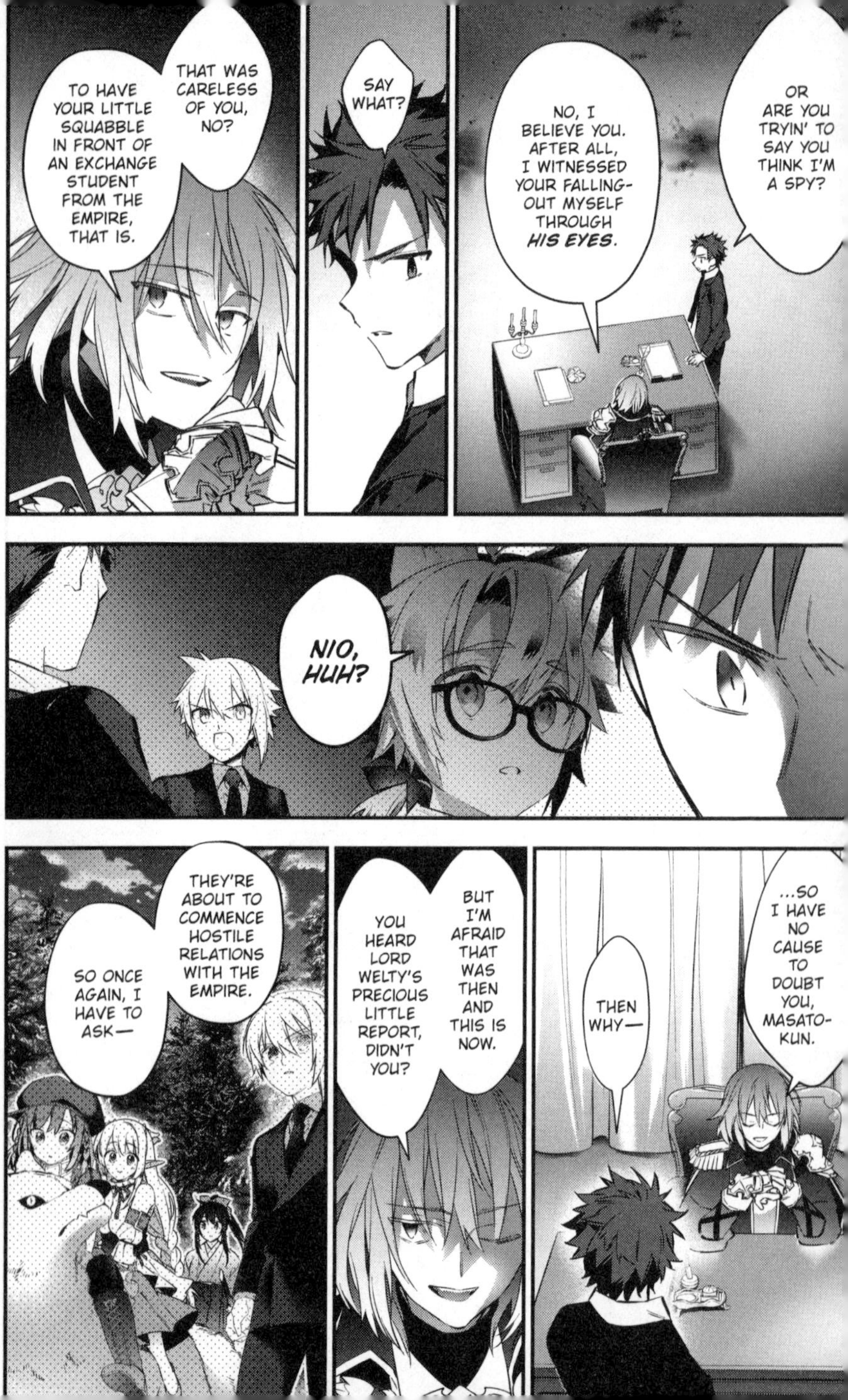
OR ARE YOU TRYIN' TO SAY YOU THINK I'M A SPY?
NO, I BELIEVE YOU. AFTER ALL, I WITNESSED YOUR FALLING-OUT MYSELF THROUGH *HIS EYES*.
SAY WHAT?
THAT WAS CARELESS OF YOU, NO?
TO HAVE YOUR LITTLE SQUABBLE IN FRONT OF AN EXCHANGE STUDENT FROM THE EMPIRE, THAT IS.
NIO, HUH?
...SO I HAVE NO CAUSE TO DOUBT YOU, MASATO-KUN.
THEN WHY—
BUT I'M AFRAID THAT WAS THEN AND THIS IS NOW.
YOU HEARD LORD WELTY'S PRECIOUS LITTLE REPORT, DIDN'T YOU?
THEY'RE ABOUT TO COMMENCE HOSTILE RELATIONS WITH THE EMPIRE.
SO ONCE AGAIN, I HAVE TO ASK—

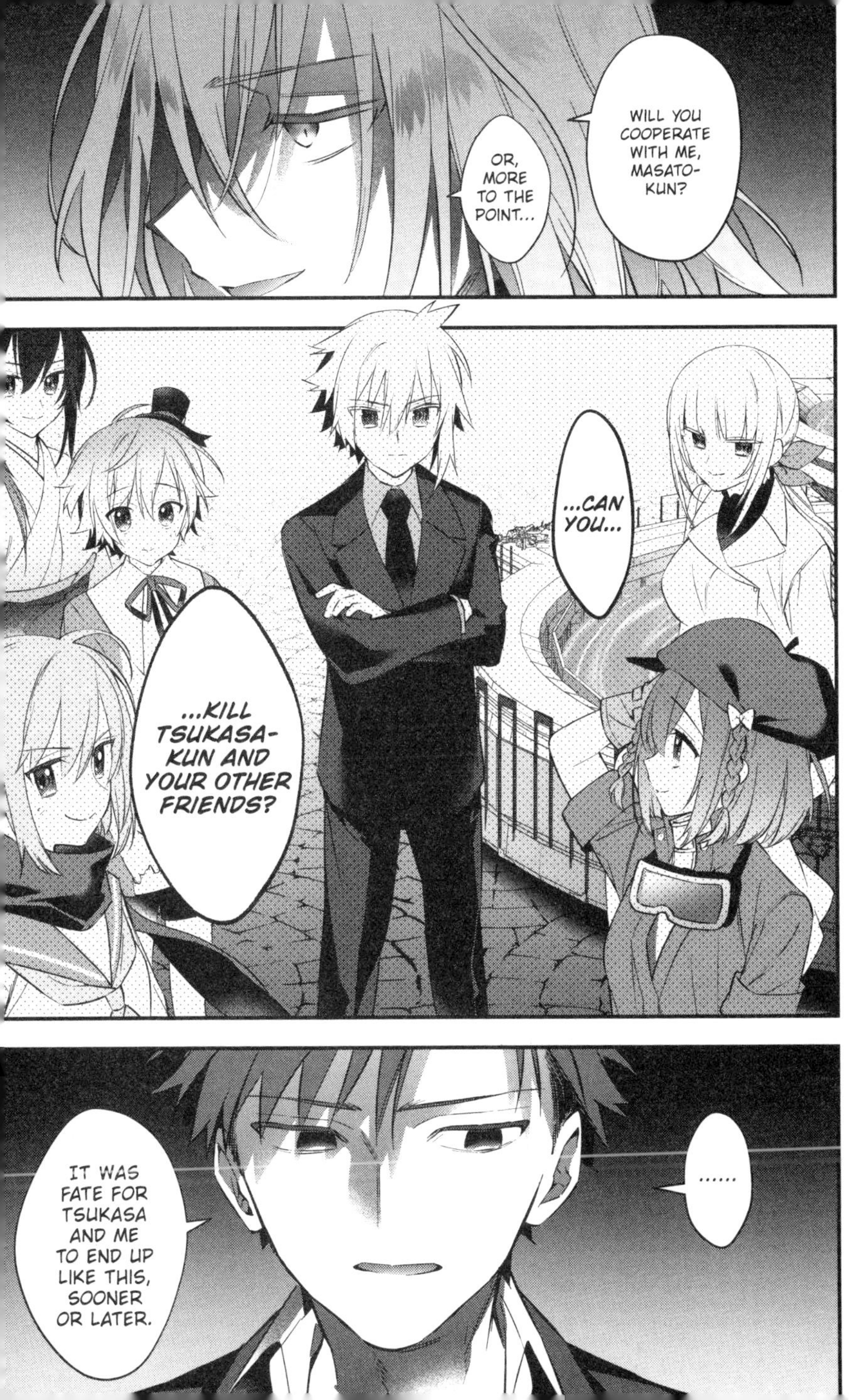
WILL YOU COOPERATE WITH ME, MASATO-KUN?
OR, MORE TO THE POINT...
...CAN YOU...
...KILL TSUKASA-KUN AND YOUR OTHER FRIENDS?
......
IT WAS FATE FOR TSUKASA AND ME TO END UP LIKE THIS, SOONER OR LATER.

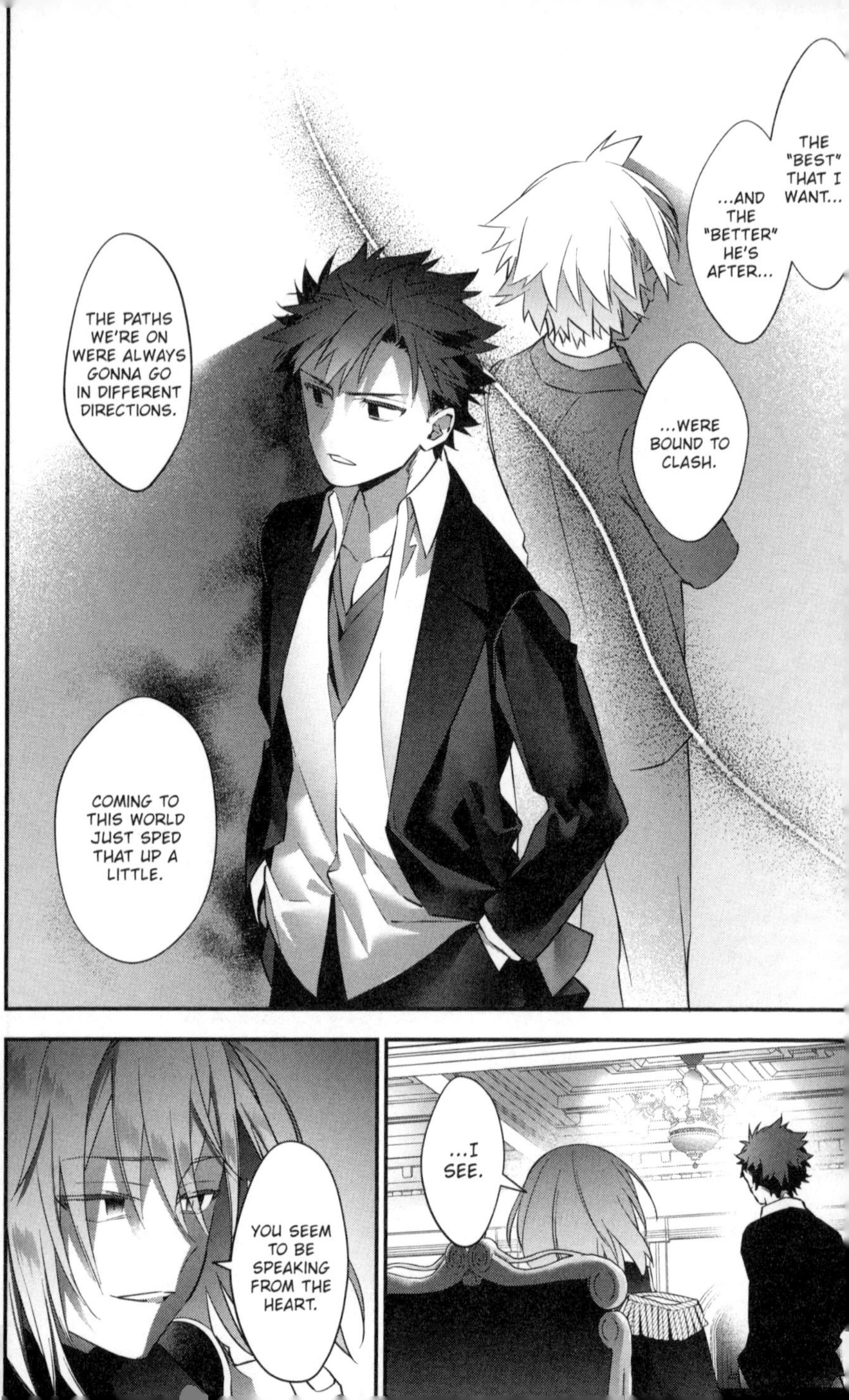
THE "BEST" THAT I WANT...
...AND THE "BETTER" HE'S AFTER...
...WERE BOUND TO CLASH.
THE PATHS WE'RE ON WERE ALWAYS GONNA GO IN DIFFERENT DIRECTIONS.
COMING TO THIS WORLD JUST SPED THAT UP A LITTLE.
...I SEE.
YOU SEEM TO BE SPEAKING FROM THE HEART.

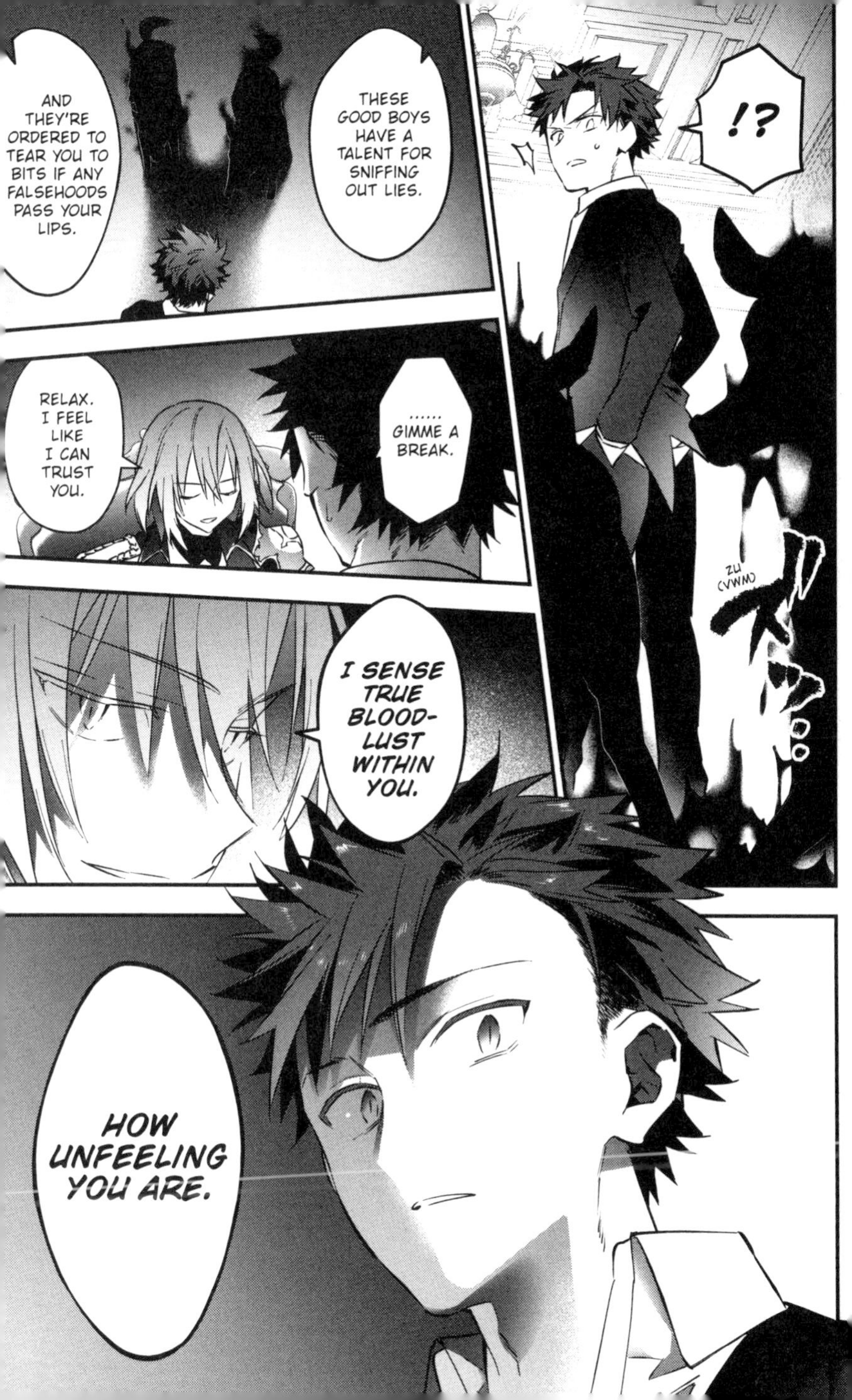

ZU (VWM)
!?
THESE GOOD BOYS HAVE A TALENT FOR SNIFFING OUT LIES.
AND THEY'RE ORDERED TO TEAR YOU TO BITS IF ANY FALSEHOODS PASS YOUR LIPS.
...... GIMME A BREAK.
RELAX. I FEEL LIKE I CAN TRUST YOU.
I SENSE TRUE BLOOD-LUST WITHIN YOU.
HOW UNFEELING YOU ARE.

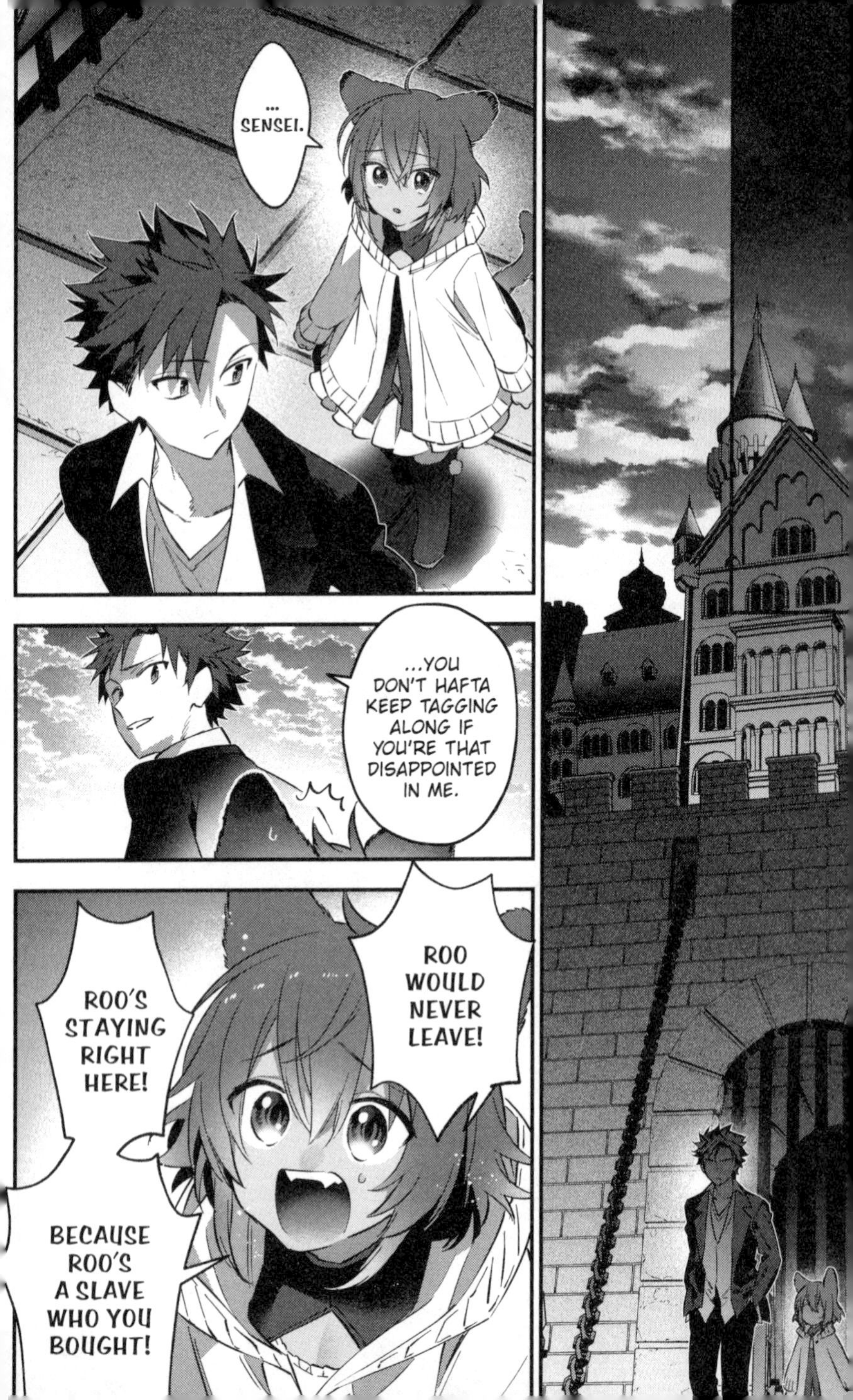
... SENSEI.
...YOU DON'T HAFTA KEEP TAGGING ALONG IF YOU'RE THAT DISAPPOINTED IN ME.
ROO WOULD NEVER LEAVE!
ROO'S STAYING RIGHT HERE!
BECAUSE ROO'S A SLAVE WHO YOU BOUGHT!

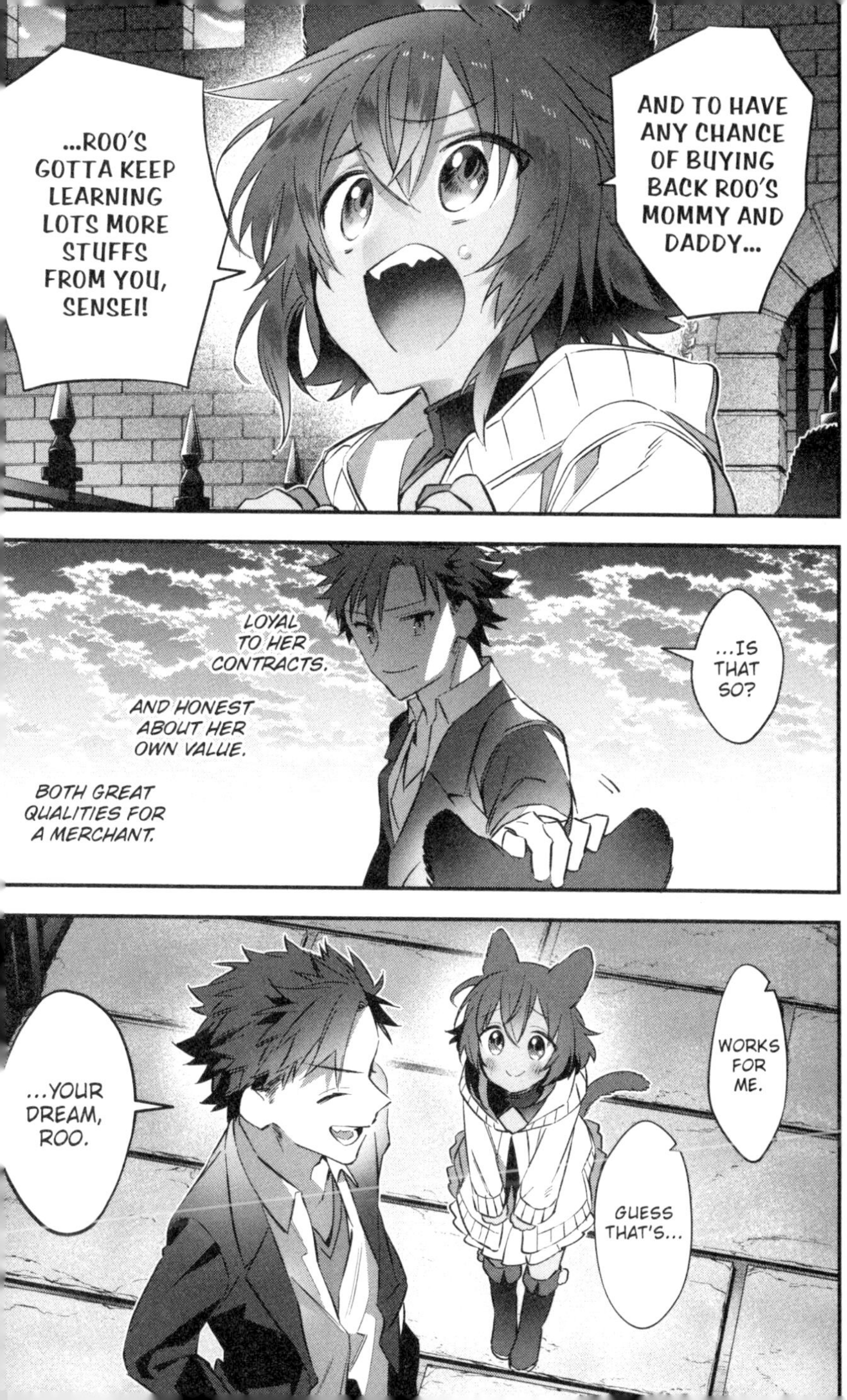
AND TO HAVE ANY CHANCE OF BUYING BACK ROO'S MOMMY AND DADDY...
...ROO'S GOTTA KEEP LEARNING LOTS MORE STUFFS FROM YOU, SENSEI!
...IS THAT SO?
LOYAL TO HER CONTRACTS.
AND HONEST ABOUT HER OWN VALUE.
BOTH GREAT QUALITIES FOR A MERCHANT.
WORKS FOR ME.
GUESS THAT'S...
...YOUR DREAM, ROO.

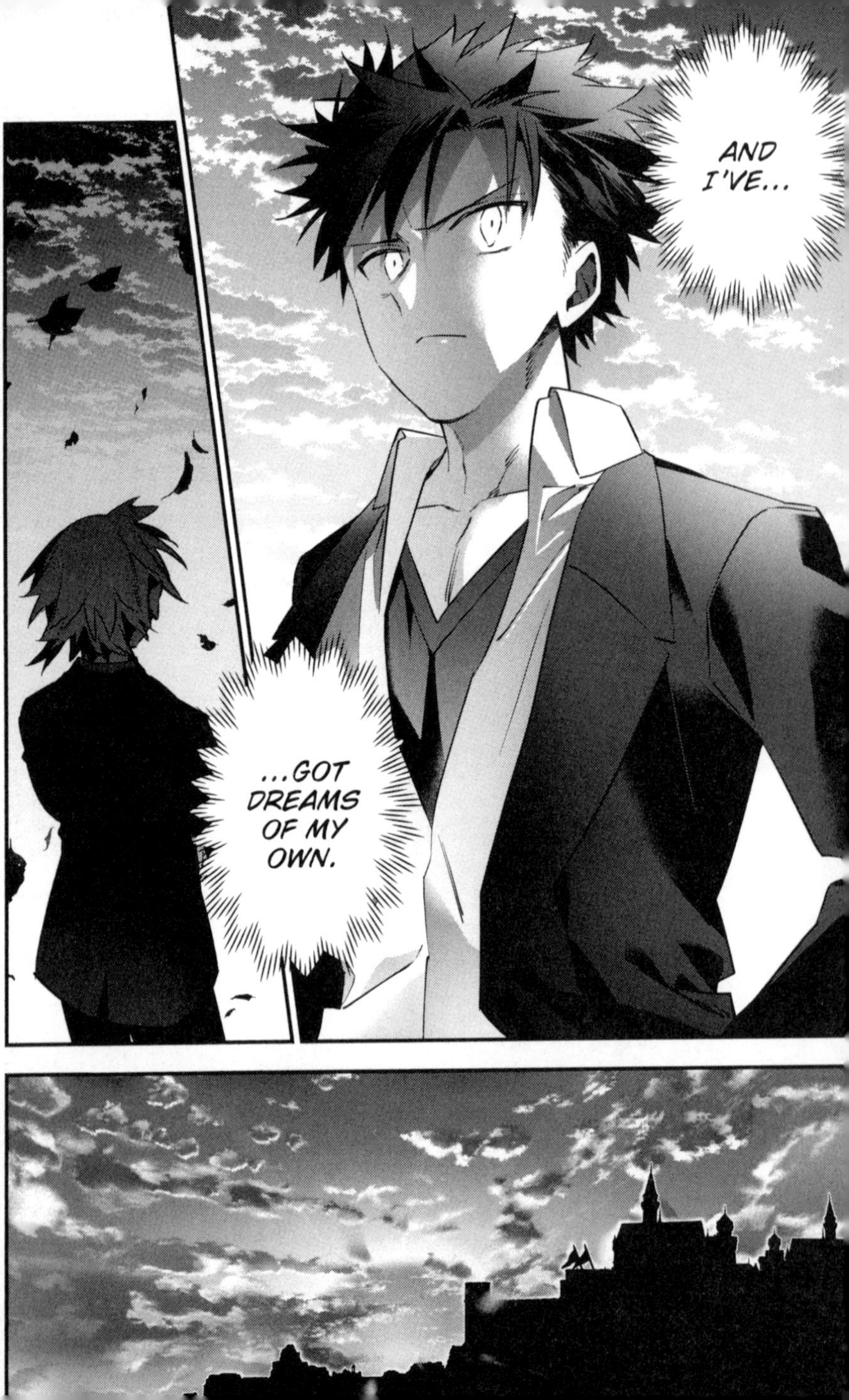
AND I'VE...
...GOT DREAMS OF MY OWN.

HIGH SCHOOL PRODIGIES HAVE IT EASY EVEN IN ANOTHER WORLD!

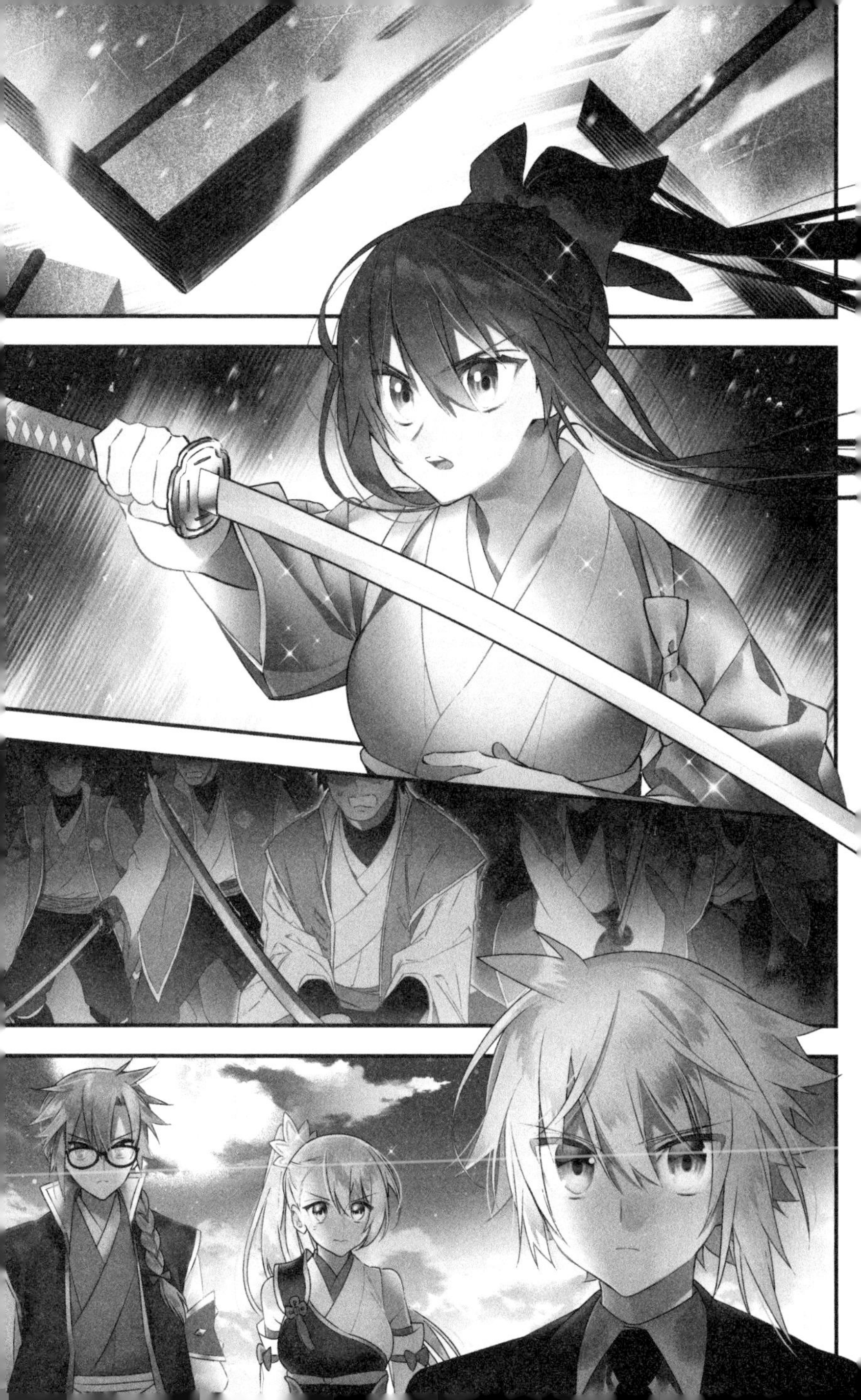

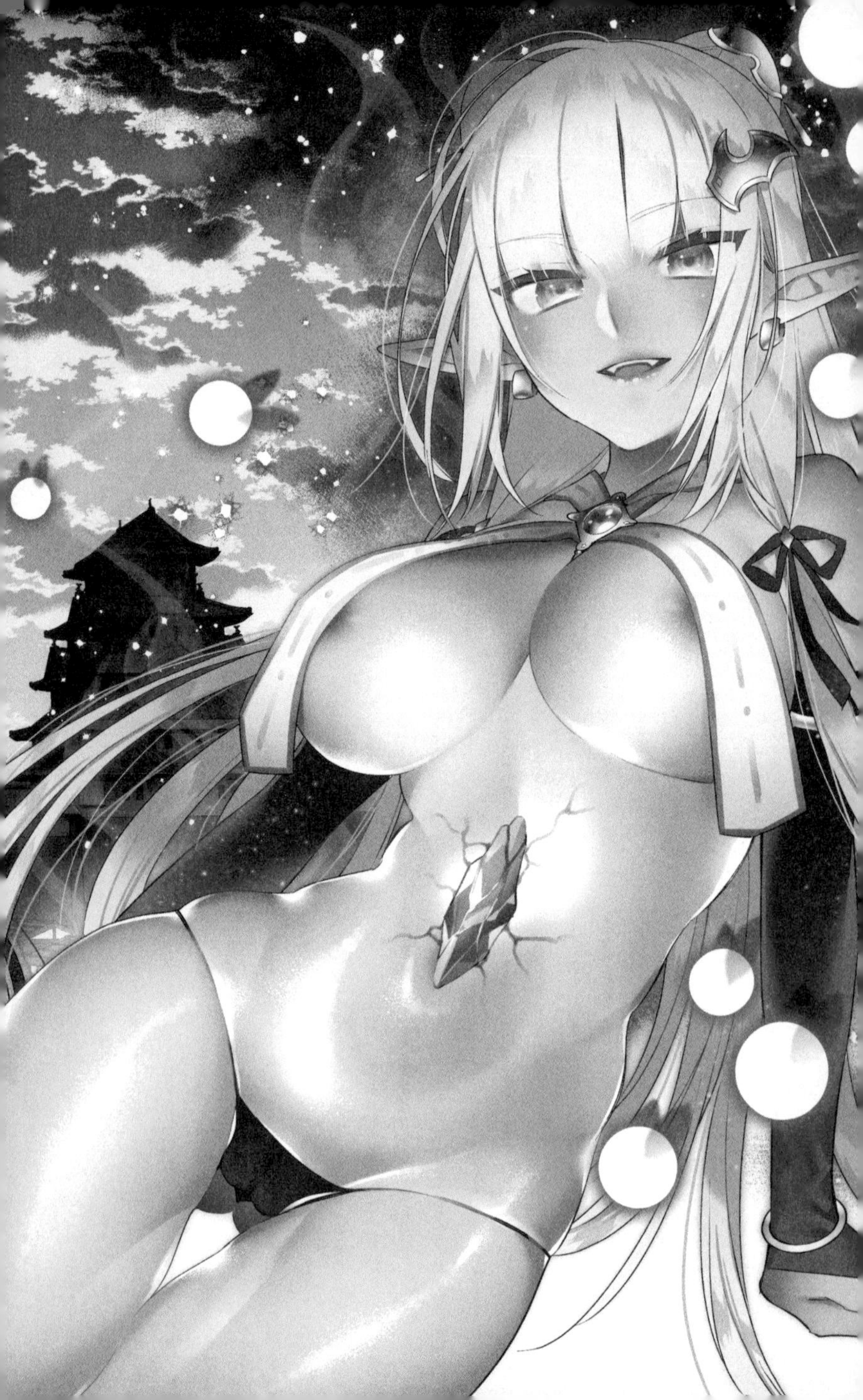

CHAPTER 80: A HINT AT THE TRUTH

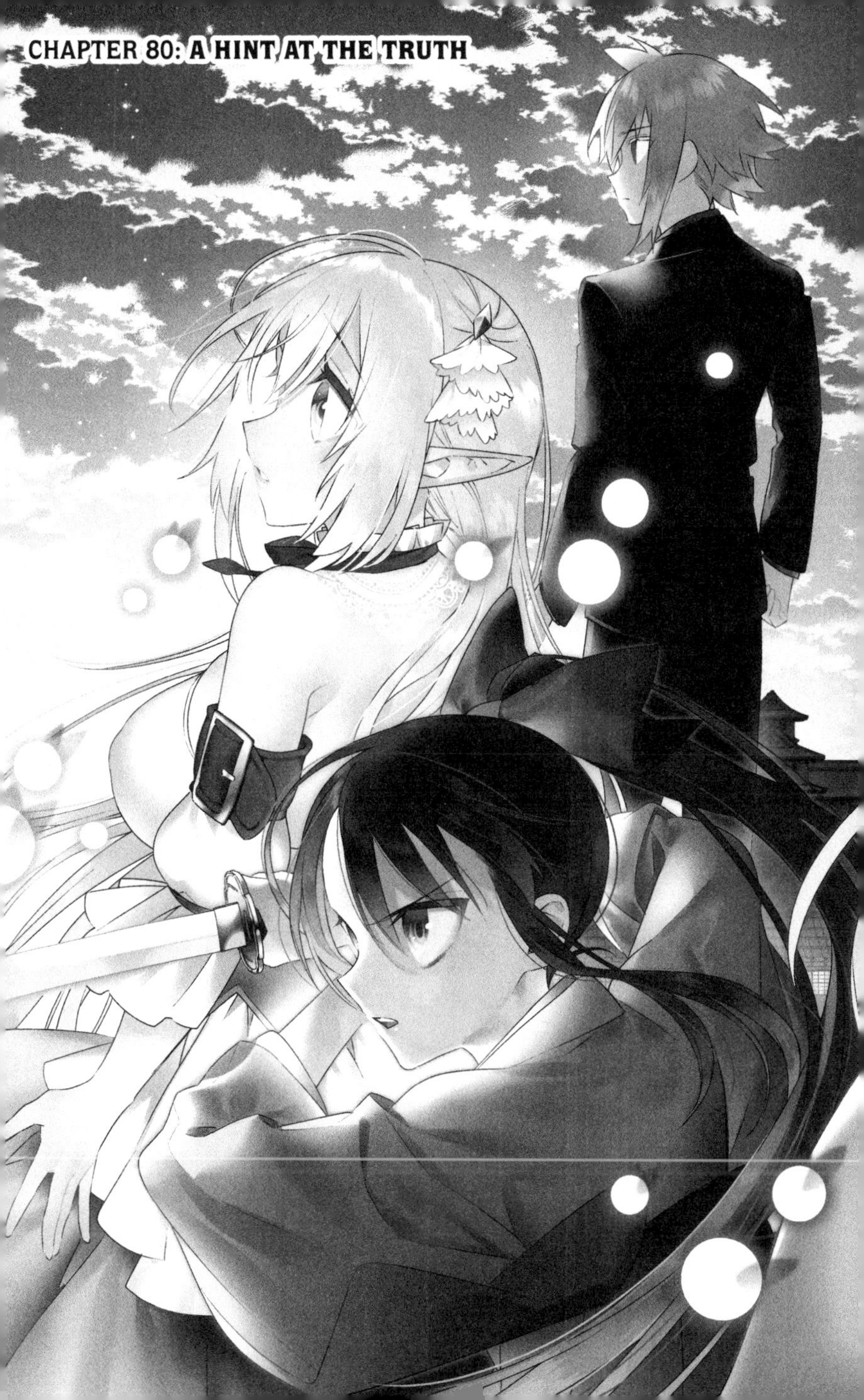

HIGH SCHOOL
PRODIGIES HAVE
IT EASY EVEN IN
ANOTHER
WORLD!

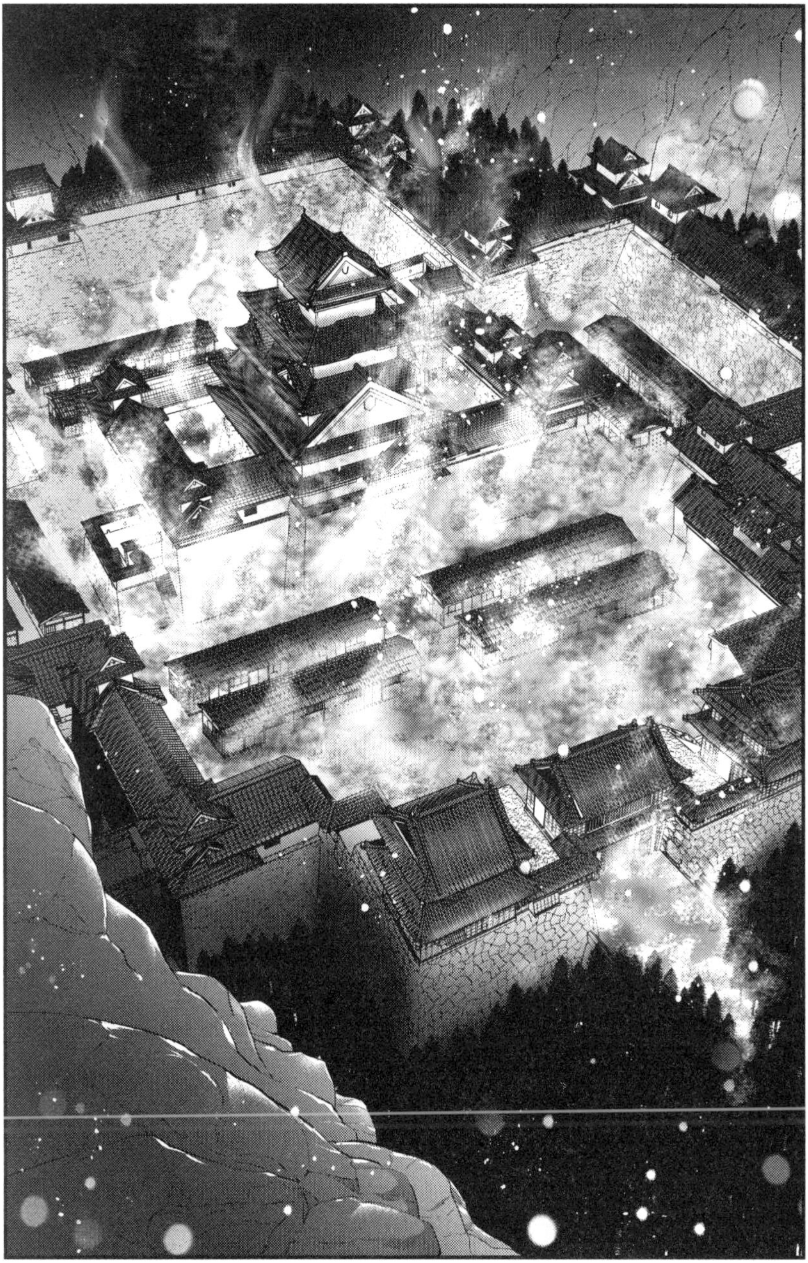

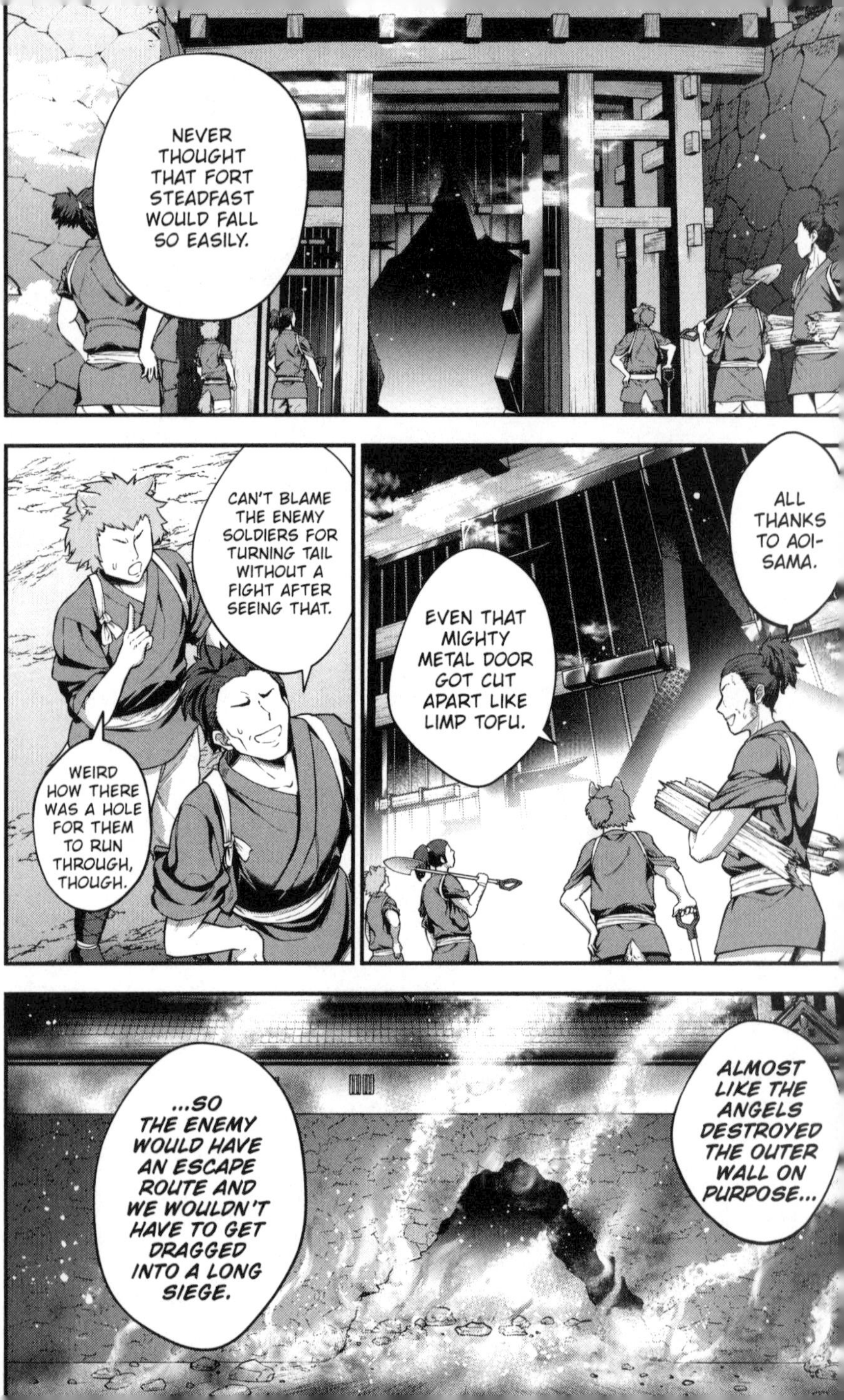
NEVER THOUGHT THAT FORT STEADFAST WOULD FALL SO EASILY.
ALL THANKS TO AOI-SAMA.
EVEN THAT MIGHTY METAL DOOR GOT CUT APART LIKE LIMP TOFU.
CAN'T BLAME THE ENEMY SOLDIERS FOR TURNING TAIL WITHOUT A FIGHT AFTER SEEING THAT.
WEIRD HOW THERE WAS A HOLE FOR THEM TO RUN THROUGH, THOUGH.
ALMOST LIKE THE ANGELS DESTROYED THE OUTER WALL ON PURPOSE...
...SO THE ENEMY WOULD HAVE AN ESCAPE ROUTE AND WE WOULDN'T HAVE TO GET DRAGGED INTO A LONG SIEGE.

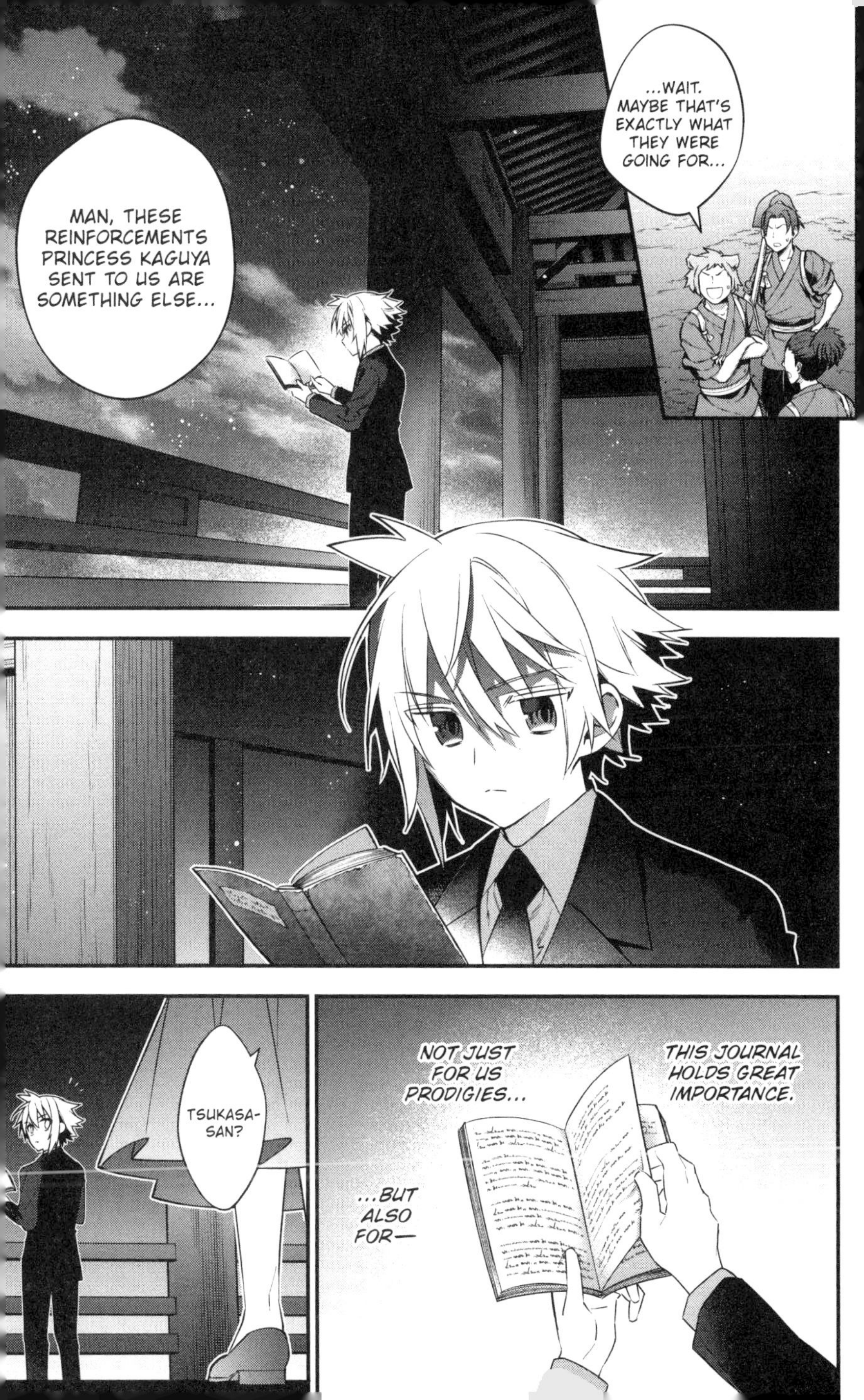
MAN, THESE REINFORCEMENTS PRINCESS KAGUYA SENT TO US ARE SOMETHING ELSE...
...WAIT. MAYBE THAT'S EXACTLY WHAT THEY WERE GOING FOR...
THIS JOURNAL HOLDS GREAT IMPORTANCE.
NOT JUST FOR US PRODIGIES...
...BUT ALSO FOR—
TSUKASA-SAN?

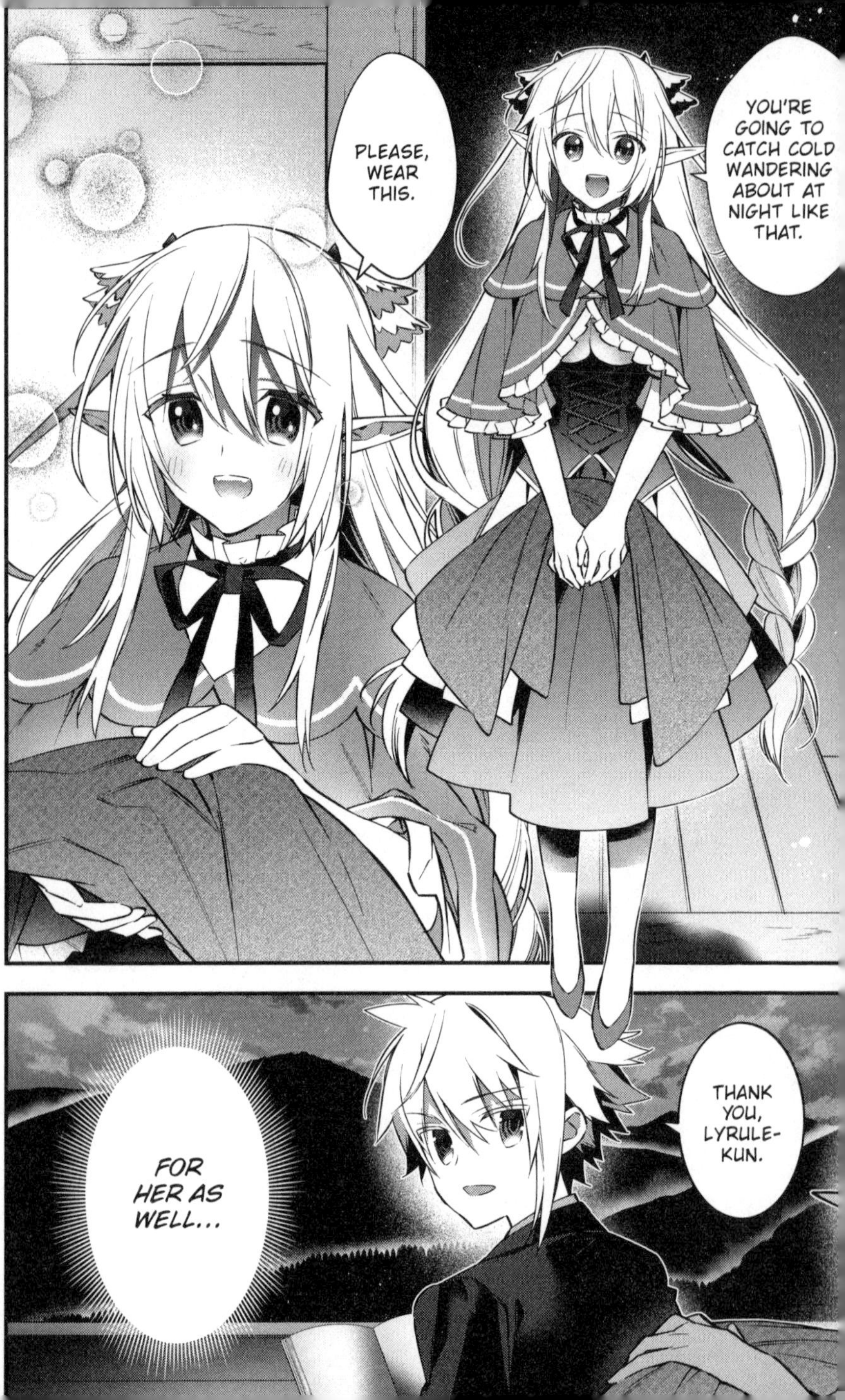
YOU'RE GOING TO CATCH COLD WANDERING ABOUT AT NIGHT LIKE THAT.
PLEASE, WEAR THIS.
THANK YOU, LYRULE-KUN.
FOR HER AS WELL...

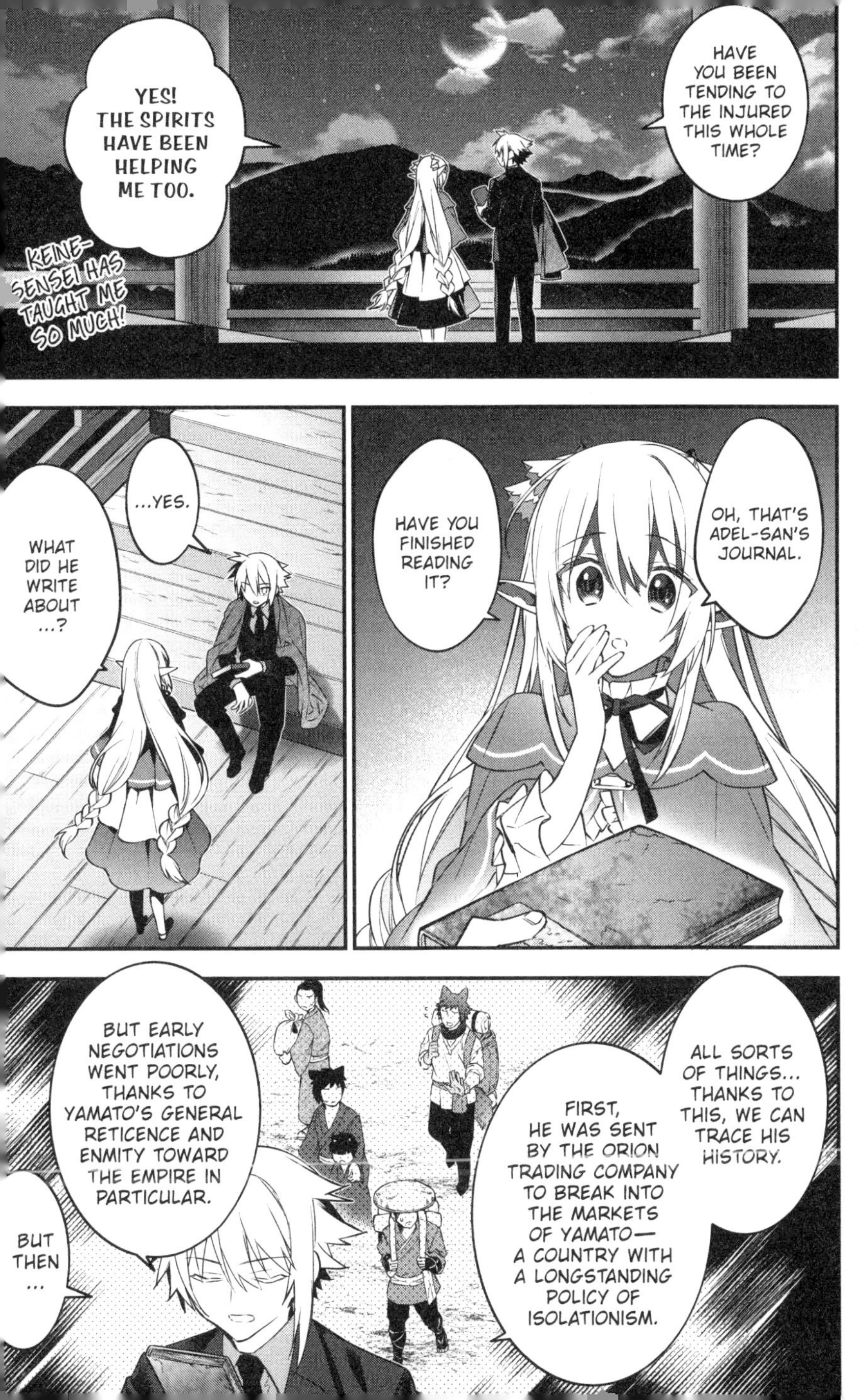
HAVE YOU BEEN TENDING TO THE INJURED THIS WHOLE TIME?
YES! THE SPIRITS HAVE BEEN HELPING ME TOO.
KEINE-SENSEI HAS TAUGHT ME SO MUCH!
OH, THAT'S ADEL-SAN'S JOURNAL.
HAVE YOU FINISHED READING IT?
...YES.
WHAT DID HE WRITE ABOUT ...?
ALL SORTS OF THINGS... THANKS TO THIS, WE CAN TRACE HIS HISTORY.
FIRST, HE WAS SENT BY THE ORION TRADING COMPANY TO BREAK INTO THE MARKETS OF YAMATO— A COUNTRY WITH A LONGSTANDING POLICY OF ISOLATIONISM.
BUT EARLY NEGOTIATIONS WENT POORLY, THANKS TO YAMATO'S GENERAL RETICENCE AND ENMITY TOWARD THE EMPIRE IN PARTICULAR.
BUT THEN ...

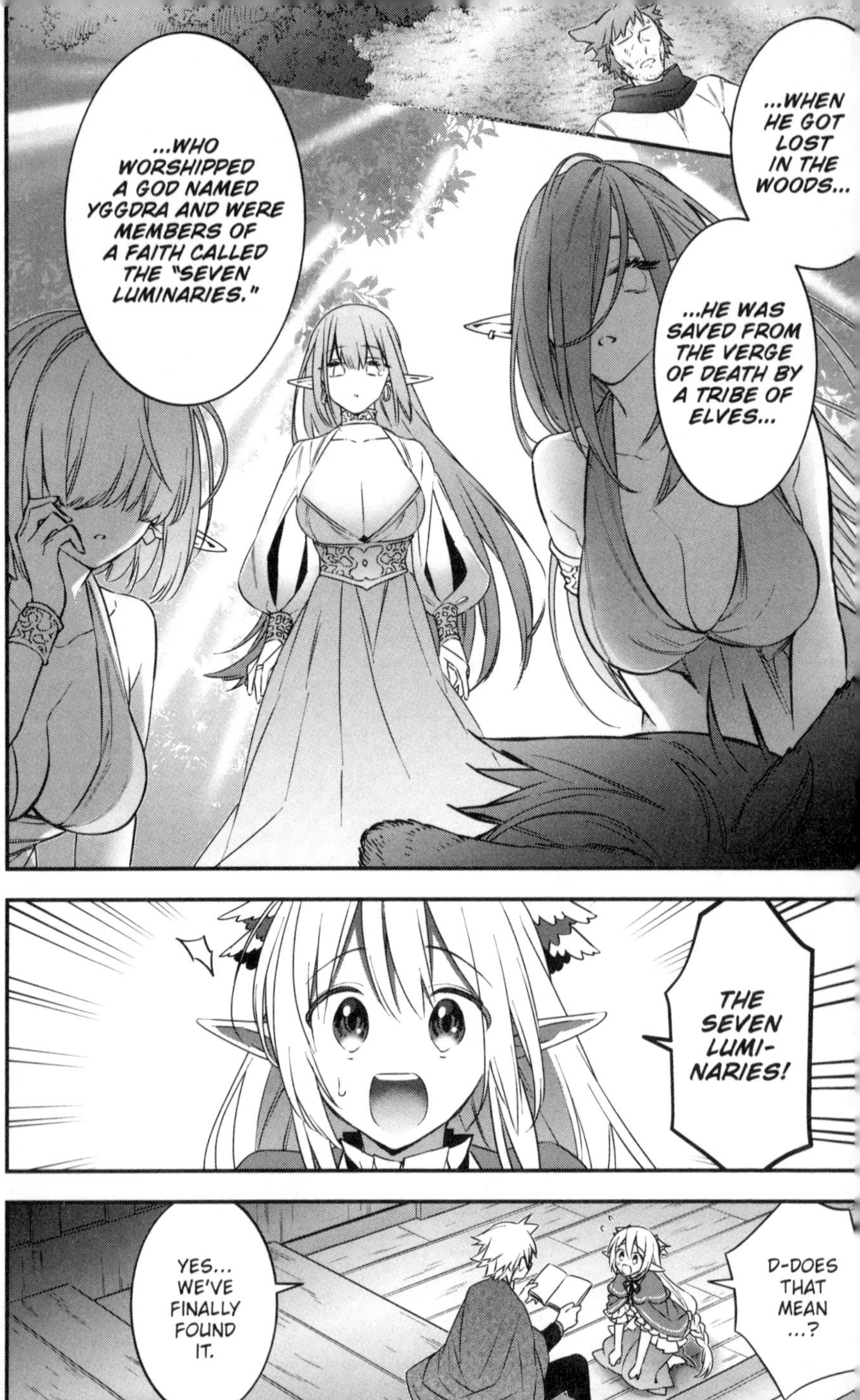
...WHEN HE GOT LOST IN THE WOODS...
...HE WAS SAVED FROM THE VERGE OF DEATH BY A TRIBE OF ELVES...
...WHO WORSHIPPED A GOD NAMED YGGDRA AND WERE MEMBERS OF A FAITH CALLED THE "SEVEN LUMINARIES."
THE SEVEN LUMI-NARIES!
D-DOES THAT MEAN ...?
YES... WE'VE FINALLY FOUND IT.

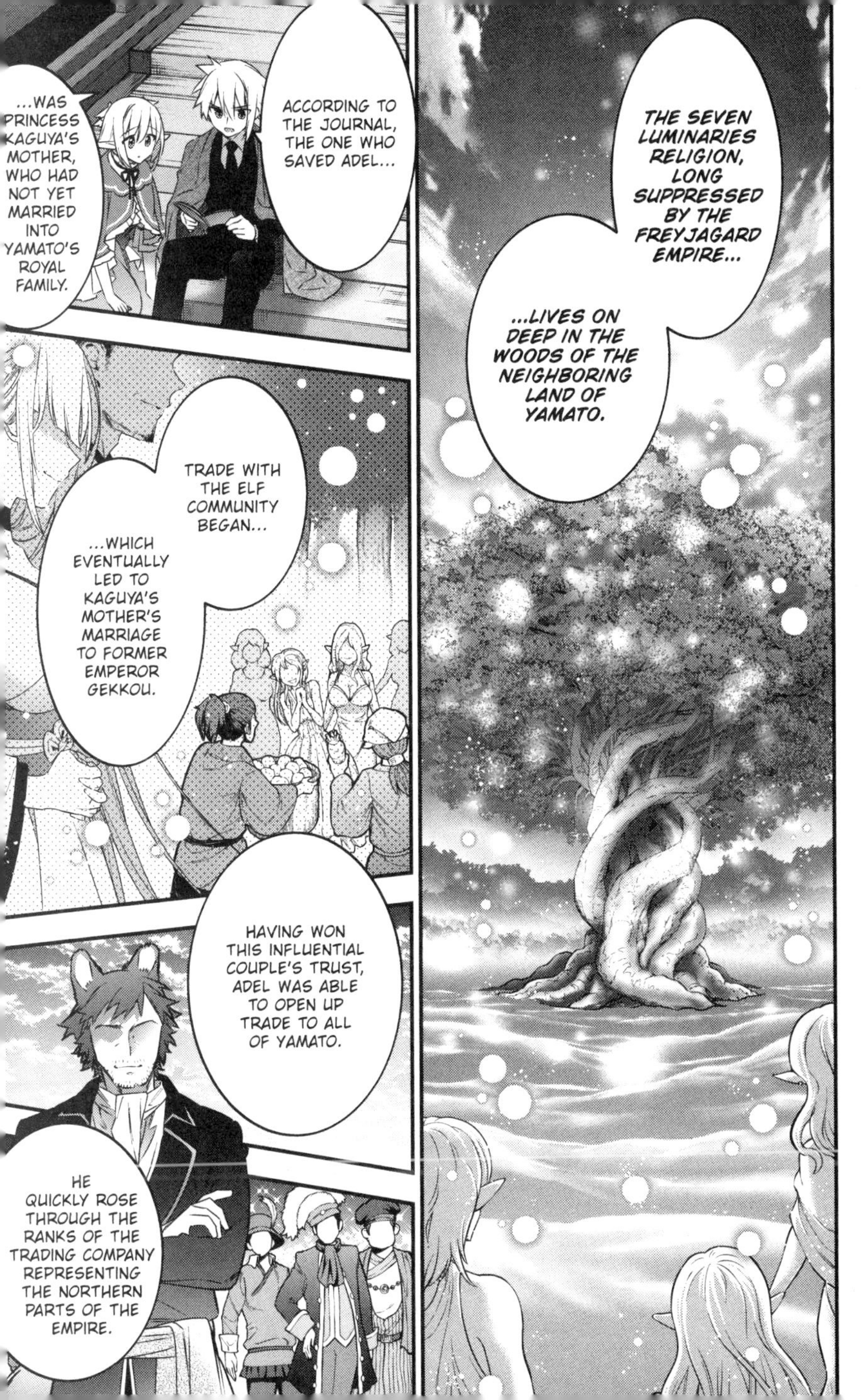
THE SEVEN LUMINARIES RELIGION, LONG SUPPRESSED BY THE FREYJAGARD EMPIRE...
...LIVES ON DEEP IN THE WOODS OF THE NEIGHBORING LAND OF YAMATO.
ACCORDING TO THE JOURNAL, THE ONE WHO SAVED ADEL...
...WAS PRINCESS KAGUYA'S MOTHER, WHO HAD NOT YET MARRIED INTO YAMATO'S ROYAL FAMILY.
TRADE WITH THE ELF COMMUNITY BEGAN...
...WHICH EVENTUALLY LED TO KAGUYA'S MOTHER'S MARRIAGE TO FORMER EMPEROR GEKKOU.
HAVING WON THIS INFLUENTIAL COUPLE'S TRUST, ADEL WAS ABLE TO OPEN UP TRADE TO ALL OF YAMATO.
HE QUICKLY ROSE THROUGH THE RANKS OF THE TRADING COMPANY REPRESENTING THE NORTHERN PARTS OF THE EMPIRE.

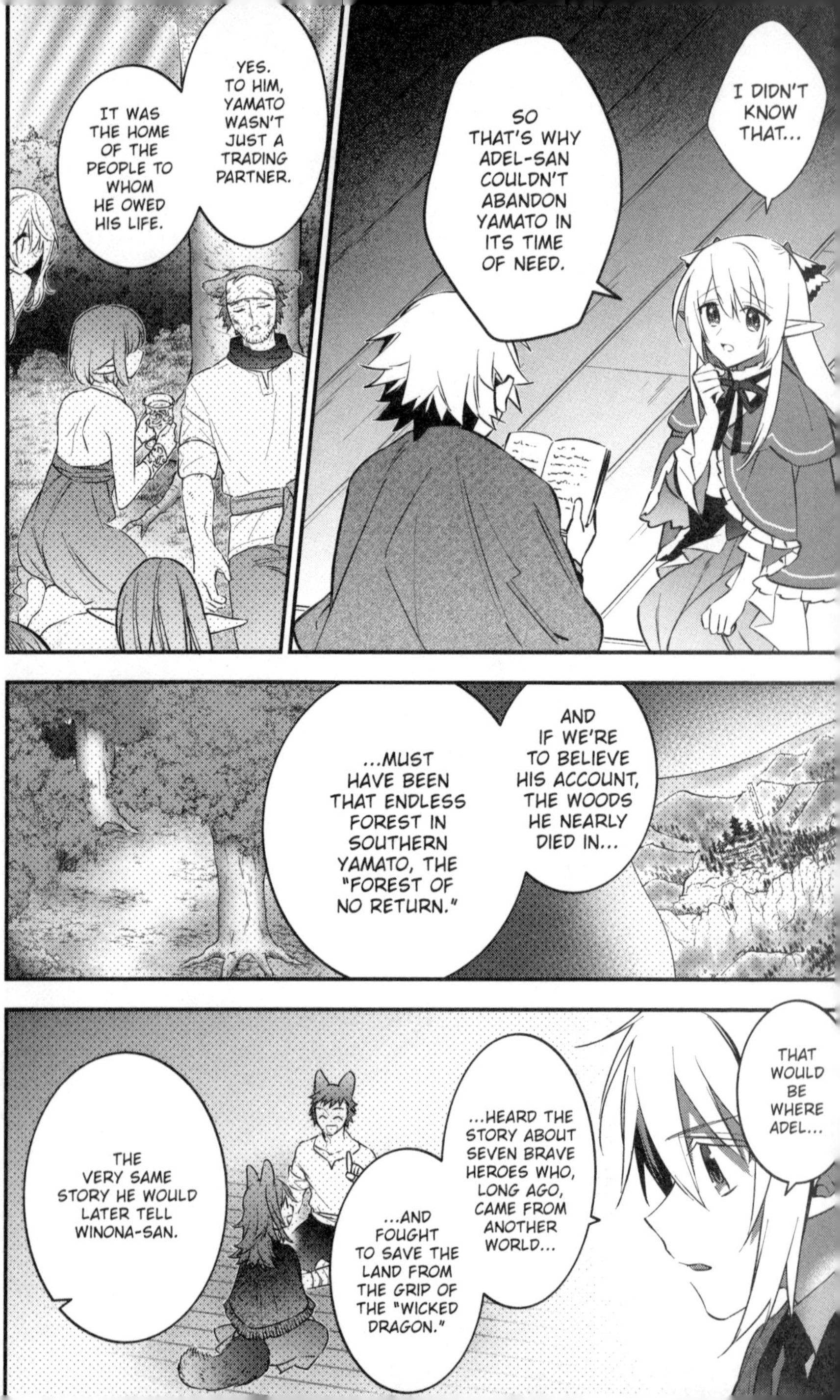
I DIDN'T KNOW THAT...
SO THAT'S WHY ADEL-SAN COULDN'T ABANDON YAMATO IN ITS TIME OF NEED.
YES. TO HIM, YAMATO WASN'T JUST A TRADING PARTNER.
IT WAS THE HOME OF THE PEOPLE TO WHOM HE OWED HIS LIFE.
AND IF WE'RE TO BELIEVE HIS ACCOUNT, THE WOODS HE NEARLY DIED IN...
...MUST HAVE BEEN THAT ENDLESS FOREST IN SOUTHERN YAMATO, THE "FOREST OF NO RETURN."
THAT WOULD BE WHERE ADEL...
...HEARD THE STORY ABOUT SEVEN BRAVE HEROES WHO, LONG AGO, CAME FROM ANOTHER WORLD...
...AND FOUGHT TO SAVE THE LAND FROM THE GRIP OF THE "WICKED DRAGON."
THE VERY SAME STORY HE WOULD LATER TELL WINONA-SAN.

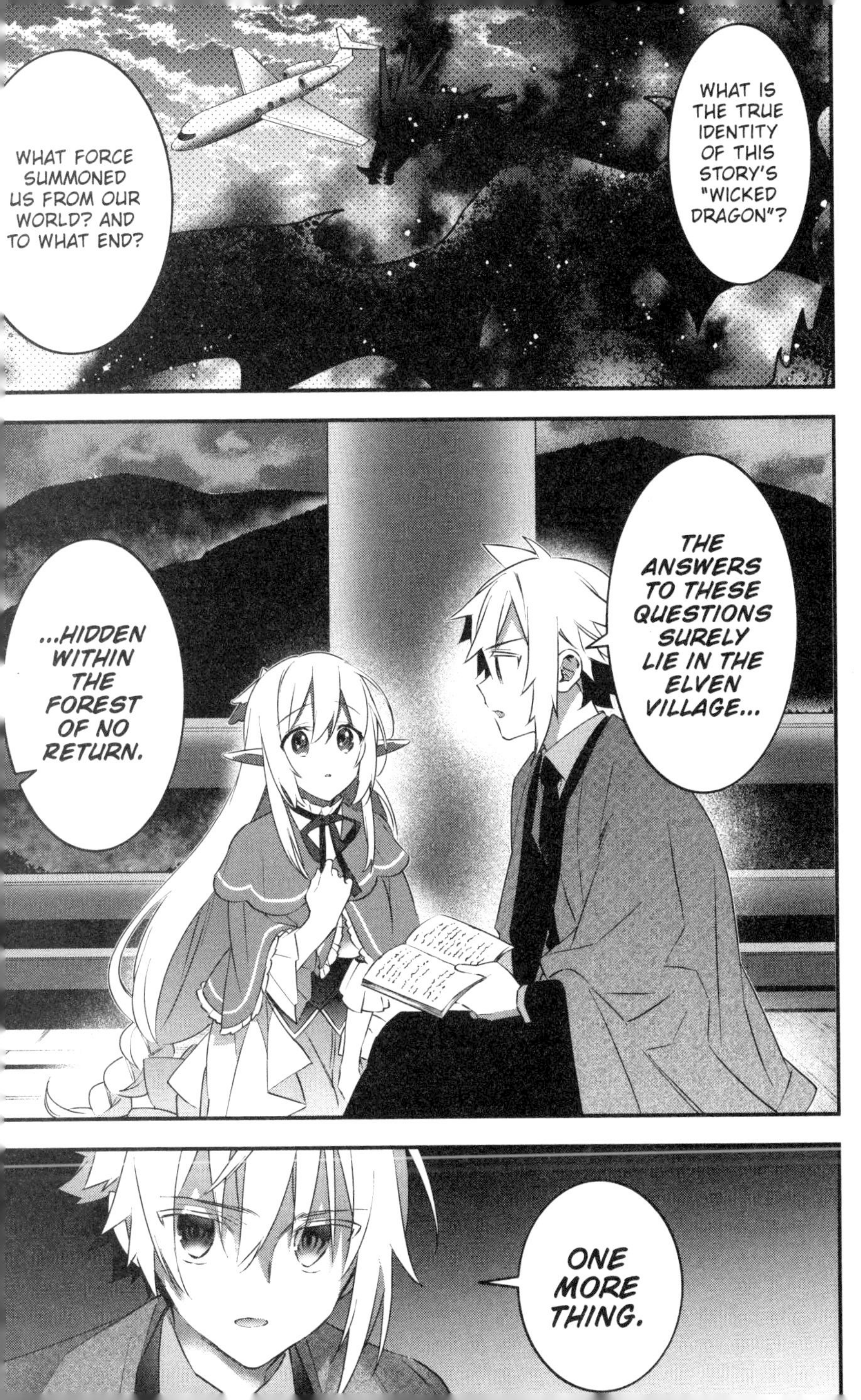
WHAT IS THE TRUE IDENTITY OF THIS STORY'S "WICKED DRAGON"?
WHAT FORCE SUMMONED US FROM OUR WORLD? AND TO WHAT END?
THE ANSWERS TO THESE QUESTIONS SURELY LIE IN THE ELVEN VILLAGE...
...HIDDEN WITHIN THE FOREST OF NO RETURN.
ONE MORE THING.

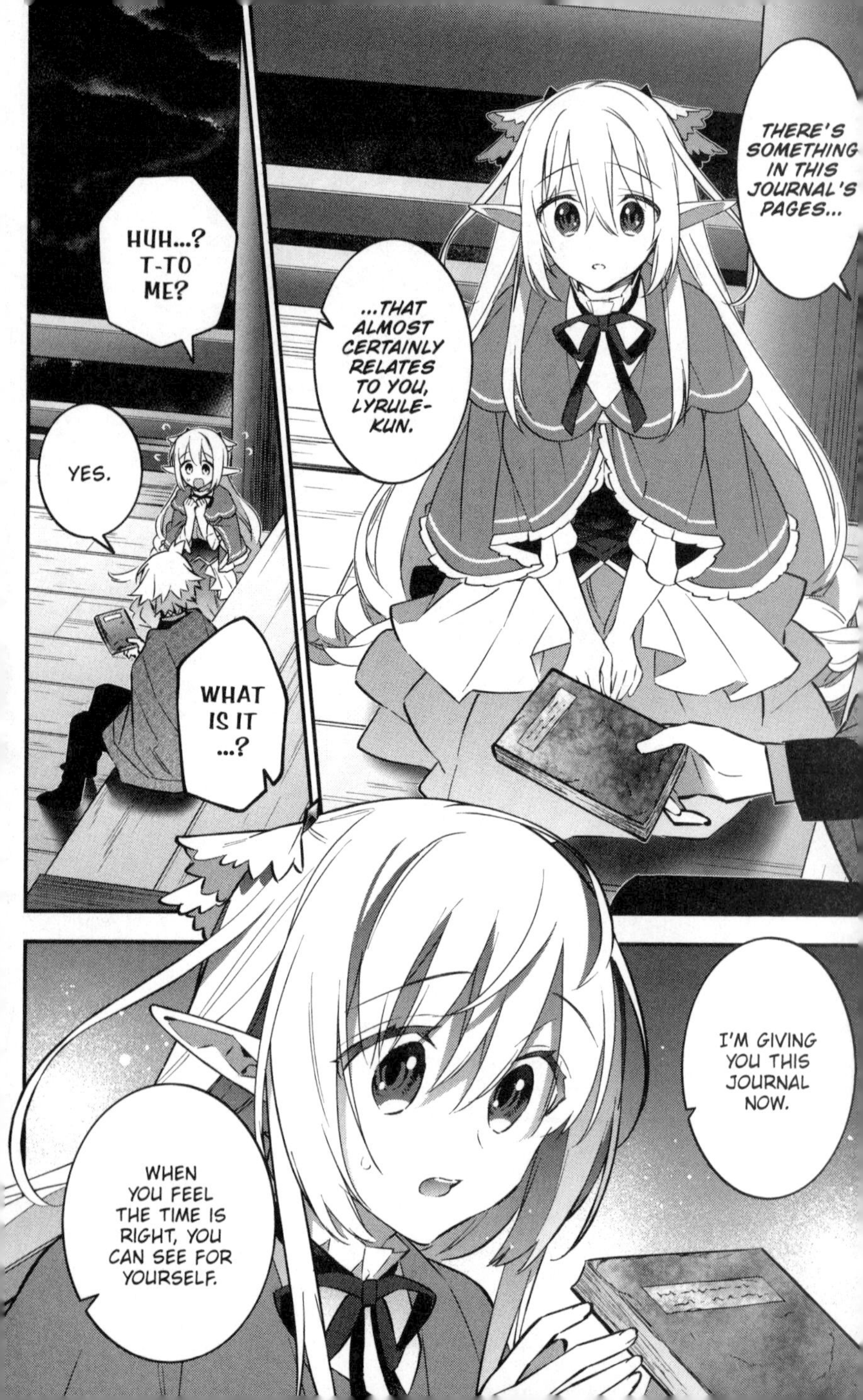
THERE'S SOMETHING IN THIS JOURNAL'S PAGES...
...THAT ALMOST CERTAINLY RELATES TO YOU, LYRULE-KUN.
HUH...? T-TO ME?
YES.
WHAT IS IT ...?
I'M GIVING YOU THIS JOURNAL NOW.
WHEN YOU FEEL THE TIME IS RIGHT, YOU CAN SEE FOR YOURSELF.

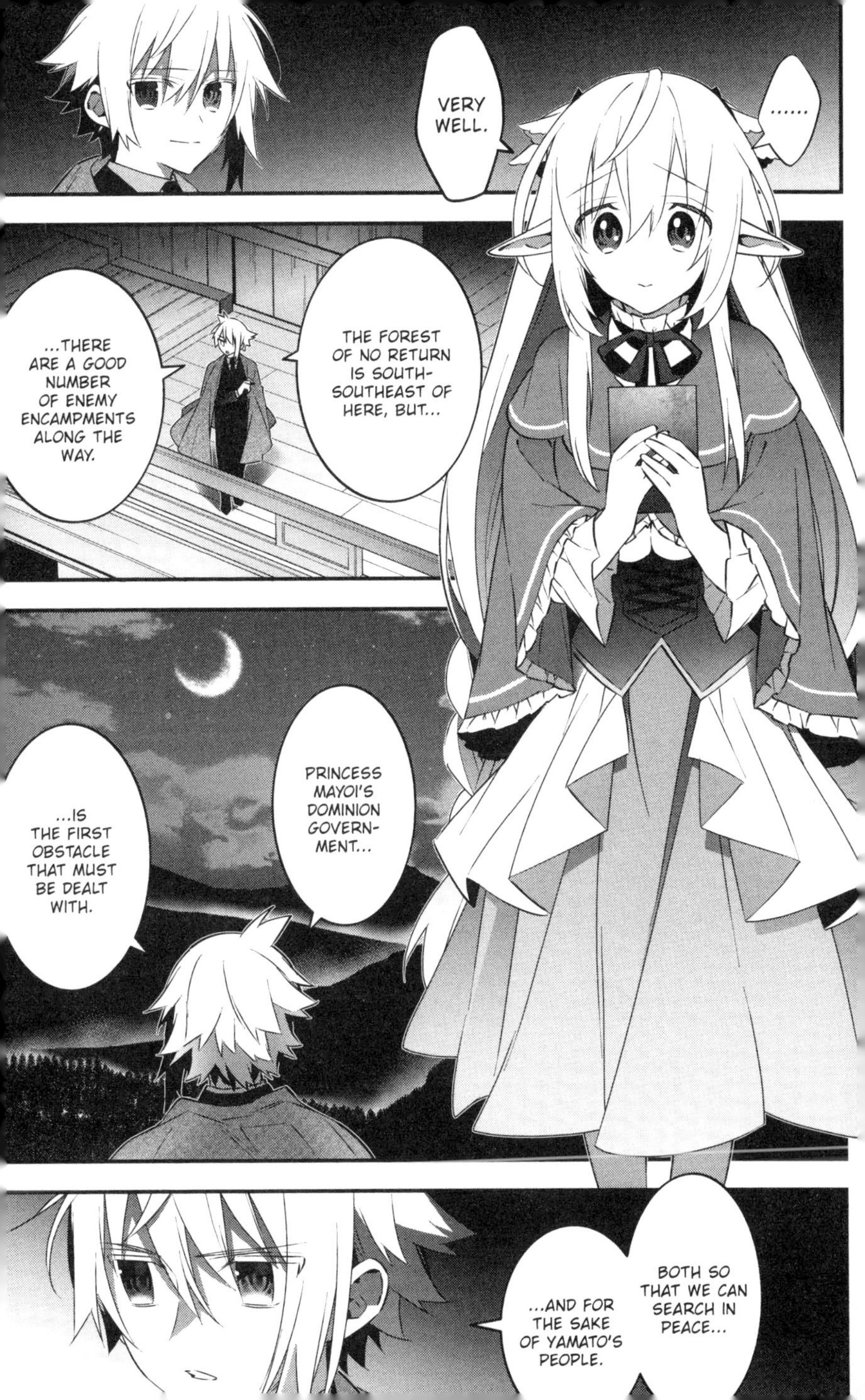
......
VERY WELL.
THE FOREST OF NO RETURN IS SOUTH-SOUTHEAST OF HERE, BUT...
...THERE ARE A GOOD NUMBER OF ENEMY ENCAMPMENTS ALONG THE WAY.
PRINCESS MAYOI'S DOMINION GOVERN-MENT...
...IS THE FIRST OBSTACLE THAT MUST BE DEALT WITH.
BOTH SO THAT WE CAN SEARCH IN PEACE...
...AND FOR THE SAKE OF YAMATO'S PEOPLE.

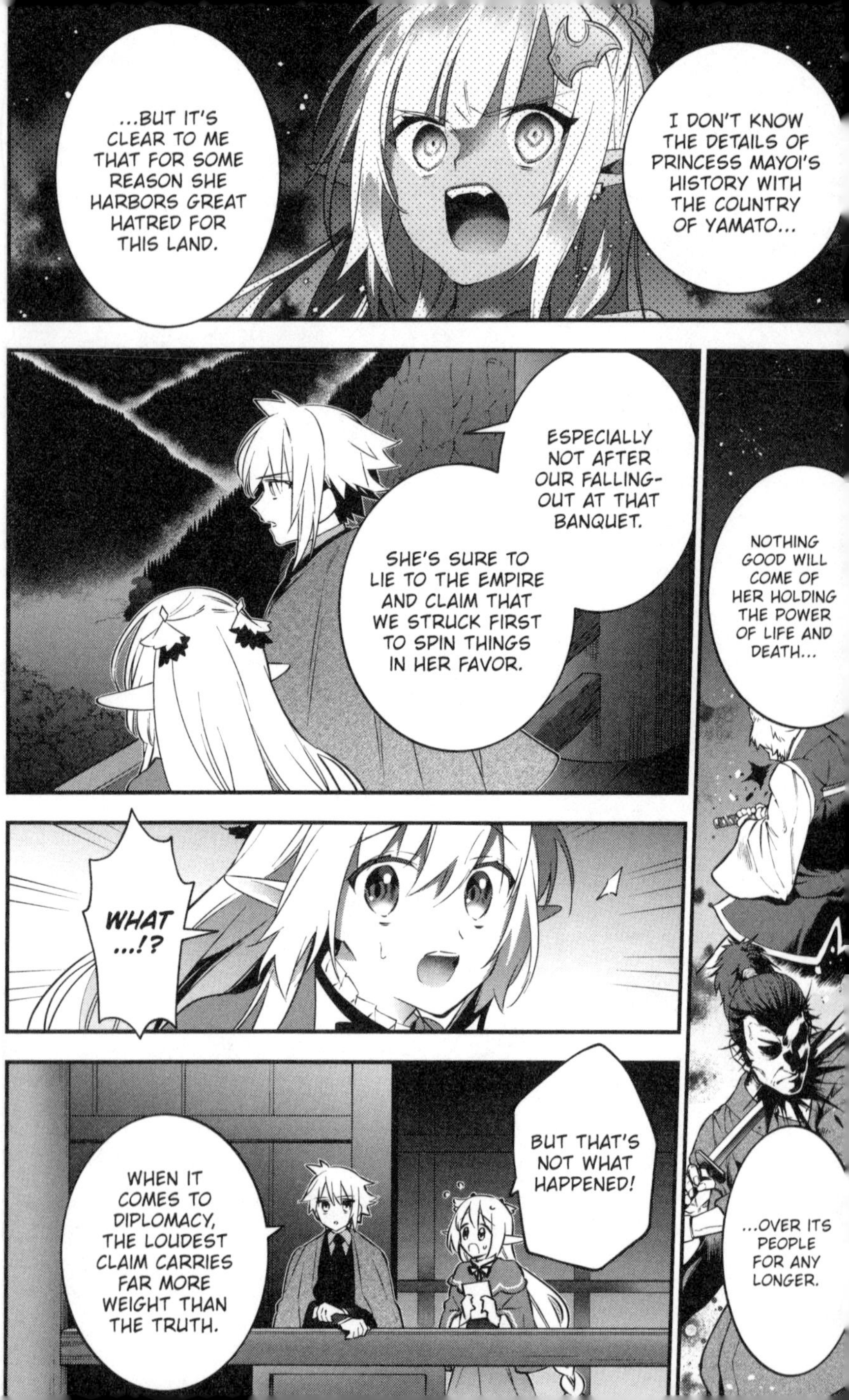
I DON'T KNOW THE DETAILS OF PRINCESS MAYOI'S HISTORY WITH THE COUNTRY OF YAMATO...
...BUT IT'S CLEAR TO ME THAT FOR SOME REASON SHE HARBORS GREAT HATRED FOR THIS LAND.
NOTHING GOOD WILL COME OF HER HOLDING THE POWER OF LIFE AND DEATH...
...OVER ITS PEOPLE FOR ANY LONGER.
ESPECIALLY NOT AFTER OUR FALLING-OUT AT THAT BANQUET.
SHE'S SURE TO LIE TO THE EMPIRE AND CLAIM THAT WE STRUCK FIRST TO SPIN THINGS IN HER FAVOR.
WHAT ...!?
BUT THAT'S NOT WHAT HAPPENED!
WHEN IT COMES TO DIPLOMACY, THE LOUDEST CLAIM CARRIES FAR MORE WEIGHT THAN THE TRUTH.

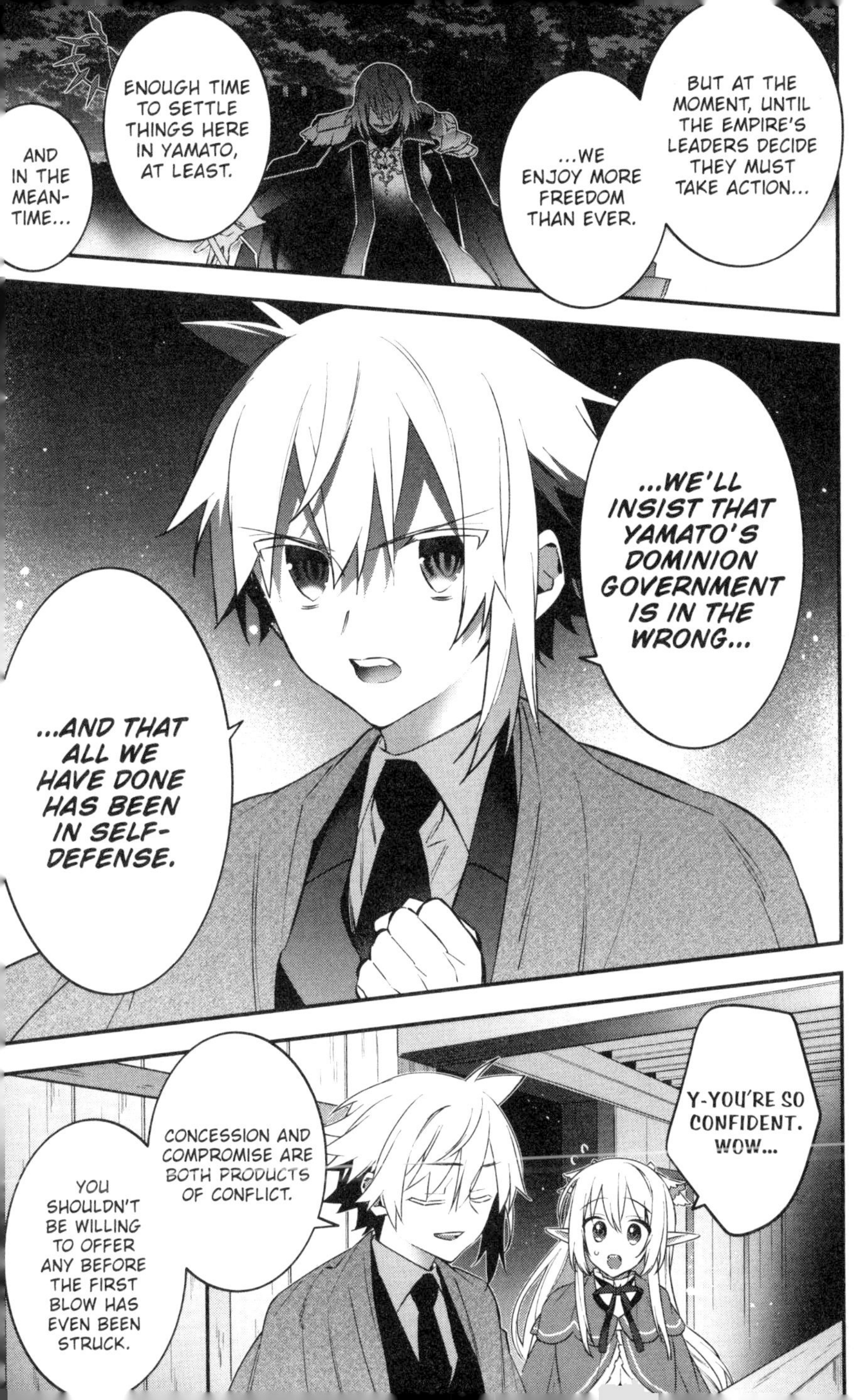
BUT AT THE MOMENT, UNTIL THE EMPIRE'S LEADERS DECIDE THEY MUST TAKE ACTION...
...WE ENJOY MORE FREEDOM THAN EVER.
ENOUGH TIME TO SETTLE THINGS HERE IN YAMATO, AT LEAST.
AND IN THE MEAN-TIME...
...WE'LL INSIST THAT YAMATO'S DOMINION GOVERNMENT IS IN THE WRONG...
...AND THAT ALL WE HAVE DONE HAS BEEN IN SELF-DEFENSE.
Y-YOU'RE SO CONFIDENT. WOW...
CONCESSION AND COMPROMISE ARE BOTH PRODUCTS OF CONFLICT.
YOU SHOULDN'T BE WILLING TO OFFER ANY BEFORE THE FIRST BLOW HAS EVEN BEEN STRUCK.

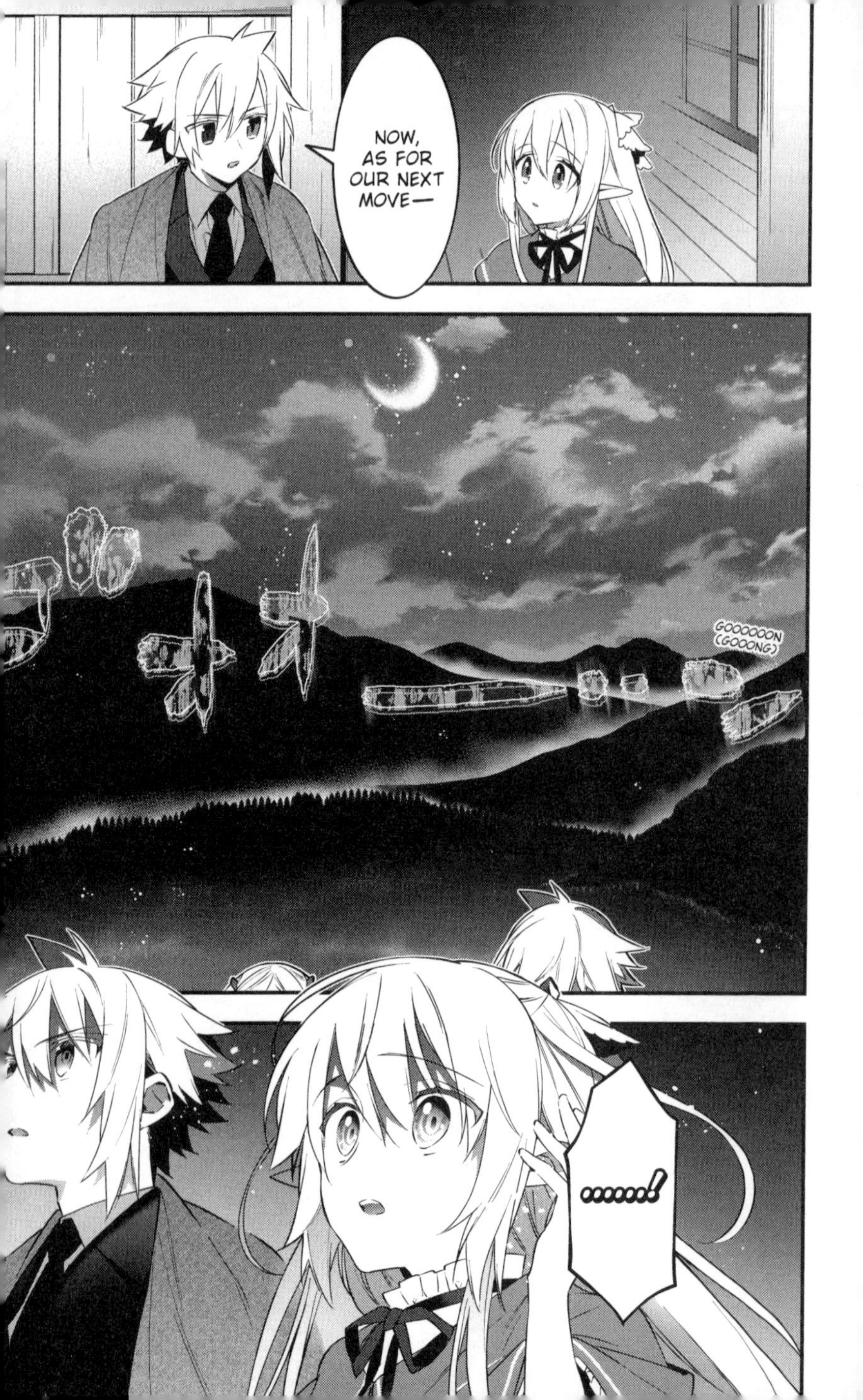
NOW, AS FOR OUR NEXT MOVE—
GOOOOOON (GOOONG)
......!

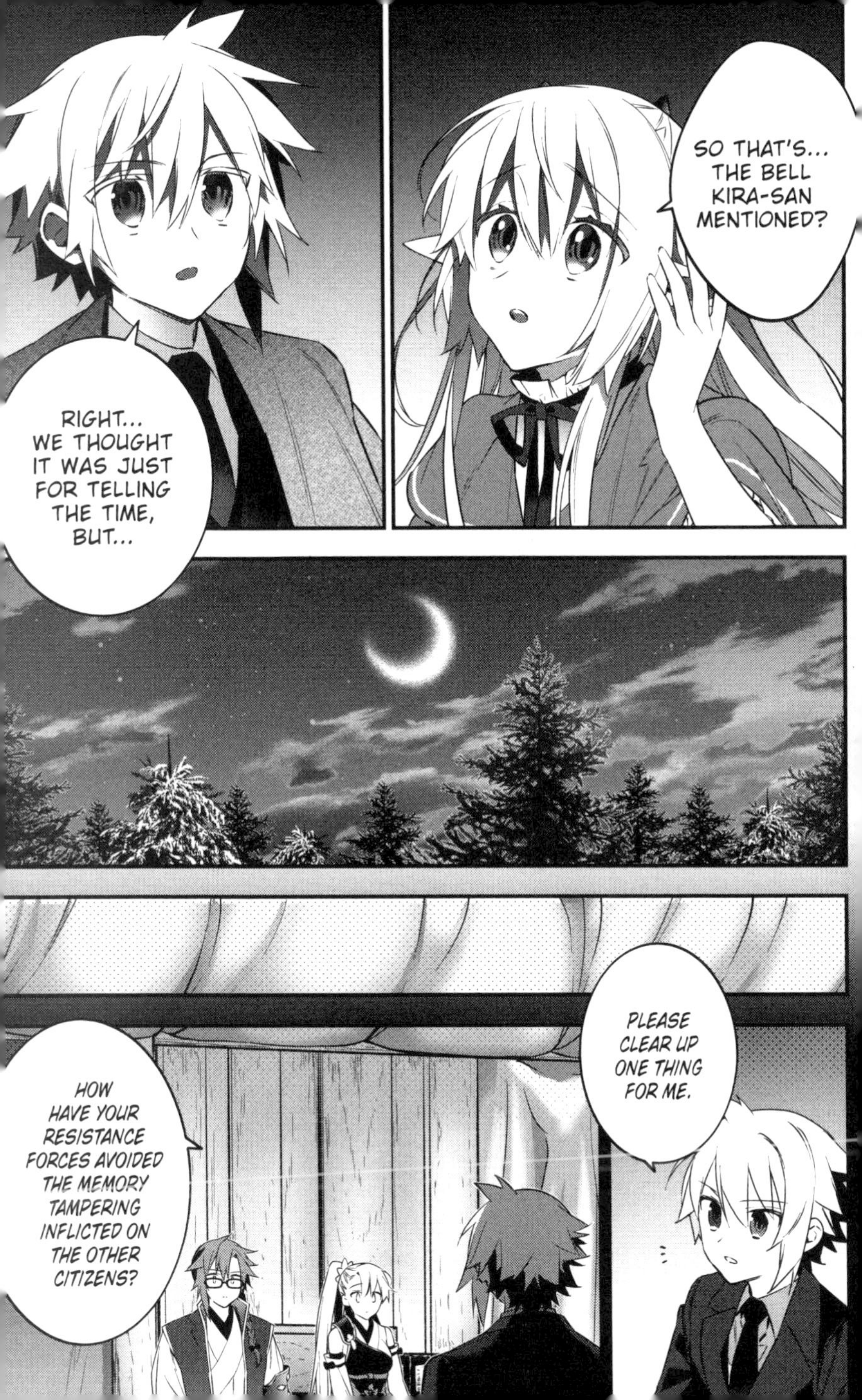
SO THAT'S... THE BELL KIRA-SAN MENTIONED?
RIGHT... WE THOUGHT IT WAS JUST FOR TELLING THE TIME, BUT...
PLEASE CLEAR UP ONE THING FOR ME.
HOW HAVE YOUR RESISTANCE FORCES AVOIDED THE MEMORY TAMPERING INFLICTED ON THE OTHER CITIZENS?

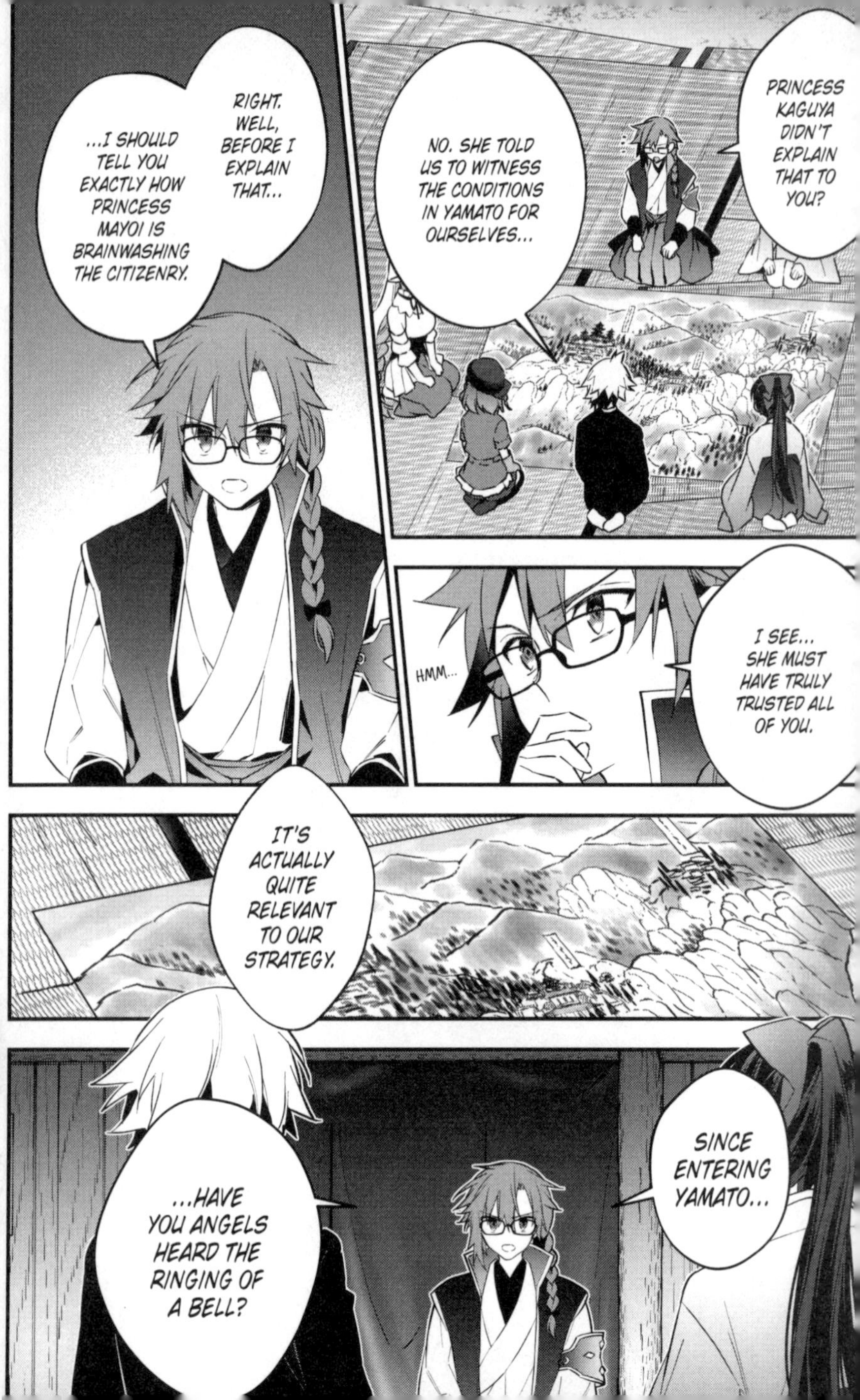
PRINCESS KAGUYA DIDN'T EXPLAIN THAT TO YOU?
NO. SHE TOLD US TO WITNESS THE CONDITIONS IN YAMATO FOR OURSELVES...
I SEE... SHE MUST HAVE TRULY TRUSTED ALL OF YOU.
HMM...
RIGHT. WELL, BEFORE I EXPLAIN THAT...
...I SHOULD TELL YOU EXACTLY HOW PRINCESS MAYOI IS BRAINWASHING THE CITIZENRY.
IT'S ACTUALLY QUITE RELEVANT TO OUR STRATEGY.
SINCE ENTERING YAMATO...
...HAVE YOU ANGELS HEARD THE RINGING OF A BELL?

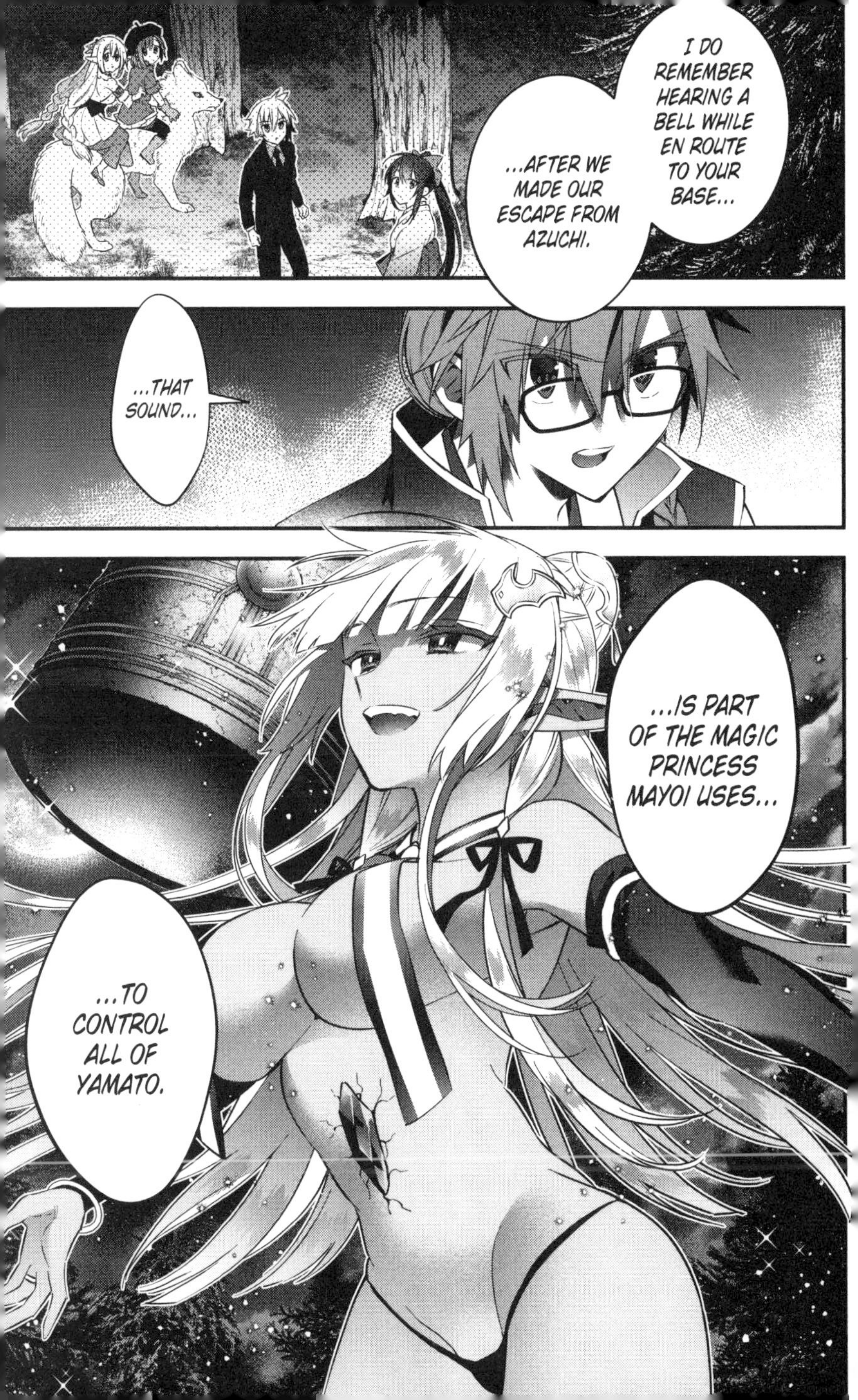
I DO REMEMBER HEARING A BELL WHILE EN ROUTE TO YOUR BASE...
...AFTER WE MADE OUR ESCAPE FROM AZUCHI.
...THAT SOUND...
...IS PART OF THE MAGIC PRINCESS MAYOI USES...
...TO CONTROL ALL OF YAMATO.

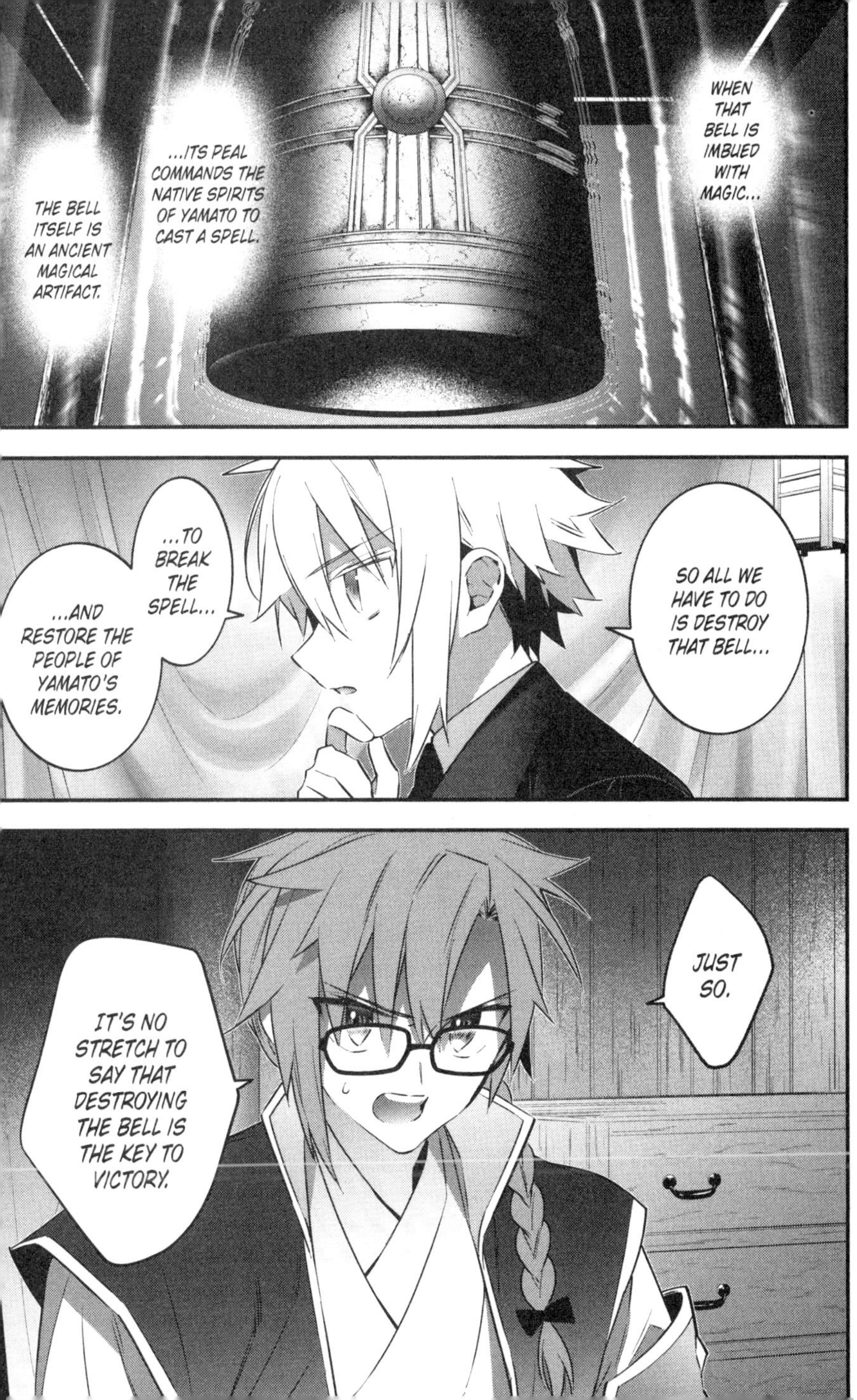
WHEN THAT BELL IS IMBUED WITH MAGIC...
...ITS PEAL COMMANDS THE NATIVE SPIRITS OF YAMATO TO CAST A SPELL.
THE BELL ITSELF IS AN ANCIENT MAGICAL ARTIFACT.
SO ALL WE HAVE TO DO IS DESTROY THAT BELL...
...TO BREAK THE SPELL...
...AND RESTORE THE PEOPLE OF YAMATO'S MEMORIES.
JUST SO.
IT'S NO STRETCH TO SAY THAT DESTROYING THE BELL IS THE KEY TO VICTORY.

CHAPTER 81: IDEALS AND RESOLVE

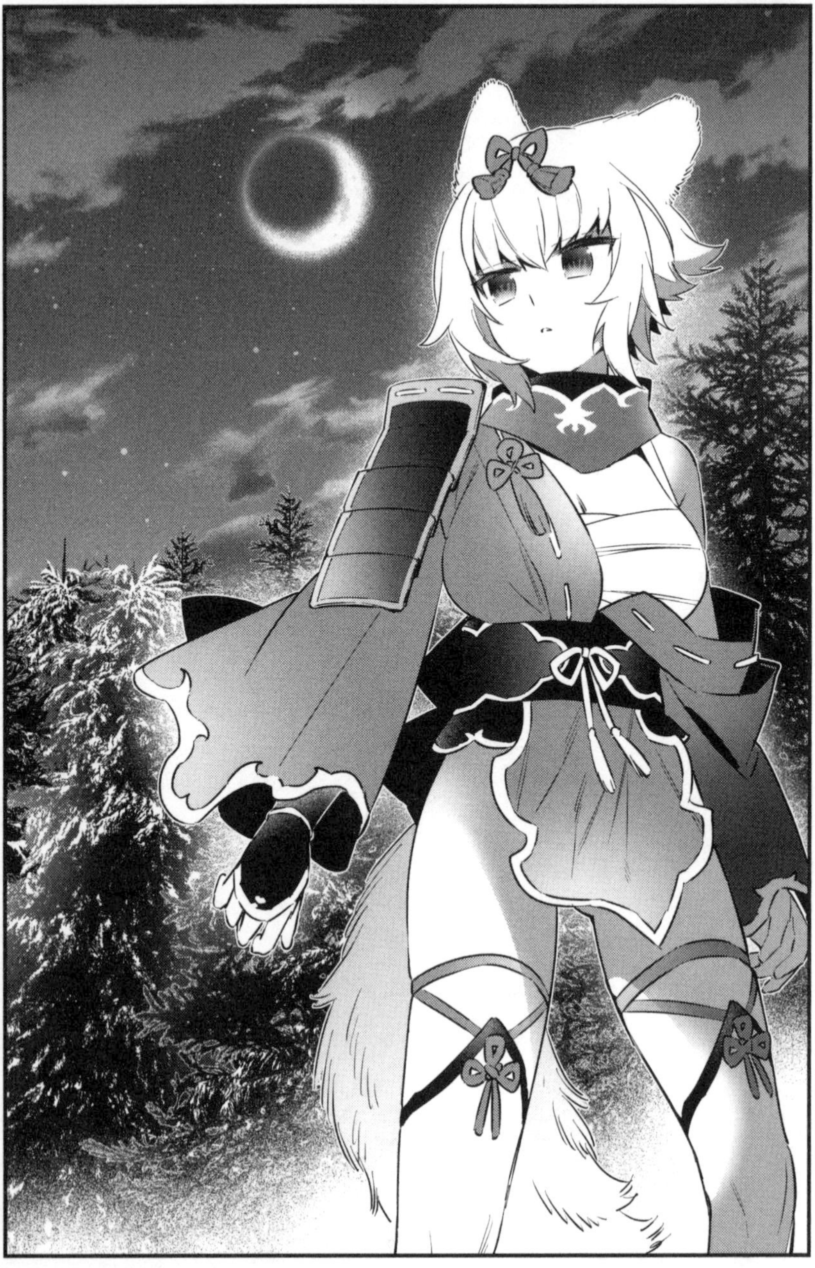

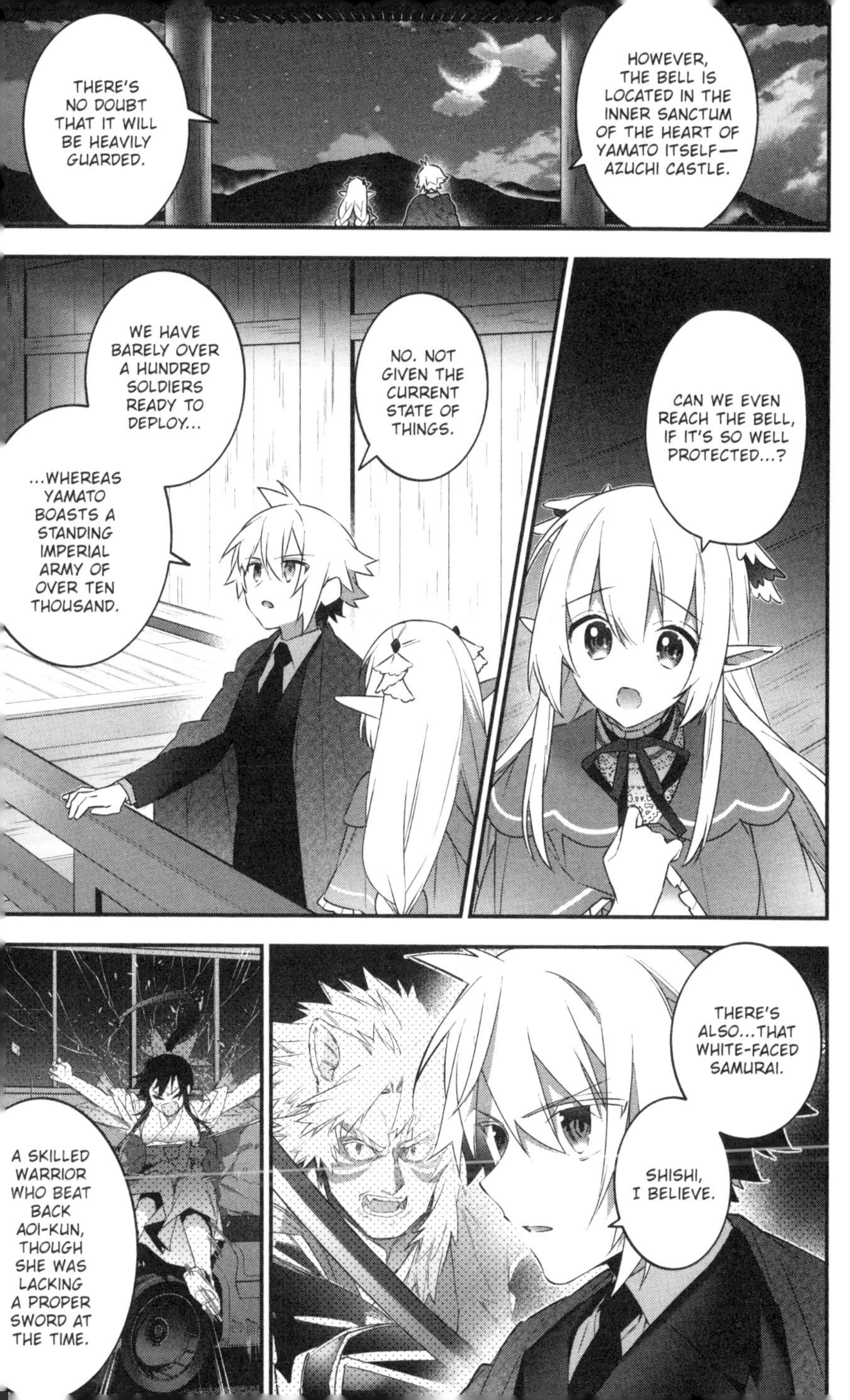
HOWEVER, THE BELL IS LOCATED IN THE INNER SANCTUM OF THE HEART OF YAMATO ITSELF—AZUCHI CASTLE.
THERE'S NO DOUBT THAT IT WILL BE HEAVILY GUARDED.
CAN WE EVEN REACH THE BELL, IF IT'S SO WELL PROTECTED...?
NO. NOT GIVEN THE CURRENT STATE OF THINGS.
WE HAVE BARELY OVER A HUNDRED SOLDIERS READY TO DEPLOY...
...WHEREAS YAMATO BOASTS A STANDING IMPERIAL ARMY OF OVER TEN THOUSAND.
THERE'S ALSO...THAT WHITE-FACED SAMURAI.
SHISHI, I BELIEVE.
A SKILLED WARRIOR WHO BEAT BACK AOI-KUN, THOUGH SHE WAS LACKING A PROPER SWORD AT THE TIME.

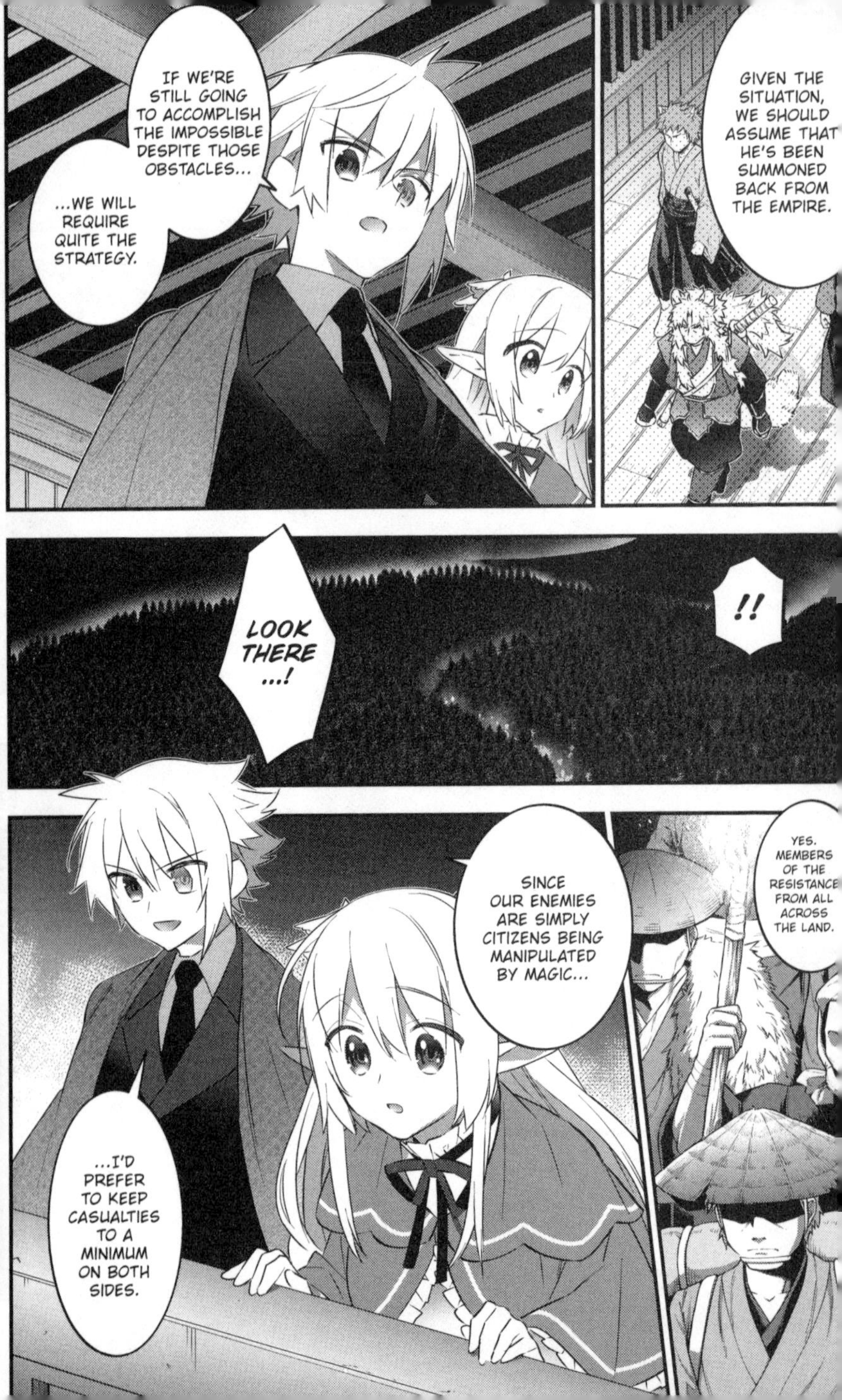
GIVEN THE SITUATION, WE SHOULD ASSUME THAT HE'S BEEN SUMMONED BACK FROM THE EMPIRE.
IF WE'RE STILL GOING TO ACCOMPLISH THE IMPOSSIBLE DESPITE THOSE OBSTACLES...
...WE WILL REQUIRE QUITE THE STRATEGY.
!!
LOOK THERE ...!
YES. MEMBERS OF THE RESISTANCE FROM ALL ACROSS THE LAND.
SINCE OUR ENEMIES ARE SIMPLY CITIZENS BEING MANIPULATED BY MAGIC...
...I'D PREFER TO KEEP CASUALTIES TO A MINIMUM ON BOTH SIDES.

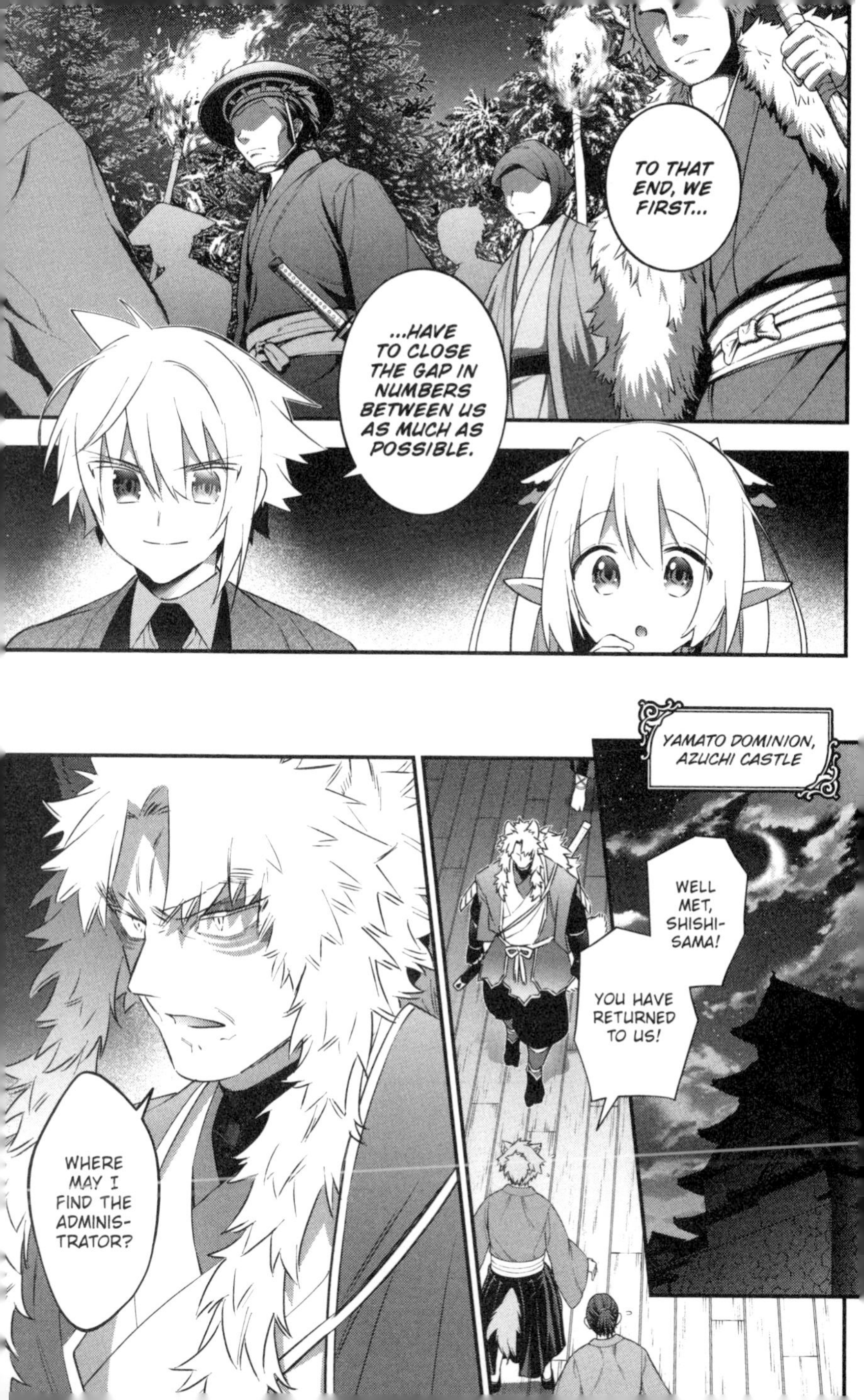
TO THAT END, WE FIRST...
...HAVE TO CLOSE THE GAP IN NUMBERS BETWEEN US AS MUCH AS POSSIBLE.
YAMATO DOMINION, AZUCHI CASTLE
WELL MET, SHISHI-SAMA!
YOU HAVE RETURNED TO US!
WHERE MAY I FIND THE ADMINISTRATOR?

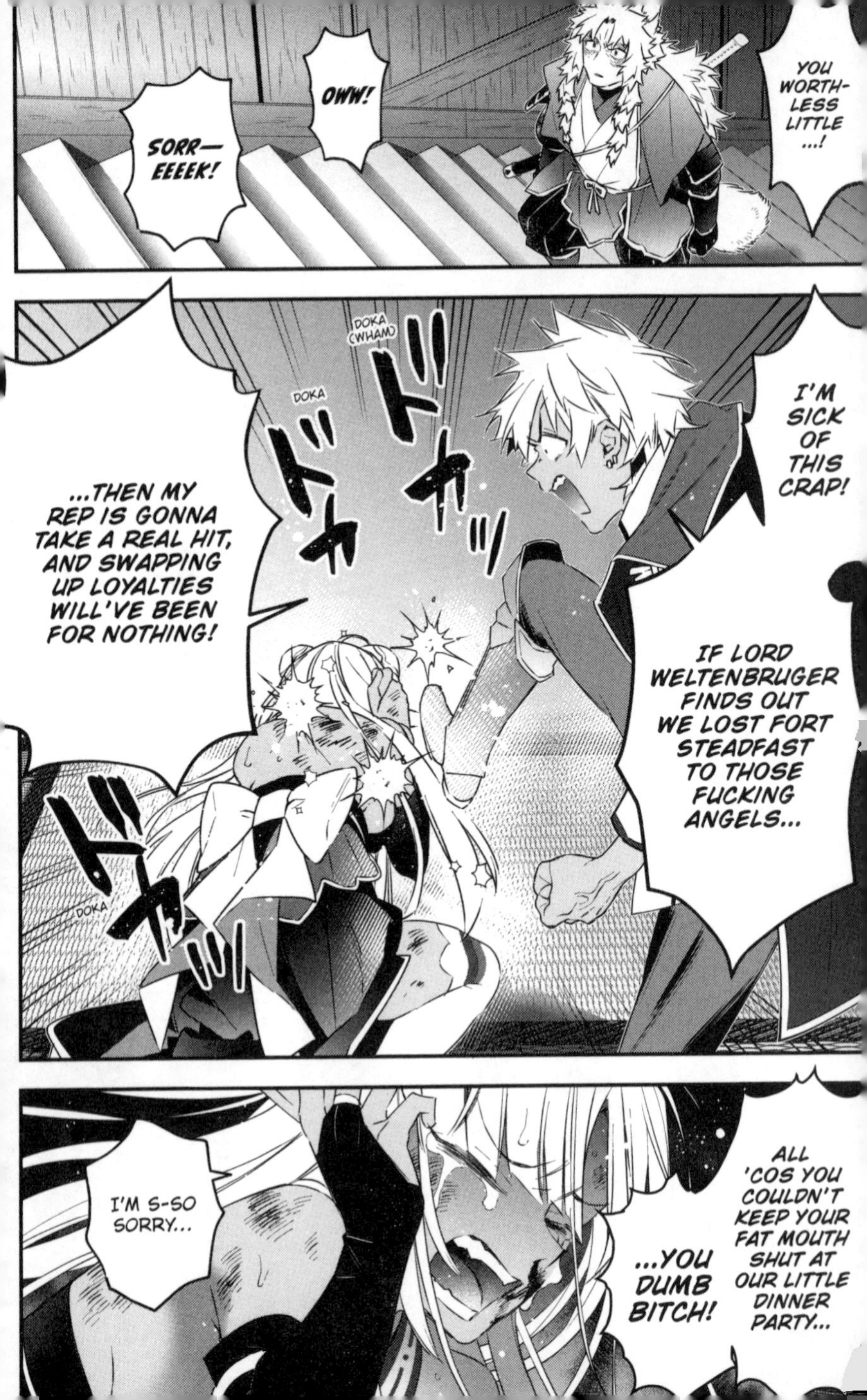
YOU WORTHLESS LITTLE...!
OWW!
SORR—EEEEK!
I'M SICK OF THIS CRAP!
DOKA (WHAM)
DOKA
IF LORD WELTENBRUGER FINDS OUT WE LOST FORT STEADFAST TO THOSE FUCKING ANGELS...
...THEN MY REP IS GONNA TAKE A REAL HIT, AND SWAPPING UP LOYALTIES WILL'VE BEEN FOR NOTHING!
DOKA
ALL 'COS YOU COULDN'T KEEP YOUR FAT MOUTH SHUT AT OUR LITTLE DINNER PARTY...
...YOU DUMB BITCH!
I'M S-SO SORRY...

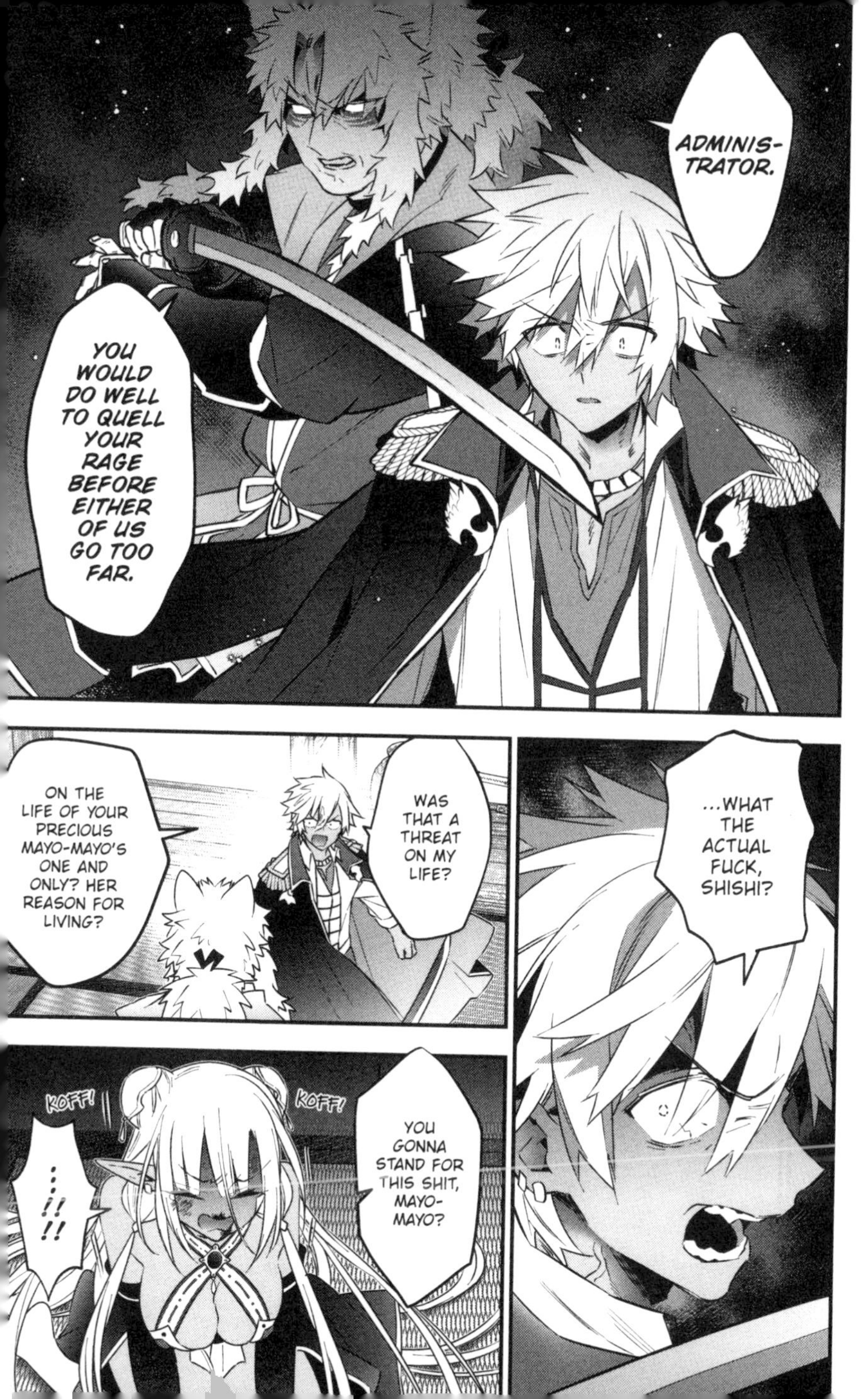
ADMINIS-TRATOR.
YOU WOULD DO WELL TO QUELL YOUR RAGE BEFORE EITHER OF US GO TOO FAR.
...WHAT THE ACTUAL FUCK, SHISHI?
WAS THAT A THREAT ON MY LIFE?
ON THE LIFE OF YOUR PRECIOUS MAYO-MAYO'S ONE AND ONLY? HER REASON FOR LIVING?
KOFF!
YOU GONNA STAND FOR THIS SHIT, MAYO-MAYO?
KOFF!
...!! !!

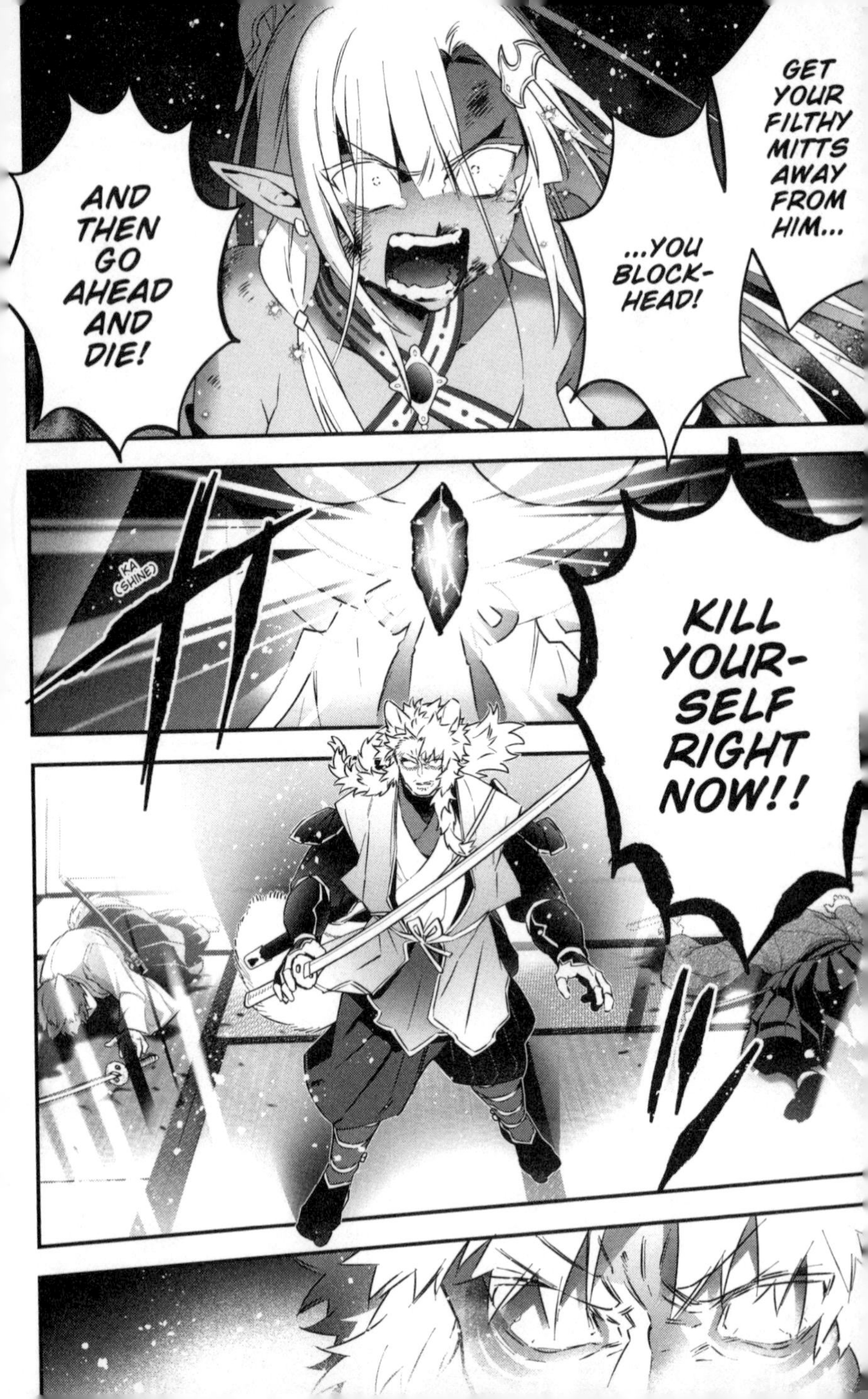
GET YOUR FILTHY MITTS AWAY FROM HIM...
...YOU BLOCK-HEAD!
AND THEN GO AHEAD AND DIE!
KILL YOUR-SELF RIGHT NOW!!
KA (SHINE)

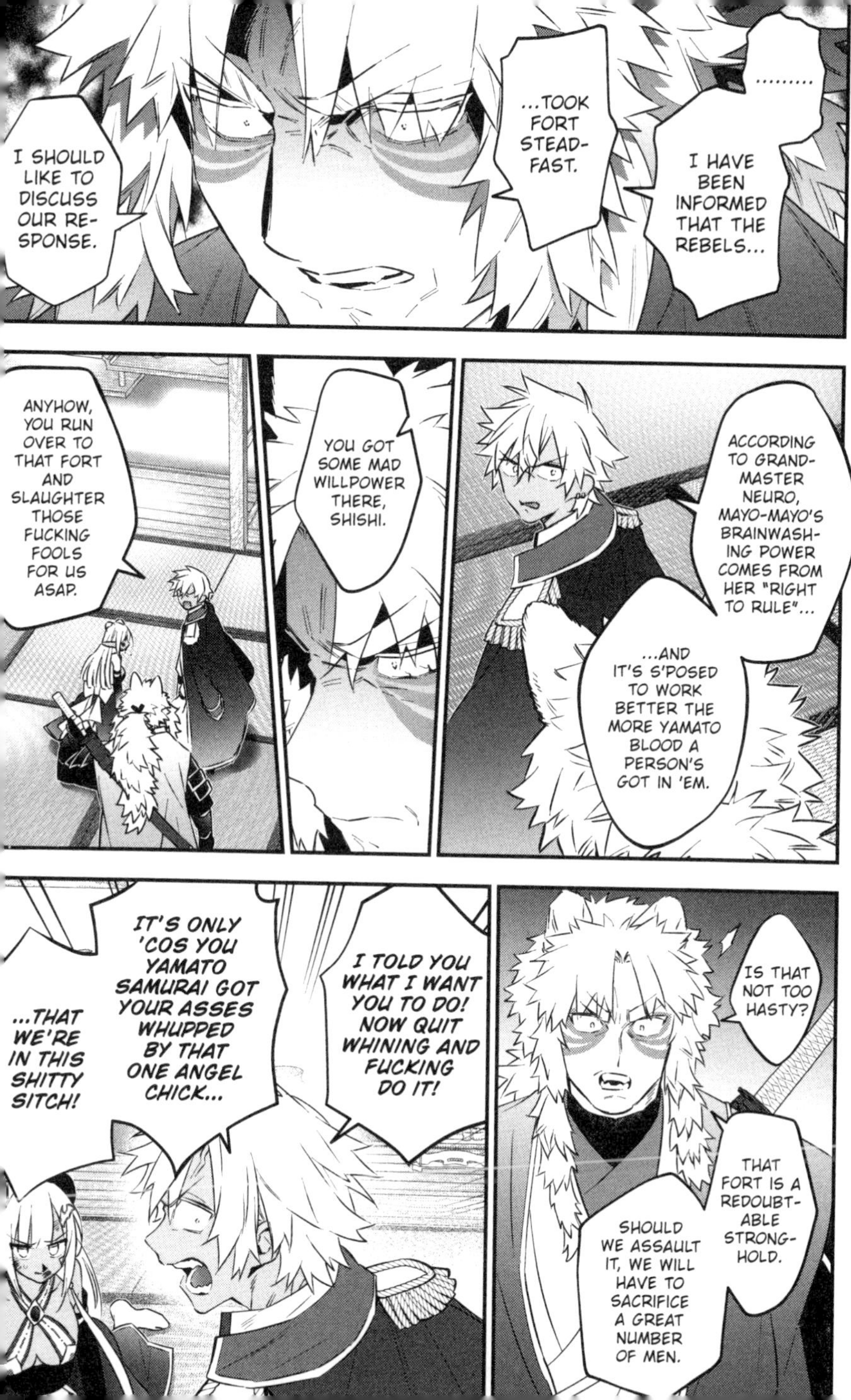
....
I HAVE BEEN INFORMED THAT THE REBELS...
...TOOK FORT STEADFAST.
I SHOULD LIKE TO DISCUSS OUR RESPONSE.
ACCORDING TO GRANDMASTER NEURO, MAYO-MAYO'S BRAINWASHING POWER COMES FROM HER "RIGHT TO RULE"...
...AND IT'S S'POSED TO WORK BETTER THE MORE YAMATO BLOOD A PERSON'S GOT IN 'EM.
YOU GOT SOME MAD WILLPOWER THERE, SHISHI.
ANYHOW, YOU RUN OVER TO THAT FORT AND SLAUGHTER THOSE FUCKING FOOLS FOR US ASAP.
IS THAT NOT TOO HASTY?
THAT FORT IS A REDOUBTABLE STRONGHOLD.
SHOULD WE ASSAULT IT, WE WILL HAVE TO SACRIFICE A GREAT NUMBER OF MEN.
I TOLD YOU WHAT I WANT YOU TO DO! NOW QUIT WHINING AND FUCKING DO IT!
IT'S ONLY 'COS YOU YAMATO SAMURAI GOT YOUR ASSES WHUPPED BY THAT ONE ANGEL CHICK...
...THAT WE'RE IN THIS SHITTY SITCH!

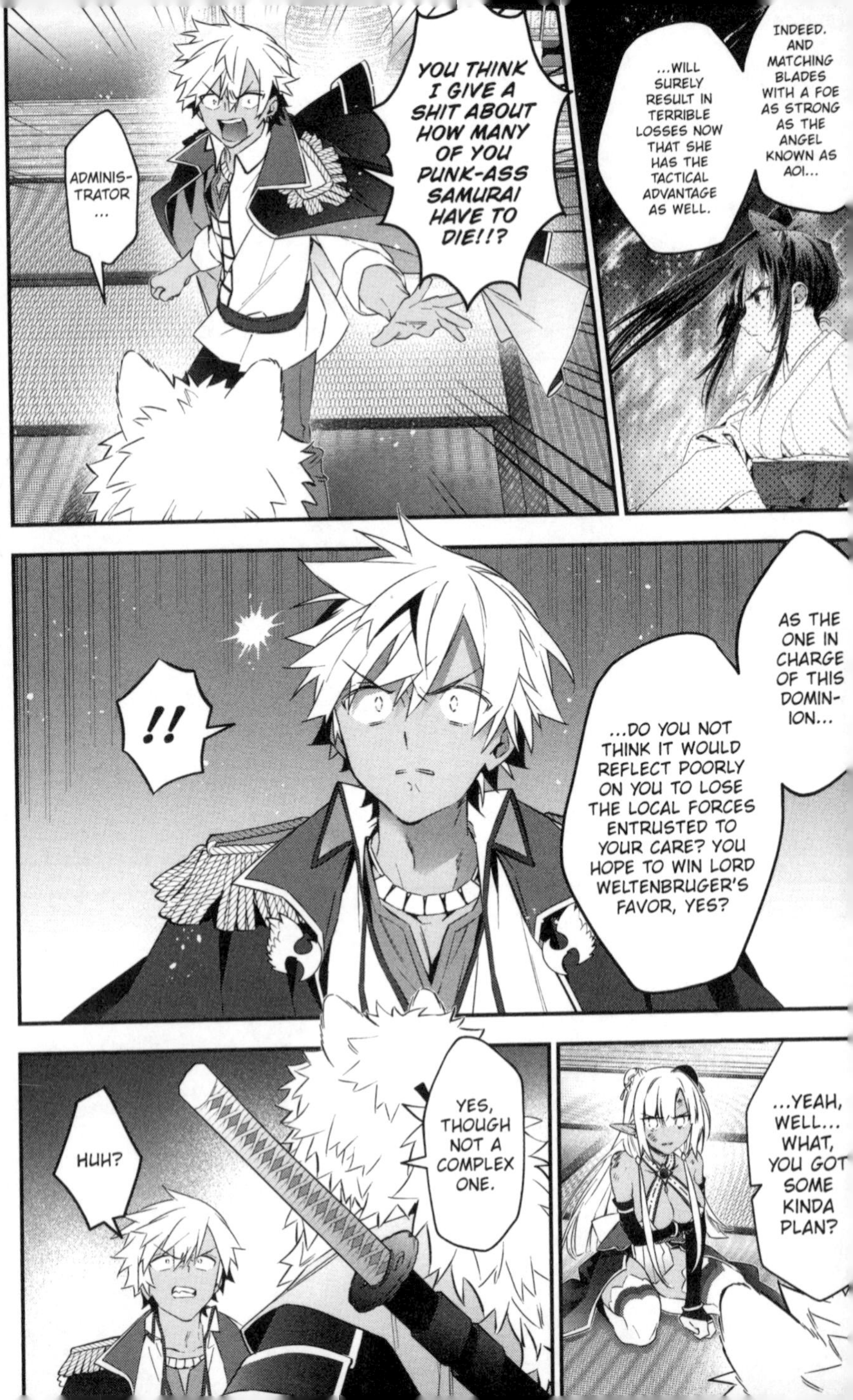
INDEED. AND MATCHING BLADES WITH A FOE AS STRONG AS THE ANGEL KNOWN AS AOI...
...WILL SURELY RESULT IN TERRIBLE LOSSES NOW THAT SHE HAS THE TACTICAL ADVANTAGE AS WELL.
YOU THINK I GIVE A SHIT ABOUT HOW MANY OF YOU PUNK-ASS SAMURAI HAVE TO DIE!!?
ADMINIS-TRATOR...
AS THE ONE IN CHARGE OF THIS DOMIN-ION...
...DO YOU NOT THINK IT WOULD REFLECT POORLY ON YOU TO LOSE THE LOCAL FORCES ENTRUSTED TO YOUR CARE? YOU HOPE TO WIN LORD WELTENBRUGER'S FAVOR, YES?
!!
...YEAH, WELL... WHAT, YOU GOT SOME KINDA PLAN?
YES, THOUGH NOT A COMPLEX ONE.
HUH?

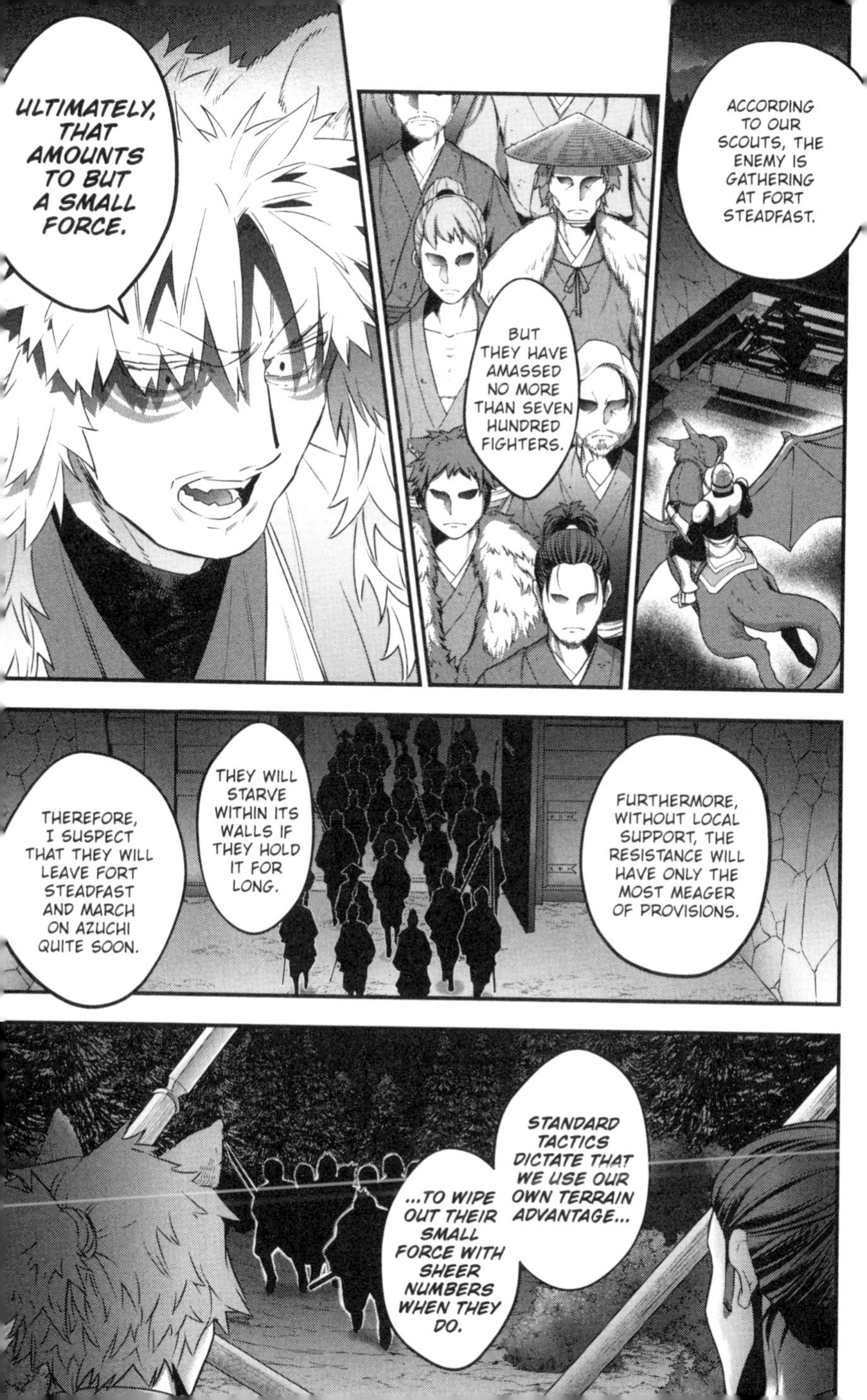
ACCORDING TO OUR SCOUTS, THE ENEMY IS GATHERING AT FORT STEADFAST.
BUT THEY HAVE AMASSED NO MORE THAN SEVEN HUNDRED FIGHTERS.
ULTIMATELY, THAT AMOUNTS TO BUT A SMALL FORCE.
FURTHERMORE, WITHOUT LOCAL SUPPORT, THE RESISTANCE WILL HAVE ONLY THE MOST MEAGER OF PROVISIONS.
THEY WILL STARVE WITHIN ITS WALLS IF THEY HOLD IT FOR LONG.
THEREFORE, I SUSPECT THAT THEY WILL LEAVE FORT STEADFAST AND MARCH ON AZUCHI QUITE SOON.
STANDARD TACTICS DICTATE THAT WE USE OUR OWN TERRAIN ADVANTAGE...
...TO WIPE OUT THEIR SMALL FORCE WITH SHEER NUMBERS WHEN THEY DO.

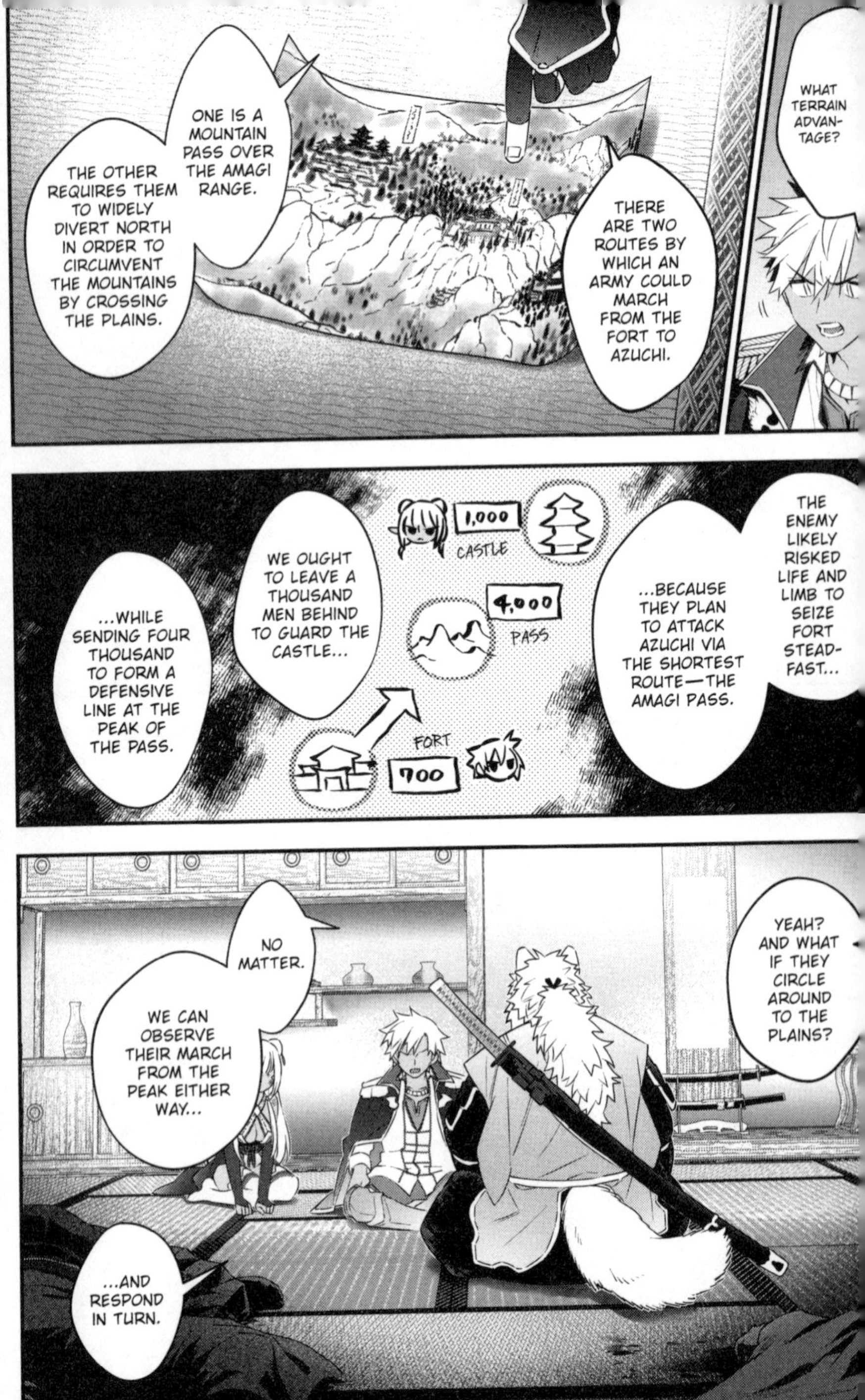
WHAT TERRAIN ADVANTAGE?
THERE ARE TWO ROUTES BY WHICH AN ARMY COULD MARCH FROM THE FORT TO AZUCHI.
ONE IS A MOUNTAIN PASS OVER THE AMAGI RANGE.
THE OTHER REQUIRES THEM TO WIDELY DIVERT NORTH IN ORDER TO CIRCUMVENT THE MOUNTAINS BY CROSSING THE PLAINS.
THE ENEMY LIKELY RISKED LIFE AND LIMB TO SEIZE FORT STEAD-FAST...
...BECAUSE THEY PLAN TO ATTACK AZUCHI VIA THE SHORTEST ROUTE—THE AMAGI PASS.
1,000
CASTLE
4,000
PASS
FORT
700
WE OUGHT TO LEAVE A THOUSAND MEN BEHIND TO GUARD THE CASTLE...
...WHILE SENDING FOUR THOUSAND TO FORM A DEFENSIVE LINE AT THE PEAK OF THE PASS.
YEAH? AND WHAT IF THEY CIRCLE AROUND TO THE PLAINS?
NO MATTER.
WE CAN OBSERVE THEIR MARCH FROM THE PEAK EITHER WAY...
...AND RESPOND IN TURN.

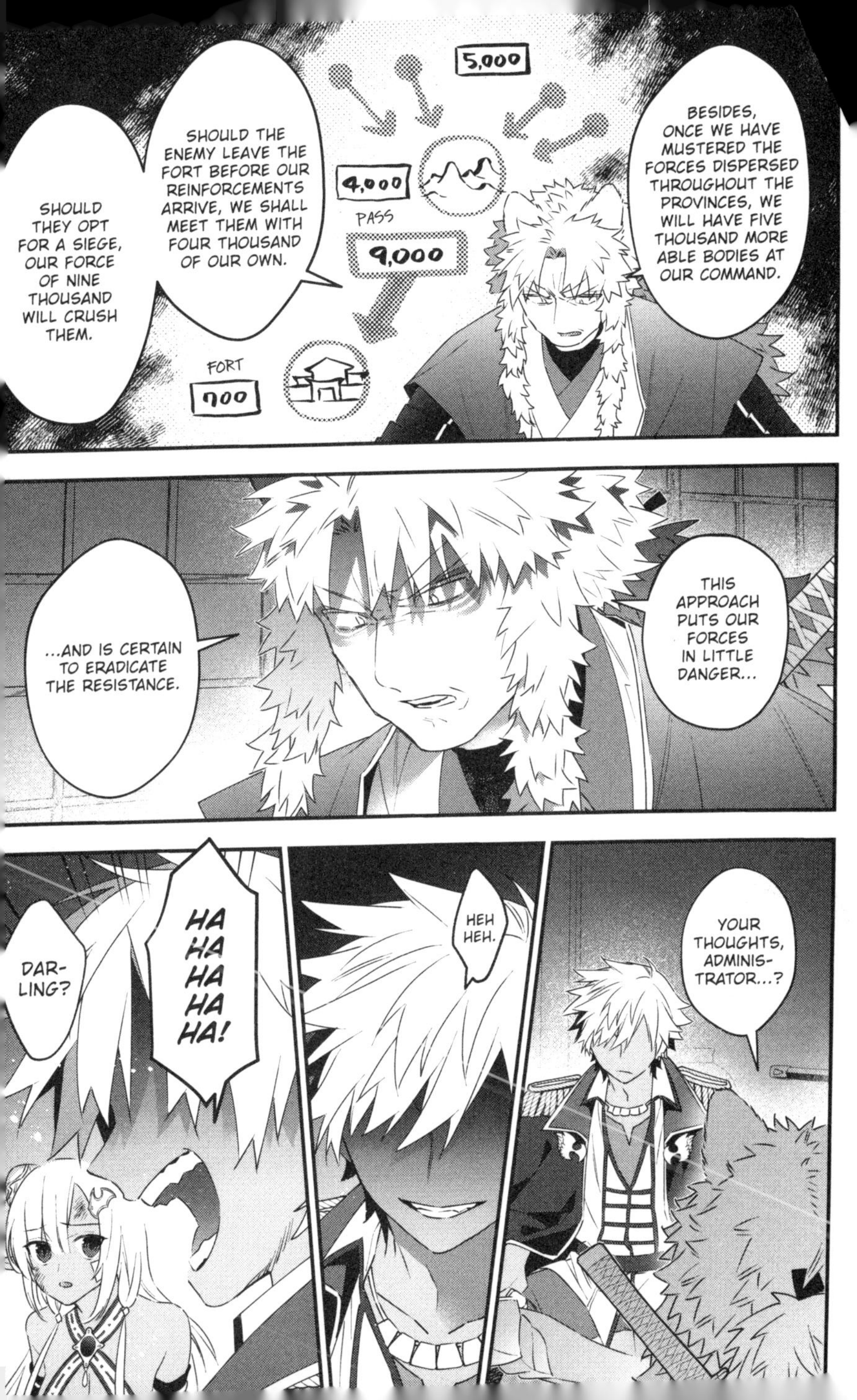
BESIDES, ONCE WE HAVE MUSTERED THE FORCES DISPERSED THROUGHOUT THE PROVINCES, WE WILL HAVE FIVE THOUSAND MORE ABLE BODIES AT OUR COMMAND.
5,000
4,000
PASS
9,000
FORT
700
SHOULD THE ENEMY LEAVE THE FORT BEFORE OUR REINFORCEMENTS ARRIVE, WE SHALL MEET THEM WITH FOUR THOUSAND OF OUR OWN.
SHOULD THEY OPT FOR A SIEGE, OUR FORCE OF NINE THOUSAND WILL CRUSH THEM.
THIS APPROACH PUTS OUR FORCES IN LITTLE DANGER...
...AND IS CERTAIN TO ERADICATE THE RESISTANCE.
YOUR THOUGHTS, ADMINISTRATOR...?
HEH HEH.
HA HA HA HA HA HA!
DARLING?

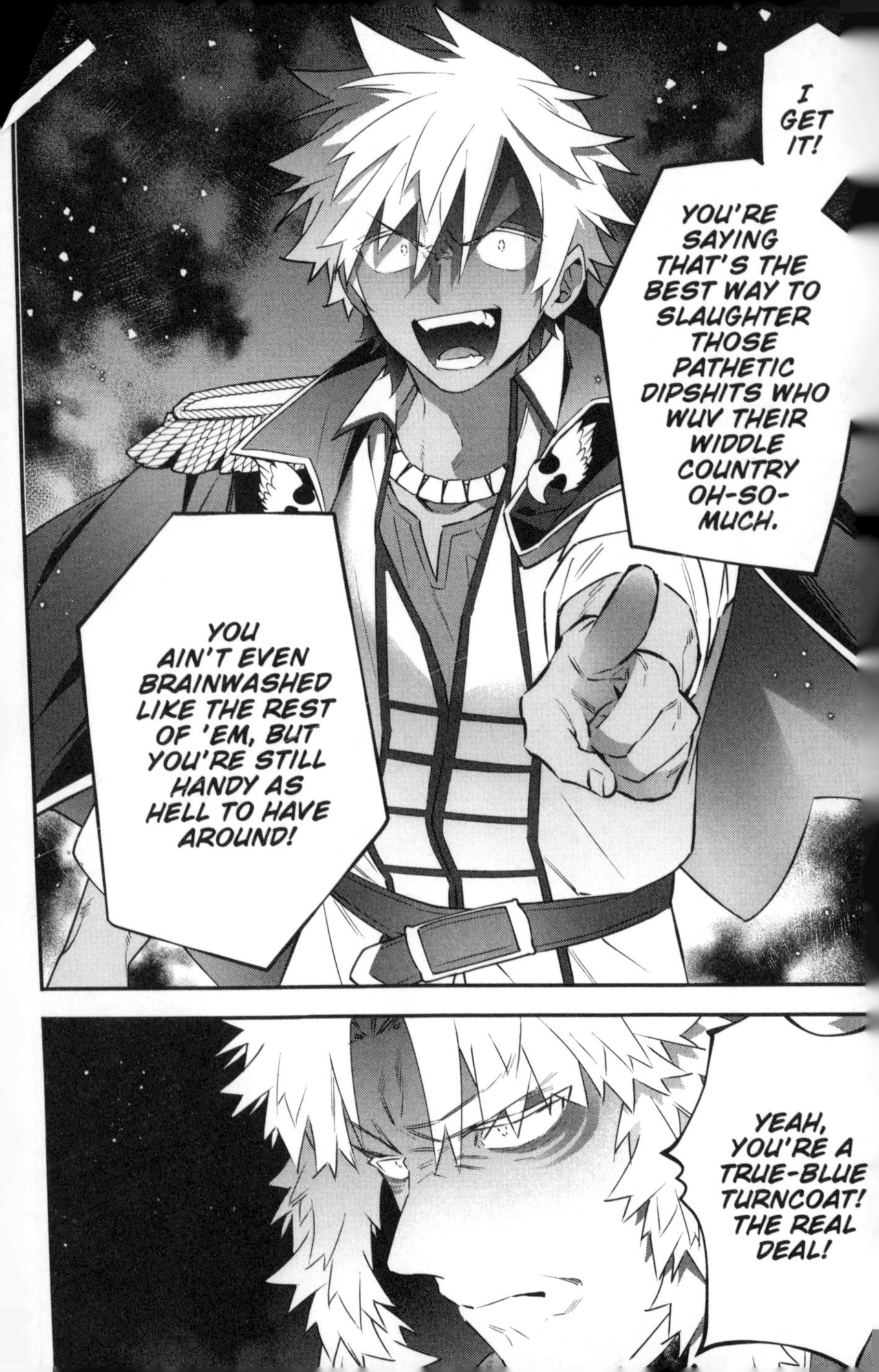
I GET IT!
YOU'RE SAYING THAT'S THE BEST WAY TO SLAUGHTER THOSE PATHETIC DIPSHITS WHO WUV THEIR WIDDLE COUNTRY OH-SO-MUCH.
YOU AIN'T EVEN BRAINWASHED LIKE THE REST OF 'EM, BUT YOU'RE STILL HANDY AS HELL TO HAVE AROUND!
YEAH, YOU'RE A TRUE-BLUE TURNCOAT! THE REAL DEAL!

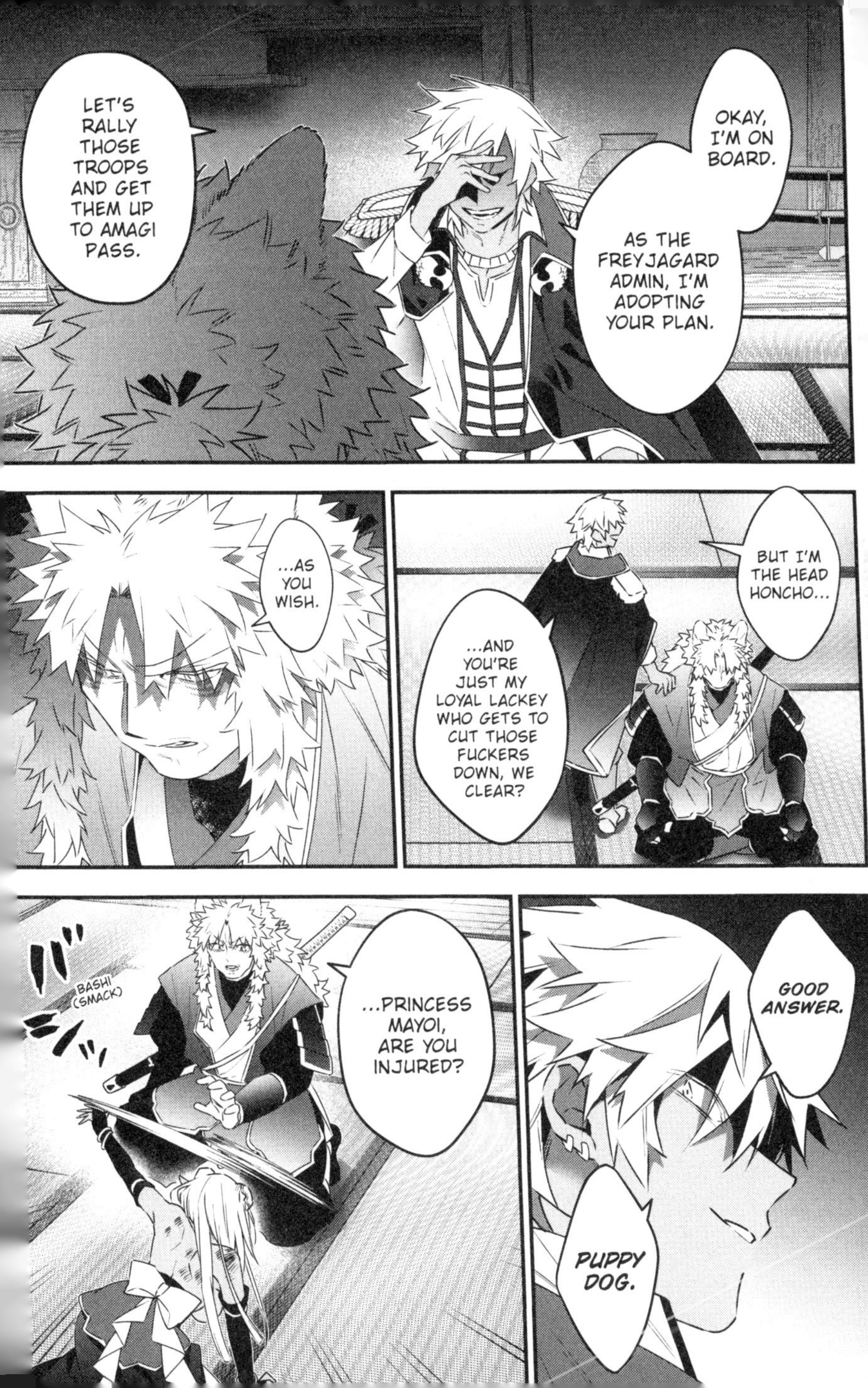
OKAY, I'M ON BOARD.
AS THE FREYJAGARD ADMIN, I'M ADOPTING YOUR PLAN.
LET'S RALLY THOSE TROOPS AND GET THEM UP TO AMAGI PASS.
BUT I'M THE HEAD HONCHO...
...AND YOU'RE JUST MY LOYAL LACKEY WHO GETS TO CUT THOSE FUCKERS DOWN, WE CLEAR?
...AS YOU WISH.
GOOD ANSWER.
PUPPY DOG.
...PRINCESS MAYOI, ARE YOU INJURED?
BASHI (SMACK)

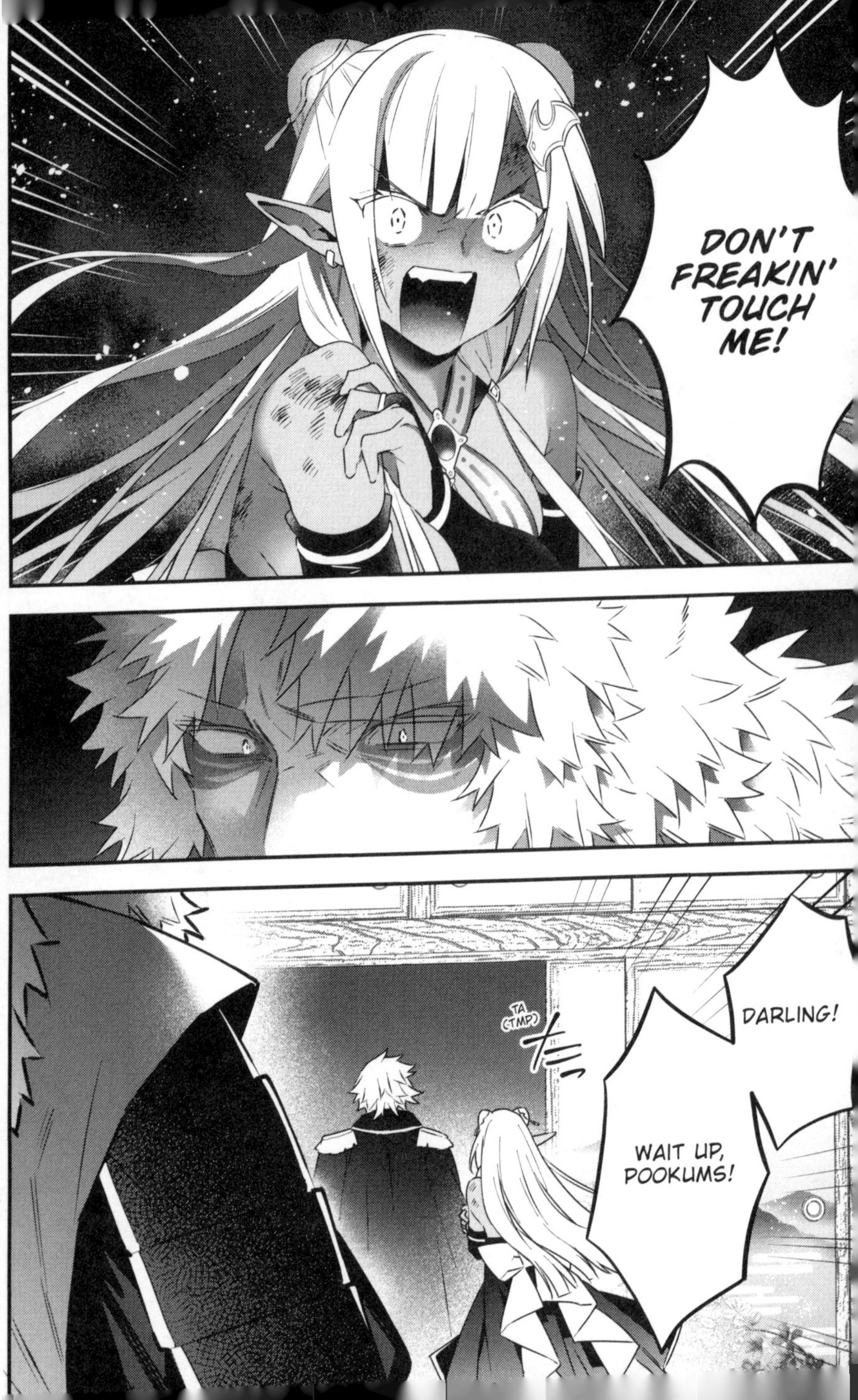
DON'T FREAKIN' TOUCH ME!
DARLING!
WAIT UP, POOKUMS!
TA (STMP)

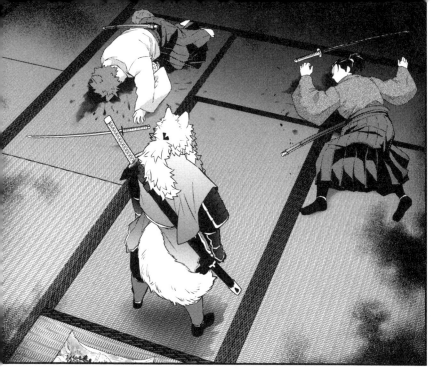

STILL YOUR TONGUE.

I'M NOT HERE TO HEAR YOU TALK.

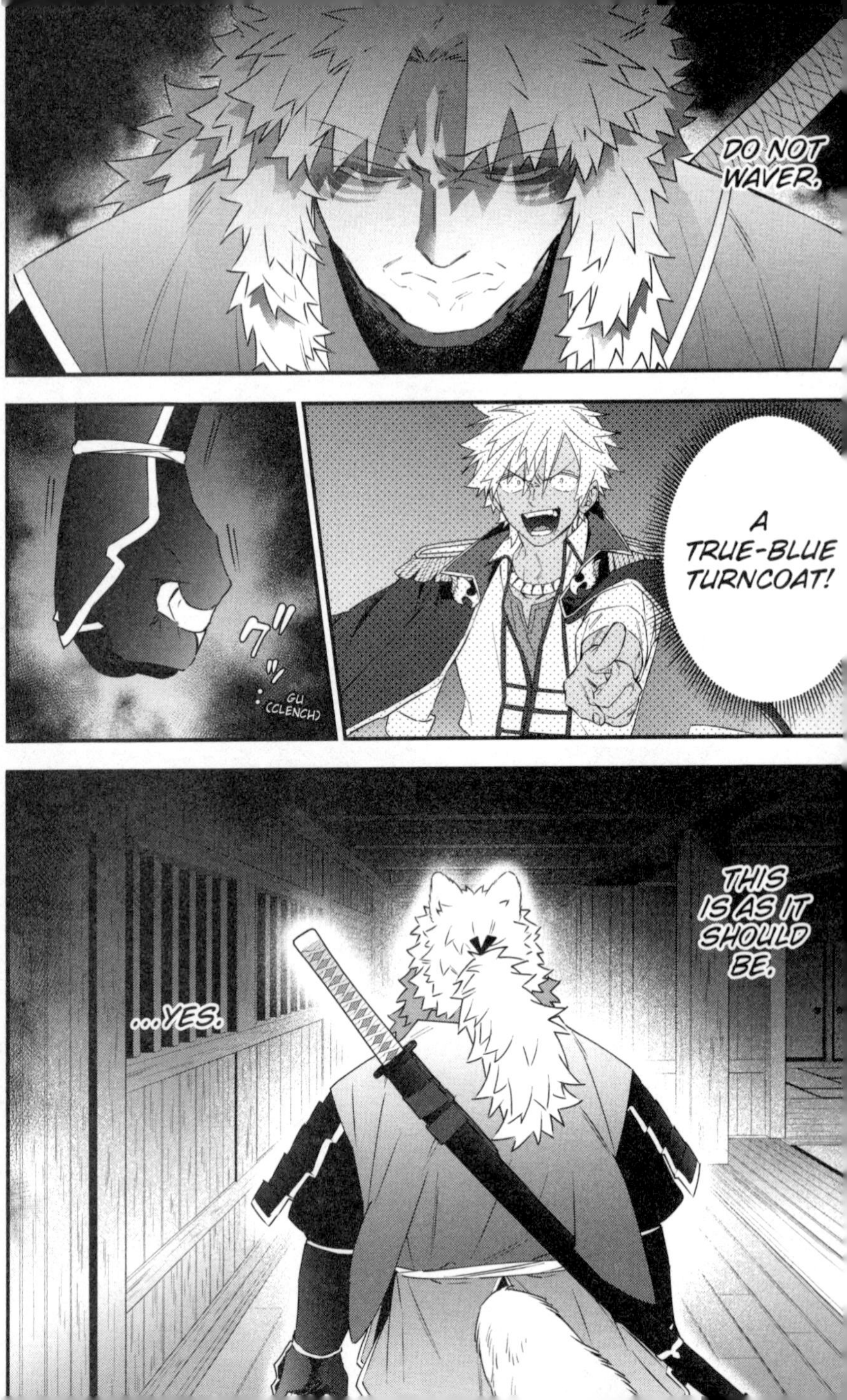
DO NOT WAVER.
A TRUE-BLUE TURNCOAT!
グッ
GU (CLENCH)
THIS IS AS IT SHOULD BE.
...YES.

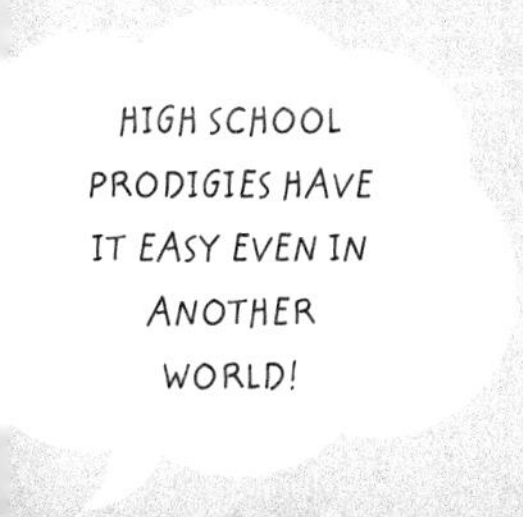
HIGH SCHOOL PRODIGIES HAVE IT EASY EVEN IN ANOTHER WORLD!

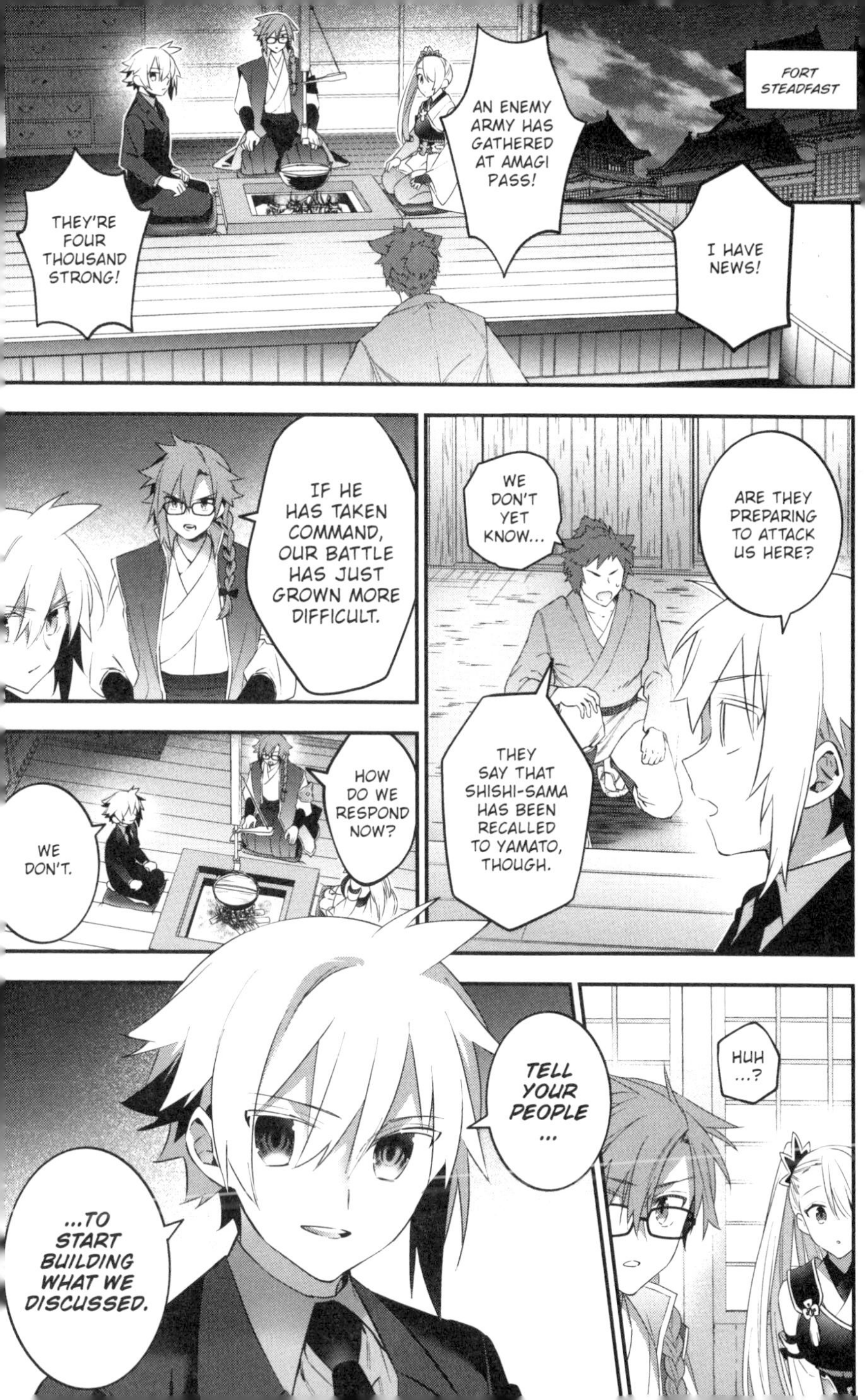
FORT STEADFAST
I HAVE NEWS!
AN ENEMY ARMY HAS GATHERED AT AMAGI PASS!
THEY'RE FOUR THOUSAND STRONG!
ARE THEY PREPARING TO ATTACK US HERE?
WE DON'T YET KNOW...
THEY SAY THAT SHISHI-SAMA HAS BEEN RECALLED TO YAMATO, THOUGH.
IF HE HAS TAKEN COMMAND, OUR BATTLE HAS JUST GROWN MORE DIFFICULT.
HOW DO WE RESPOND NOW?
WE DON'T.
HUH ...?
TELL YOUR PEOPLE ...
...TO START BUILDING WHAT WE DISCUSSED.

CHAPTER 82: **UNEXPECTED**

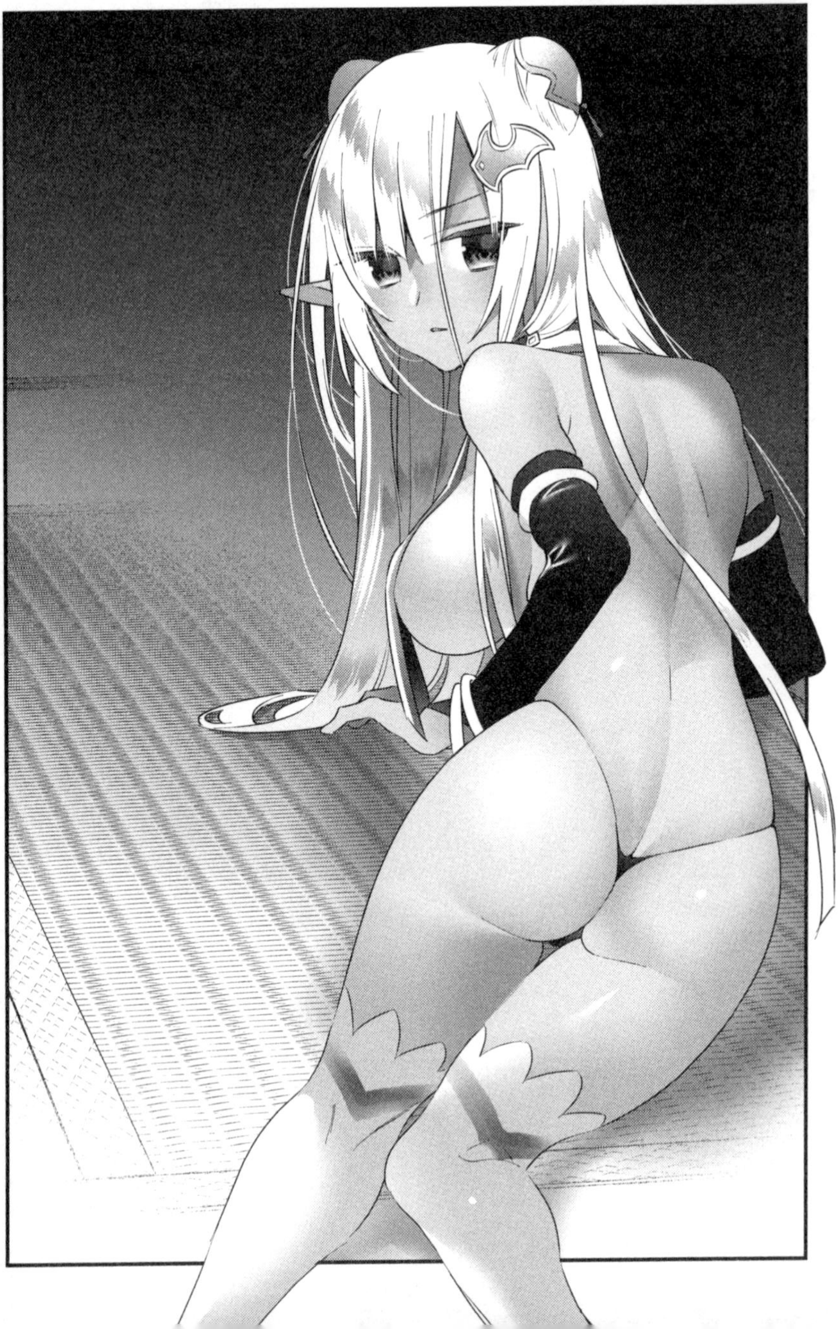

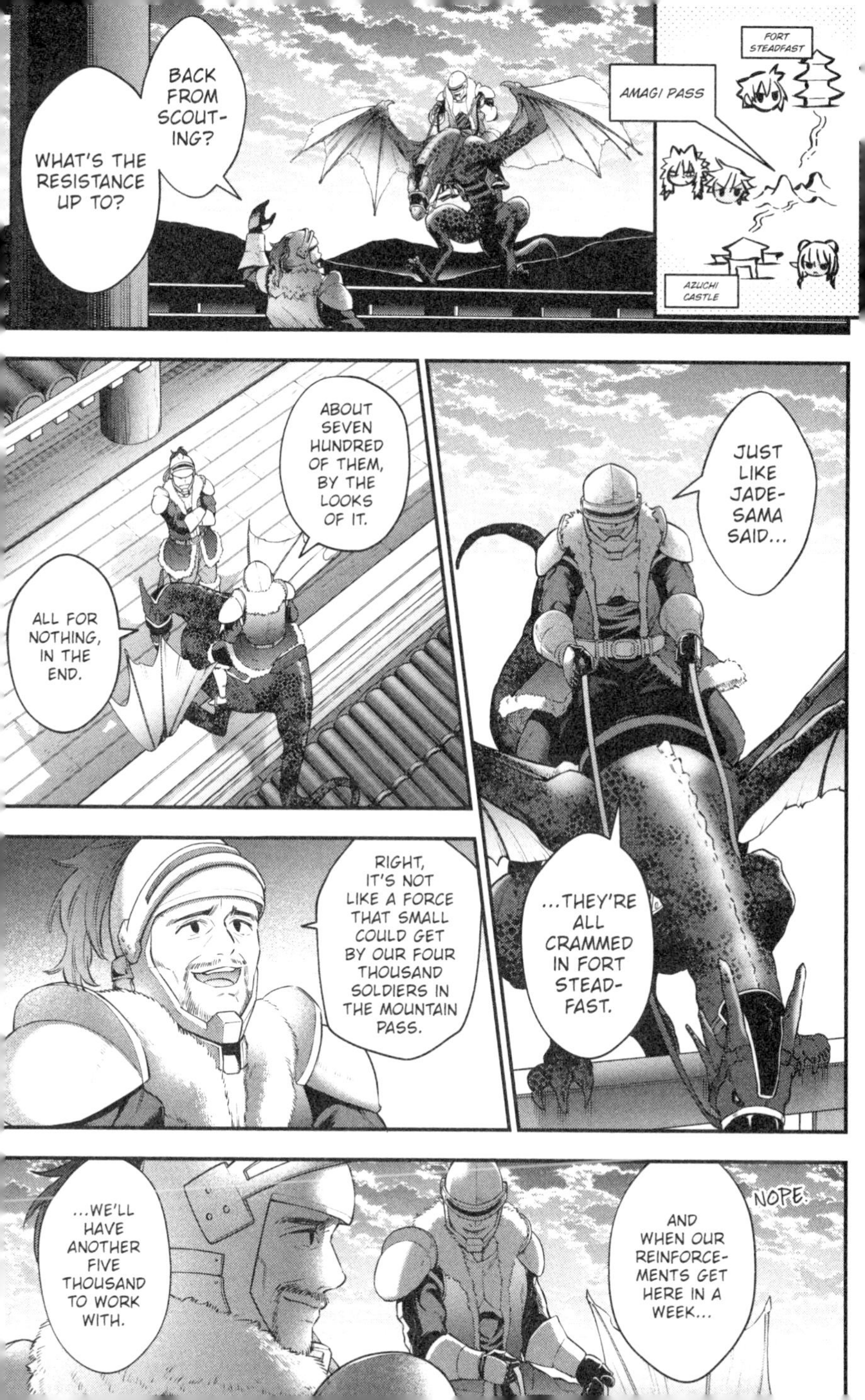
FORT STEADFAST
AMAGI PASS
AZUCHI CASTLE
BACK FROM SCOUT-ING?
WHAT'S THE RESISTANCE UP TO?
JUST LIKE JADE-SAMA SAID...
...THEY'RE ALL CRAMMED IN FORT STEAD-FAST.
ABOUT SEVEN HUNDRED OF THEM, BY THE LOOKS OF IT.
ALL FOR NOTHING, IN THE END.
RIGHT, IT'S NOT LIKE A FORCE THAT SMALL COULD GET BY OUR FOUR THOUSAND SOLDIERS IN THE MOUNTAIN PASS.
NOPE.
AND WHEN OUR REINFORCE-MENTS GET HERE IN A WEEK...
...WE'LL HAVE ANOTHER FIVE THOUSAND TO WORK WITH.

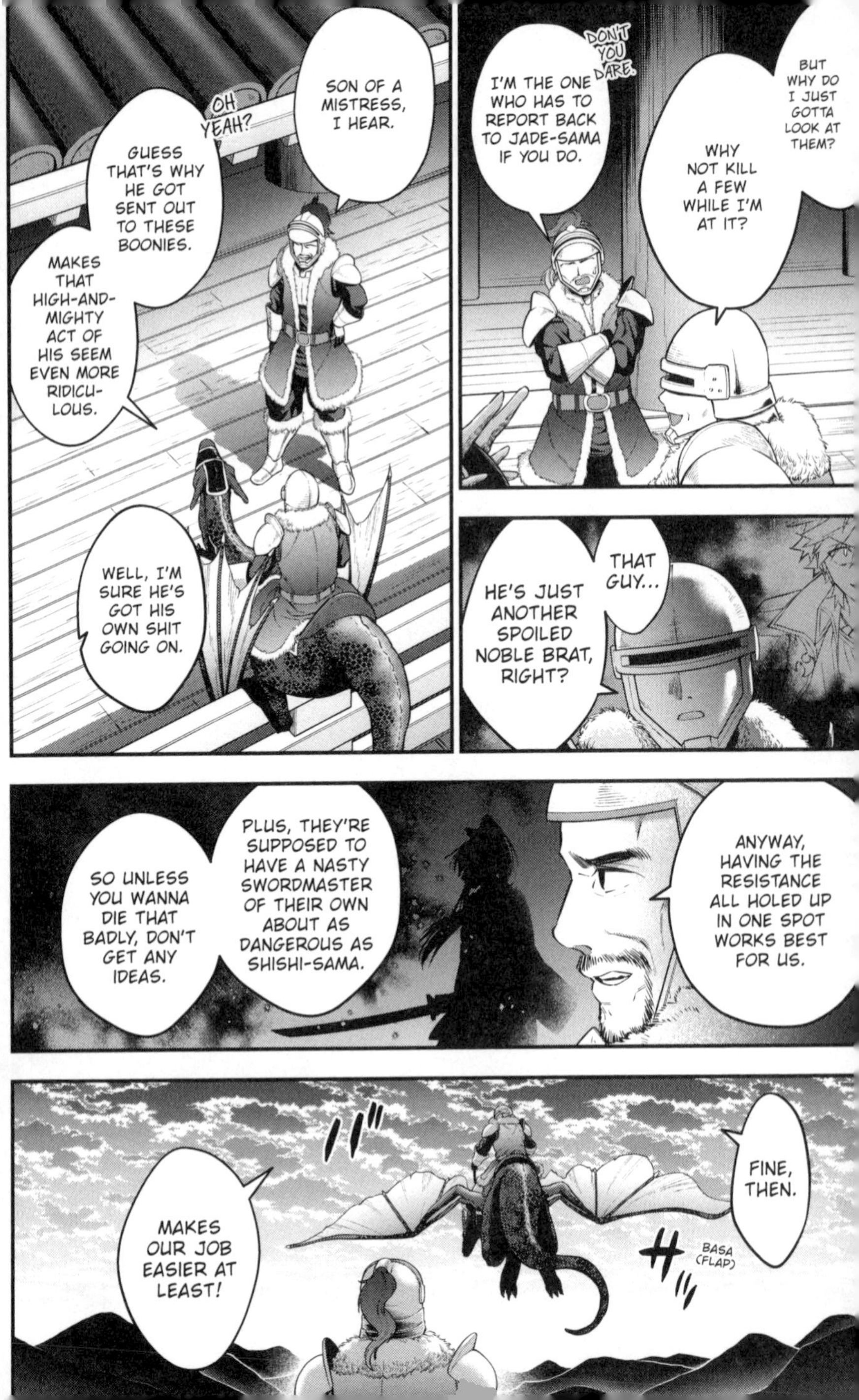
BUT WHY DO I JUST GOTTA LOOK AT THEM?
WHY NOT KILL A FEW WHILE I'M AT IT?
DON'T YOU DARE.
I'M THE ONE WHO HAS TO REPORT BACK TO JADE-SAMA IF YOU DO.
THAT GUY...
HE'S JUST ANOTHER SPOILED NOBLE BRAT, RIGHT?
SON OF A MISTRESS, I HEAR.
OH YEAH?
GUESS THAT'S WHY HE GOT SENT OUT TO THESE BOONIES.
MAKES THAT HIGH-AND-MIGHTY ACT OF HIS SEEM EVEN MORE RIDICULOUS.
WELL, I'M SURE HE'S GOT HIS OWN SHIT GOING ON.
ANYWAY, HAVING THE RESISTANCE ALL HOLED UP IN ONE SPOT WORKS BEST FOR US.
PLUS, THEY'RE SUPPOSED TO HAVE A NASTY SWORDMASTER OF THEIR OWN ABOUT AS DANGEROUS AS SHISHI-SAMA.
SO UNLESS YOU WANNA DIE THAT BADLY, DON'T GET ANY IDEAS.
FINE, THEN.
BASA (FLAP)
MAKES OUR JOB EASIER AT LEAST!

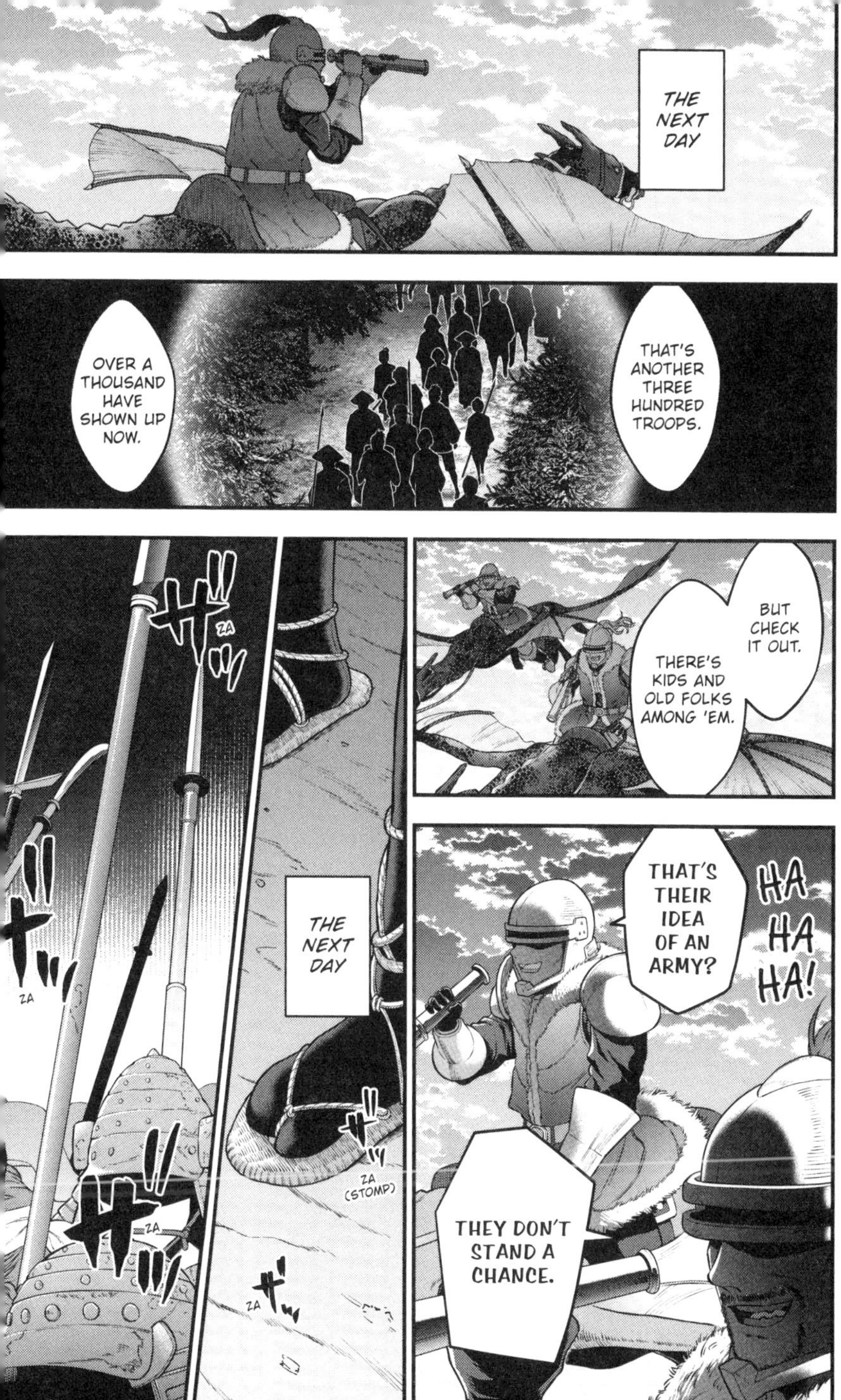
THE NEXT DAY
THAT'S ANOTHER THREE HUNDRED TROOPS.
OVER A THOUSAND HAVE SHOWN UP NOW.
BUT CHECK IT OUT.
THERE'S KIDS AND OLD FOLKS AMONG 'EM.
HA HA HA!
THAT'S THEIR IDEA OF AN ARMY?
THEY DON'T STAND A CHANCE.
THE NEXT DAY
ZA (STOMP)
ZA
ZA
ZA
ZA

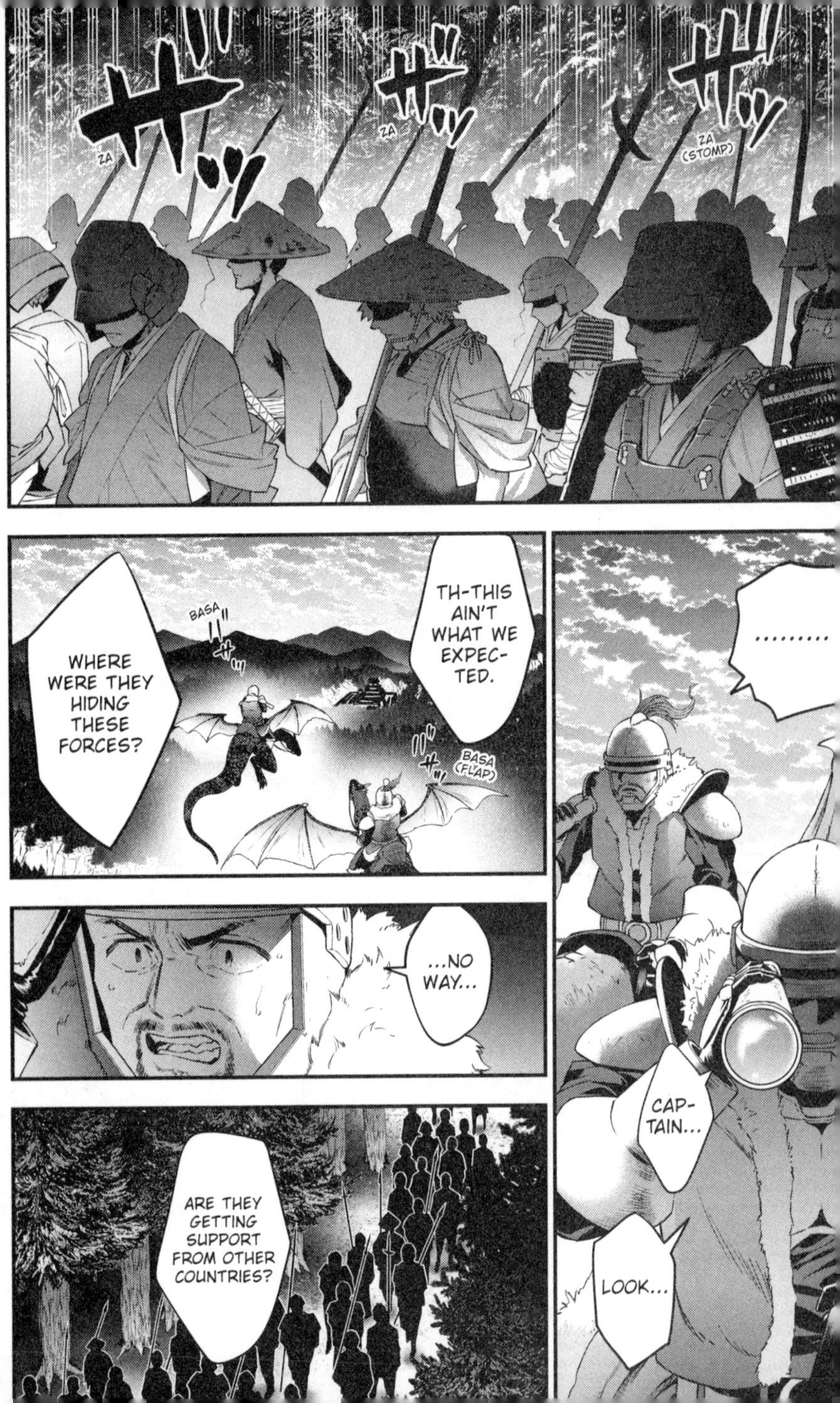
ZA (STOMP)
ZA
ZA
....
CAP-TAIN...
LOOK...
TH-THIS AIN'T WHAT WE EXPEC-TED.
BASA
WHERE WERE THEY HIDING THESE FORCES?
BASA (FLAP)
...NO WAY...
ARE THEY GETTING SUPPORT FROM OTHER COUNTRIES?

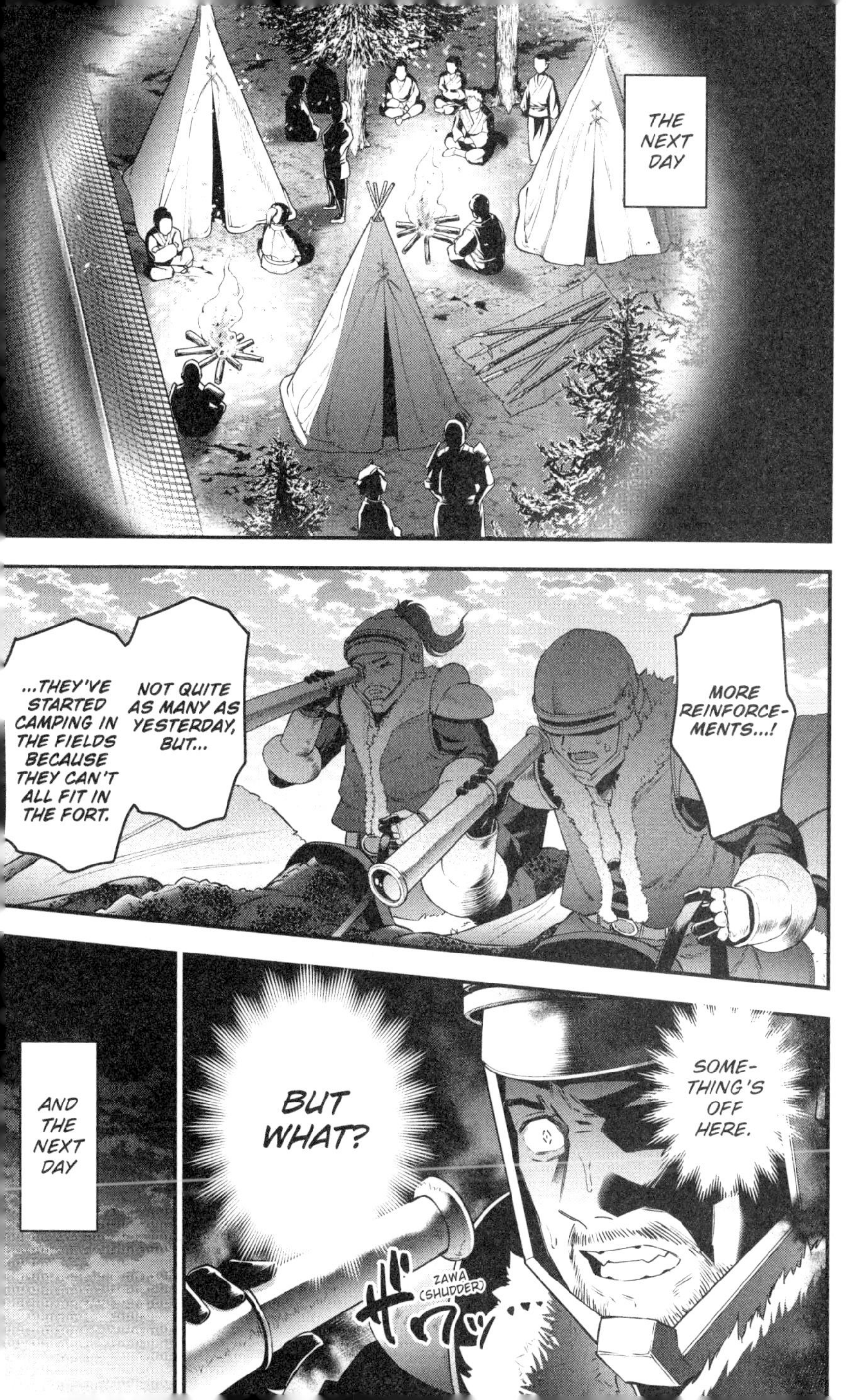
THE NEXT DAY
MORE REINFORCEMENTS...!
NOT QUITE AS MANY AS YESTERDAY, BUT...
...THEY'VE STARTED CAMPING IN THE FIELDS BECAUSE THEY CAN'T ALL FIT IN THE FORT.
SOMETHING'S OFF HERE.
BUT WHAT?
ZAWA (SHUDDER)
AND THE NEXT DAY

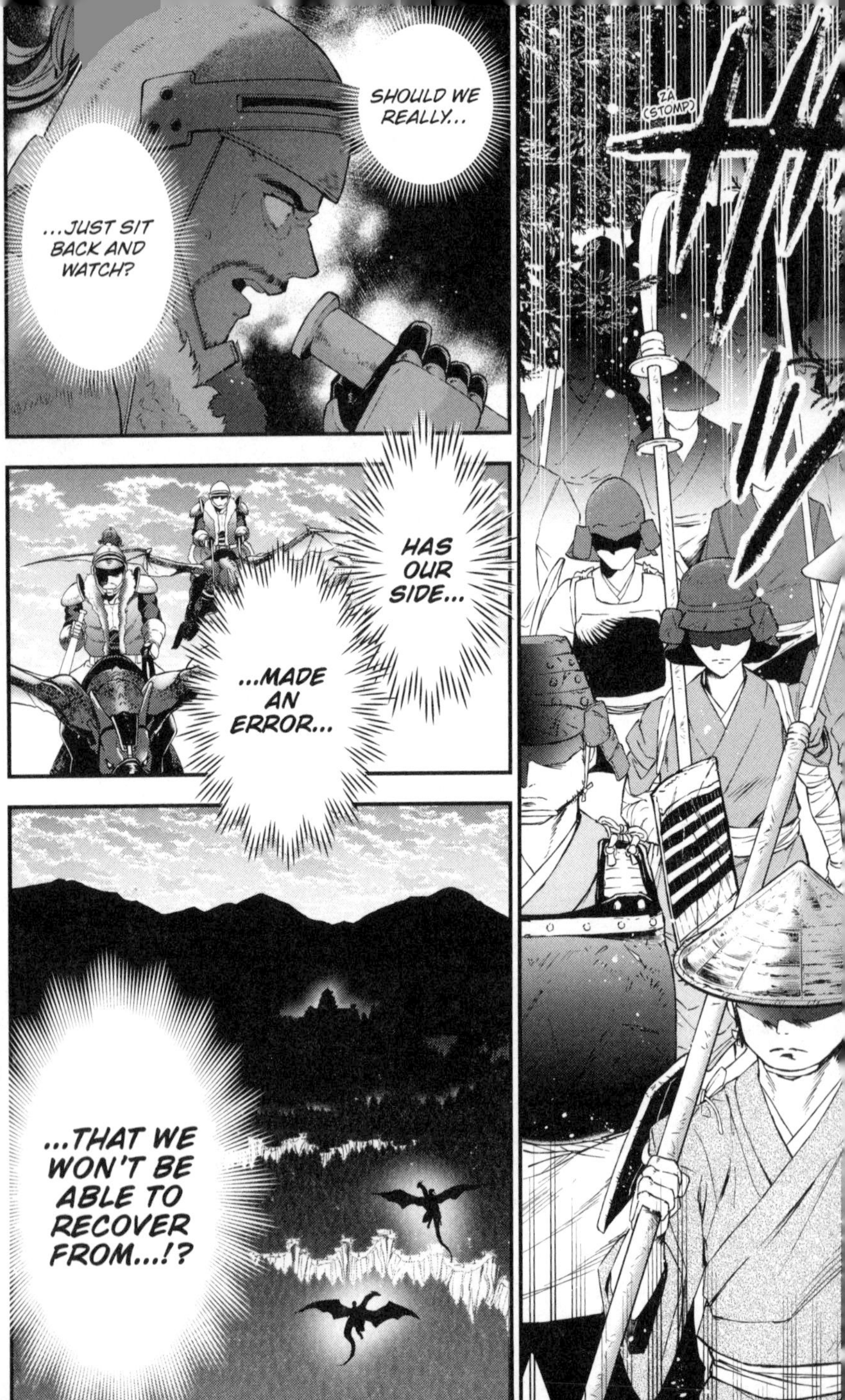
ZA (STOMP)
SHOULD WE REALLY...
...JUST SIT BACK AND WATCH?
HAS OUR SIDE...
...MADE AN ERROR...
...THAT WE WON'T BE ABLE TO RECOVER FROM...!?

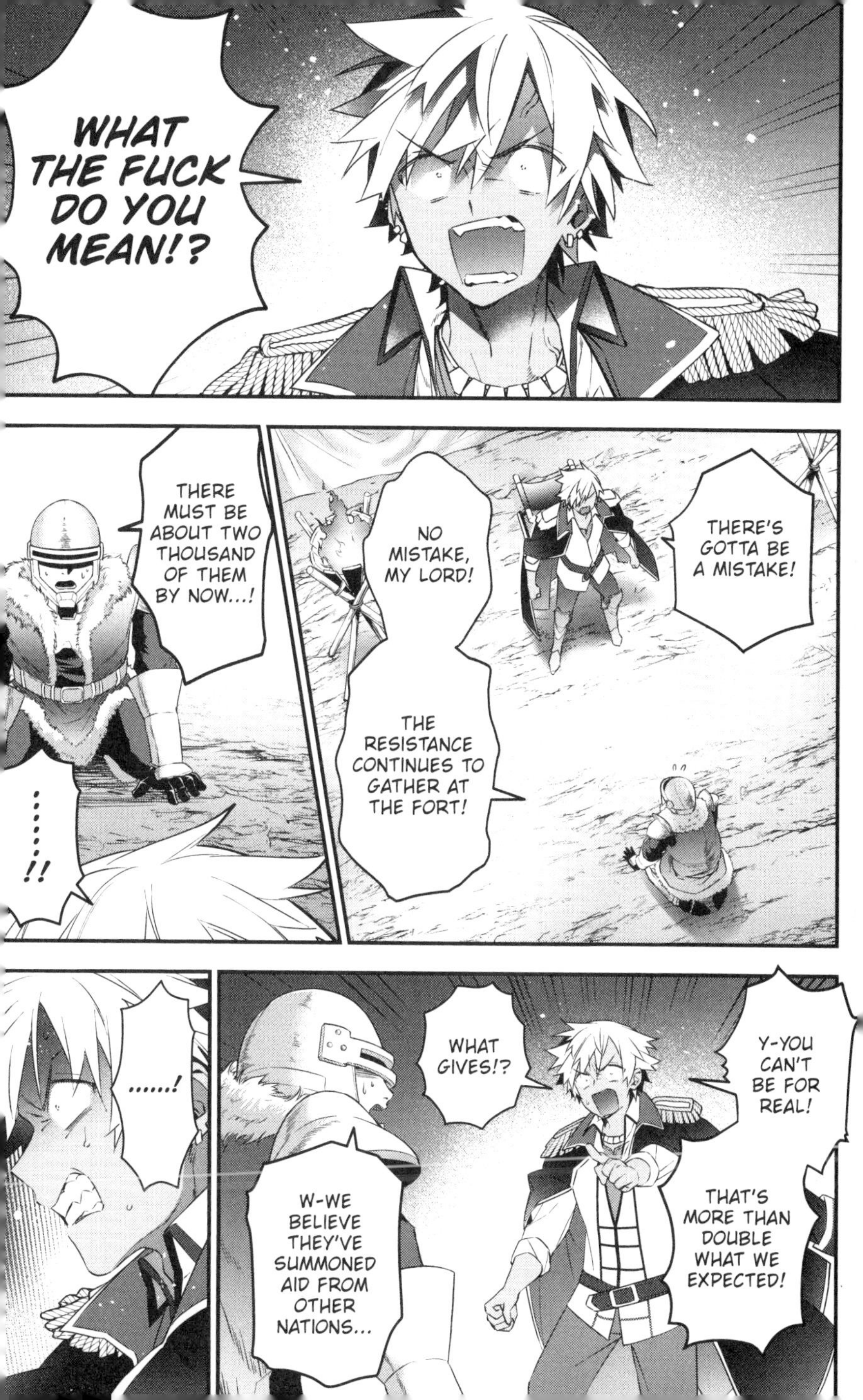
WHAT THE FUCK DO YOU MEAN!?
THERE'S GOTTA BE A MISTAKE!
NO MISTAKE, MY LORD!
THE RESISTANCE CONTINUES TO GATHER AT THE FORT!
THERE MUST BE ABOUT TWO THOUSAND OF THEM BY NOW...!
......!!
Y-YOU CAN'T BE FOR REAL!
WHAT GIVES!?
THAT'S MORE THAN DOUBLE WHAT WE EXPECTED!
W-WE BELIEVE THEY'VE SUMMONED AID FROM OTHER NATIONS...
......!

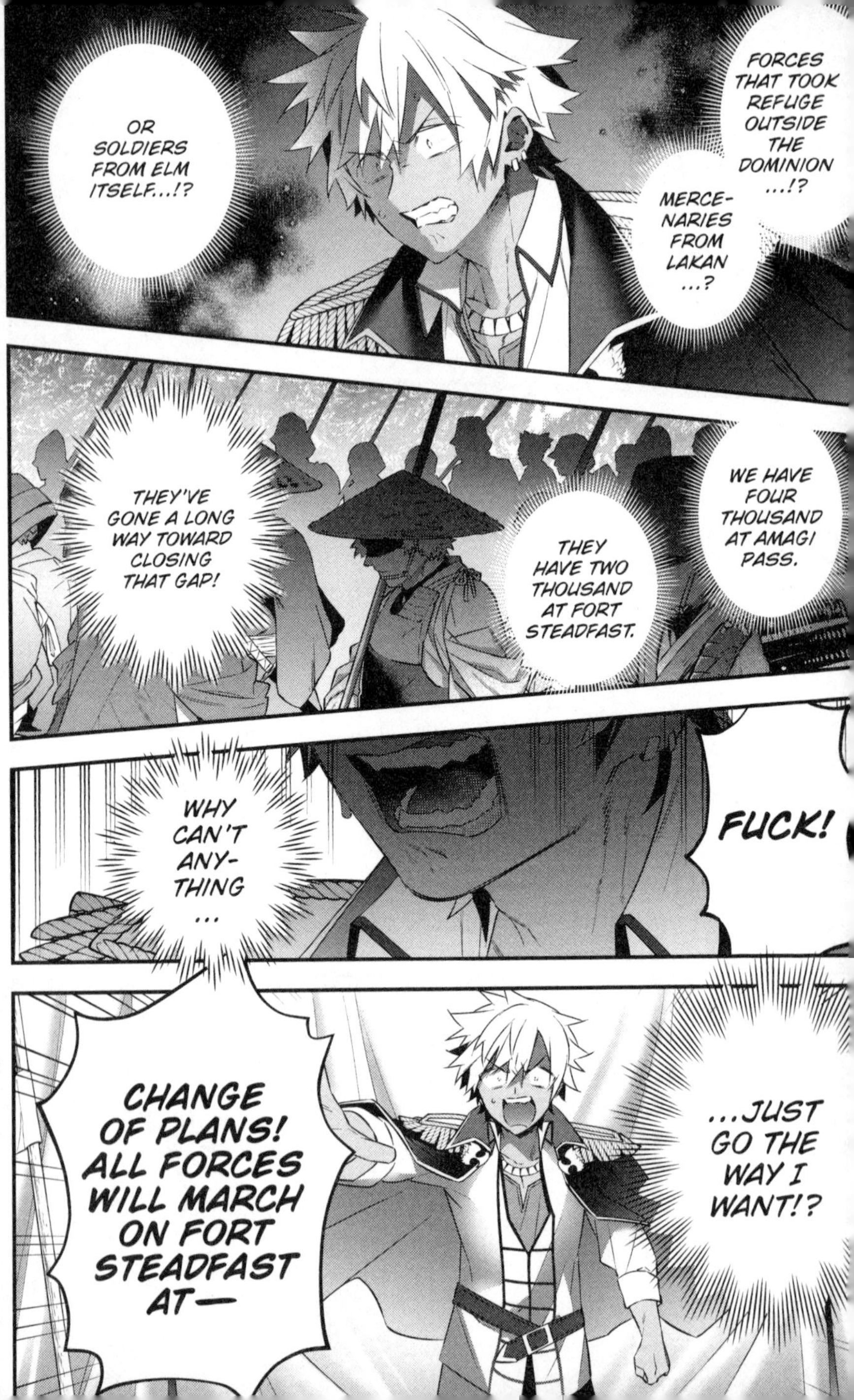
FORCES THAT TOOK REFUGE OUTSIDE THE DOMINION...!?
MERCE-NARIES FROM LAKAN...?
OR SOLDIERS FROM ELM ITSELF...!?
WE HAVE FOUR THOUSAND AT AMAGI PASS.
THEY HAVE TWO THOUSAND AT FORT STEADFAST.
THEY'VE GONE A LONG WAY TOWARD CLOSING THAT GAP!
FUCK!
WHY CAN'T ANY-THING...
...JUST GO THE WAY I WANT!?
CHANGE OF PLANS! ALL FORCES WILL MARCH ON FORT STEADFAST AT—

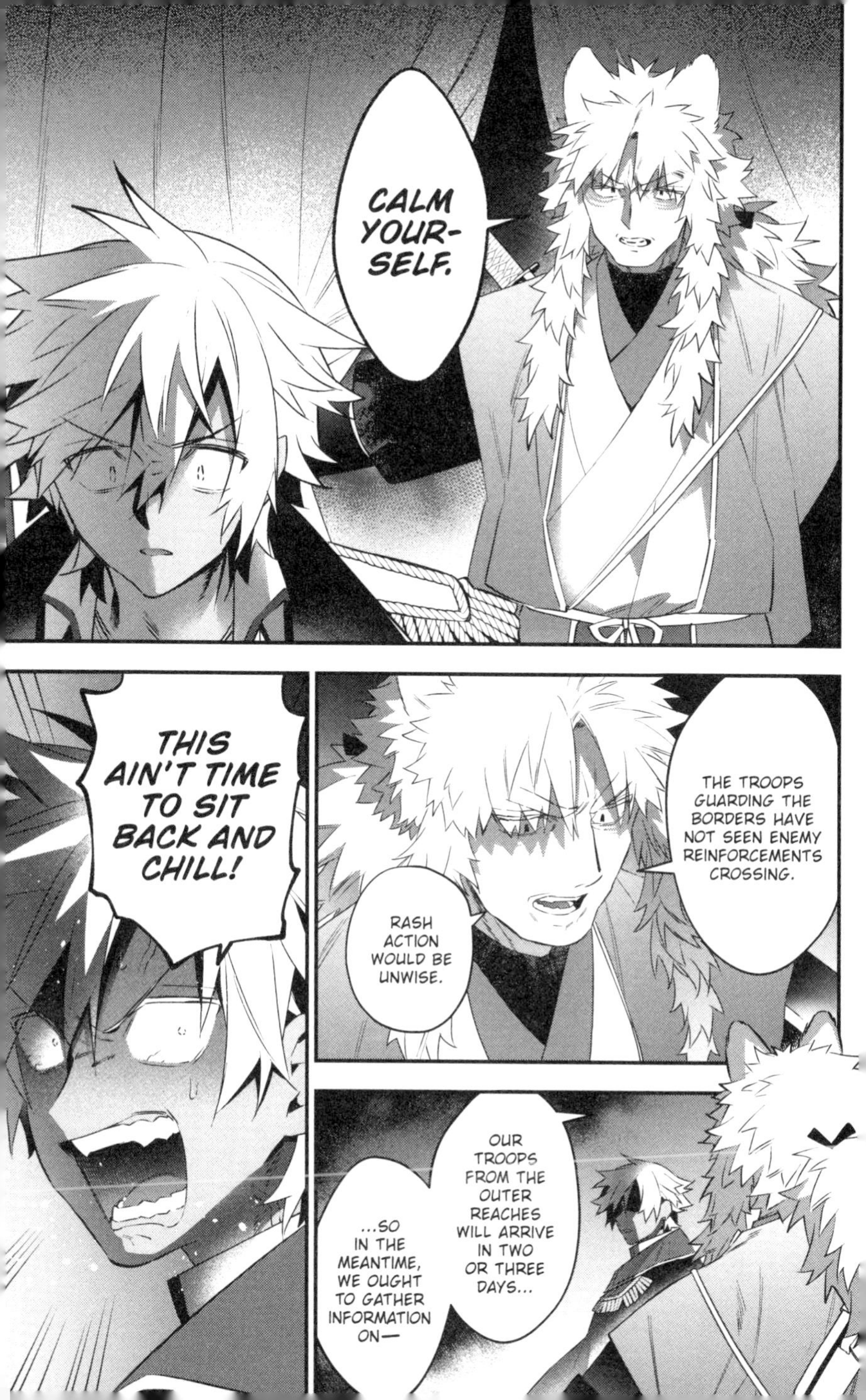
CALM YOURSELF.
THE TROOPS GUARDING THE BORDERS HAVE NOT SEEN ENEMY REINFORCEMENTS CROSSING.
RASH ACTION WOULD BE UNWISE.
OUR TROOPS FROM THE OUTER REACHES WILL ARRIVE IN TWO OR THREE DAYS...
...SO IN THE MEANTIME, WE OUGHT TO GATHER INFORMATION ON—
THIS AIN'T TIME TO SIT BACK AND CHILL!

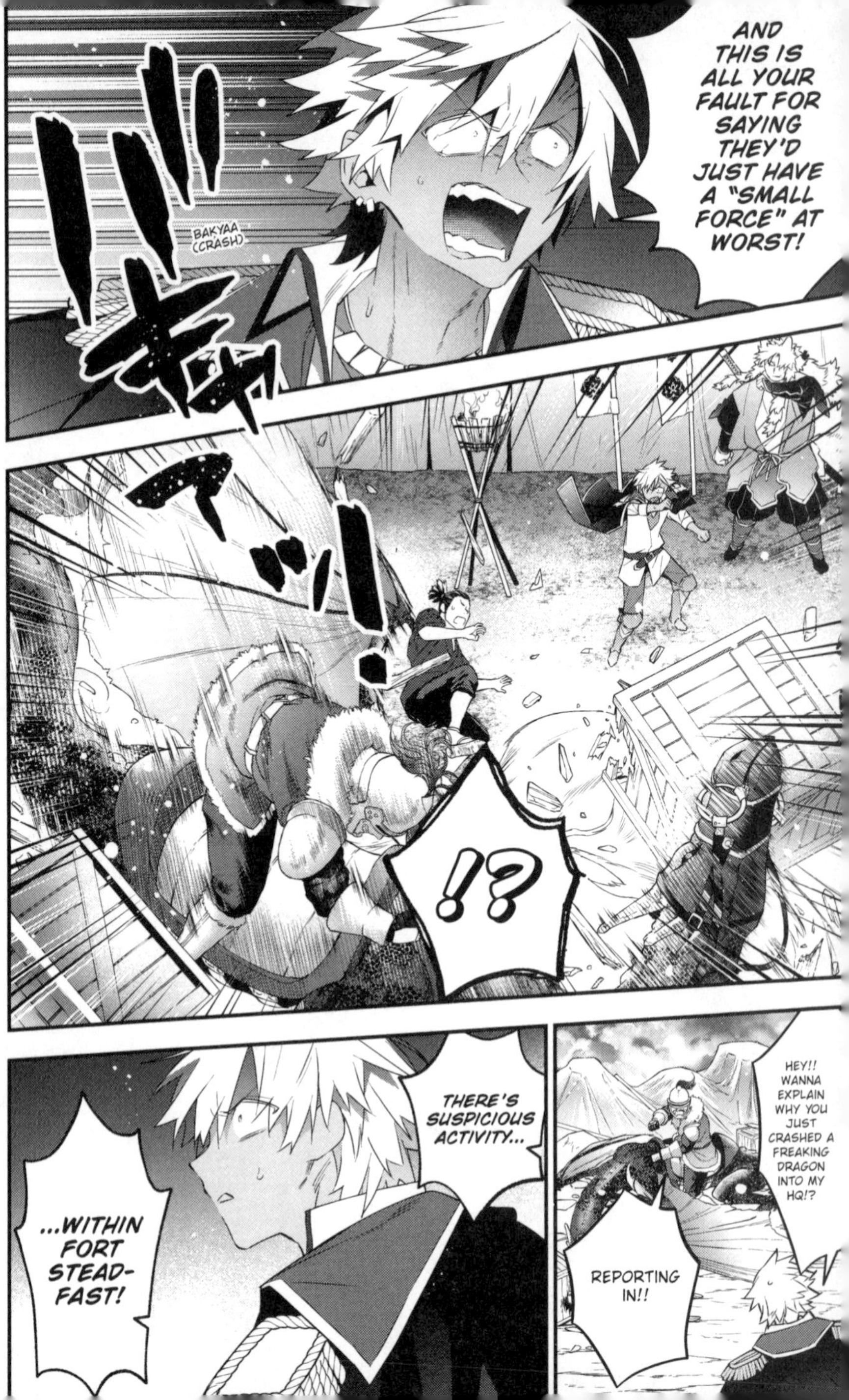
AND THIS IS ALL YOUR FAULT FOR SAYING THEY'D JUST HAVE A "SMALL FORCE" AT WORST!
BAKYAA (CRASH)
!?
HEY!! WANNA EXPLAIN WHY YOU JUST CRASHED A FREAKING DRAGON INTO MY HQ!?
REPORTING IN!!
THERE'S SUSPICIOUS ACTIVITY...
...WITHIN FORT STEAD-FAST!

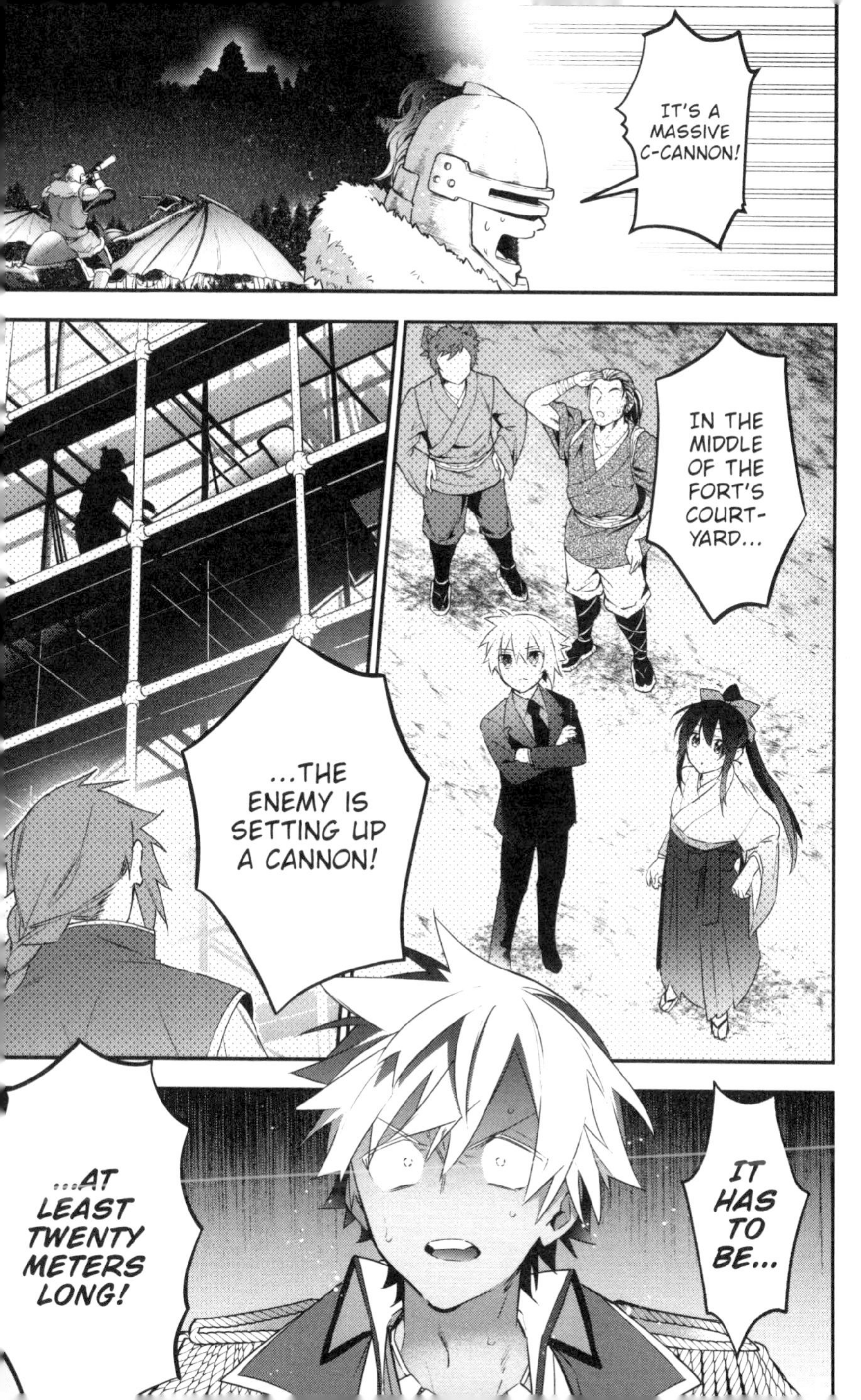
IT'S A MASSIVE C-CANNON!
IN THE MIDDLE OF THE FORT'S COURT-YARD...
...THE ENEMY IS SETTING UP A CANNON!
IT HAS TO BE...
...AT LEAST TWENTY METERS LONG!

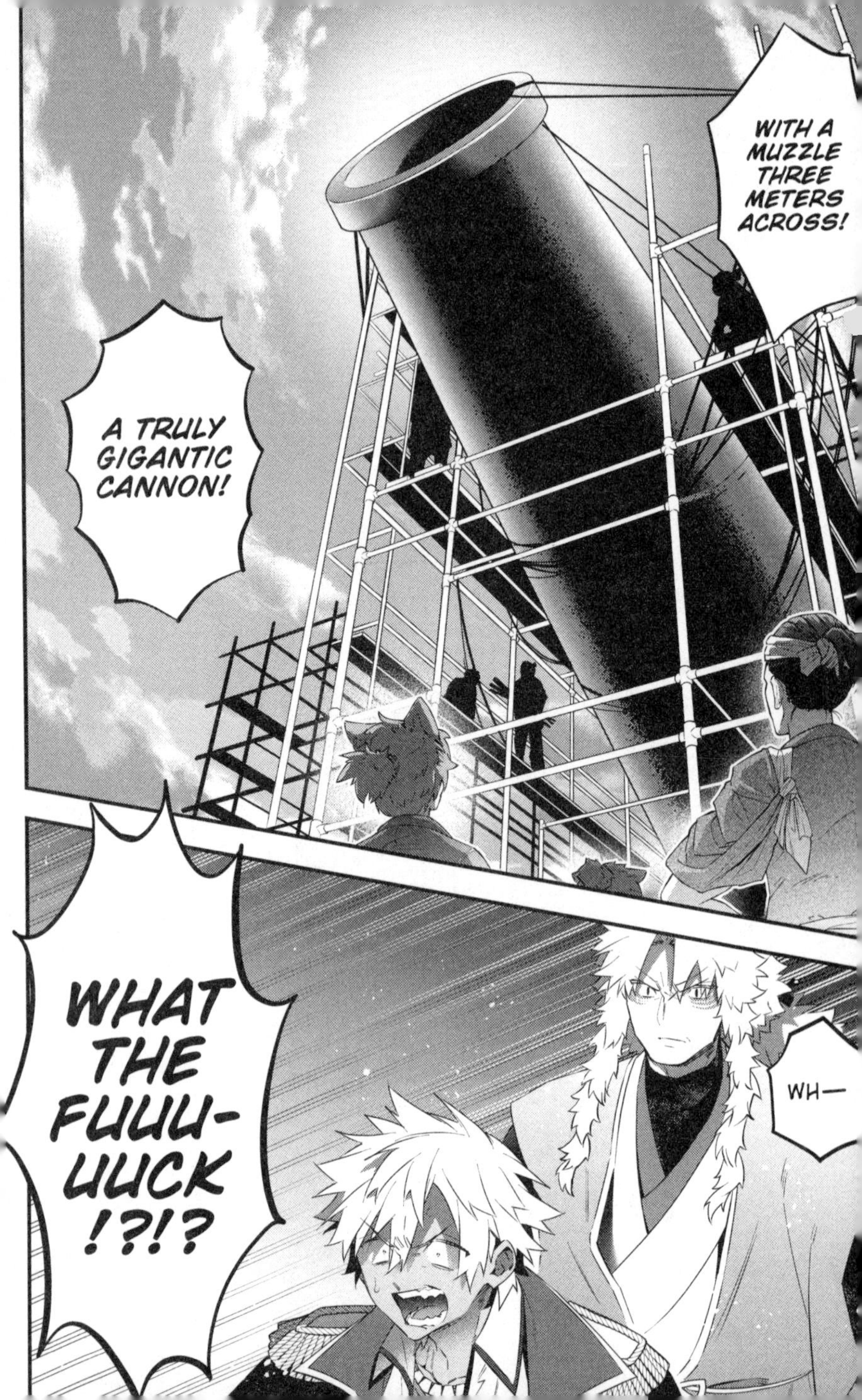
WITH A MUZZLE THREE METERS ACROSS!
A TRULY GIGANTIC CANNON!
WH—
WHAT THE FUUU-UUCK!?!?

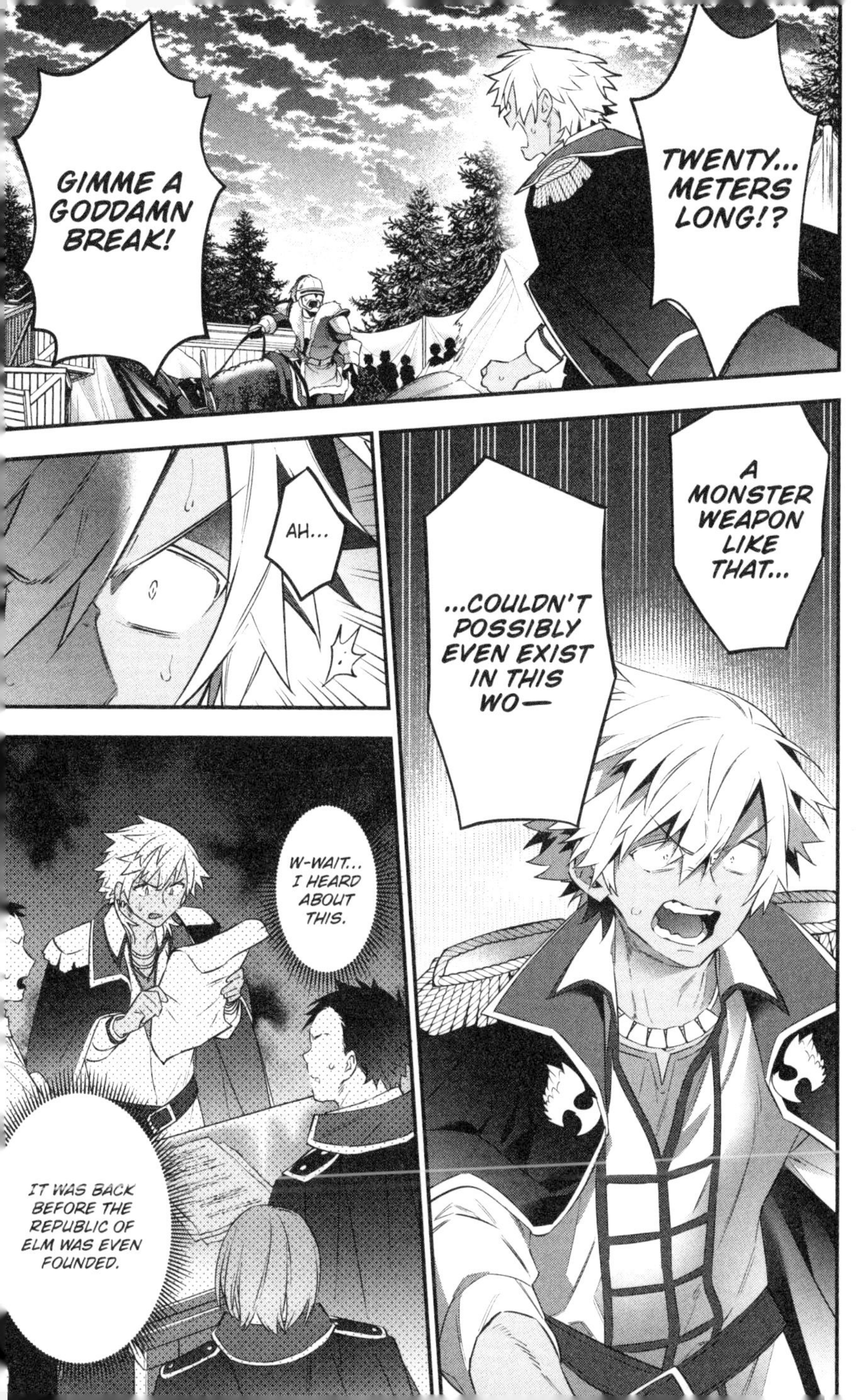
TWENTY... METERS LONG!?
GIMME A GODDAMN BREAK!
A MONSTER WEAPON LIKE THAT...
...COULDN'T POSSIBLY EVEN EXIST IN THIS WO—
AH...
W-WAIT... I HEARD ABOUT THIS.
IT WAS BACK BEFORE THE REPUBLIC OF ELM WAS EVEN FOUNDED.

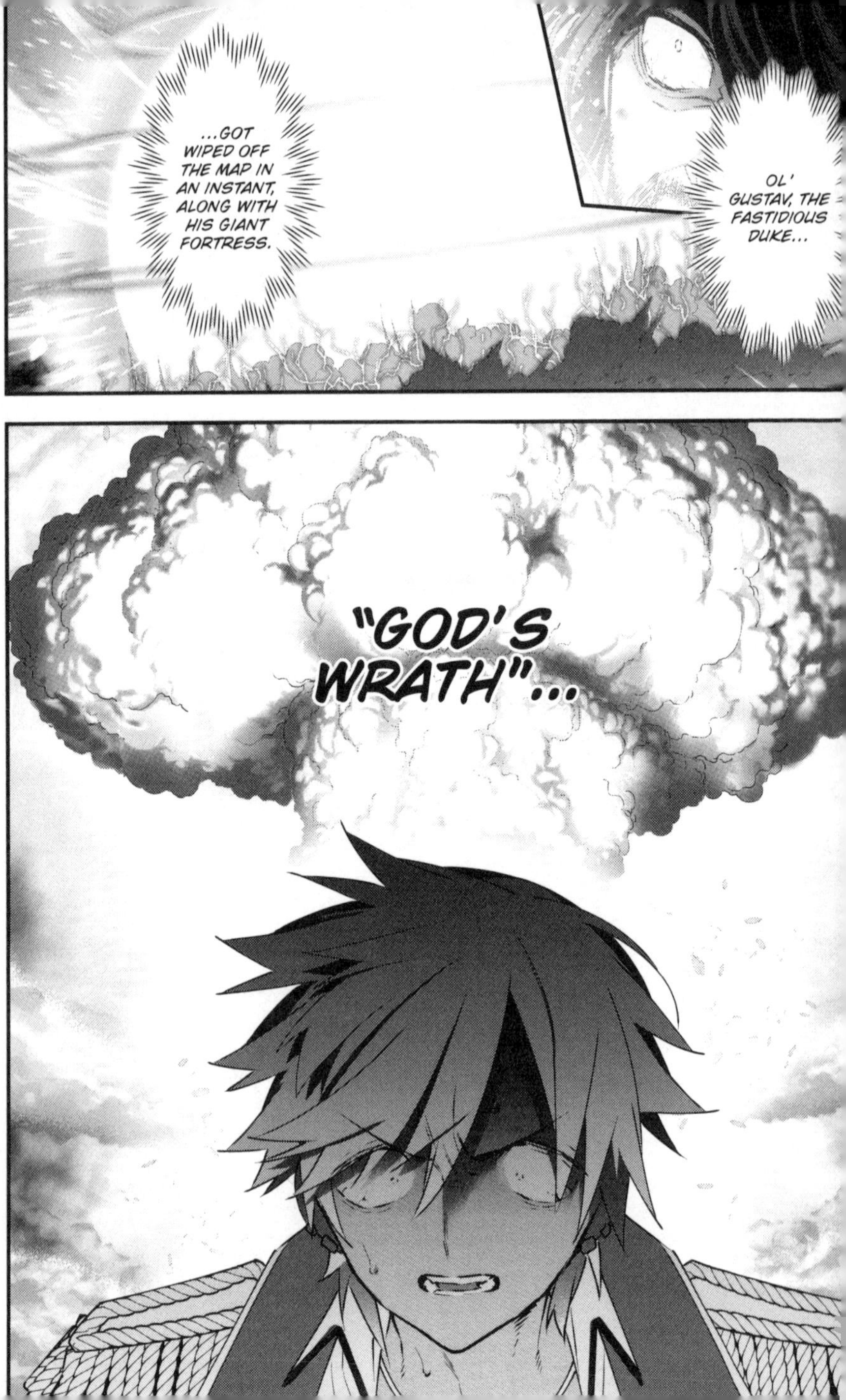
OL' GUSTAV, THE FASTIDIOUS DUKE...
...GOT WIPED OFF THE MAP IN AN INSTANT, ALONG WITH HIS GIANT FORTRESS.
"GOD'S WRATH"...

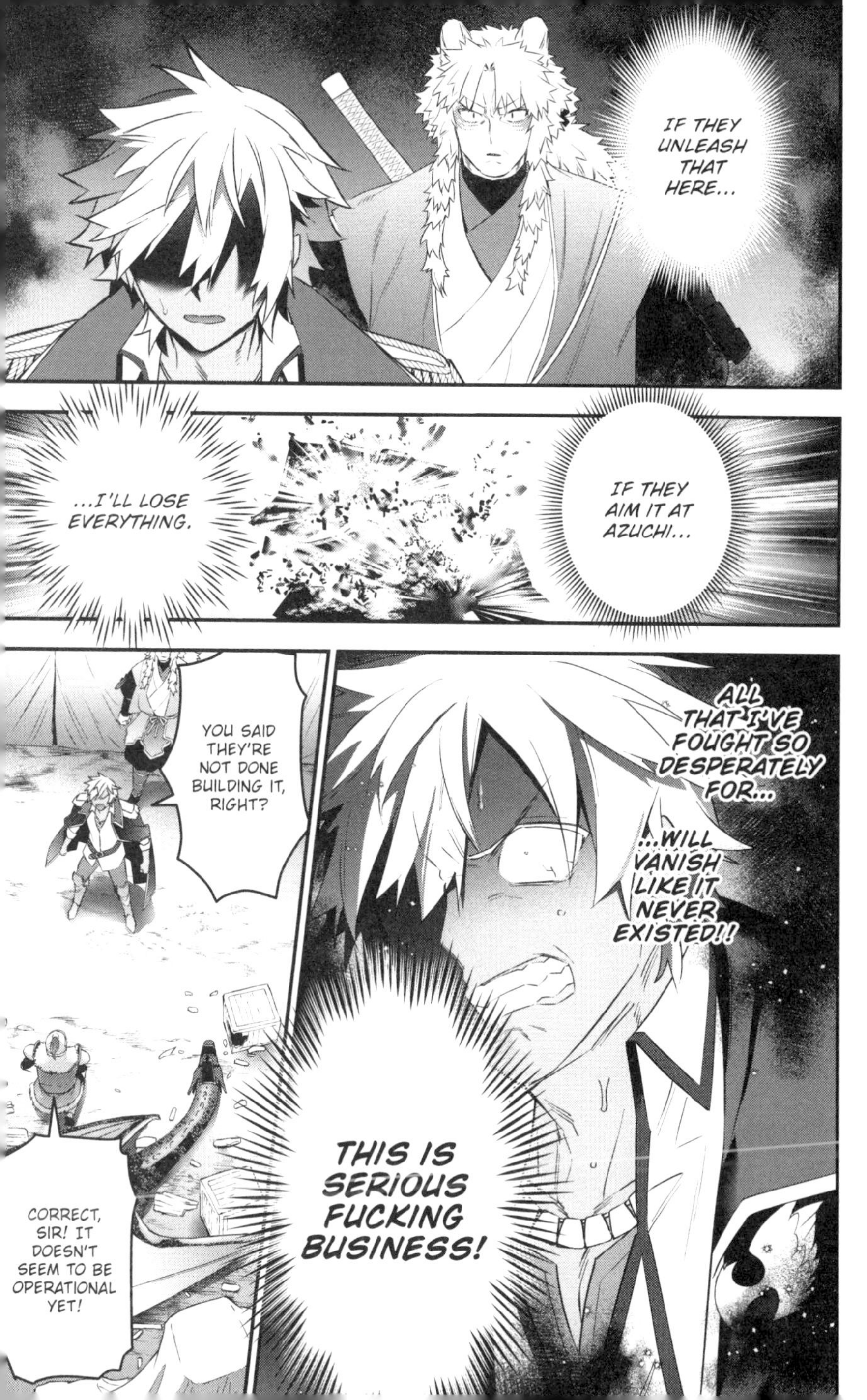
IF THEY UNLEASH THAT HERE...
IF THEY AIM IT AT AZUCHI...
...I'LL LOSE EVERYTHING.
ALL THAT I'VE FOUGHT SO DESPERATELY FOR...
...WILL VANISH LIKE IT NEVER EXISTED!!
THIS IS SERIOUS FUCKING BUSINESS!
YOU SAID THEY'RE NOT DONE BUILDING IT, RIGHT?
CORRECT, SIR! IT DOESN'T SEEM TO BE OPERATIONAL YET!

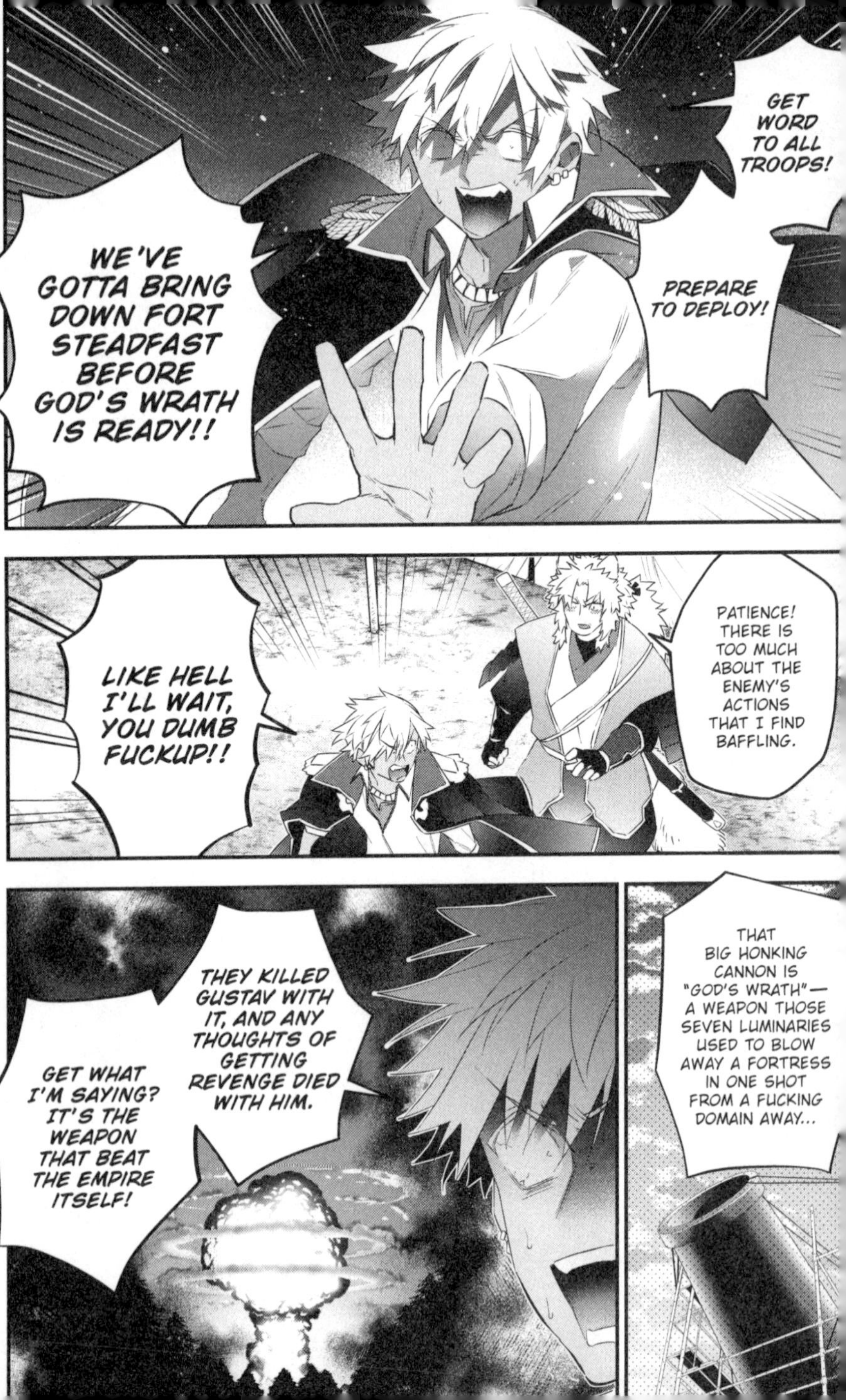
GET WORD TO ALL TROOPS!
PREPARE TO DEPLOY!
WE'VE GOTTA BRING DOWN FORT STEADFAST BEFORE GOD'S WRATH IS READY!!
PATIENCE! THERE IS TOO MUCH ABOUT THE ENEMY'S ACTIONS THAT I FIND BAFFLING.
LIKE HELL I'LL WAIT, YOU DUMB FUCKUP!!
THAT BIG HONKING CANNON IS "GOD'S WRATH"—A WEAPON THOSE SEVEN LUMINARIES USED TO BLOW AWAY A FORTRESS IN ONE SHOT FROM A FUCKING DOMAIN AWAY...
THEY KILLED GUSTAV WITH IT, AND ANY THOUGHTS OF GETTING REVENGE DIED WITH HIM.
GET WHAT I'M SAYING? IT'S THE WEAPON THAT BEAT THE EMPIRE ITSELF!

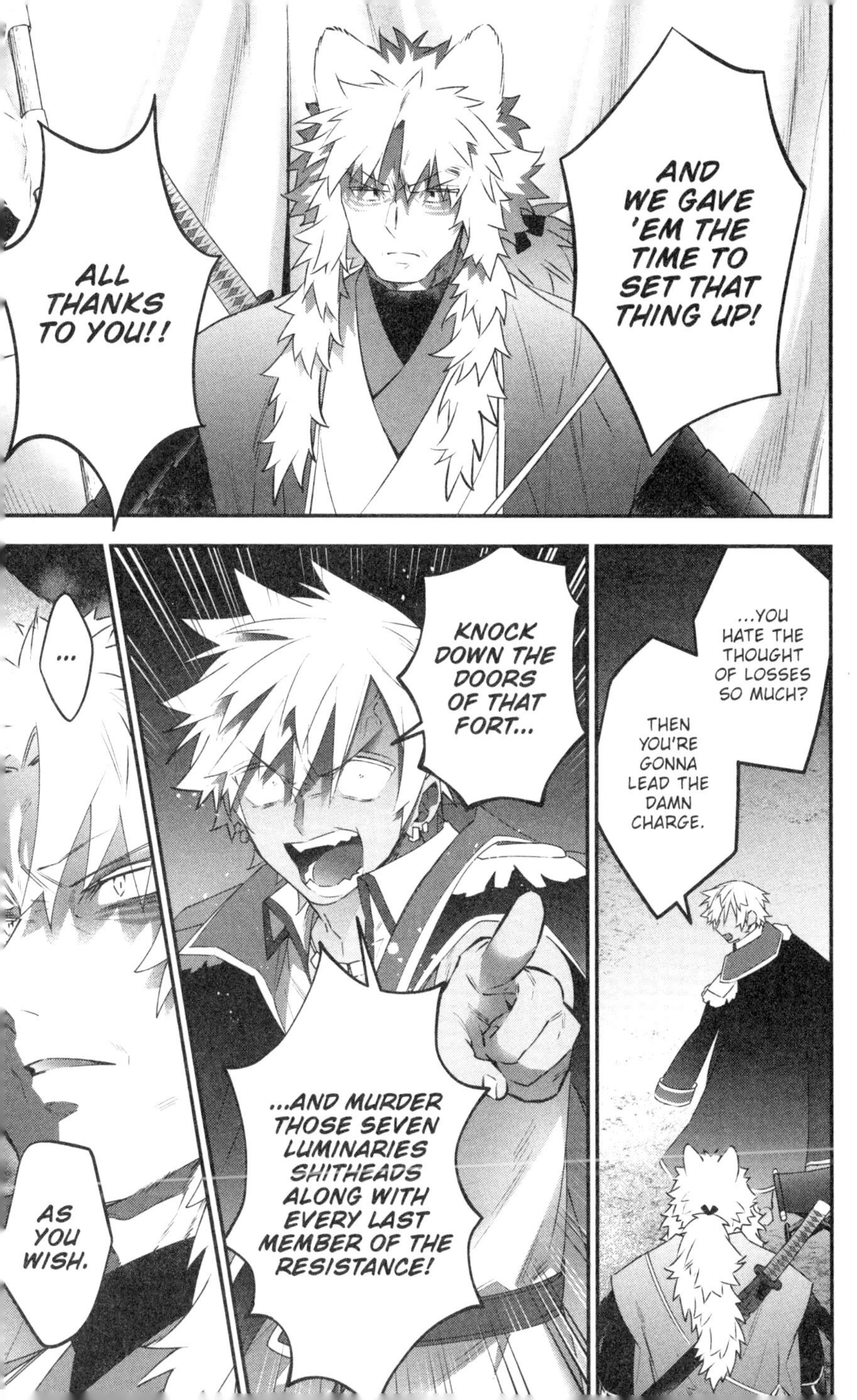
AND WE GAVE 'EM THE TIME TO SET THAT THING UP!
ALL THANKS TO YOU!!
...YOU HATE THE THOUGHT OF LOSSES SO MUCH?
THEN YOU'RE GONNA LEAD THE DAMN CHARGE.
KNOCK DOWN THE DOORS OF THAT FORT...
...AND MURDER THOSE SEVEN LUMINARIES SHITHEADS ALONG WITH EVERY LAST MEMBER OF THE RESISTANCE!
...
AS YOU WISH.

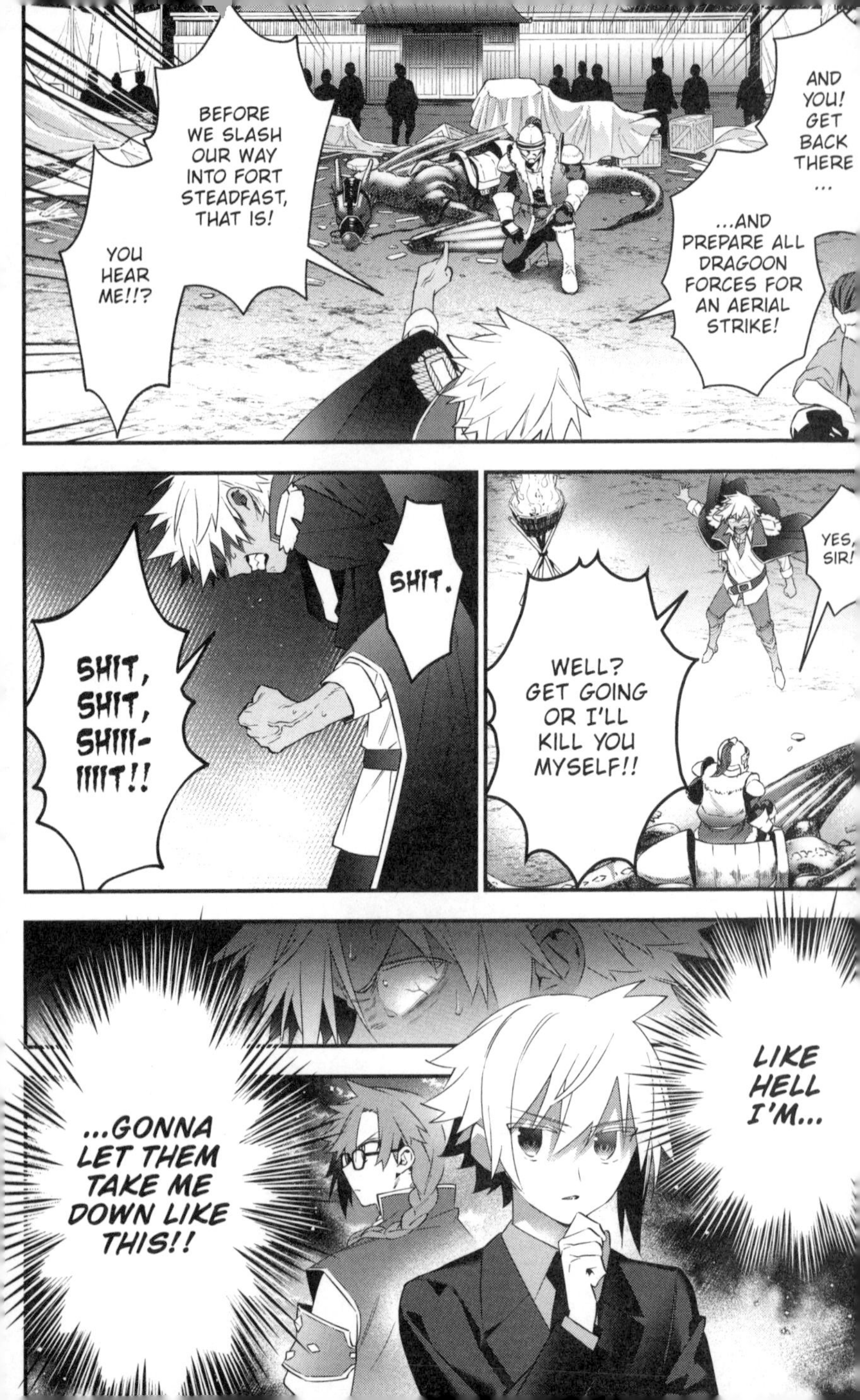
AND YOU! GET BACK THERE...
...AND PREPARE ALL DRAGOON FORCES FOR AN AERIAL STRIKE!
BEFORE WE SLASH OUR WAY INTO FORT STEADFAST, THAT IS!
YOU HEAR ME!!?
YES, SIR!
WELL? GET GOING OR I'LL KILL YOU MYSELF!!
SHIT.
SHIT, SHIT, SHIIII-IIIIT!!
LIKE HELL I'M...
...GONNA LET THEM TAKE ME DOWN LIKE THIS!!

HIGH SCHOOL
PRODIGIES HAVE
IT EASY EVEN IN
ANOTHER
WORLD!

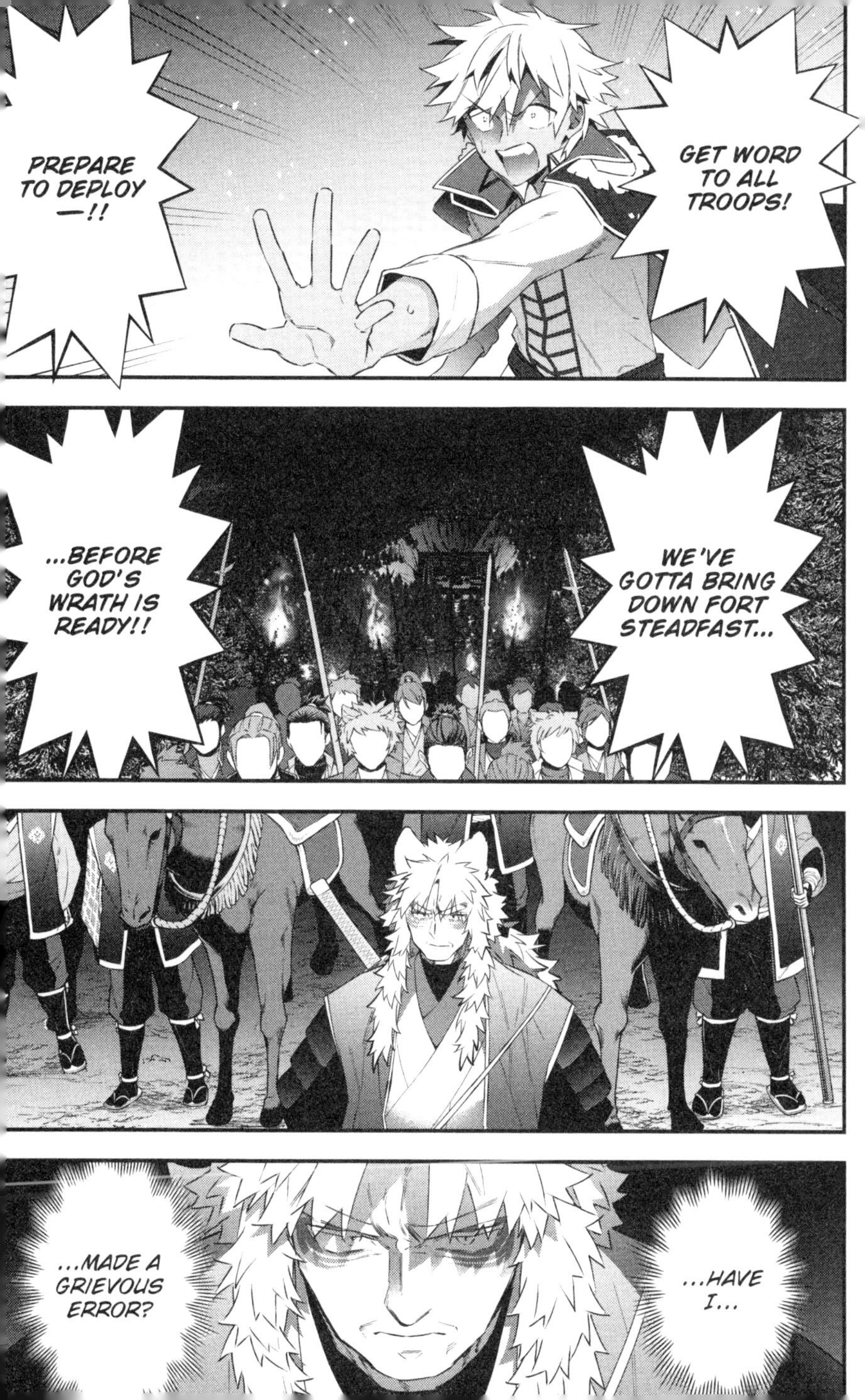
GET WORD TO ALL TROOPS!
PREPARE TO DEPLOY —!!
WE'VE GOTTA BRING DOWN FORT STEADFAST...
...BEFORE GOD'S WRATH IS READY!!
...HAVE I...
...MADE A GRIEVOUS ERROR?

CHAPTER 83: **CLEVER SCHEMES**

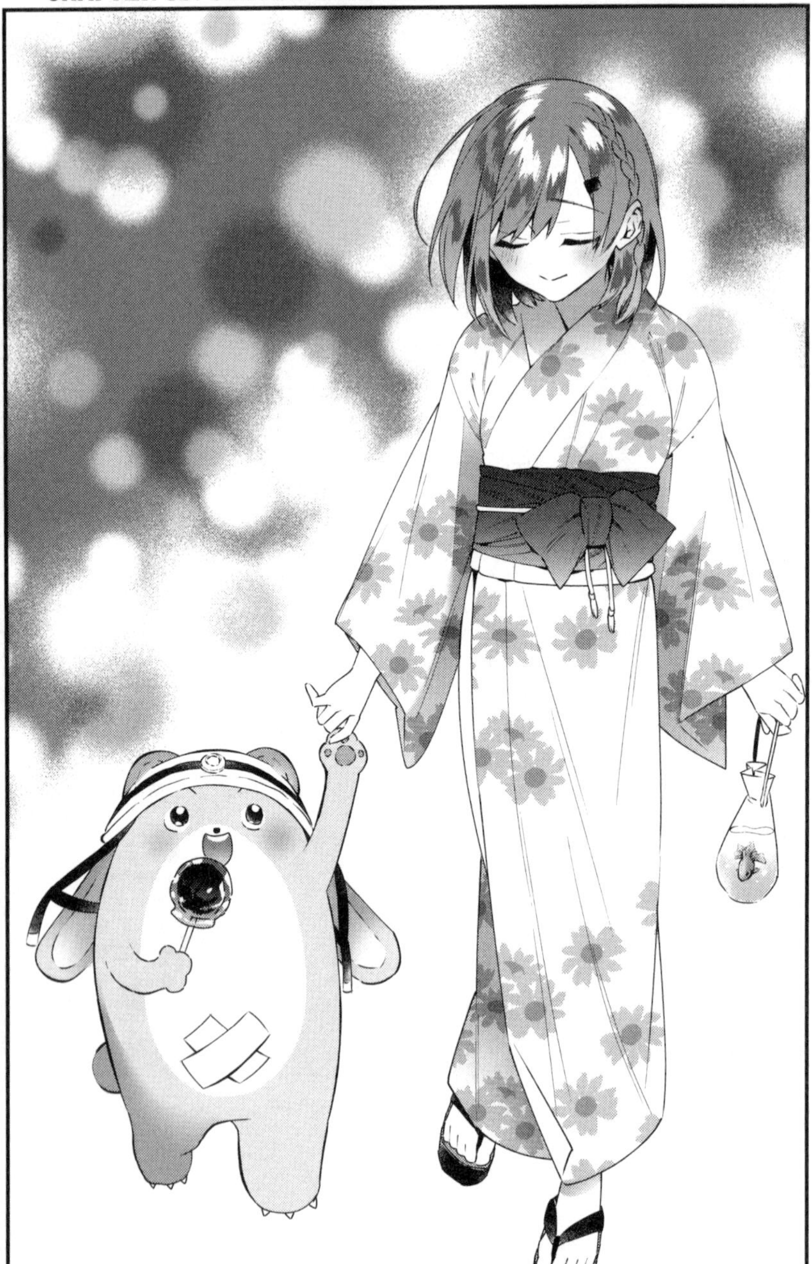

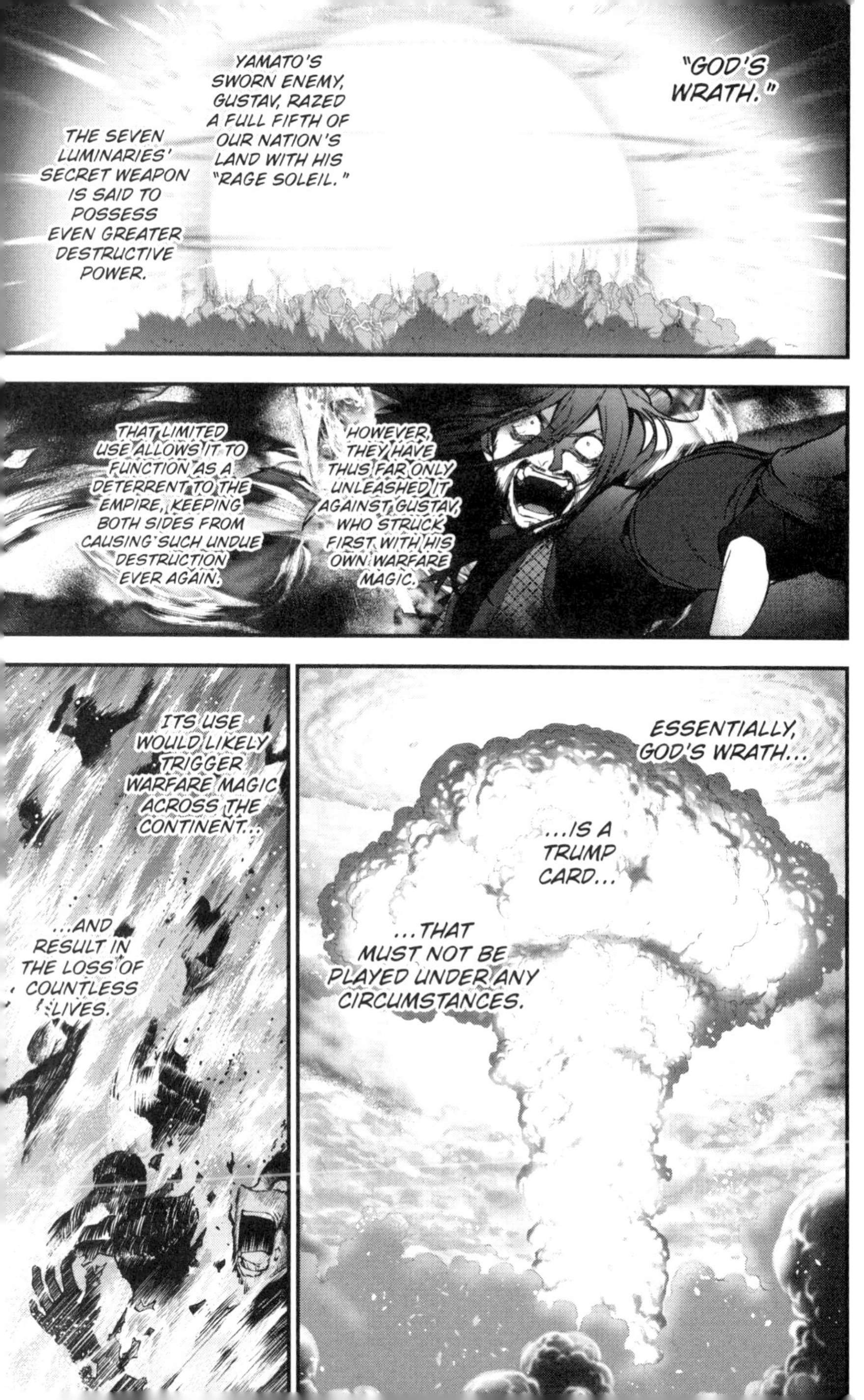
"GOD'S WRATH."
YAMATO'S SWORN ENEMY, GUSTAV, RAZED A FULL FIFTH OF OUR NATION'S LAND WITH HIS "RAGE SOLEIL."
THE SEVEN LUMINARIES' SECRET WEAPON IS SAID TO POSSESS EVEN GREATER DESTRUCTIVE POWER.
HOWEVER, THEY HAVE THUS FAR ONLY UNLEASHED IT AGAINST GUSTAV, WHO STRUCK FIRST WITH HIS OWN WARFARE MAGIC.
THAT LIMITED USE ALLOWS IT TO FUNCTION AS A DETERRENT TO THE EMPIRE, KEEPING BOTH SIDES FROM CAUSING SUCH UNDUE DESTRUCTION EVER AGAIN.
ESSENTIALLY, GOD'S WRATH...
...IS A TRUMP CARD...
...THAT MUST NOT BE PLAYED UNDER ANY CIRCUMSTANCES.
ITS USE WOULD LIKELY TRIGGER WARFARE MAGIC ACROSS THE CONTINENT...
...AND RESULT IN THE LOSS OF COUNTLESS LIVES.

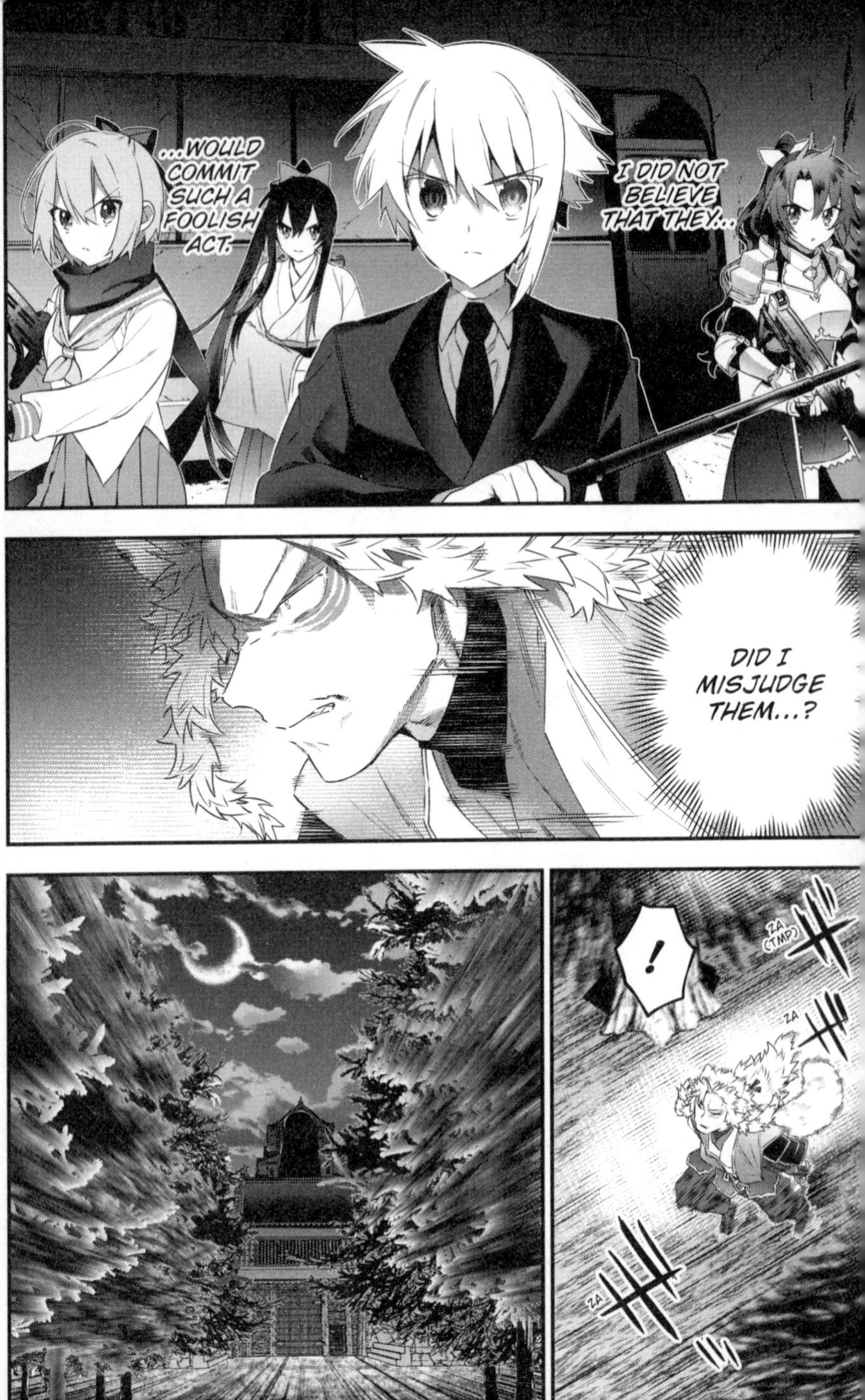
I DID NOT BELIEVE THAT THEY...
...WOULD COMMIT SUCH A FOOLISH ACT.
DID I MISJUDGE THEM...?
!
ZA (TMP)
ZA
ZA

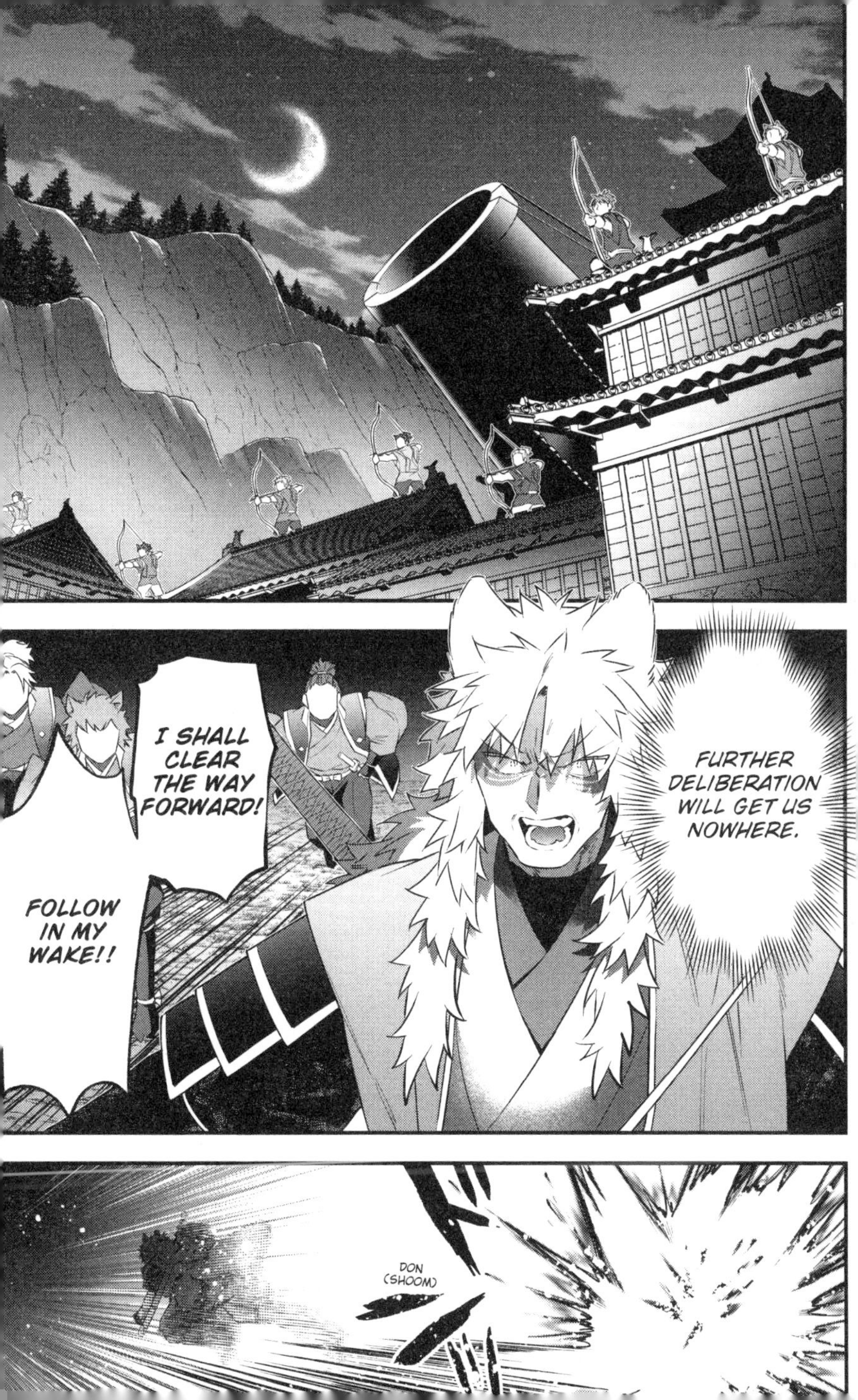
FURTHER DELIBERATION WILL GET US NOWHERE.
I SHALL CLEAR THE WAY FORWARD!
FOLLOW IN MY WAKE!!
DON (SHOOM)

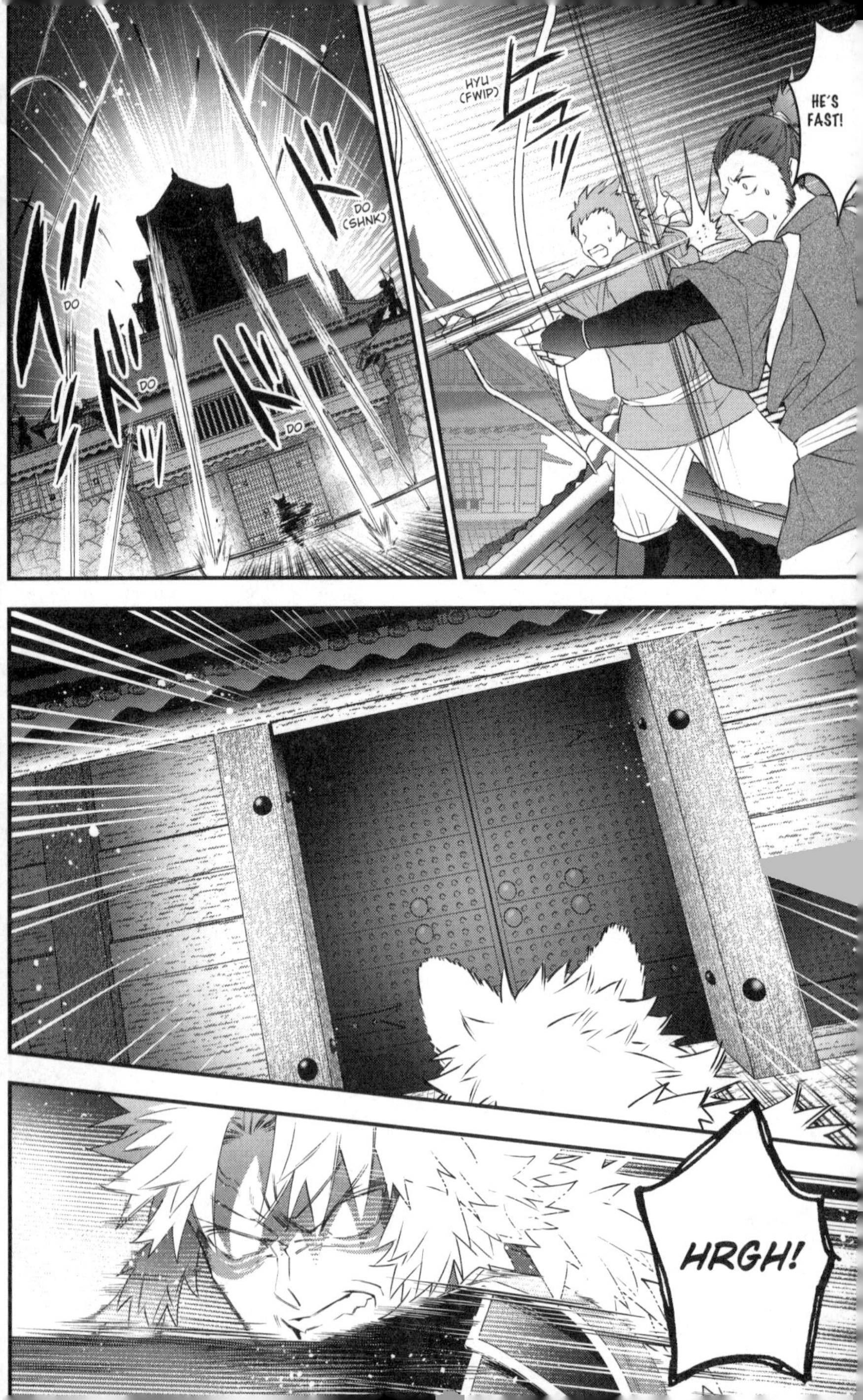
HE'S FAST!
HYU (FWIP)
DO (SHNK)
DO
DO
DO
HRGH!

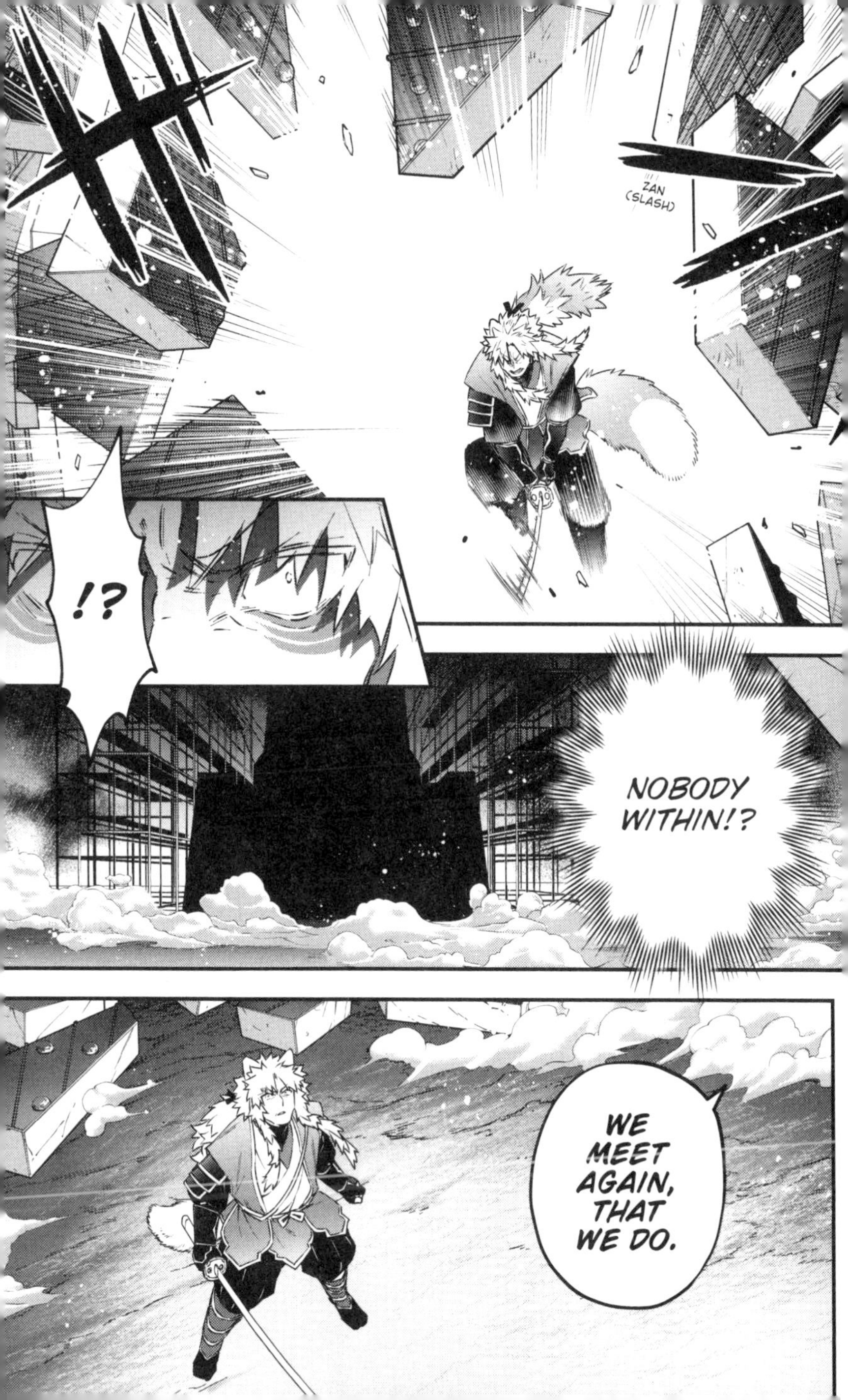
ZAN (SLASH)
!?
NOBODY WITHIN!?
WE MEET AGAIN, THAT WE DO.

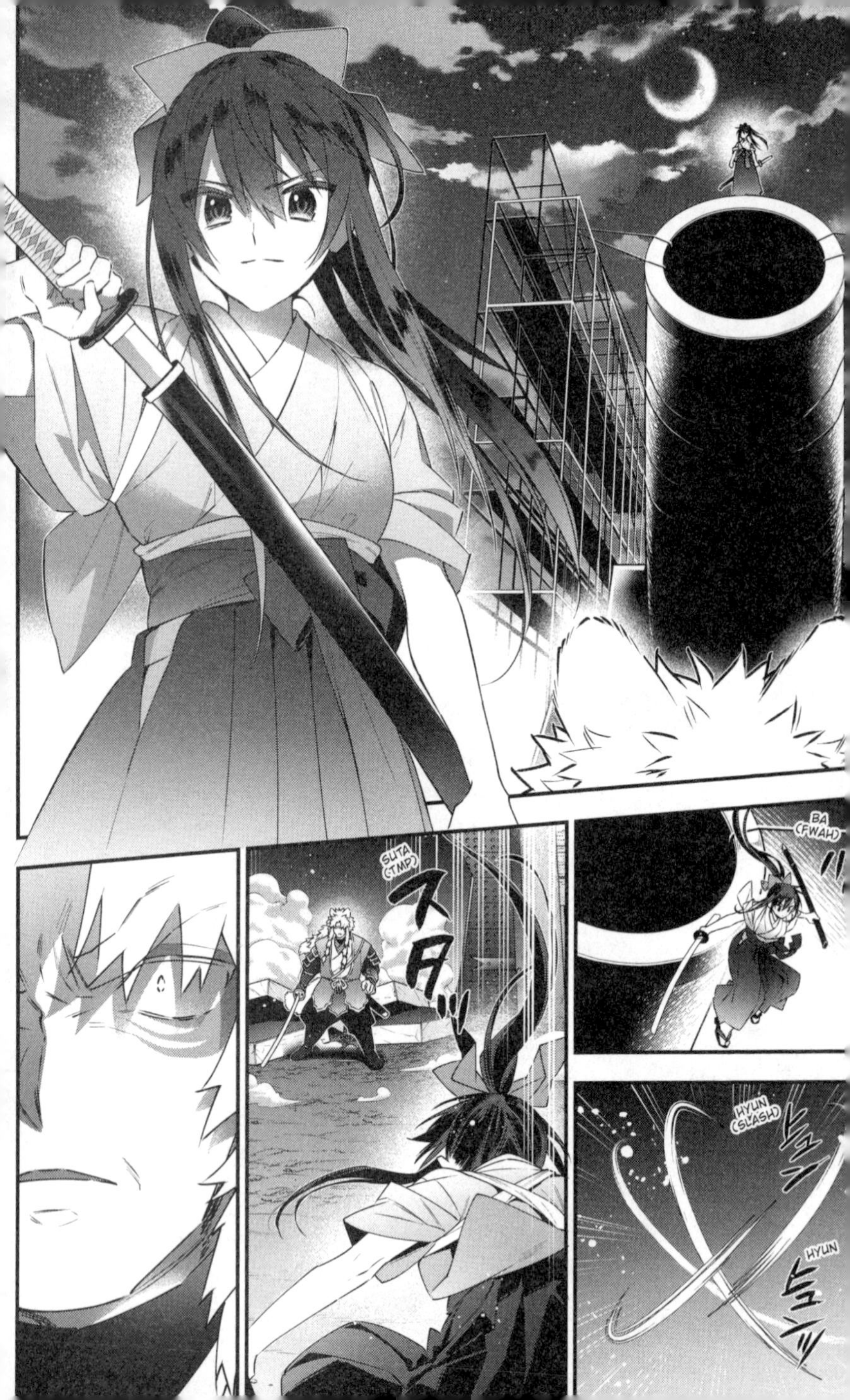

BA (FWAH)
HYUN (SLASH)
HYUN
SUTA (TMP)

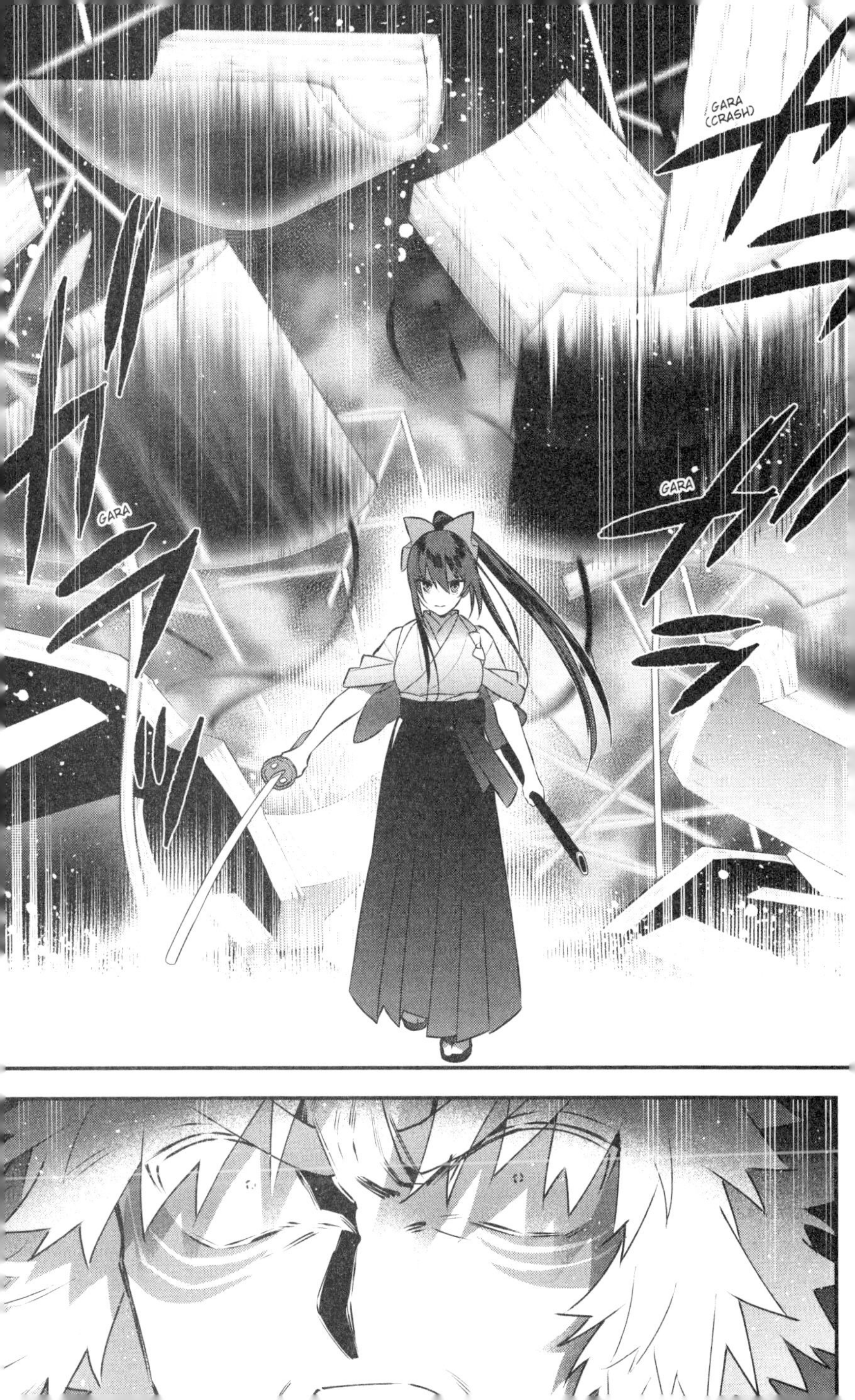
GARA (CRASH)
GARA
GARA

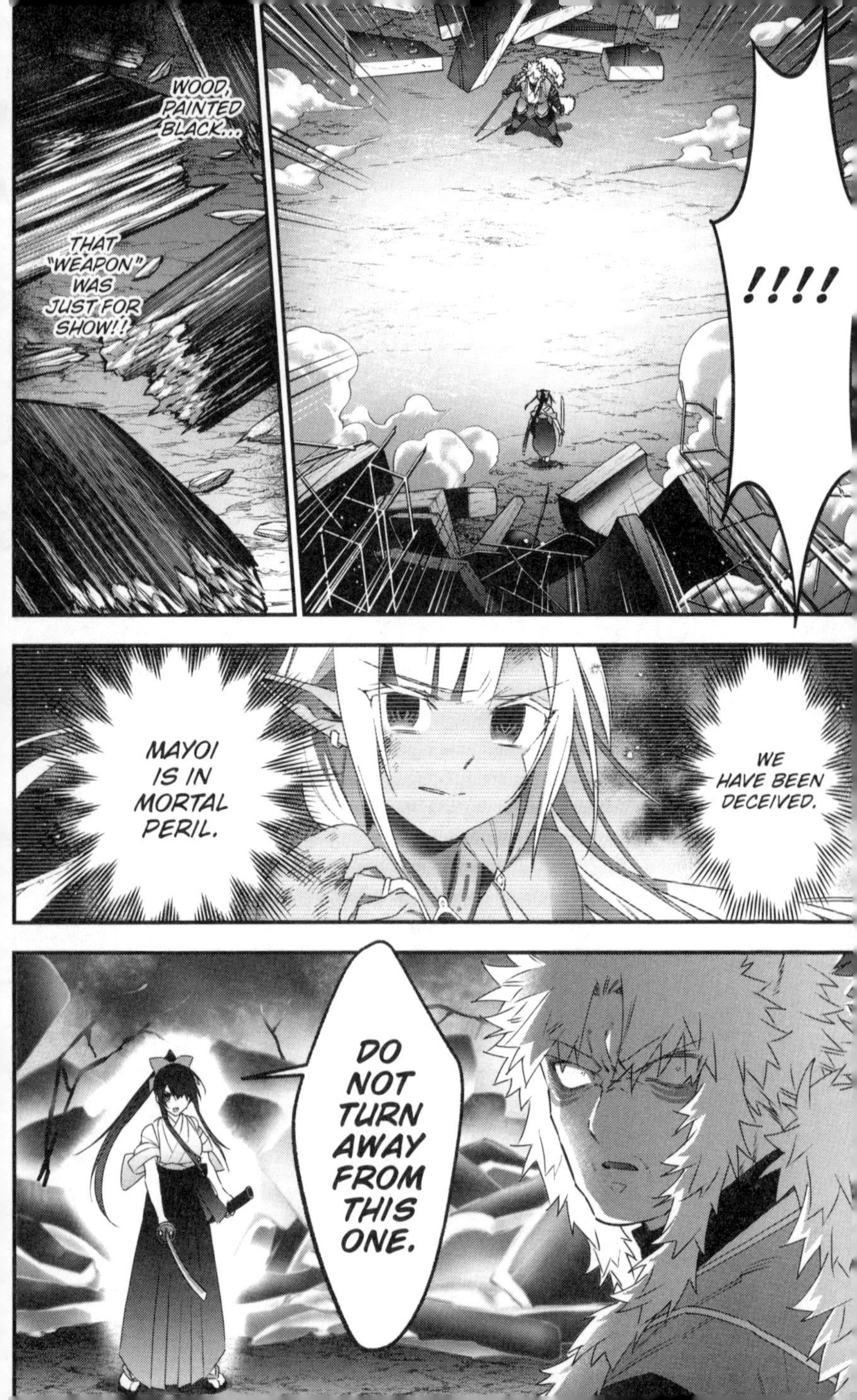
!!!!
WOOD, PAINTED BLACK...
THAT "WEAPON" WAS JUST FOR SHOW!!
WE HAVE BEEN DECEIVED.
MAYOI IS IN MORTAL PERIL.
DO NOT TURN AWAY FROM THIS ONE.

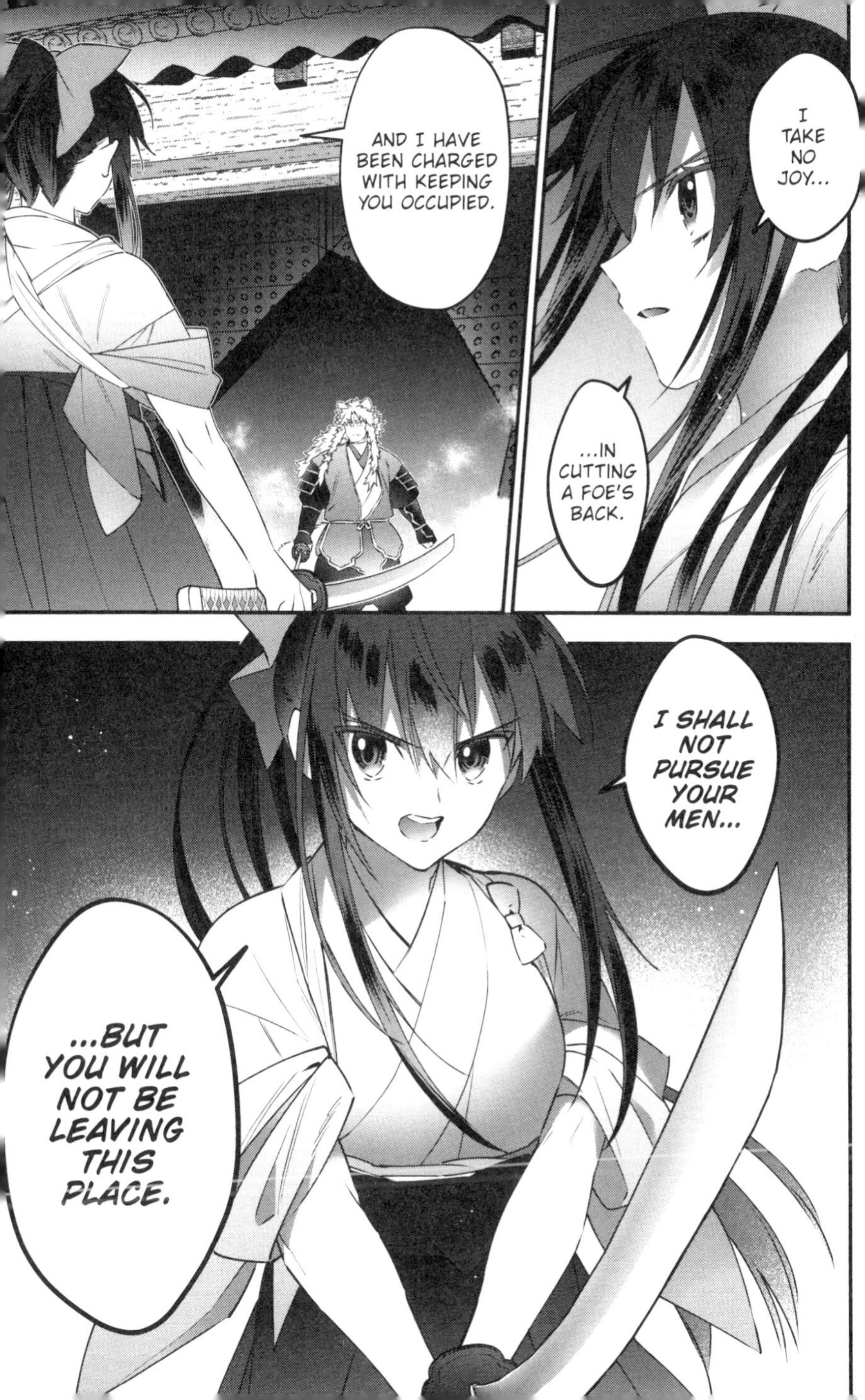
I TAKE NO JOY...
...IN CUTTING A FOE'S BACK.
AND I HAVE BEEN CHARGED WITH KEEPING YOU OCCUPIED.
I SHALL NOT PURSUE YOUR MEN...
...BUT YOU WILL NOT BE LEAVING THIS PLACE.

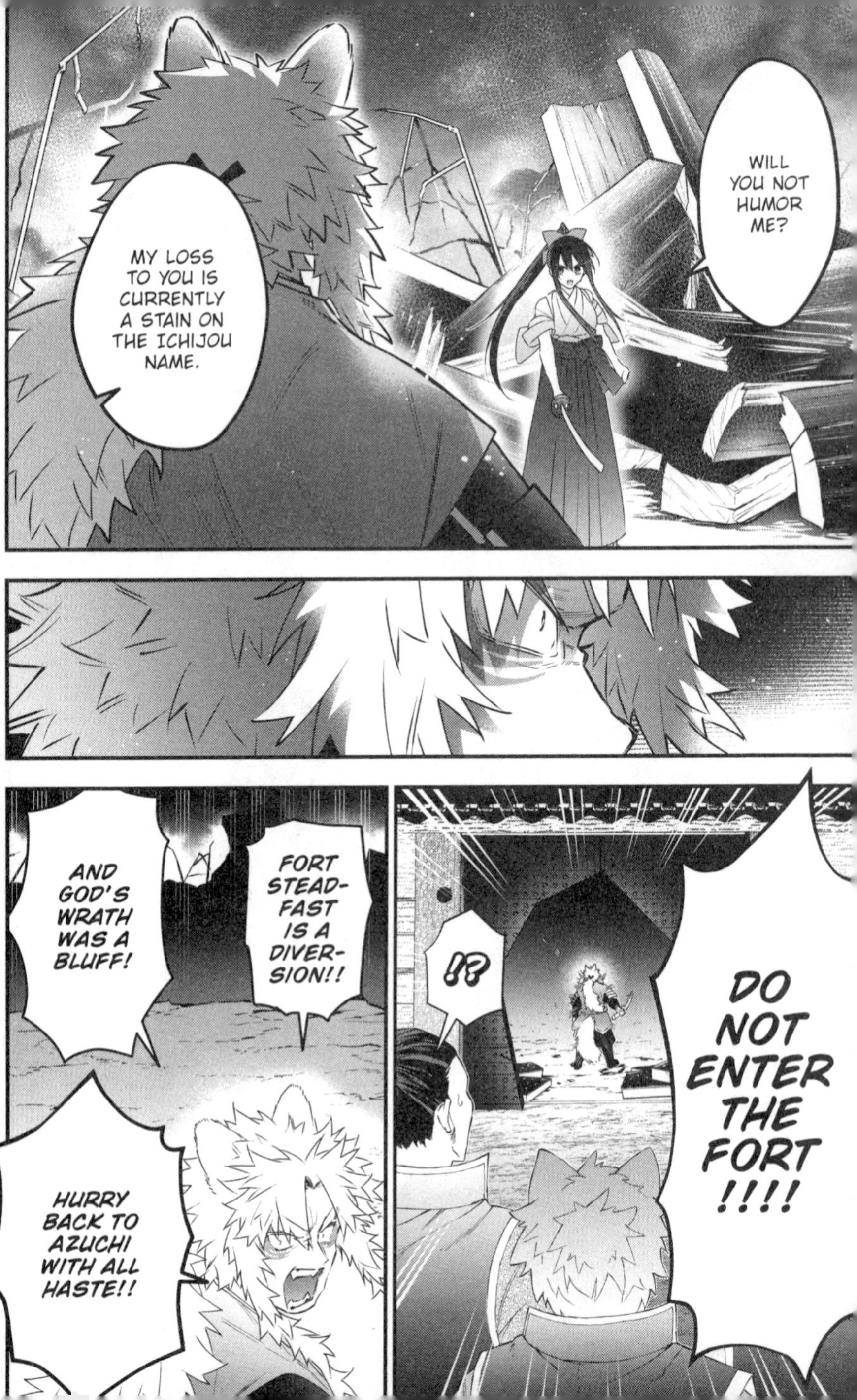
WILL YOU NOT HUMOR ME?
MY LOSS TO YOU IS CURRENTLY A STAIN ON THE ICHIJOU NAME.
DO NOT ENTER THE FORT!!!!
!?
FORT STEAD-FAST IS A DIVER-SION!!
AND GOD'S WRATH WAS A BLUFF!
HURRY BACK TO AZUCHI WITH ALL HASTE!!

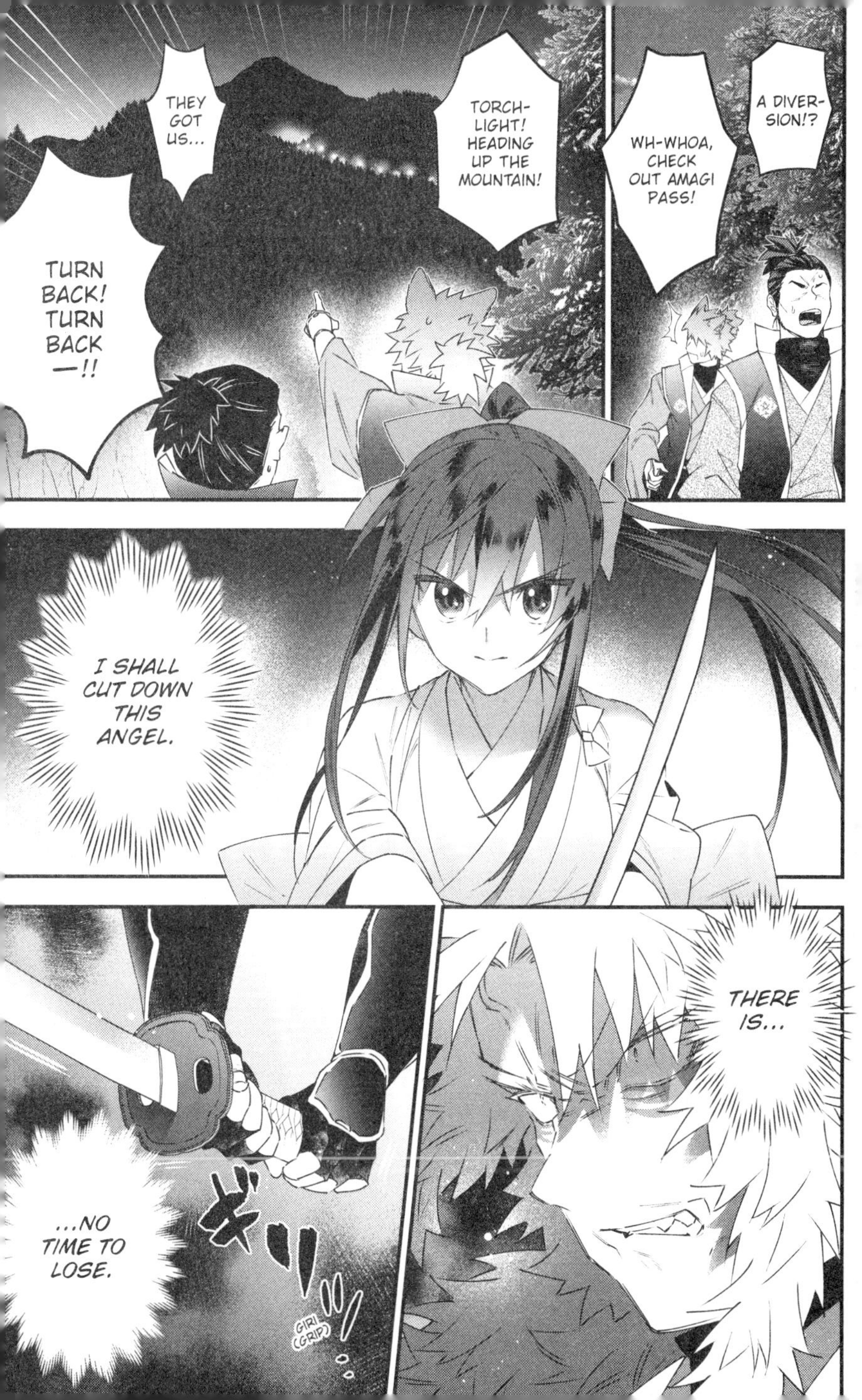
A DIVERSION!?
WH-WHOA, CHECK OUT AMAGI PASS!
TORCHLIGHT! HEADING UP THE MOUNTAIN!
THEY GOT US...
TURN BACK! TURN BACK—!!
I SHALL CUT DOWN THIS ANGEL.
THERE IS...
...NO TIME TO LOSE.
GIRI (GRIP)

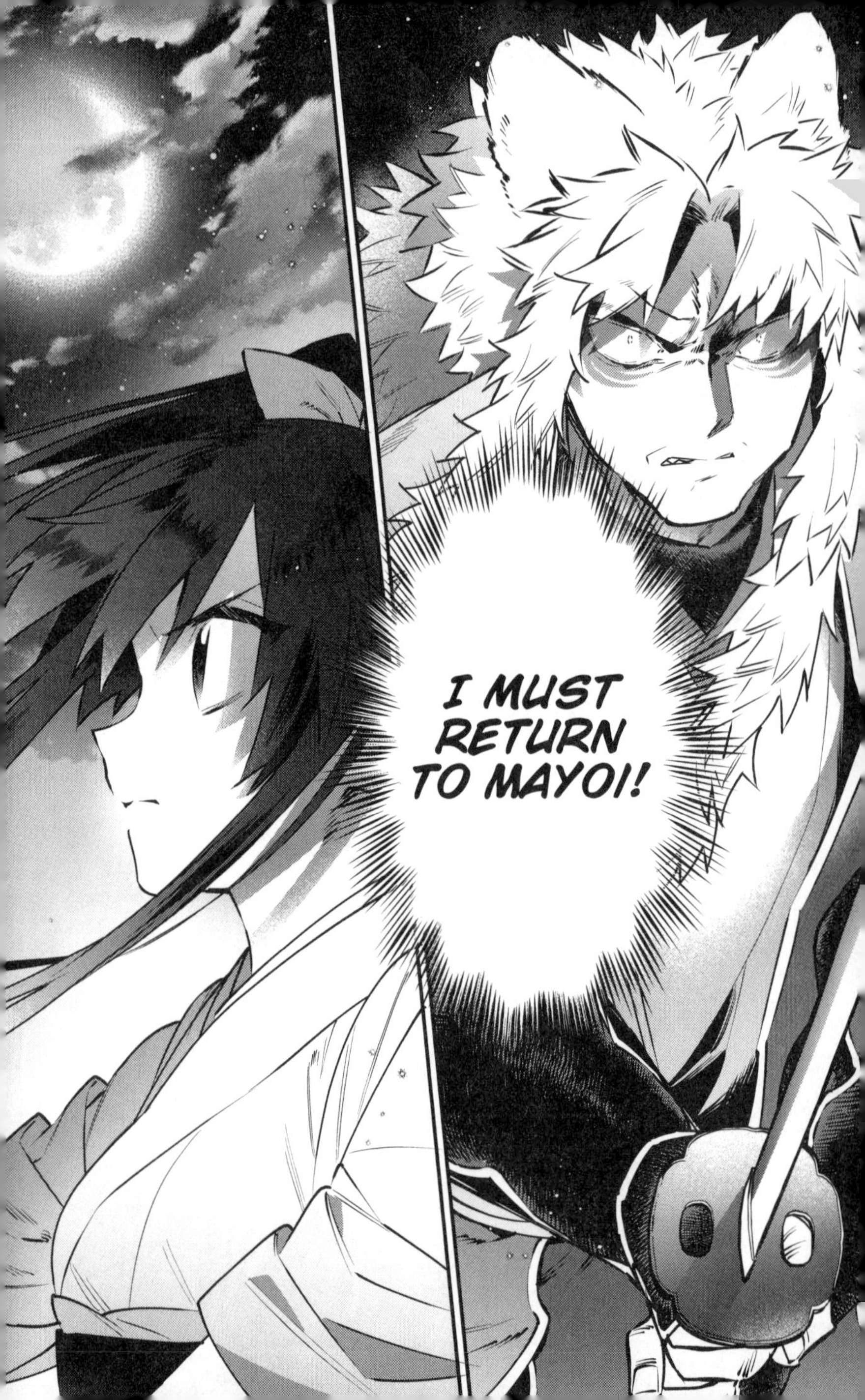
I MUST RETURN TO MAYOI!

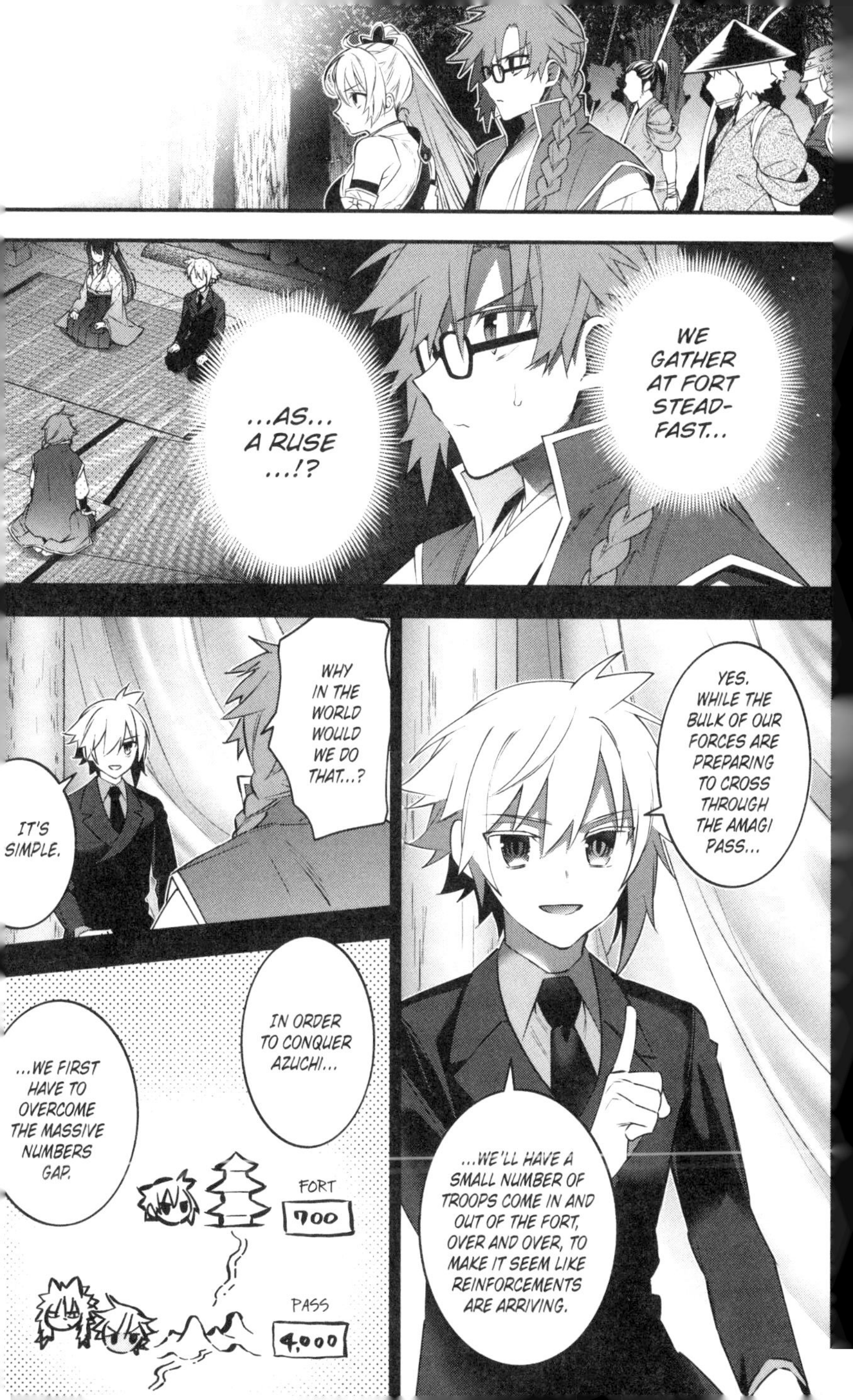
WE GATHER AT FORT STEAD-FAST...
...AS... A RUSE ...!?
YES. WHILE THE BULK OF OUR FORCES ARE PREPARING TO CROSS THROUGH THE AMAGI PASS...
...WE'LL HAVE A SMALL NUMBER OF TROOPS COME IN AND OUT OF THE FORT, OVER AND OVER, TO MAKE IT SEEM LIKE REINFORCEMENTS ARE ARRIVING.
WHY IN THE WORLD WOULD WE DO THAT...?
IT'S SIMPLE.
IN ORDER TO CONQUER AZUCHI...
...WE FIRST HAVE TO OVERCOME THE MASSIVE NUMBERS GAP.
FORT
700
PASS
4,000

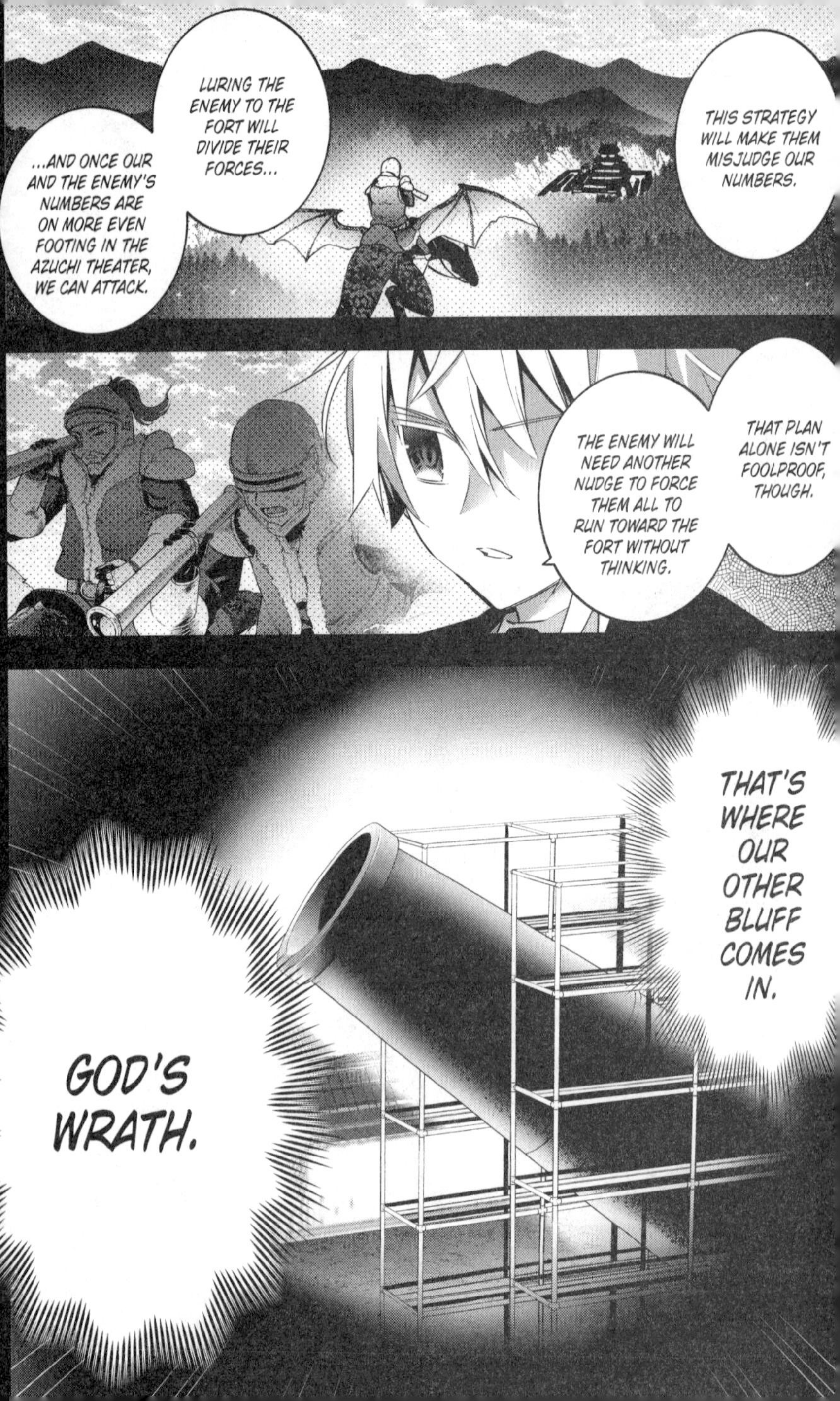
THIS STRATEGY WILL MAKE THEM MISJUDGE OUR NUMBERS.
LURING THE ENEMY TO THE FORT WILL DIVIDE THEIR FORCES...
...AND ONCE OUR AND THE ENEMY'S NUMBERS ARE ON MORE EVEN FOOTING IN THE AZUCHI THEATER, WE CAN ATTACK.
THAT PLAN ALONE ISN'T FOOLPROOF, THOUGH.
THE ENEMY WILL NEED ANOTHER NUDGE TO FORCE THEM ALL TO RUN TOWARD THE FORT WITHOUT THINKING.
THAT'S WHERE OUR OTHER BLUFF COMES IN.
GOD'S WRATH.

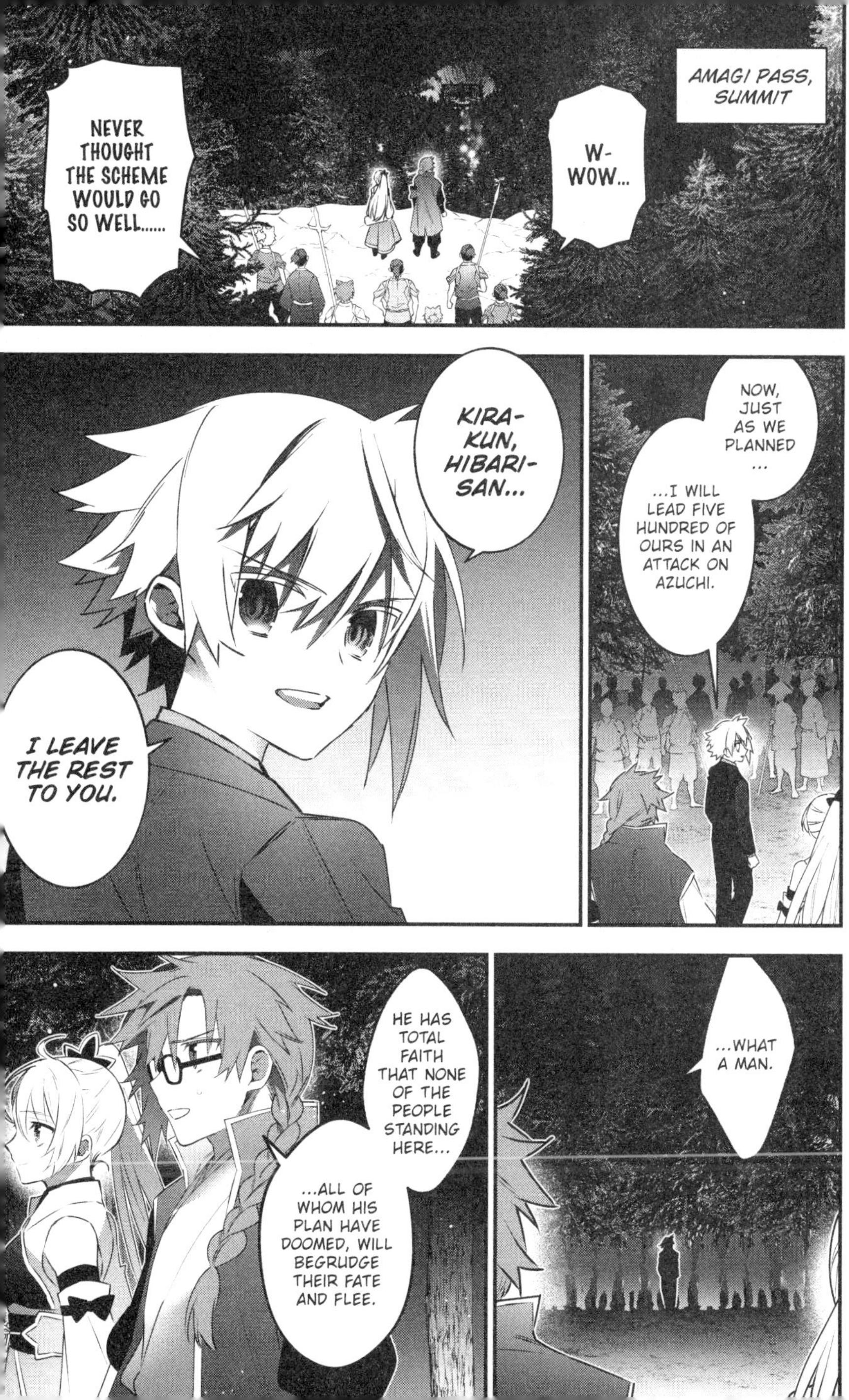
AMAGI PASS, SUMMIT
W-WOW...
NEVER THOUGHT THE SCHEME WOULD GO SO WELL......
NOW, JUST AS WE PLANNED...
...I WILL LEAD FIVE HUNDRED OF OURS IN AN ATTACK ON AZUCHI.
KIRA-KUN, HIBARI-SAN...
I LEAVE THE REST TO YOU.
...WHAT A MAN.
HE HAS TOTAL FAITH THAT NONE OF THE PEOPLE STANDING HERE...
...ALL OF WHOM HIS PLAN HAVE DOOMED, WILL BEGRUDGE THEIR FATE AND FLEE.

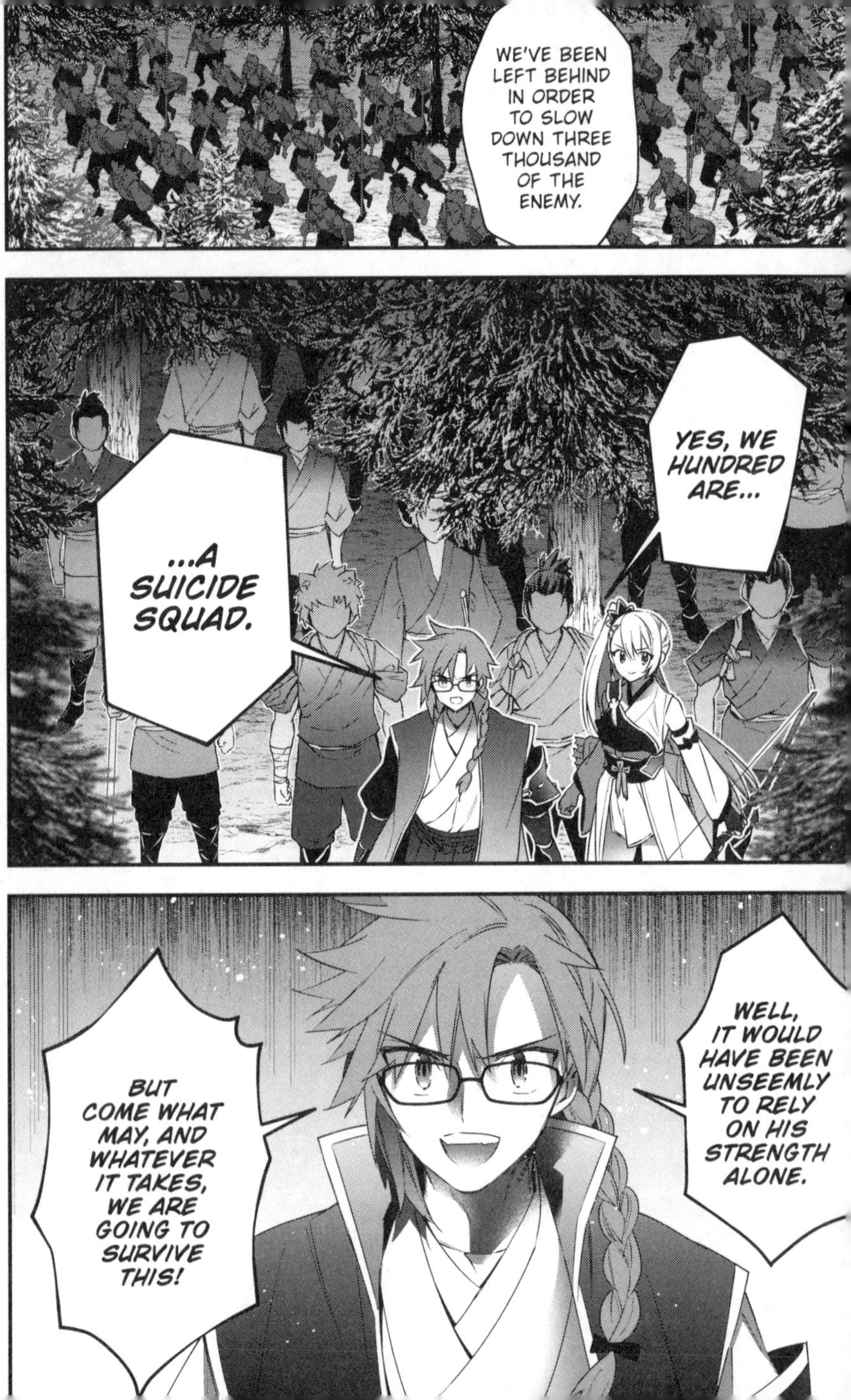
WE'VE BEEN LEFT BEHIND IN ORDER TO SLOW DOWN THREE THOUSAND OF THE ENEMY.
YES, WE HUNDRED ARE...
...A SUICIDE SQUAD.
WELL, IT WOULD HAVE BEEN UNSEEMLY TO RELY ON HIS STRENGTH ALONE.
BUT COME WHAT MAY, AND WHATEVER IT TAKES, WE ARE GOING TO SURVIVE THIS!

HIGH SCHOOL PRODIGIES HAVE IT EASY EVEN IN ANOTHER WORLD!

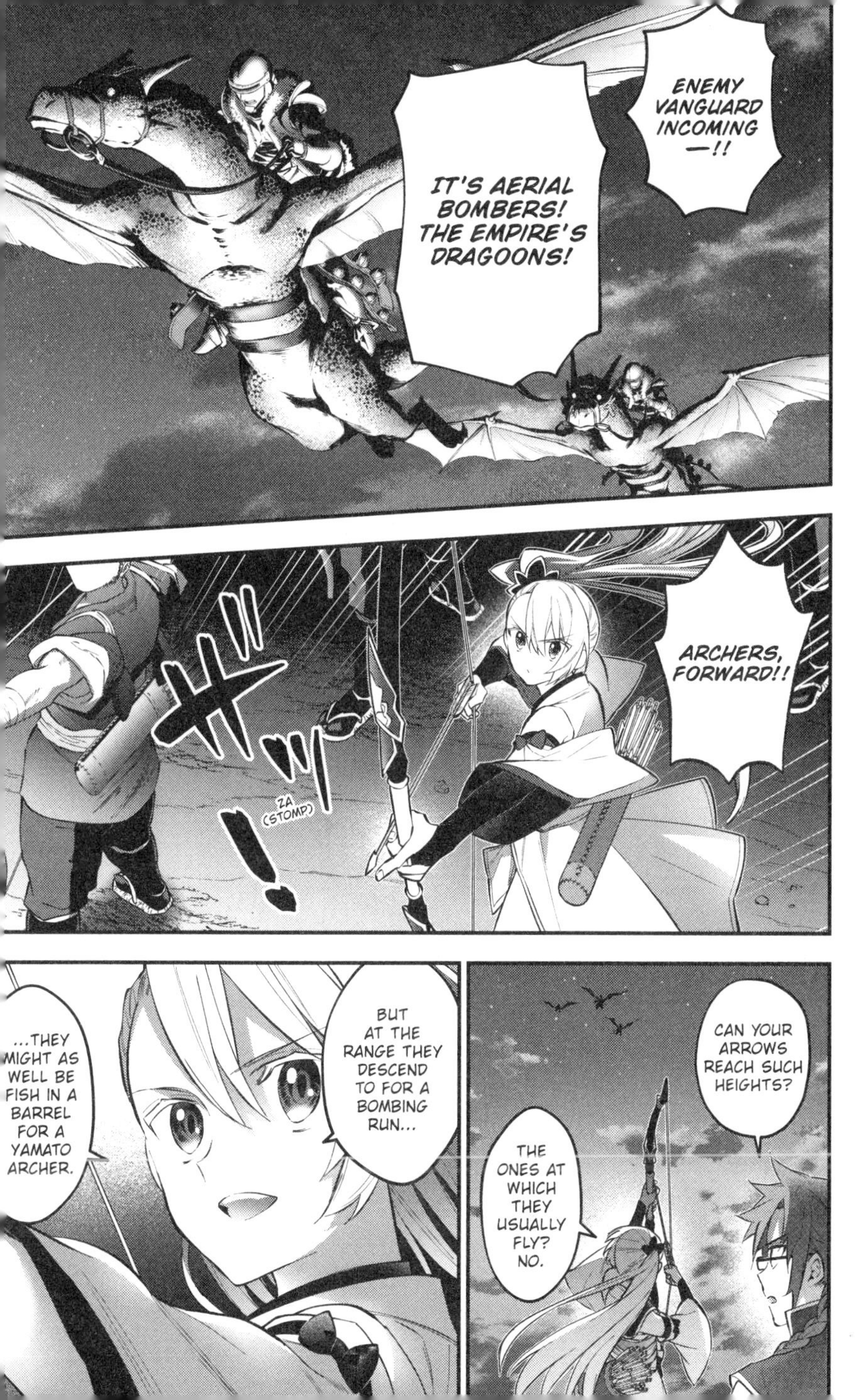
ENEMY VANGUARD INCOMING—!!
IT'S AERIAL BOMBERS! THE EMPIRE'S DRAGOONS!
ARCHERS, FORWARD!!
ZA (STOMP)
CAN YOUR ARROWS REACH SUCH HEIGHTS?
THE ONES AT WHICH THEY USUALLY FLY? NO.
BUT AT THE RANGE THEY DESCEND TO FOR A BOMBING RUN...
...THEY MIGHT AS WELL BE FISH IN A BARREL FOR A YAMATO ARCHER.

CHAPTER 84: CLASH

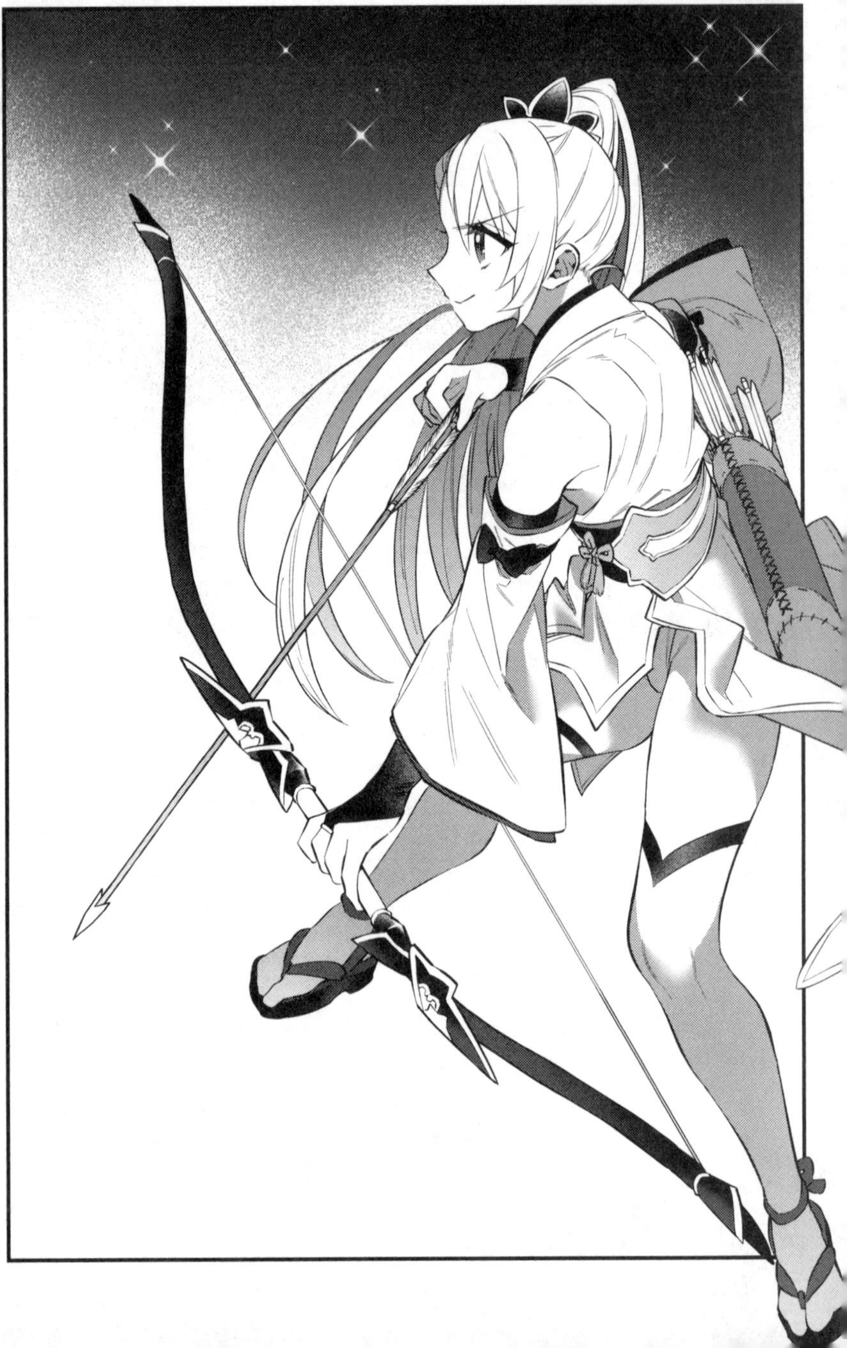

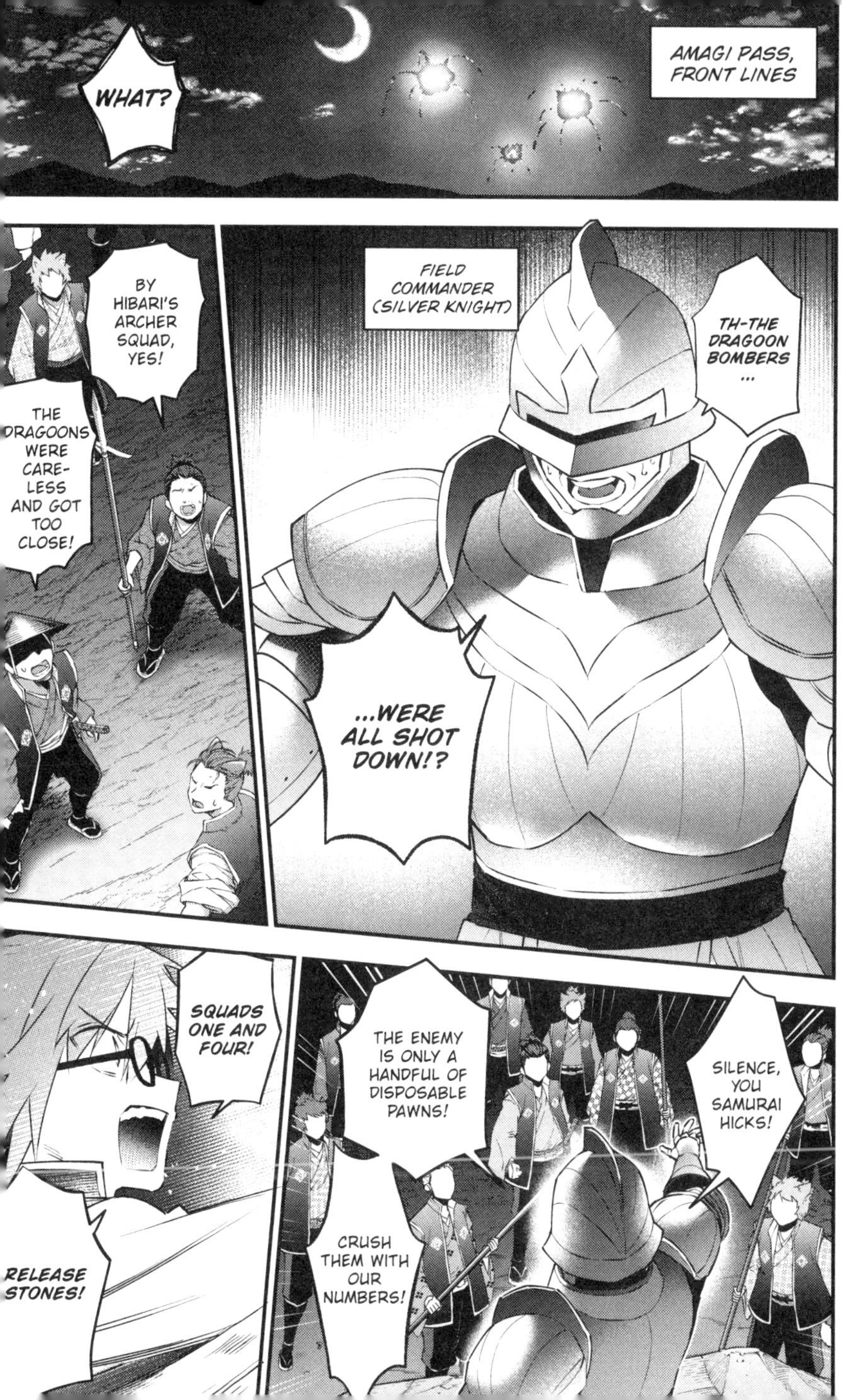
AMAGI PASS, FRONT LINES
WHAT?
FIELD COMMANDER (SILVER KNIGHT)
TH-THE DRAGOON BOMBERS...
...WERE ALL SHOT DOWN!?
BY HIBARI'S ARCHER SQUAD, YES!
THE DRAGOONS WERE CARE-LESS AND GOT TOO CLOSE!
SILENCE, YOU SAMURAI HICKS!
THE ENEMY IS ONLY A HANDFUL OF DISPOSABLE PAWNS!
CRUSH THEM WITH OUR NUMBERS!
SQUADS ONE AND FOUR!
RELEASE STONES!

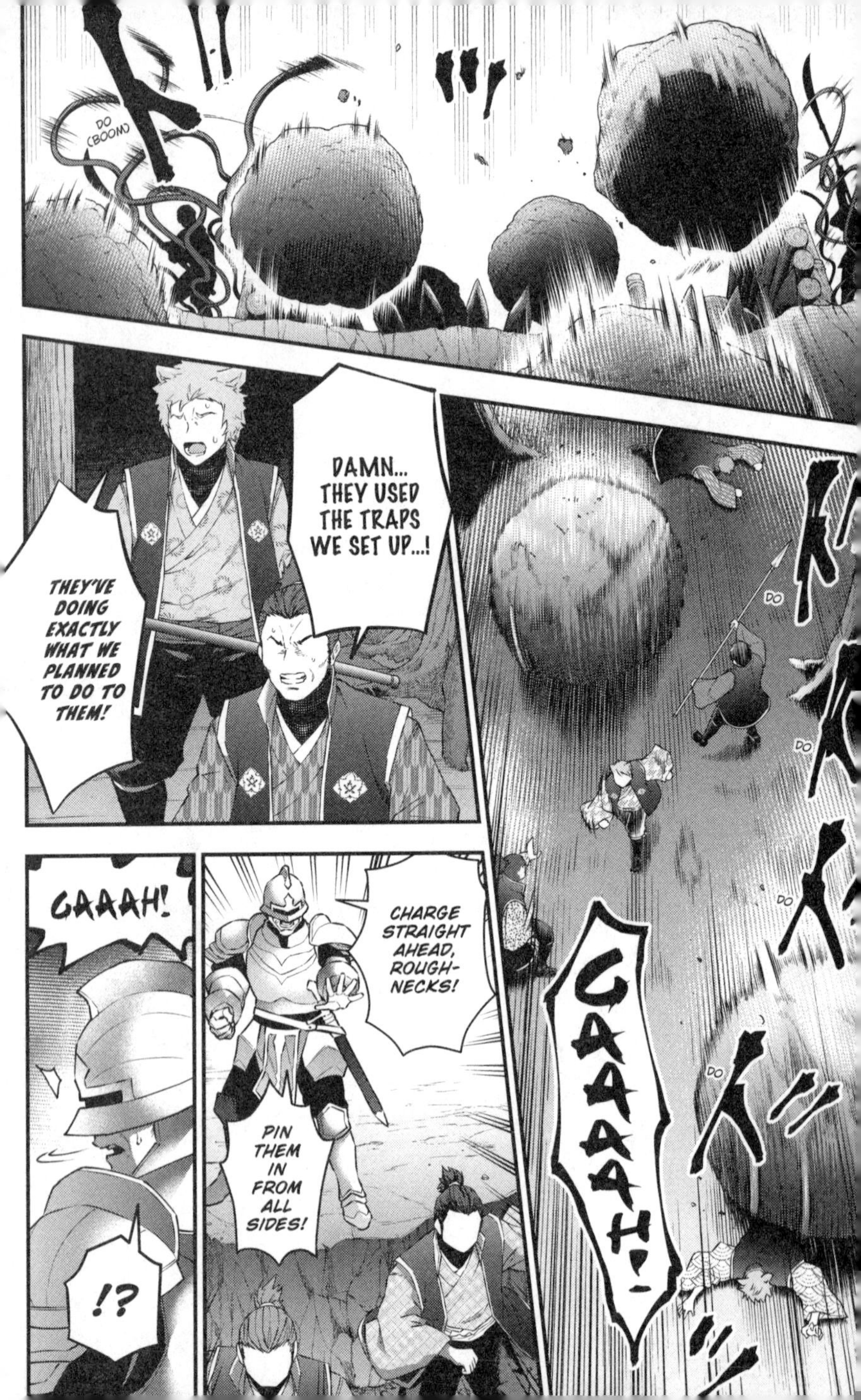
DO (BOOM)
DO
DO
DO
GAAAAH!
DO
DAMN... THEY USED THE TRAPS WE SET UP...!
THEY'VE DOING EXACTLY WHAT WE PLANNED TO DO TO THEM!
CHARGE STRAIGHT AHEAD, ROUGH-NECKS!
PIN THEM IN FROM ALL SIDES!
GAAAH!
!?

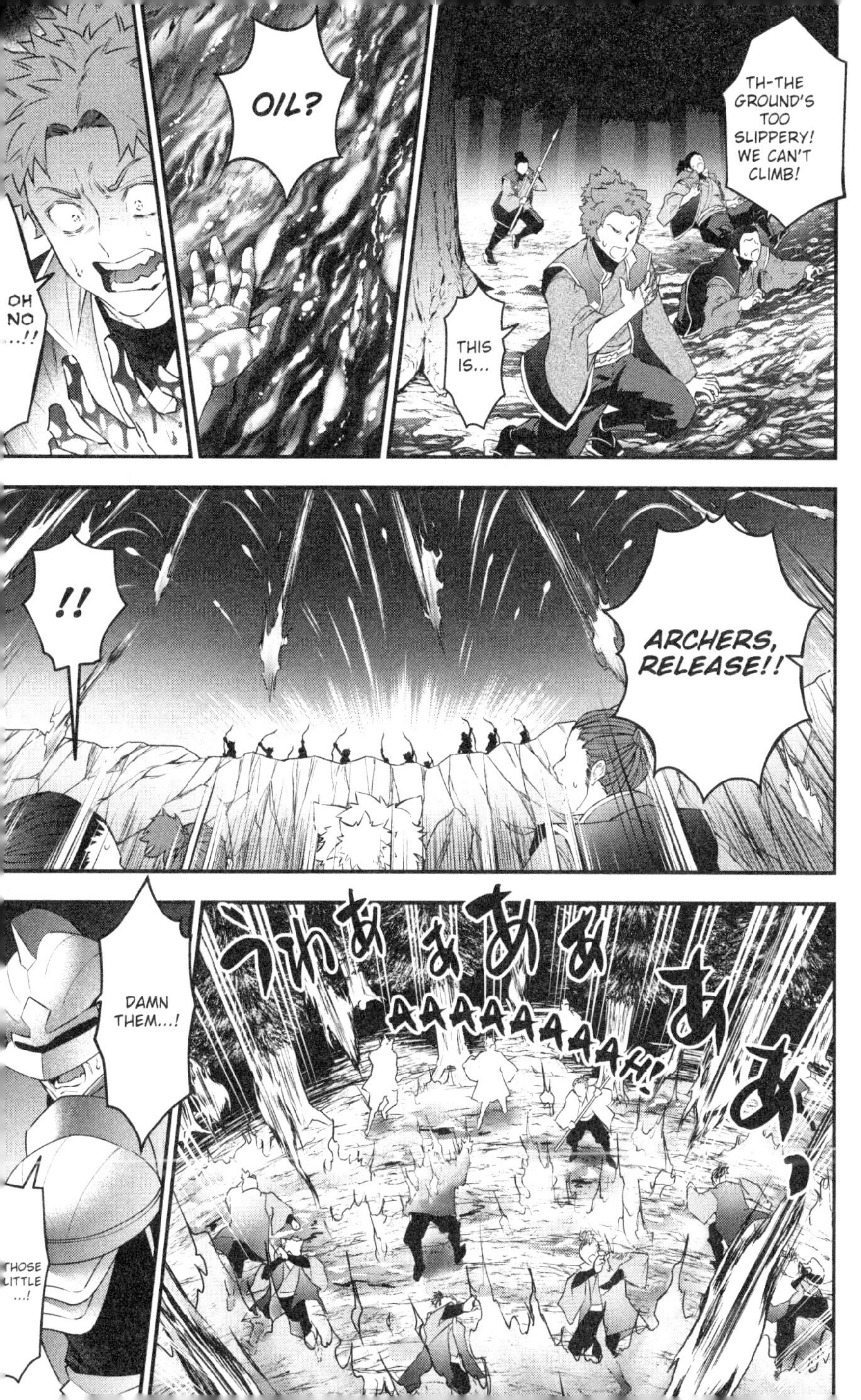
TH-THE GROUND'S TOO SLIPPERY! WE CAN'T CLIMB!
THIS IS...
OIL?
OH NO ...!!
ARCHERS, RELEASE!!
!!
うわあああああああ
AAAAAAAAAAH!!
DAMN THEM...!
THOSE LITTLE ...!

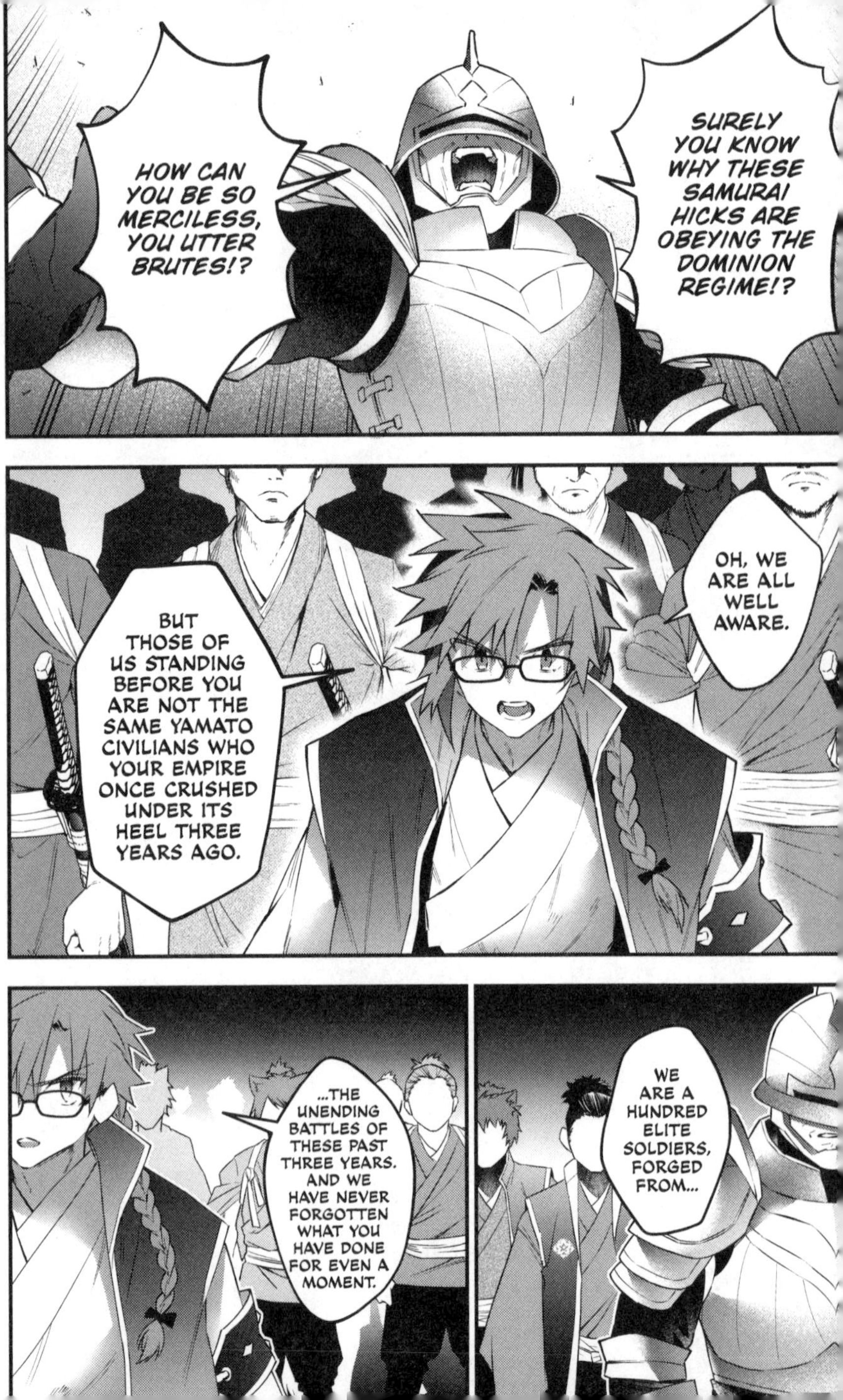
SURELY YOU KNOW WHY THESE SAMURAI HICKS ARE OBEYING THE DOMINION REGIME!?
HOW CAN YOU BE SO MERCILESS, YOU UTTER BRUTES!?
OH, WE ARE ALL WELL AWARE.
BUT THOSE OF US STANDING BEFORE YOU ARE NOT THE SAME YAMATO CIVILIANS WHO YOUR EMPIRE ONCE CRUSHED UNDER ITS HEEL THREE YEARS AGO.
WE ARE A HUNDRED ELITE SOLDIERS, FORGED FROM...
...THE UNENDING BATTLES OF THESE PAST THREE YEARS. AND WE HAVE NEVER FORGOTTEN WHAT YOU HAVE DONE FOR EVEN A MOMENT.

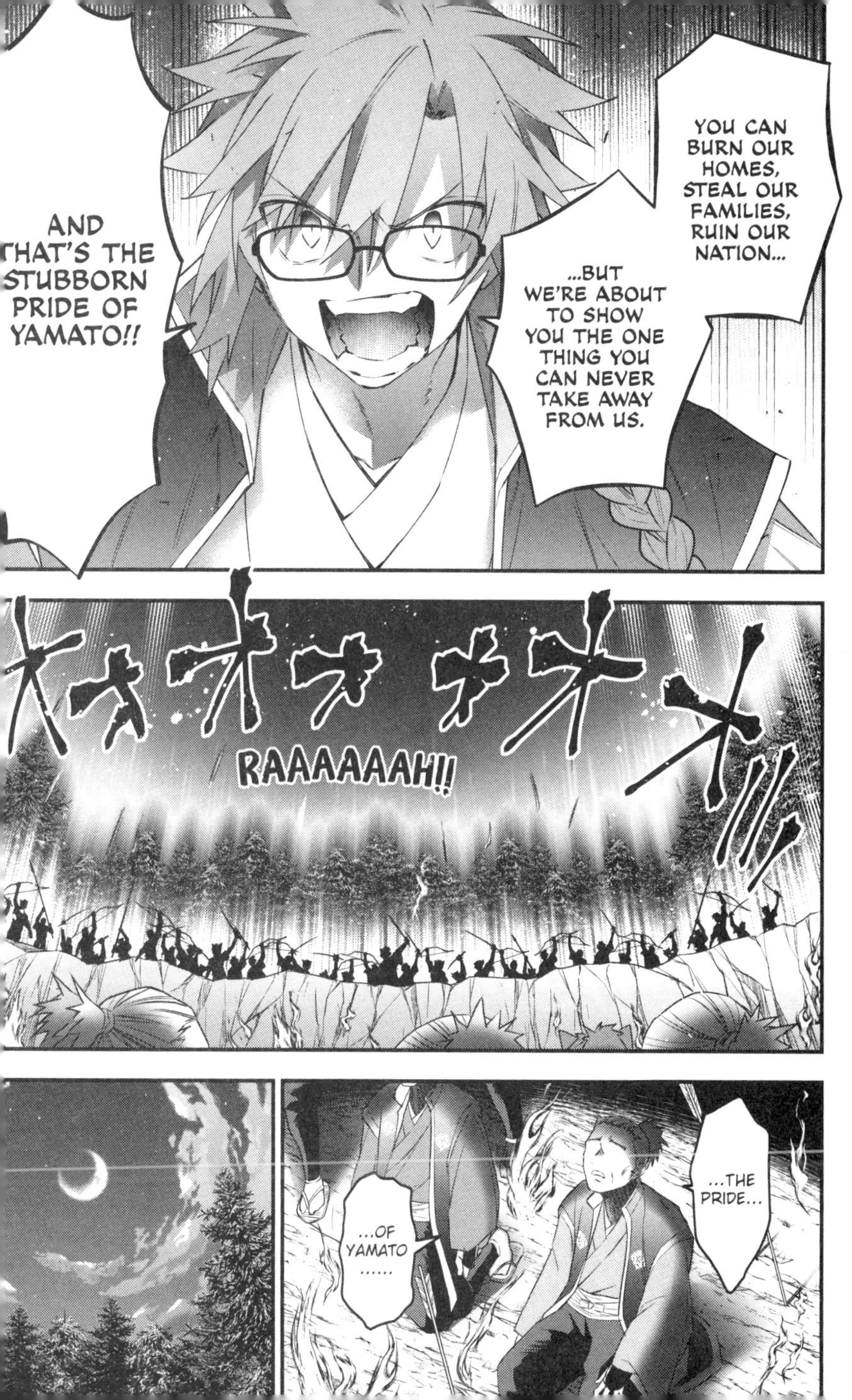
YOU CAN BURN OUR HOMES, STEAL OUR FAMILIES, RUIN OUR NATION...
...BUT WE'RE ABOUT TO SHOW YOU THE ONE THING YOU CAN NEVER TAKE AWAY FROM US.
AND THAT'S THE STUBBORN PRIDE OF YAMATO!!
RAAAAAAH!!
...THE PRIDE...
...OF YAMATO ......

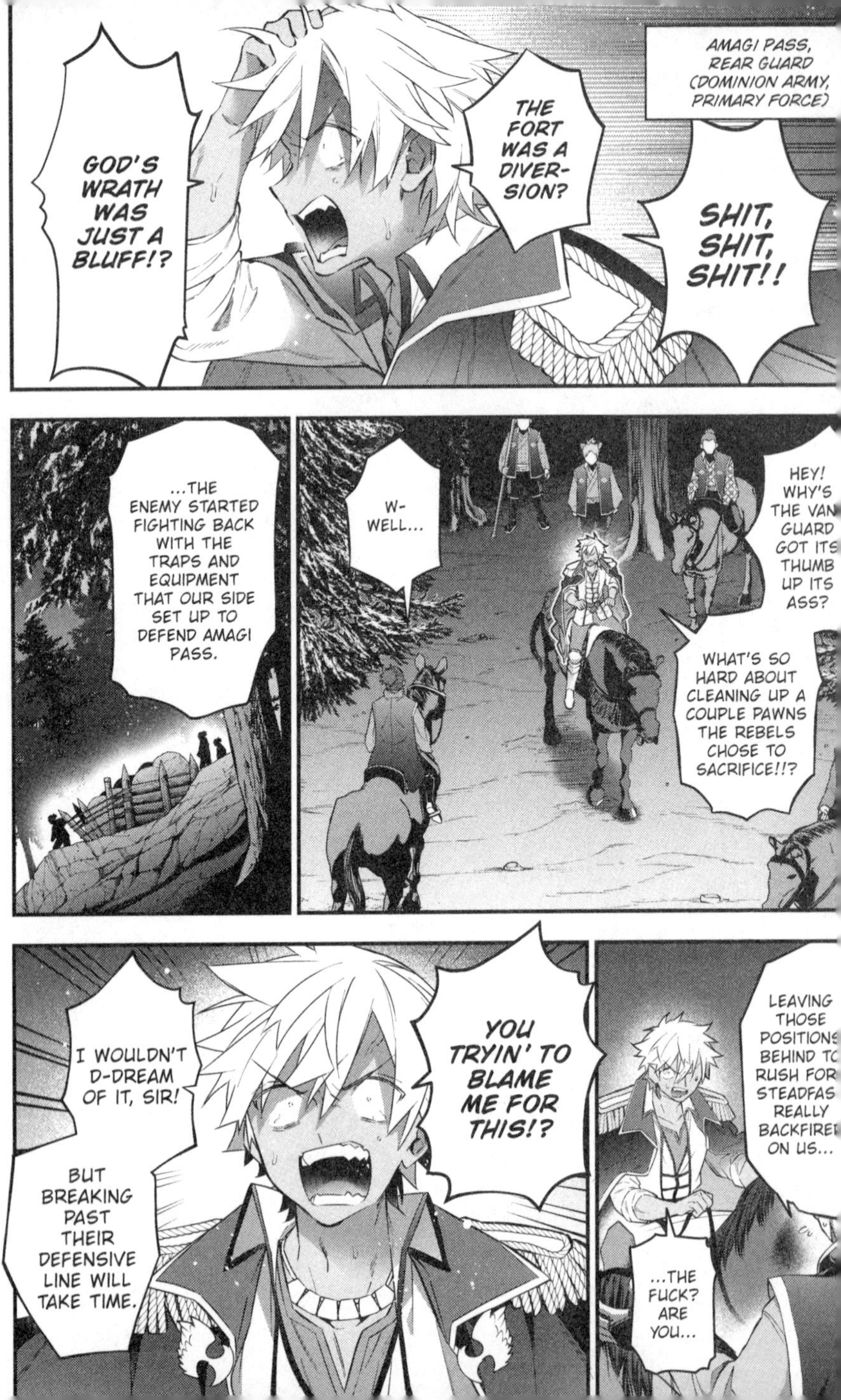
AMAGI PASS, REAR GUARD (DOMINION ARMY, PRIMARY FORCE)
SHIT, SHIT, SHIT!!
THE FORT WAS A DIVERSION?
GOD'S WRATH WAS JUST A BLUFF!?
HEY! WHY'S THE VAN GUARD GOT ITS THUMB UP ITS ASS?
WHAT'S SO HARD ABOUT CLEANING UP A COUPLE PAWNS THE REBELS CHOSE TO SACRIFICE!!?
W-WELL...
...THE ENEMY STARTED FIGHTING BACK WITH THE TRAPS AND EQUIPMENT THAT OUR SIDE SET UP TO DEFEND AMAGI PASS.
LEAVING THOSE POSITIONS BEHIND TO RUSH FOR STEADFAS REALLY BACKFIRE ON US...
...THE FUCK? ARE YOU...
YOU TRYIN' TO BLAME ME FOR THIS!?
I WOULDN'T D-DREAM OF IT, SIR!
BUT BREAKING PAST THEIR DEFENSIVE LINE WILL TAKE TIME.

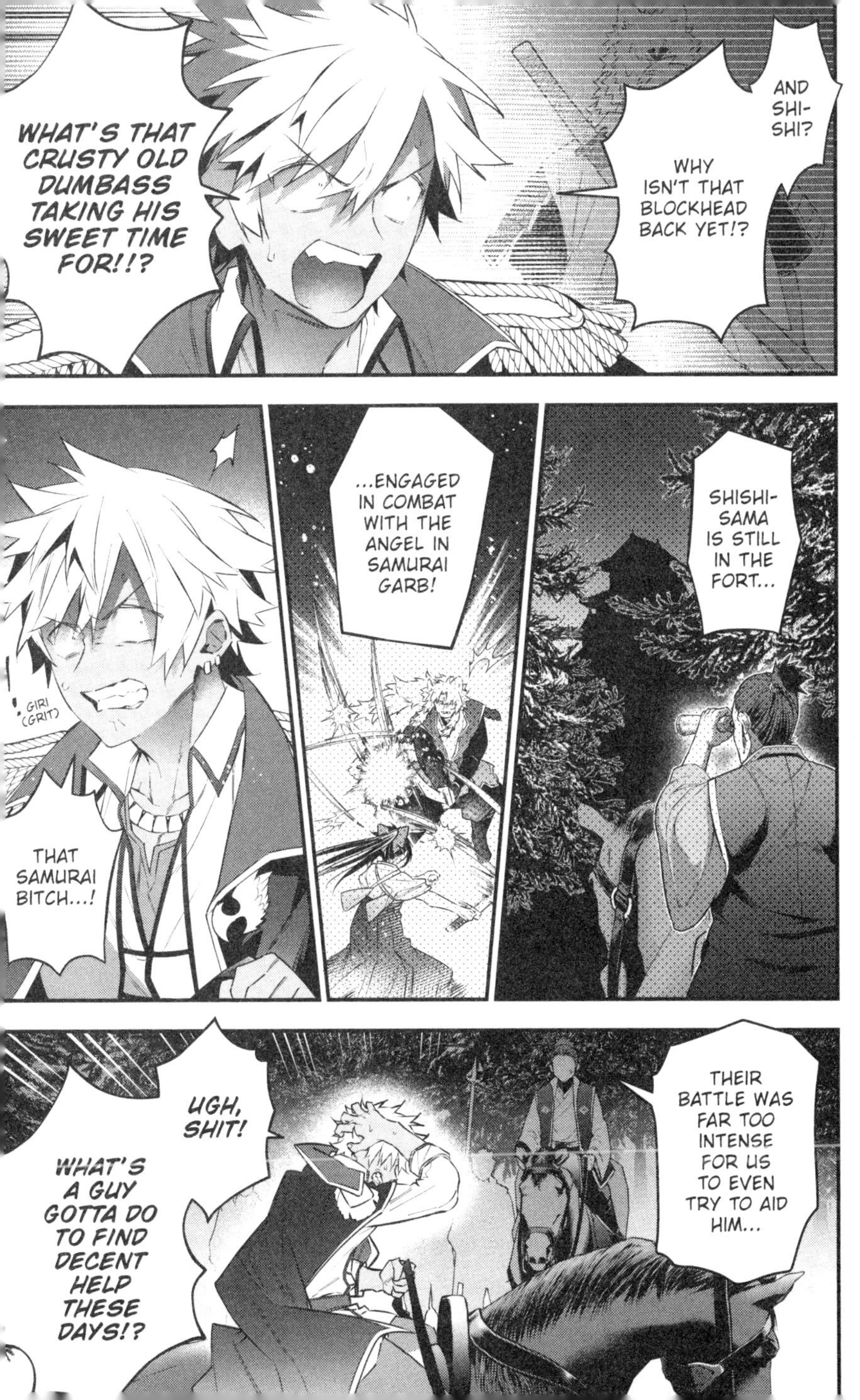
AND SHI-SHI?
WHY ISN'T THAT BLOCKHEAD BACK YET!?
WHAT'S THAT CRUSTY OLD DUMBASS TAKING HIS SWEET TIME FOR!!?
SHISHI-SAMA IS STILL IN THE FORT...
...ENGAGED IN COMBAT WITH THE ANGEL IN SAMURAI GARB!
GIRI (GRIT)
THAT SAMURAI BITCH...!
THEIR BATTLE WAS FAR TOO INTENSE FOR US TO EVEN TRY TO AID HIM...
UGH, SHIT!
WHAT'S A GUY GOTTA DO TO FIND DECENT HELP THESE DAYS!?

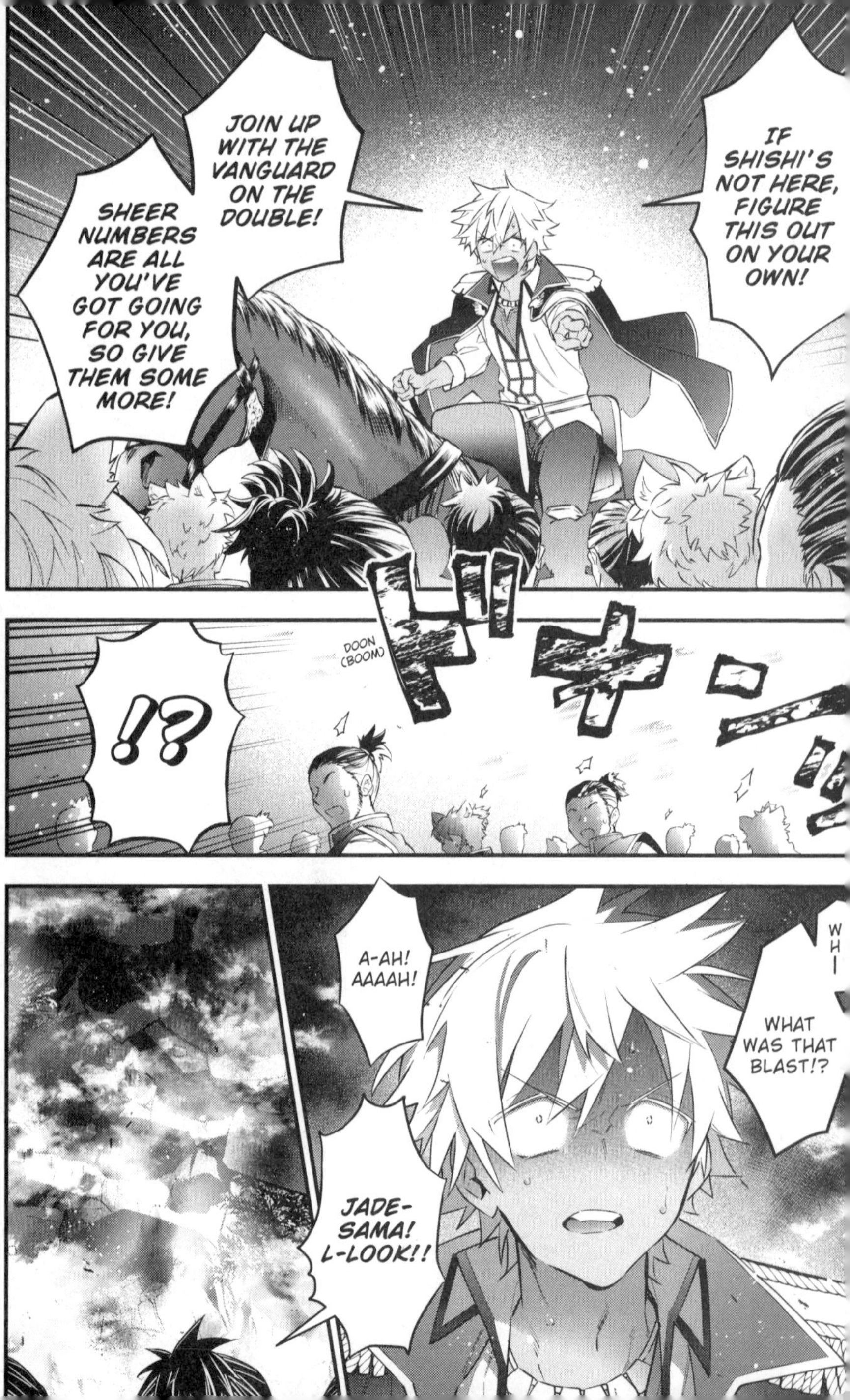
IF SHISHI'S NOT HERE, FIGURE THIS OUT ON YOUR OWN!
JOIN UP WITH THE VANGUARD ON THE DOUBLE!
SHEER NUMBERS ARE ALL YOU'VE GOT GOING FOR YOU, SO GIVE THEM SOME MORE!
DOON (BOOM)
!?
WHI—
WHAT WAS THAT BLAST!?
A-AH! AAAAH!
JADE-SAMA! L-LOOK!!

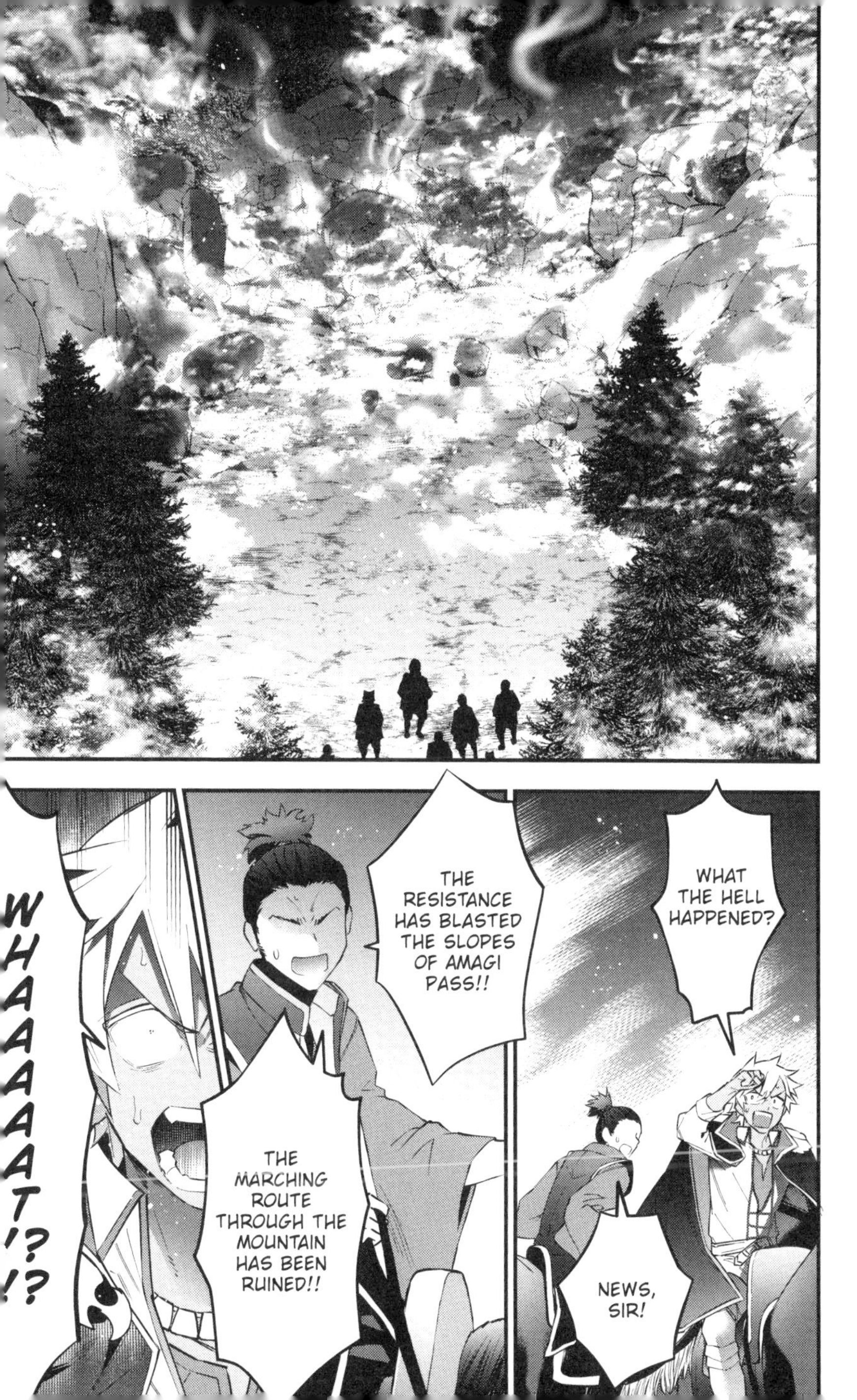
WHAT THE HELL HAPPENED?
NEWS, SIR!
THE RESISTANCE HAS BLASTED THE SLOPES OF AMAGI PASS!!
THE MARCHING ROUTE THROUGH THE MOUNTAIN HAS BEEN RUINED!!
WHAAAAAAAT!?!?

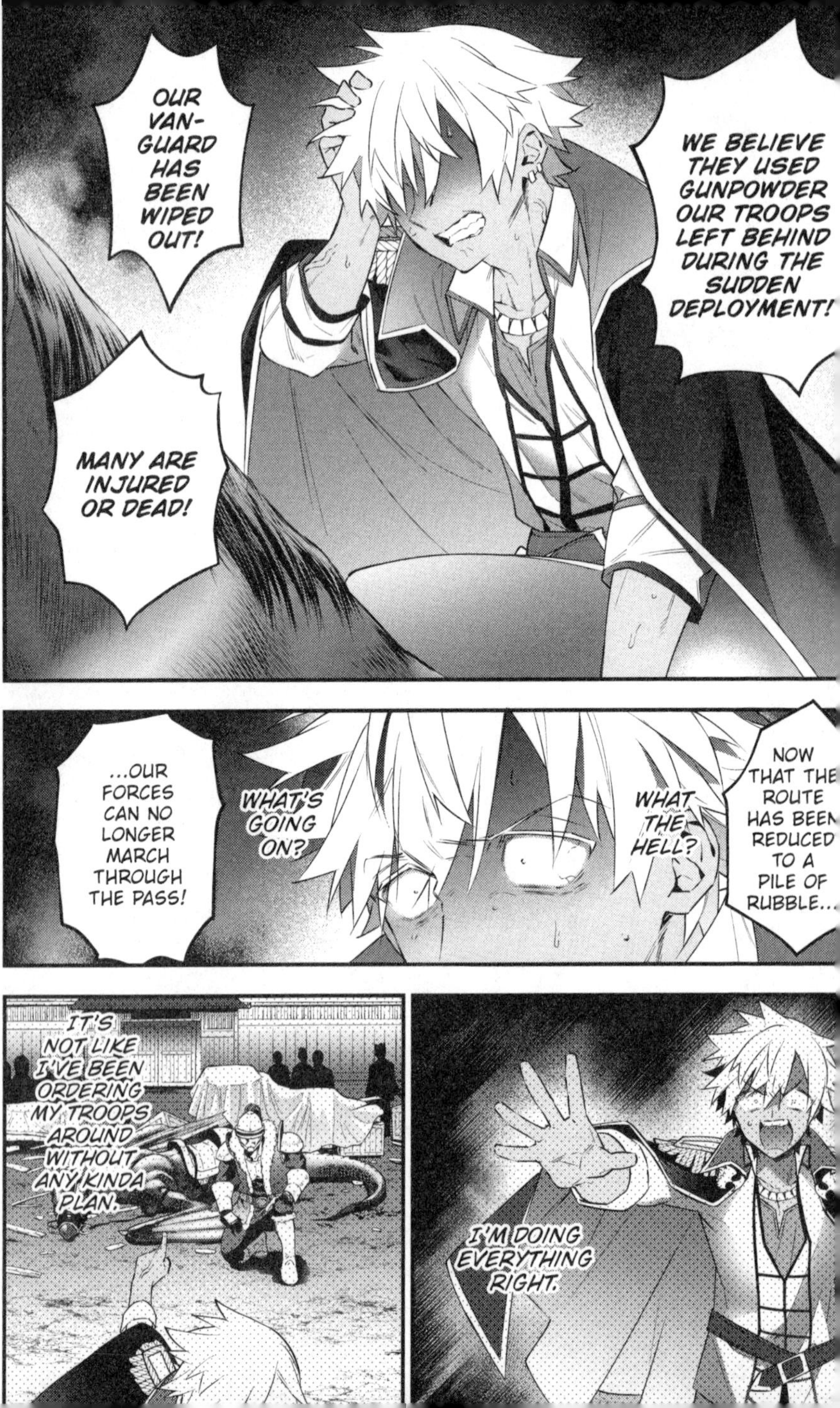
WE BELIEVE THEY USED GUNPOWDER OUR TROOPS LEFT BEHIND DURING THE SUDDEN DEPLOYMENT!
OUR VAN-GUARD HAS BEEN WIPED OUT!
MANY ARE INJURED OR DEAD!
NOW THAT THE ROUTE HAS BEEN REDUCED TO A PILE OF RUBBLE...
WHAT THE HELL?
WHAT'S GOING ON?
...OUR FORCES CAN NO LONGER MARCH THROUGH THE PASS!
I'M DOING EVERYTHING RIGHT.
IT'S NOT LIKE I'VE BEEN ORDERING MY TROOPS AROUND WITHOUT ANY KINDA PLAN.

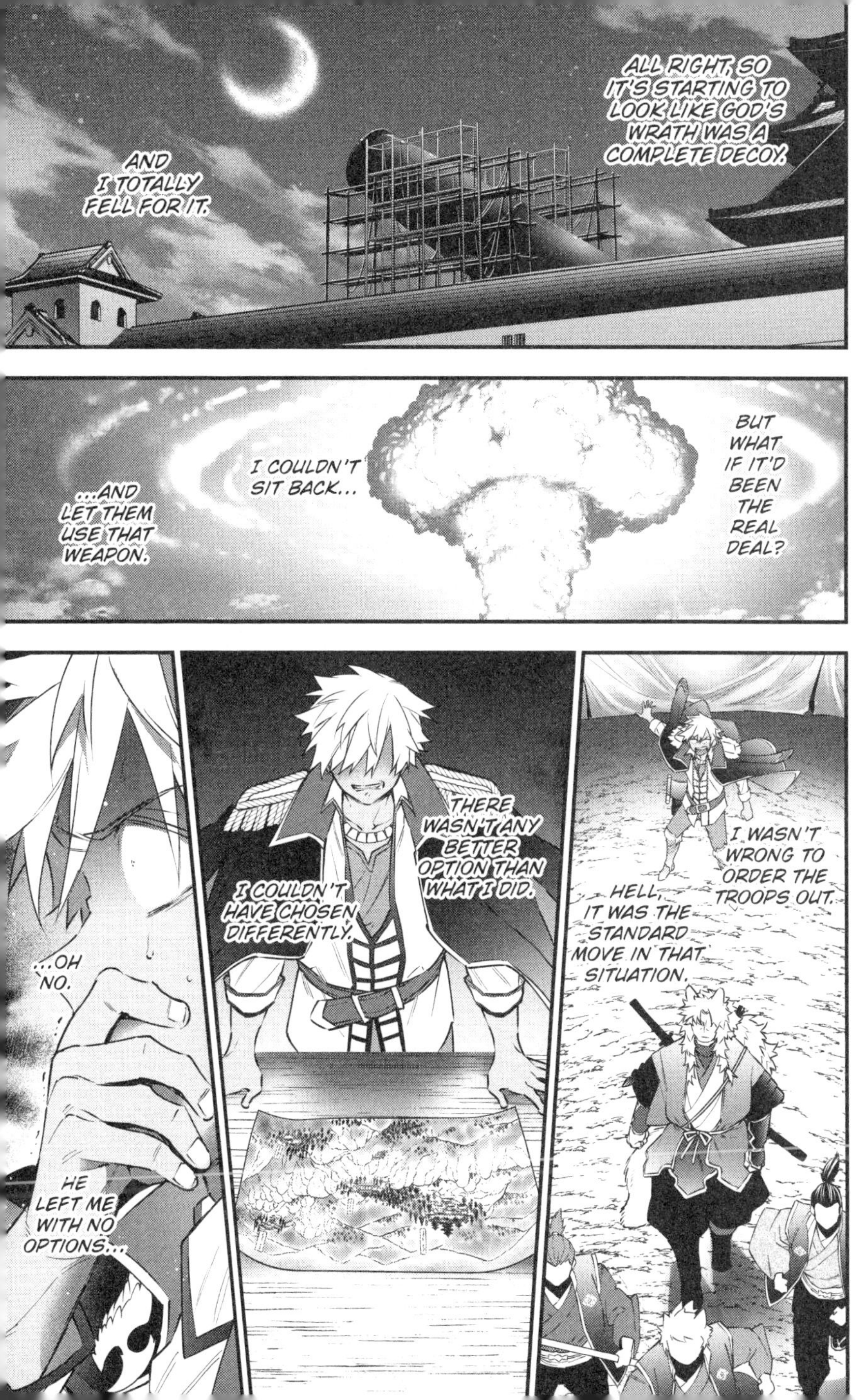
ALL RIGHT, SO IT'S STARTING TO LOOK LIKE GOD'S WRATH WAS A COMPLETE DECOY.
AND I TOTALLY FELL FOR IT.
BUT WHAT IF IT'D BEEN THE REAL DEAL?
I COULDN'T SIT BACK...
...AND LET THEM USE THAT WEAPON.
I WASN'T WRONG TO ORDER THE TROOPS OUT.
HELL, IT WAS THE STANDARD MOVE IN THAT SITUATION.
THERE WASN'T ANY BETTER OPTION THAN WHAT I DID.
I COULDN'T HAVE CHOSEN DIFFERENTLY.
...OH NO.
HE LEFT ME WITH NO OPTIONS...

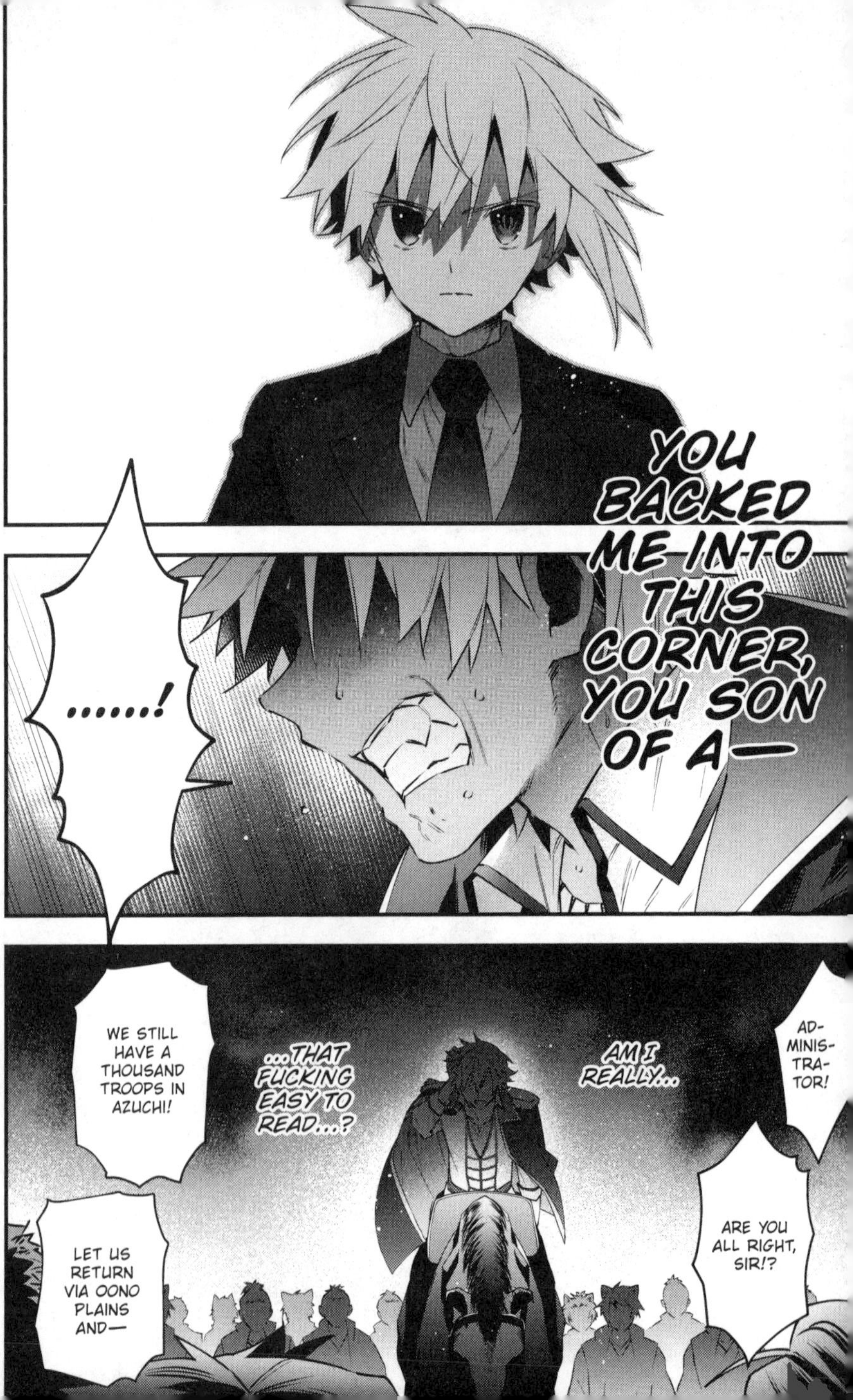
YOU BACKED ME INTO THIS CORNER, YOU SON OF A—
......!
AD-MINIS-TRA-TOR!
ARE YOU ALL RIGHT, SIR!?
AM I REALLY...
...THAT FUCKING EASY TO READ...?
WE STILL HAVE A THOUSAND TROOPS IN AZUCHI!
LET US RETURN VIA OONO PLAINS AND—

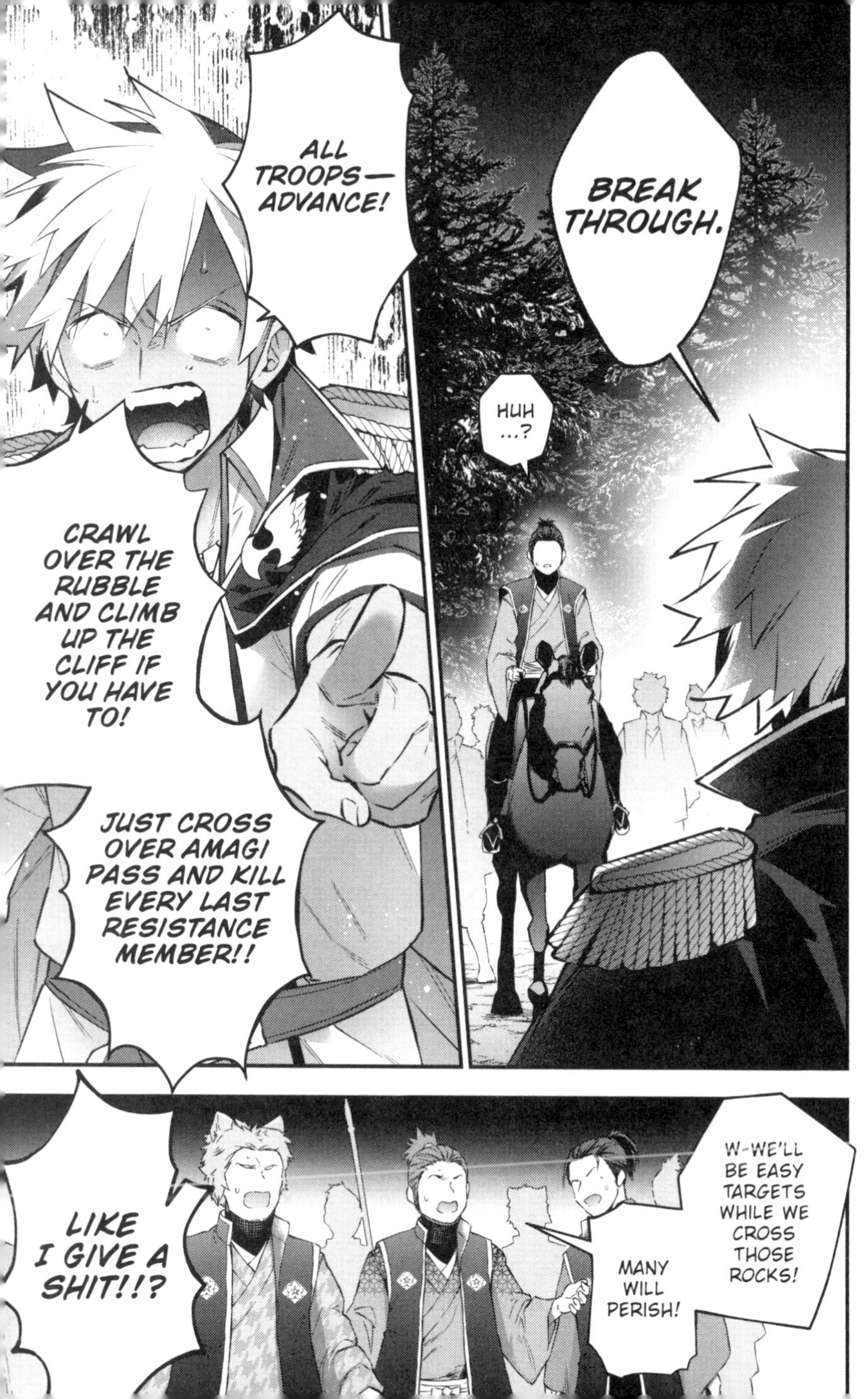
BREAK THROUGH.
HUH ...?
ALL TROOPS—ADVANCE!
CRAWL OVER THE RUBBLE AND CLIMB UP THE CLIFF IF YOU HAVE TO!
JUST CROSS OVER AMAGI PASS AND KILL EVERY LAST RESISTANCE MEMBER!!
W-WE'LL BE EASY TARGETS WHILE WE CROSS THOSE ROCKS!
MANY WILL PERISH!
LIKE I GIVE A SHIT!!?

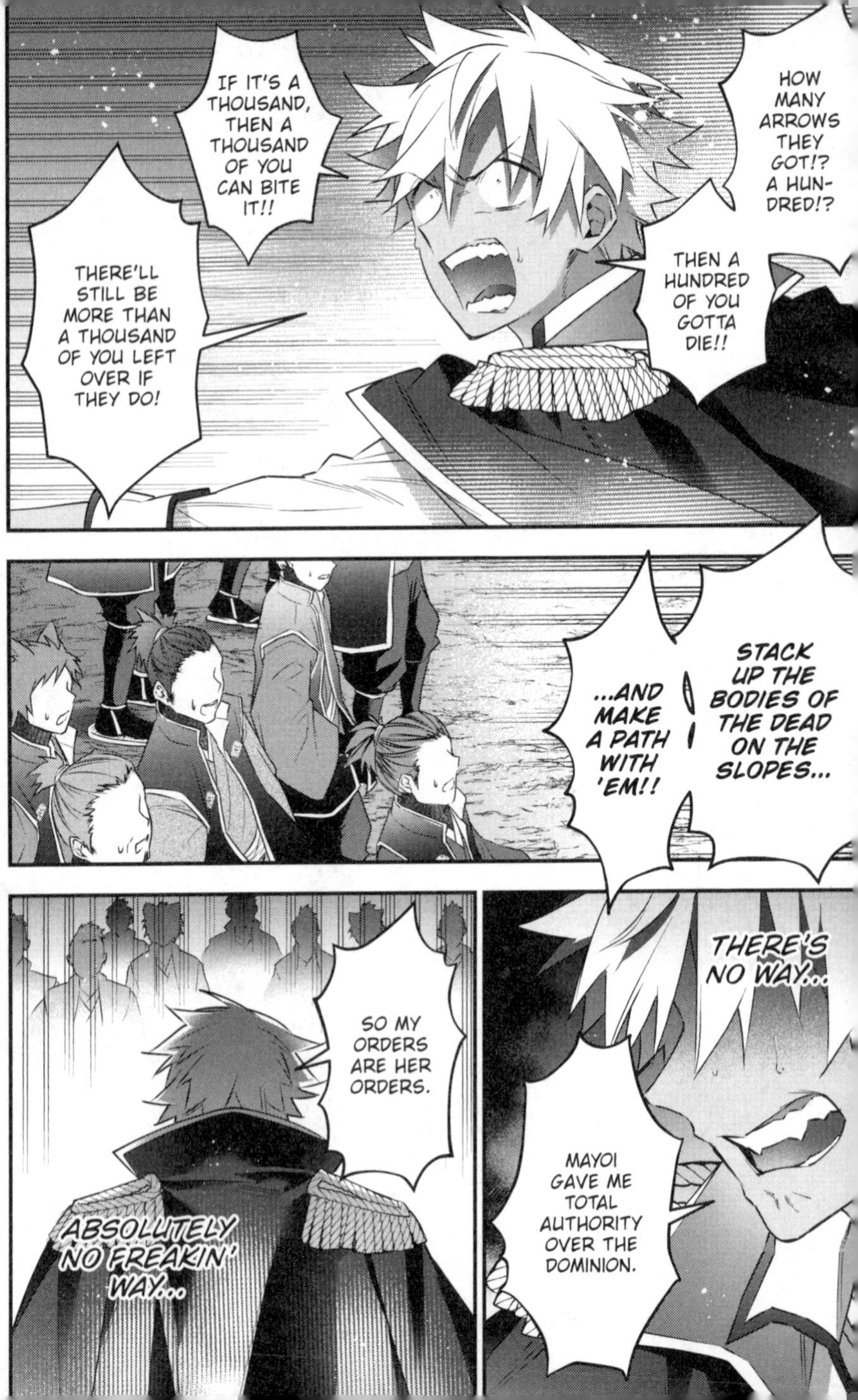
HOW MANY ARROWS THEY GOT!? A HUN-DRED!?
THEN A HUNDRED OF YOU GOTTA DIE!!
IF IT'S A THOUSAND, THEN A THOUSAND OF YOU CAN BITE IT!!
THERE'LL STILL BE MORE THAN A THOUSAND OF YOU LEFT OVER IF THEY DO!
STACK UP THE BODIES OF THE DEAD ON THE SLOPES...
...AND MAKE A PATH WITH 'EM!!
THERE'S NO WAY...
MAYOI GAVE ME TOTAL AUTHORITY OVER THE DOMINION.
SO MY ORDERS ARE HER ORDERS.
ABSOLUTELY NO FREAKIN' WAY...

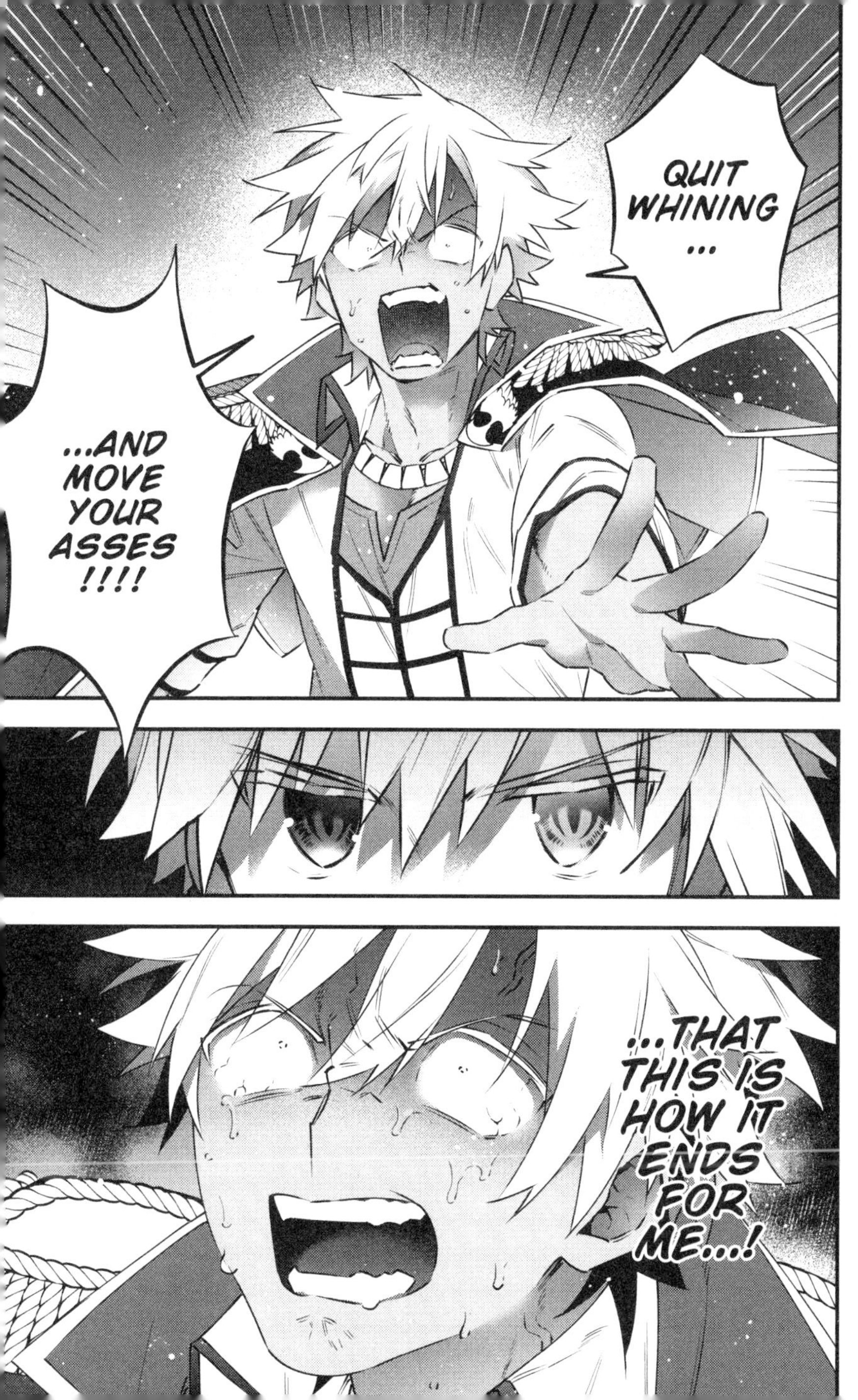
QUIT WHINING ...
...AND MOVE YOUR ASSES !!!!
...THAT THIS IS HOW IT ENDS FOR ME...!

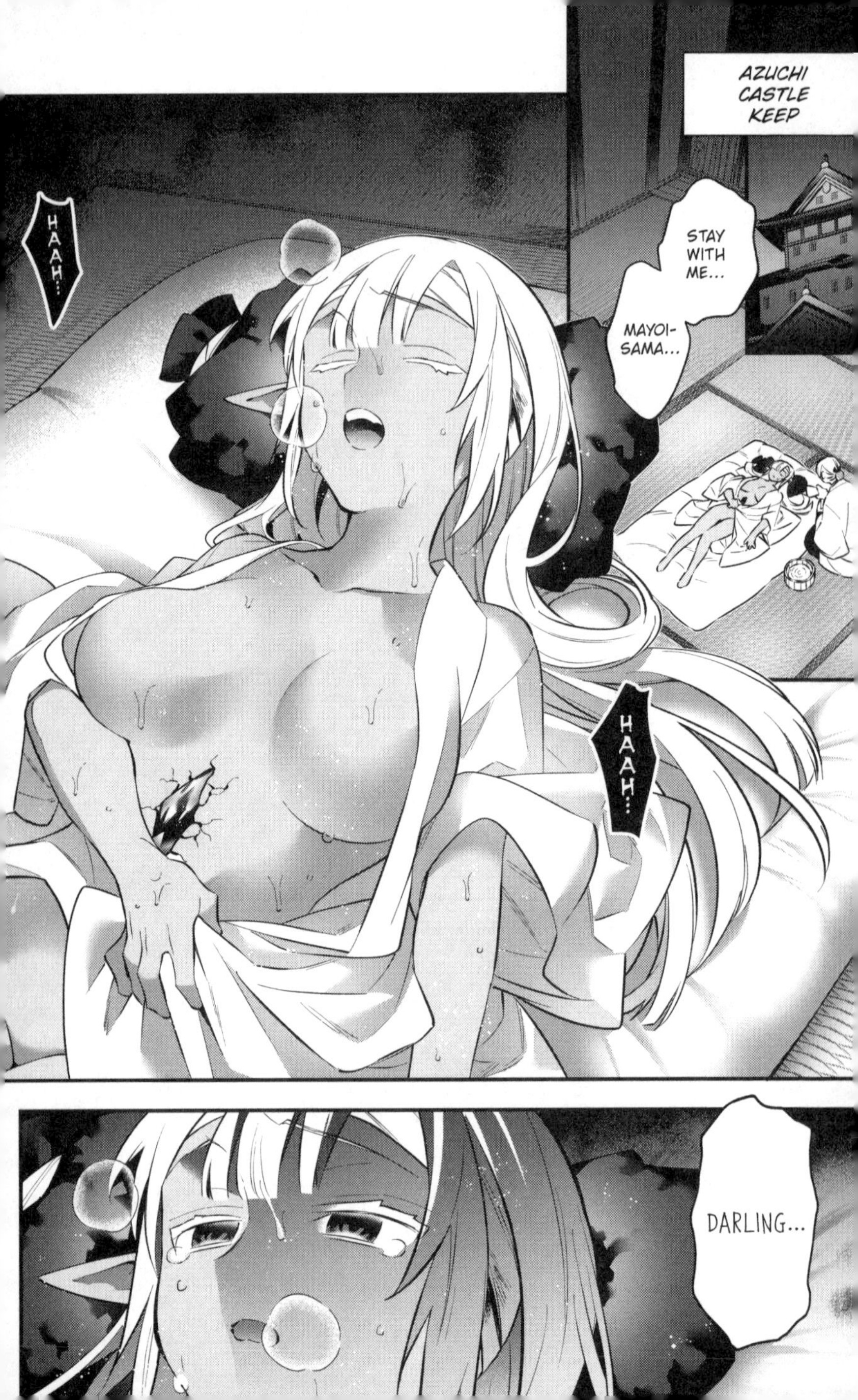
AZUCHI CASTLE KEEP
STAY WITH ME...
MAYOI-SAMA...
HAAH...
HAAH...
DARLING...

HIGH SCHOOL PRODIGIES HAVE IT EASY EVEN IN ANOTHER WORLD!

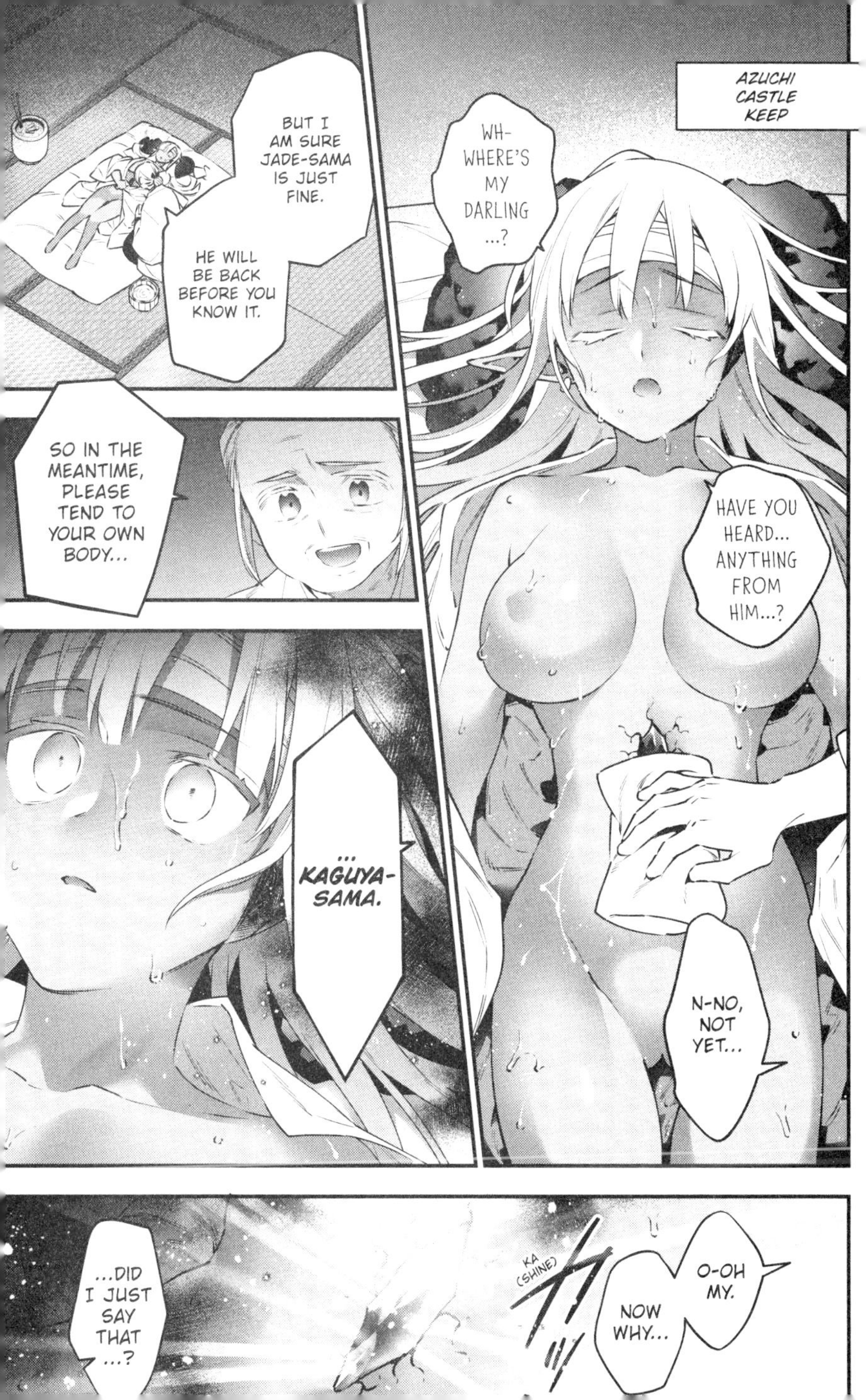
AZUCHI CASTLE KEEP
WH- WHERE'S MY DARLING ...?
HAVE YOU HEARD... ANYTHING FROM HIM...?
N-NO, NOT YET...
BUT I AM SURE JADE-SAMA IS JUST FINE.
HE WILL BE BACK BEFORE YOU KNOW IT.
SO IN THE MEANTIME, PLEASE TEND TO YOUR OWN BODY...
... KAGUYA-SAMA.
O-OH MY.
NOW WHY...
KA (SHINE)
...DID I JUST SAY THAT ...?

CHAPTER 85: **GROUNDWORK**

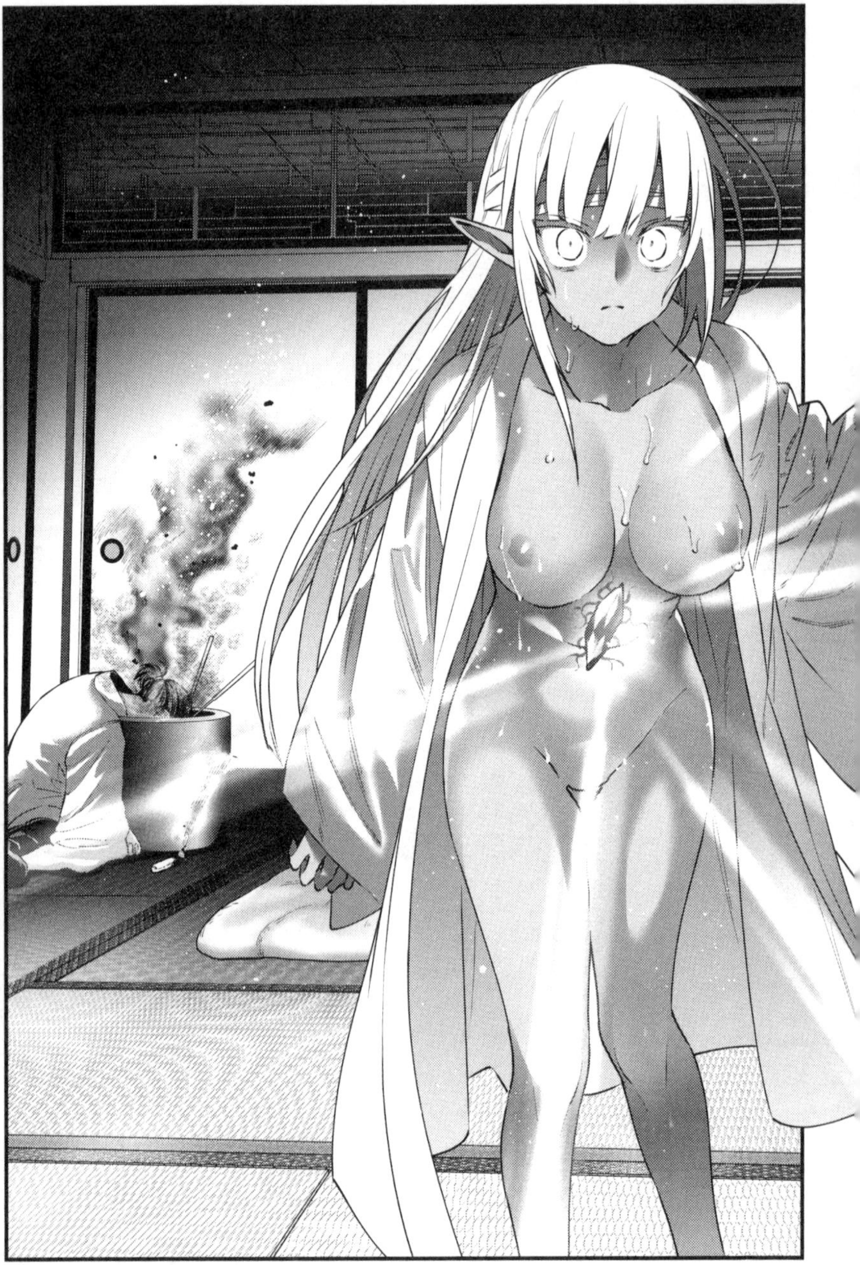

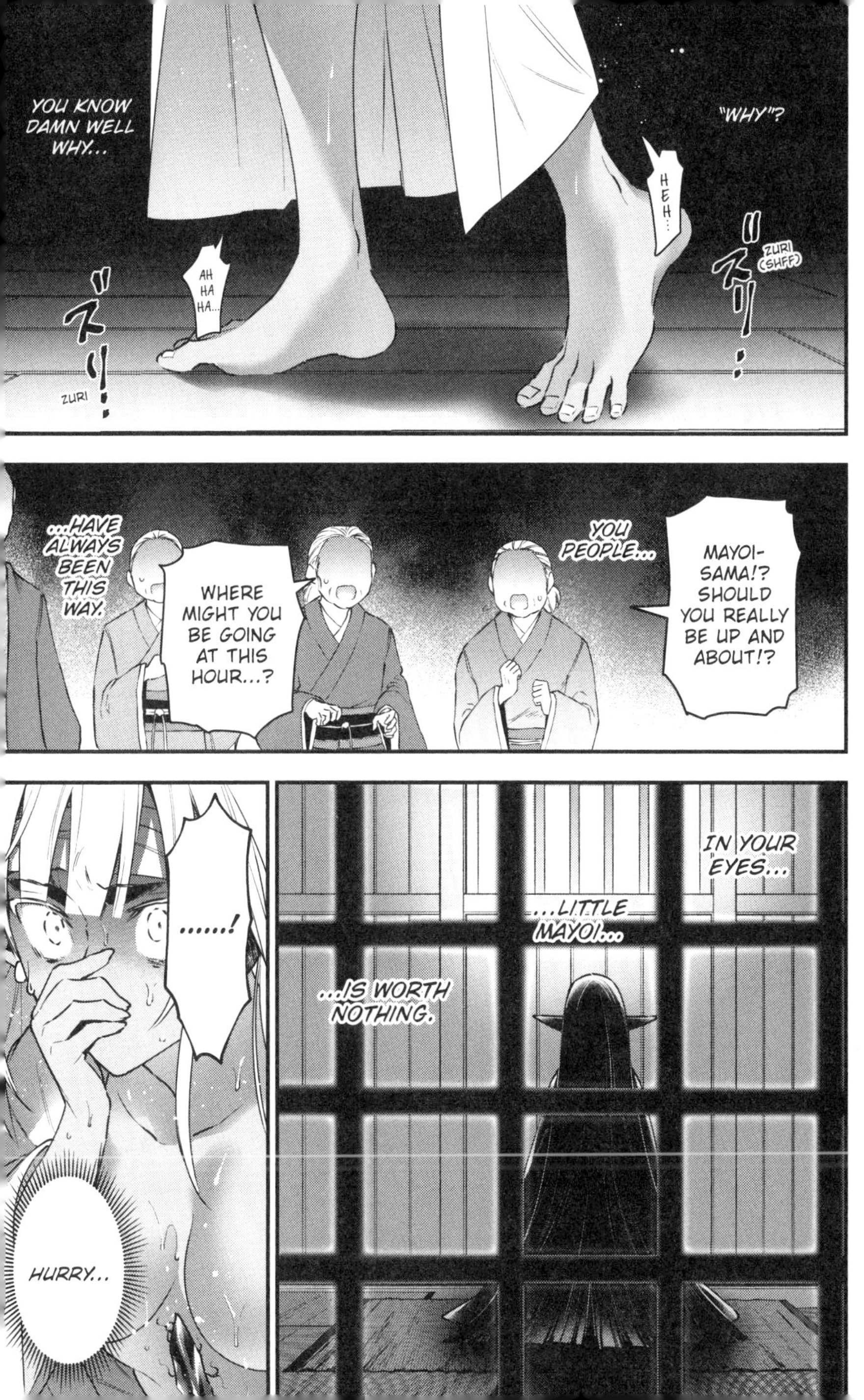
"WHY"?
HEH...
ZURI (SHFF)
YOU KNOW DAMN WELL WHY...
AH HA HA...
ZURI
MAYOI-SAMA!? SHOULD YOU REALLY BE UP AND ABOUT!?
YOU PEOPLE...
WHERE MIGHT YOU BE GOING AT THIS HOUR...?
...HAVE ALWAYS BEEN THIS WAY.
IN YOUR EYES...
...LITTLE MAYOI...
...IS WORTH NOTHING.
......!
HURRY...

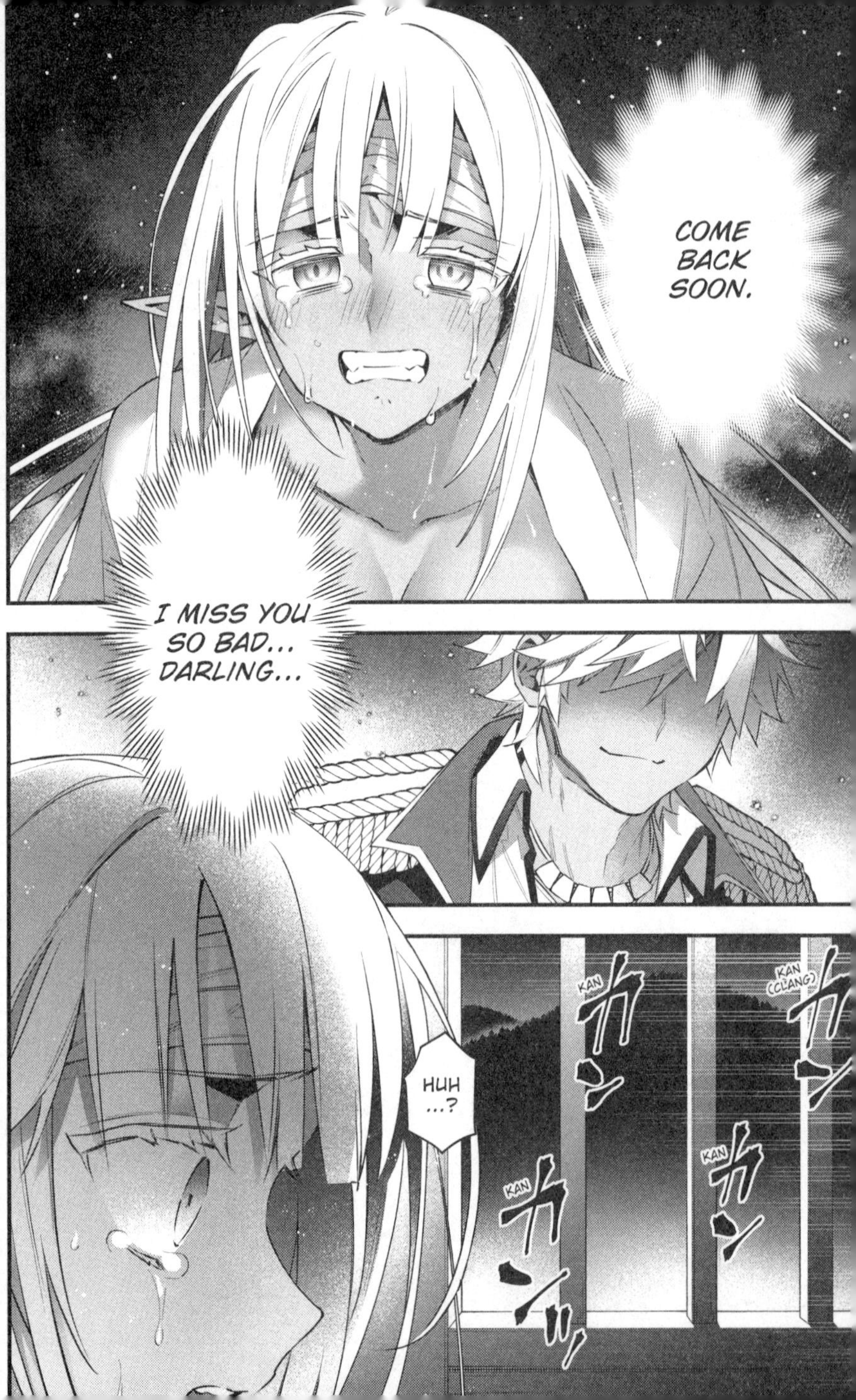
COME BACK SOON.
I MISS YOU SO BAD... DARLING...
KAN (CLANG)
KAN
KAN
KAN
HUH ...?

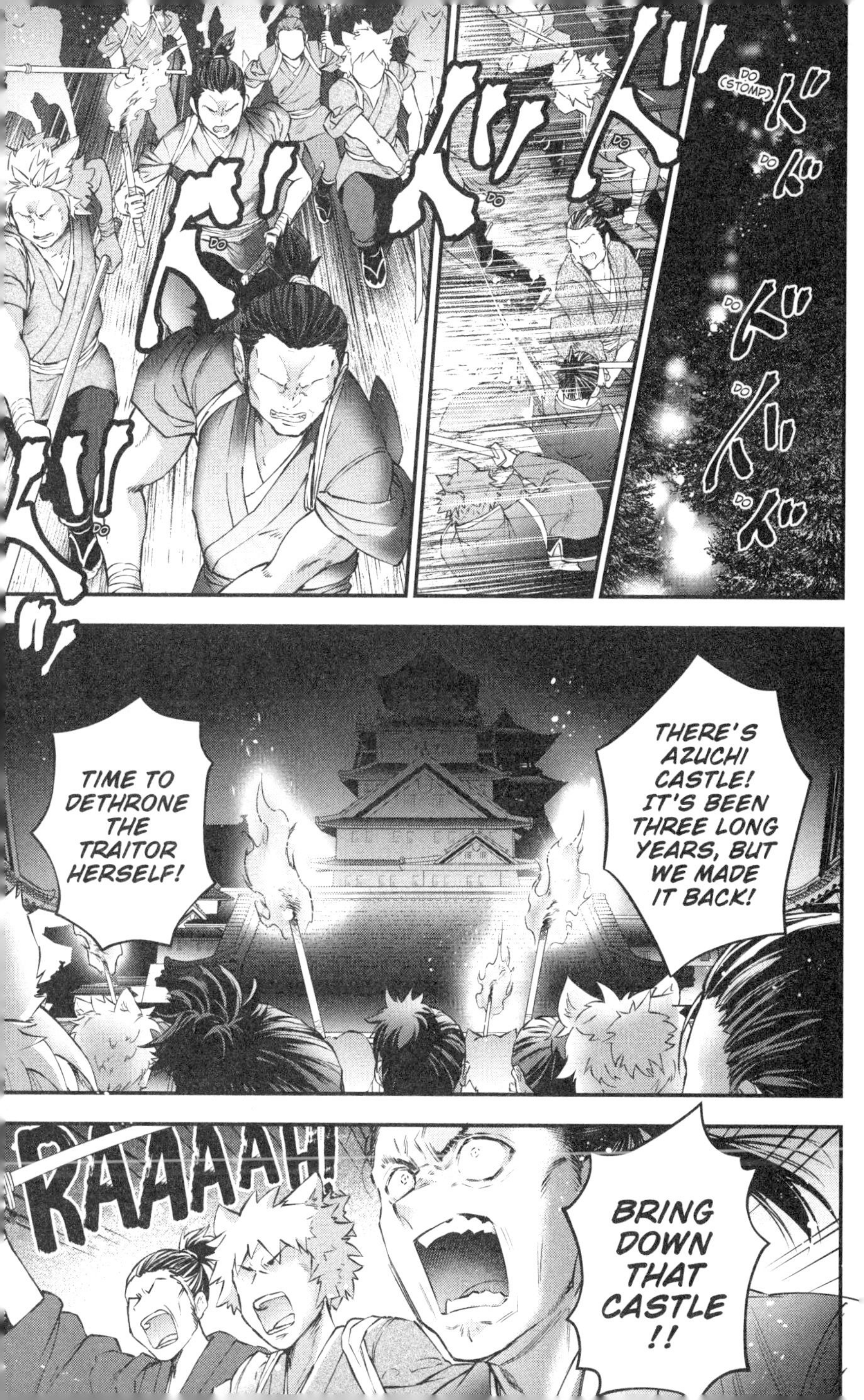
DO (STOMP)
DO
DO
DO
DO
DO
DO
DO
DO
THERE'S AZUCHI CASTLE! IT'S BEEN THREE LONG YEARS, BUT WE MADE IT BACK!
TIME TO DETHRONE THE TRAITOR HERSELF!
BRING DOWN THAT CASTLE!!
RAAAAAH!

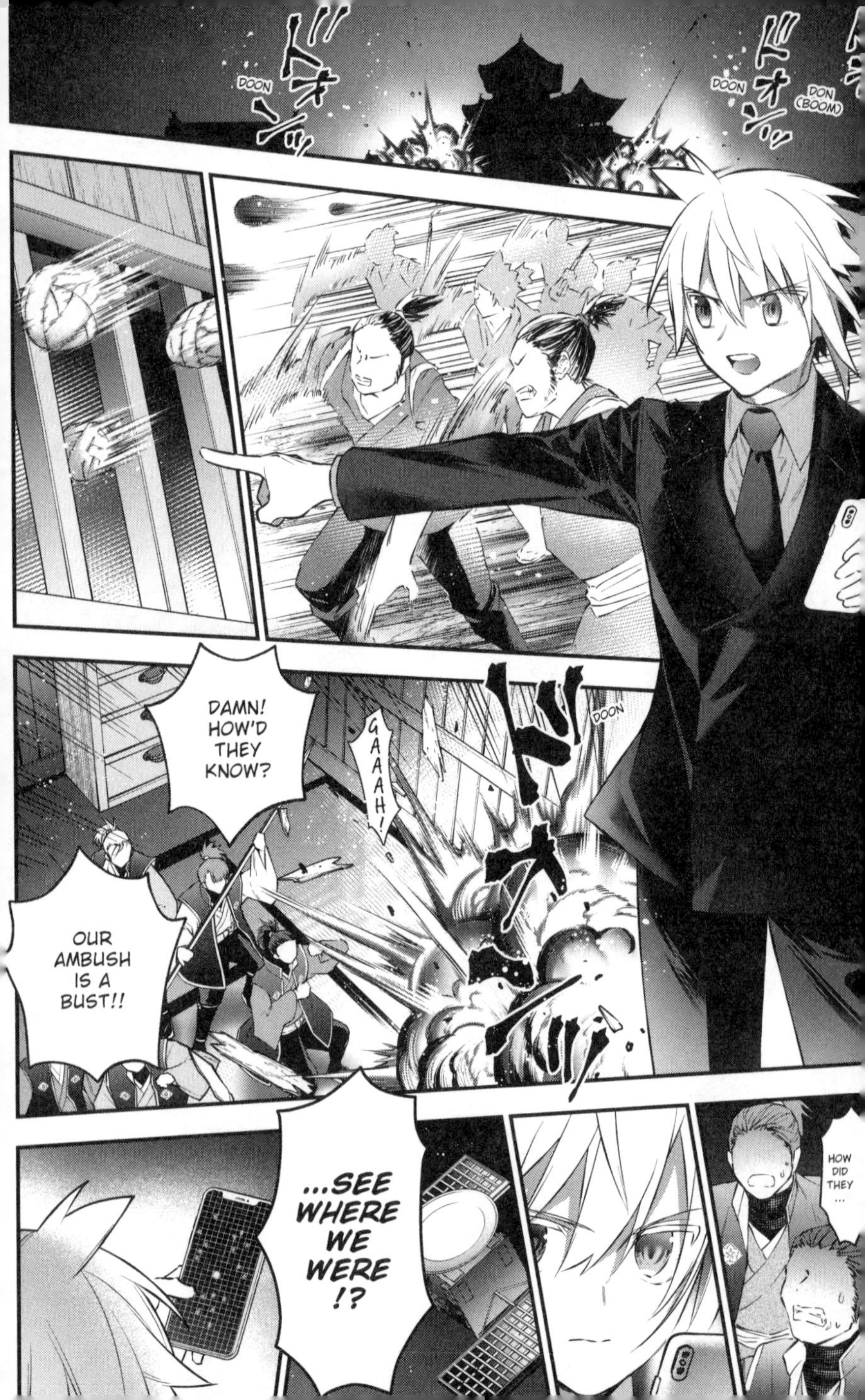
DON (BOOM)
DOON
DOON
DOON
GAAAAH!
DAMN! HOW'D THEY KNOW?
OUR AMBUSH IS A BUST!!
HOW DID THEY ...
...SEE WHERE WE WERE!?

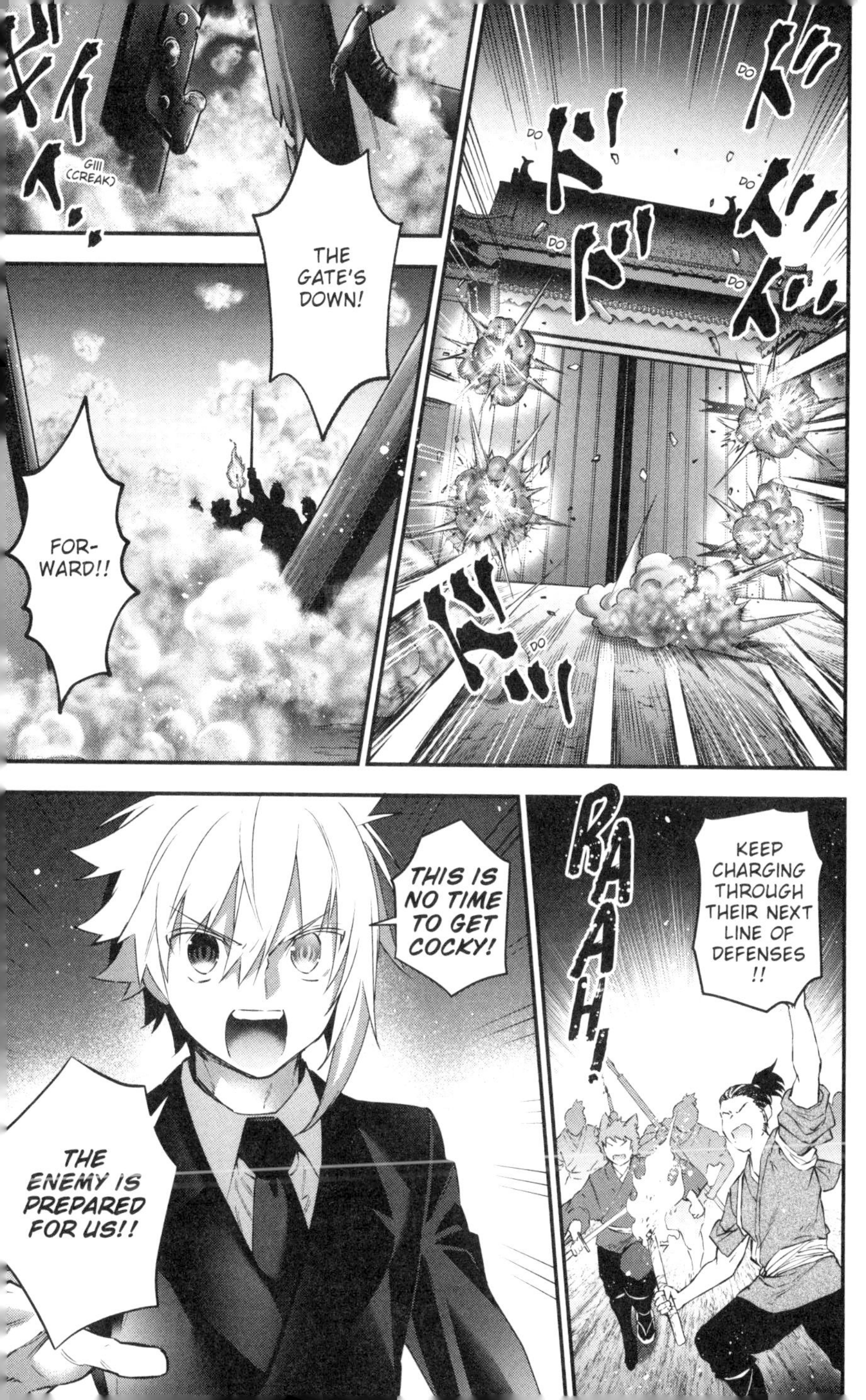
DO
DO
DO
DO
DO
DO
GIII (CREAK)
THE GATE'S DOWN!
FOR-WARD!!
KEEP CHARGING THROUGH THEIR NEXT LINE OF DEFENSES!!
RAAH!
THIS IS NO TIME TO GET COCKY!
THE ENEMY IS PREPARED FOR US!!

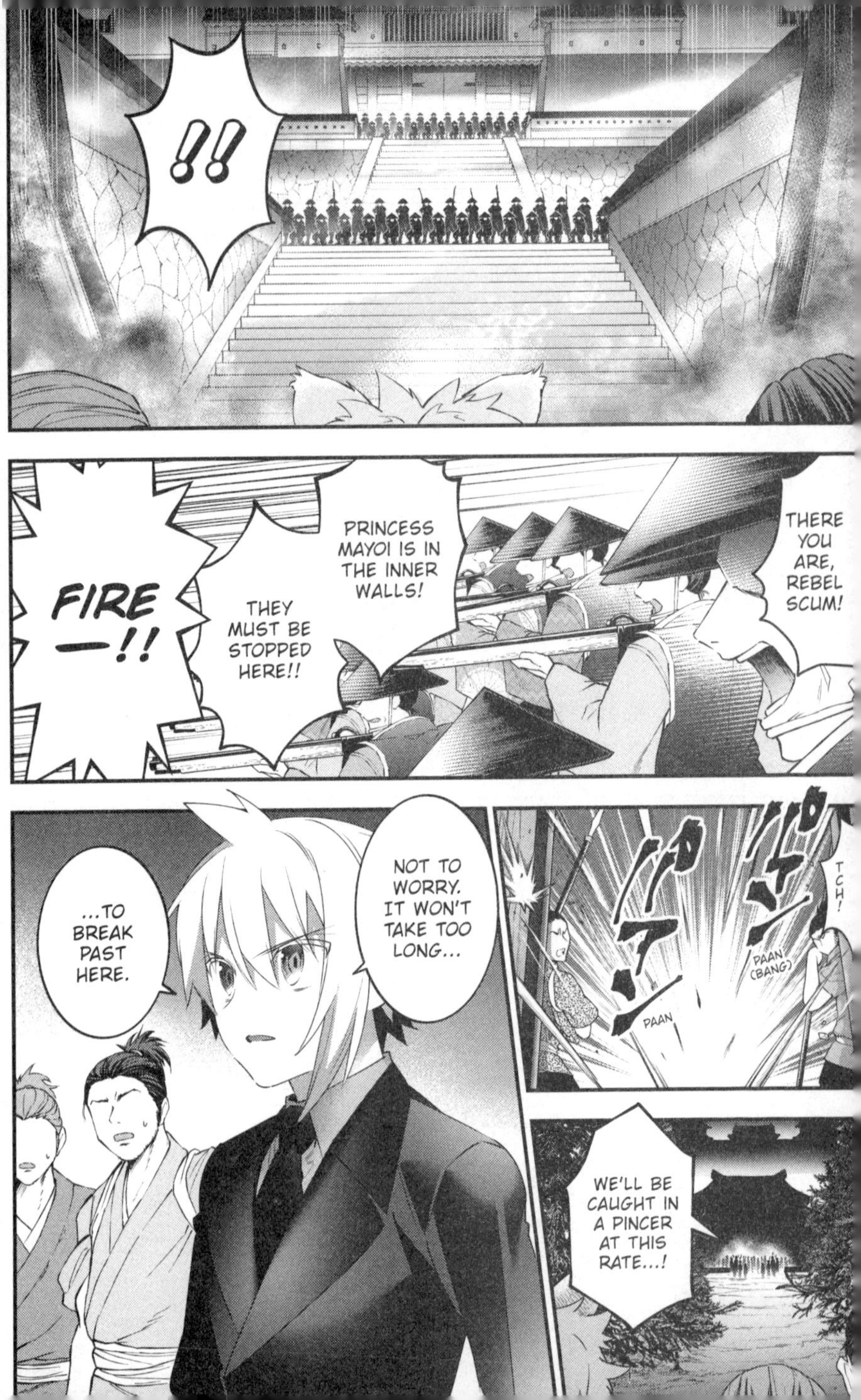
!!
THERE YOU ARE, REBEL SCUM!
PRINCESS MAYOI IS IN THE INNER WALLS!
THEY MUST BE STOPPED HERE!!
FIRE—!!
TCH!
PAAN (BANG)
PAAN
WE'LL BE CAUGHT IN A PINCER AT THIS RATE...!
NOT TO WORRY. IT WON'T TAKE TOO LONG...
...TO BREAK PAST HERE.

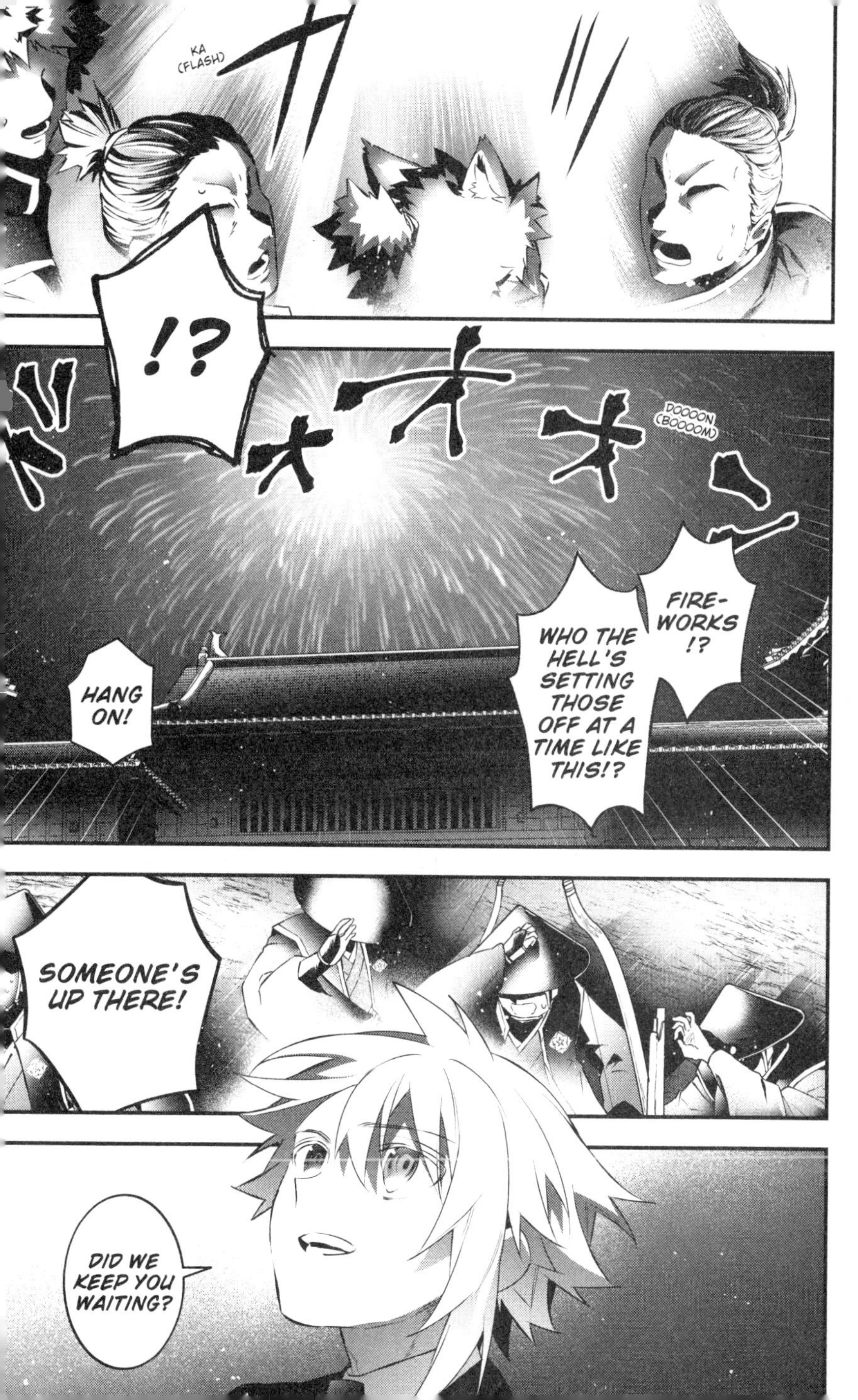
KA (FLASH)
!?
DOOOON (BOOOOM)
FIRE-WORKS!?
WHO THE HELL'S SETTING THOSE OFF AT A TIME LIKE THIS!?
HANG ON!
SOMEONE'S UP THERE!
DID WE KEEP YOU WAITING?

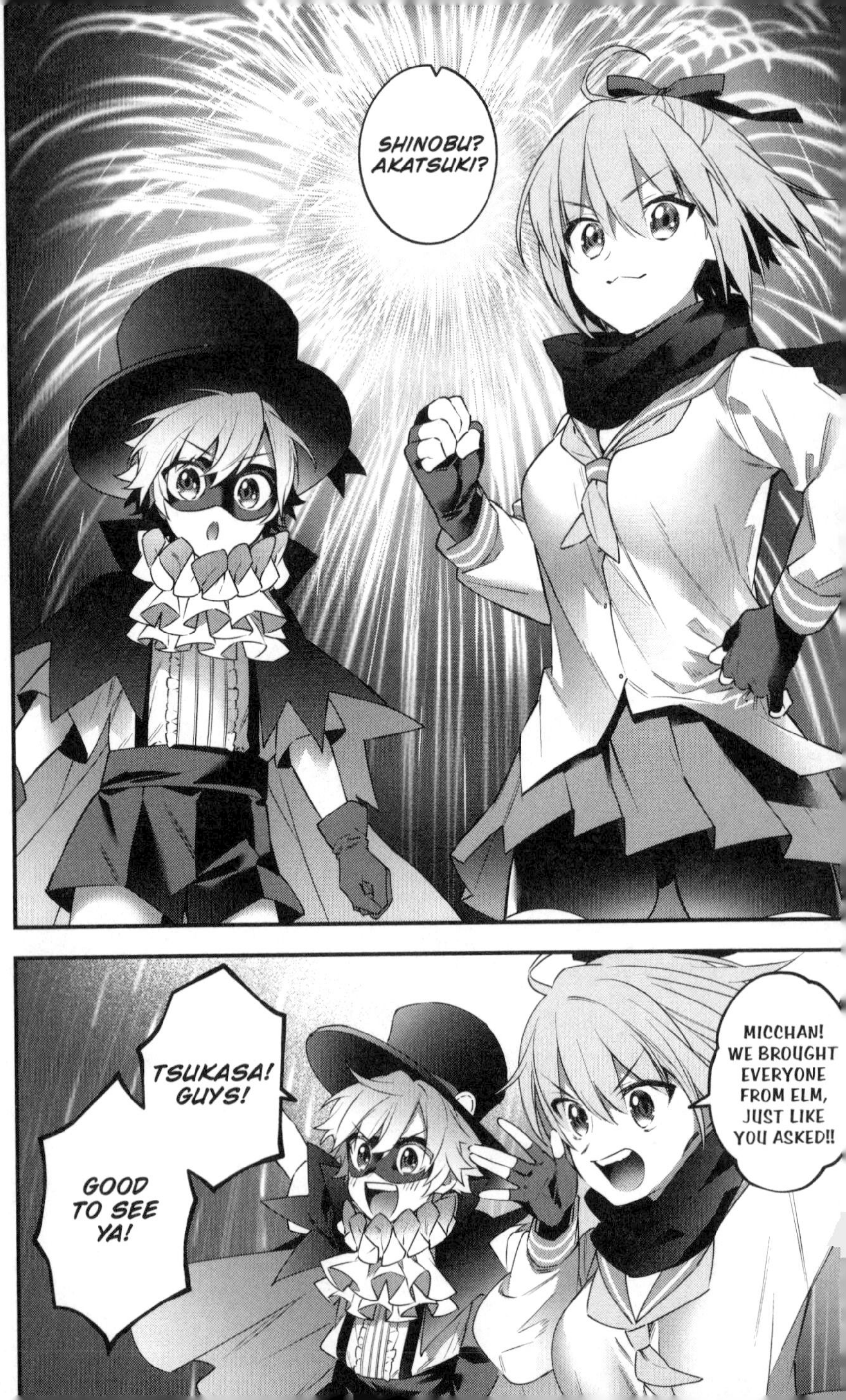
SHINOBU? AKATSUKI?
MICCHAN! WE BROUGHT EVERYONE FROM ELM, JUST LIKE YOU ASKED!!
TSUKASA! GUYS!
GOOD TO SEE YA!

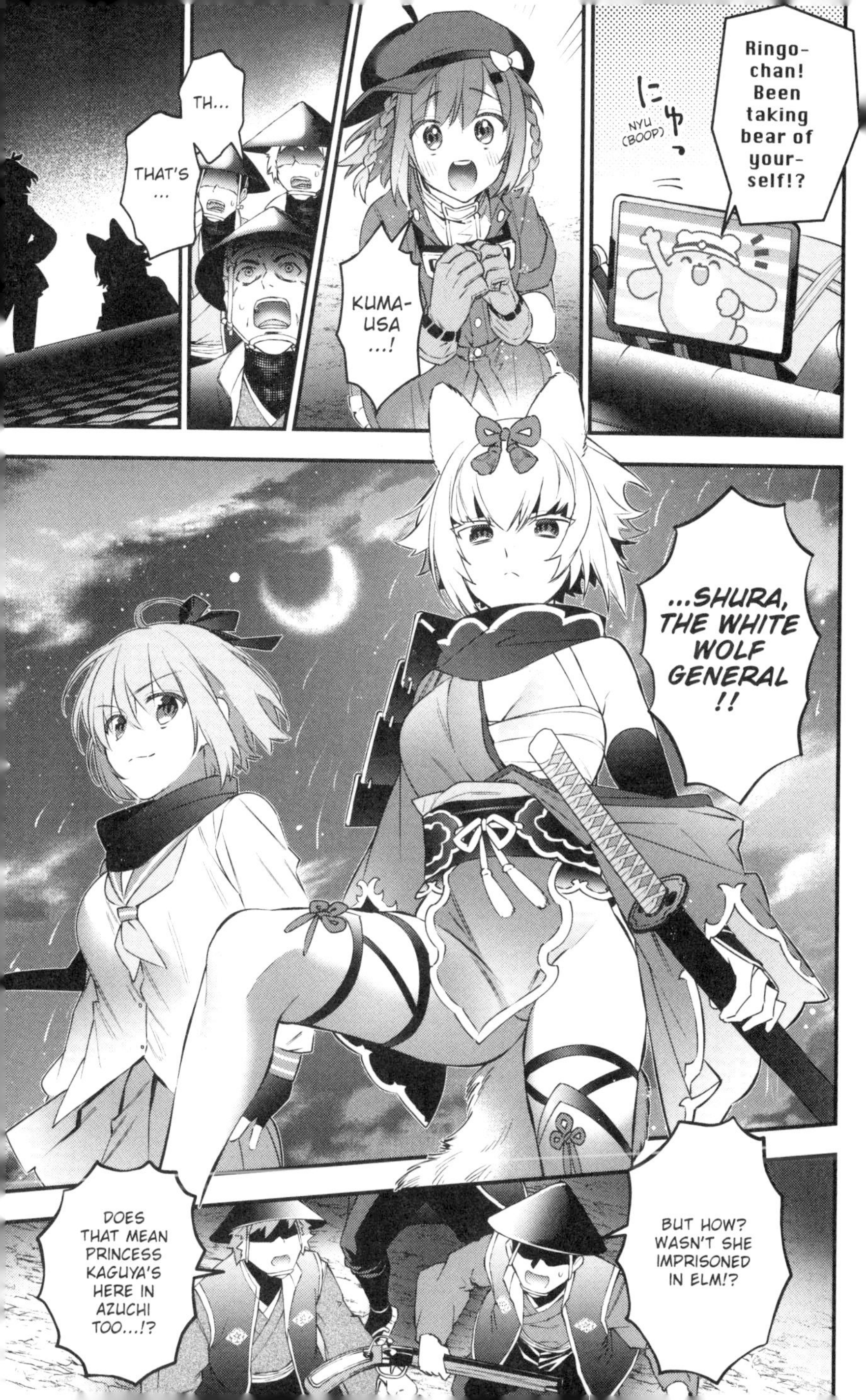
Ringo-chan! Been taking bear of your-self!?
にゅっ
NYU (BOOP)
KUMA-USA ...!
TH...
THAT'S ...
...SHURA, THE WHITE WOLF GENERAL !!
BUT HOW? WASN'T SHE IMPRISONED IN ELM!?
DOES THAT MEAN PRINCESS KAGUYA'S HERE IN AZUCHI TOO...!?

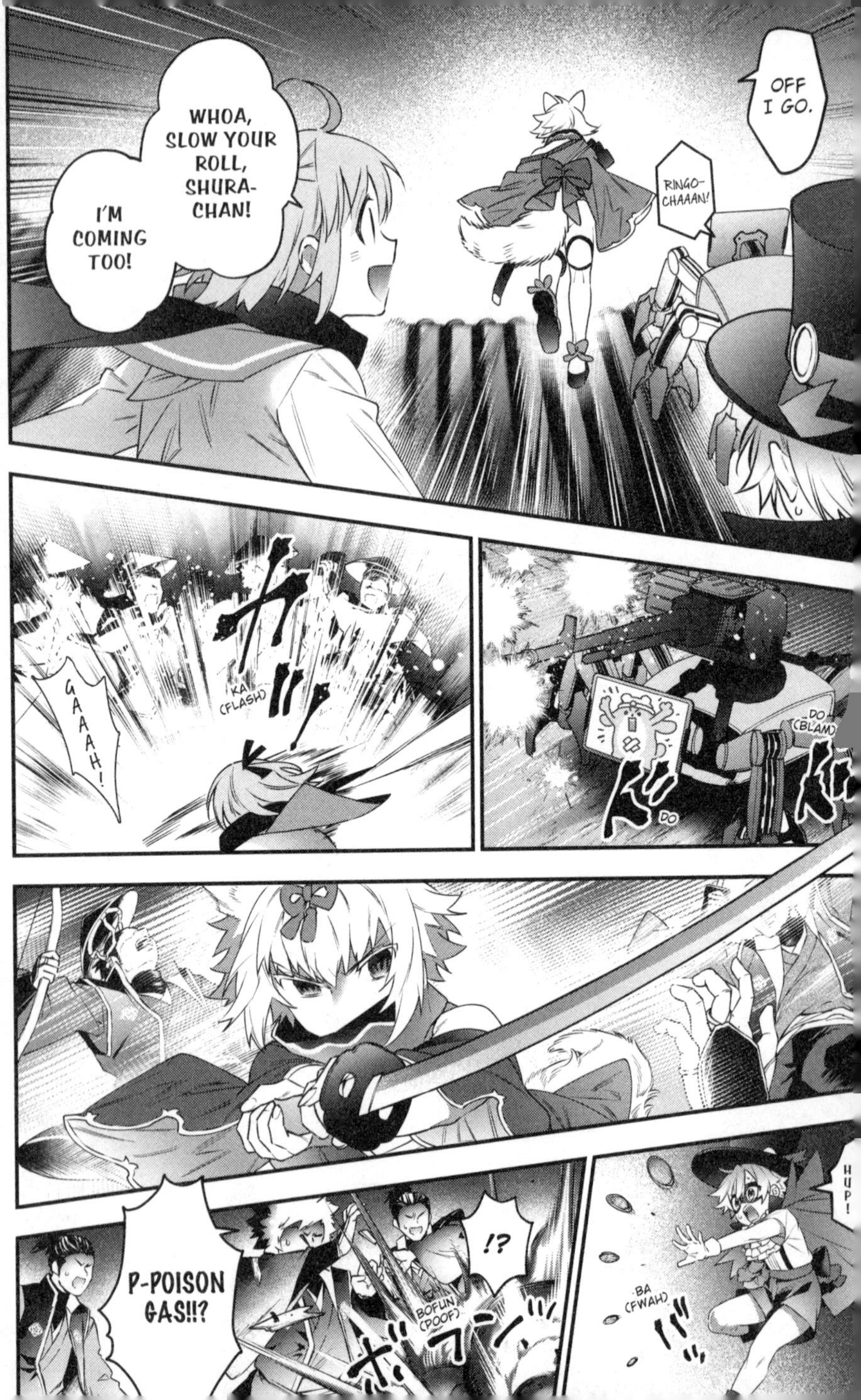
OFF I GO.
RINGO-CHAAAN!
WHOA, SLOW YOUR ROLL, SHURA-CHAN!
I'M COMING TOO!
DO (BLAM)
DO
KA (FLASH)
GAAAAH!
HUP!
BA (FWAH)
!?
BOFUN (POOF)
P-POISON GAS!!?

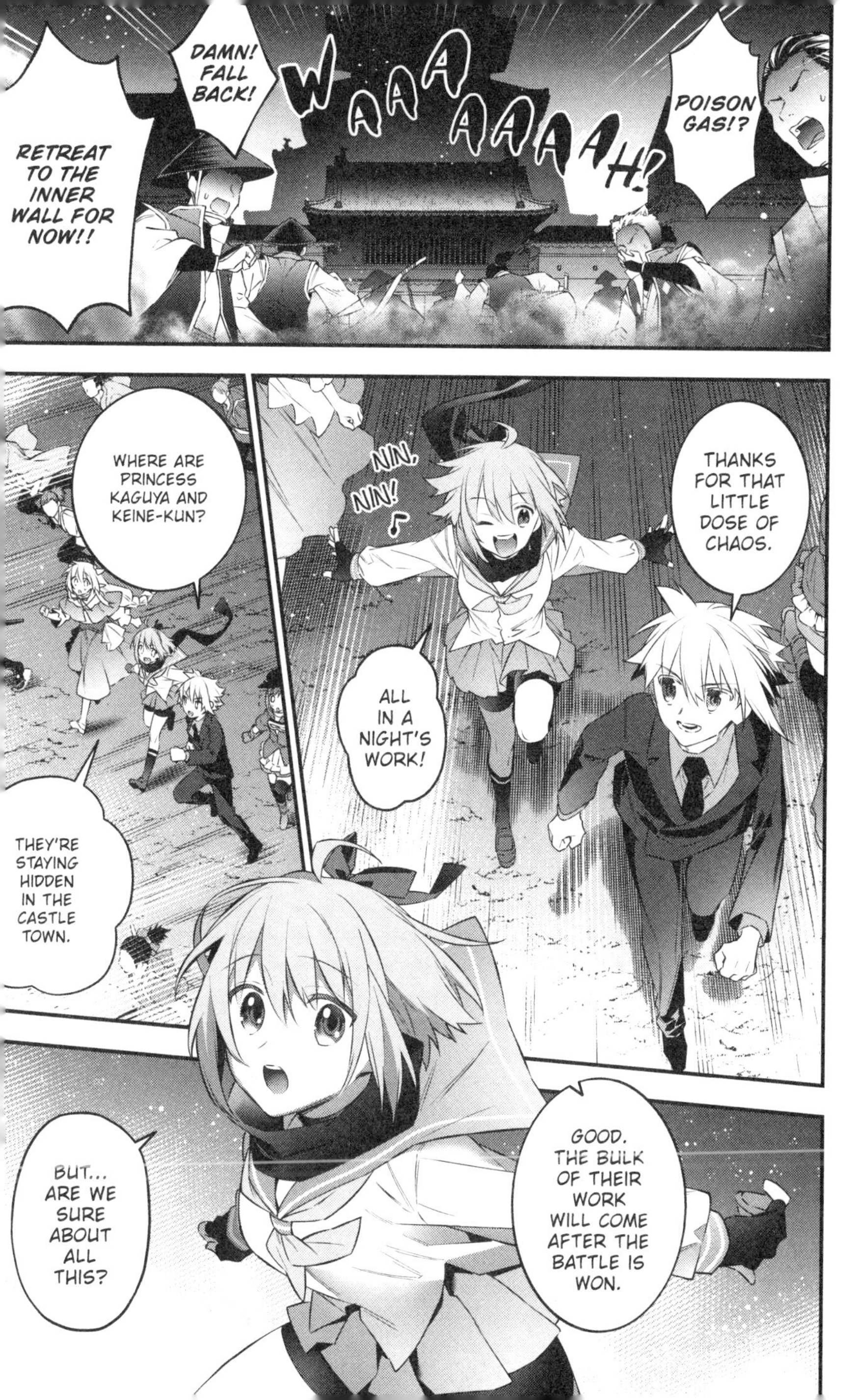

POISON GAS!?
WAAAAAAAAH!
DAMN! FALL BACK!
RETREAT TO THE INNER WALL FOR NOW!!
THANKS FOR THAT LITTLE DOSE OF CHAOS.
NIN, NIN! ♪
ALL IN A NIGHT'S WORK!
WHERE ARE PRINCESS KAGUYA AND KEINE-KUN?
THEY'RE STAYING HIDDEN IN THE CASTLE TOWN.
GOOD. THE BULK OF THEIR WORK WILL COME AFTER THE BATTLE IS WON.
BUT... ARE WE SURE ABOUT ALL THIS?

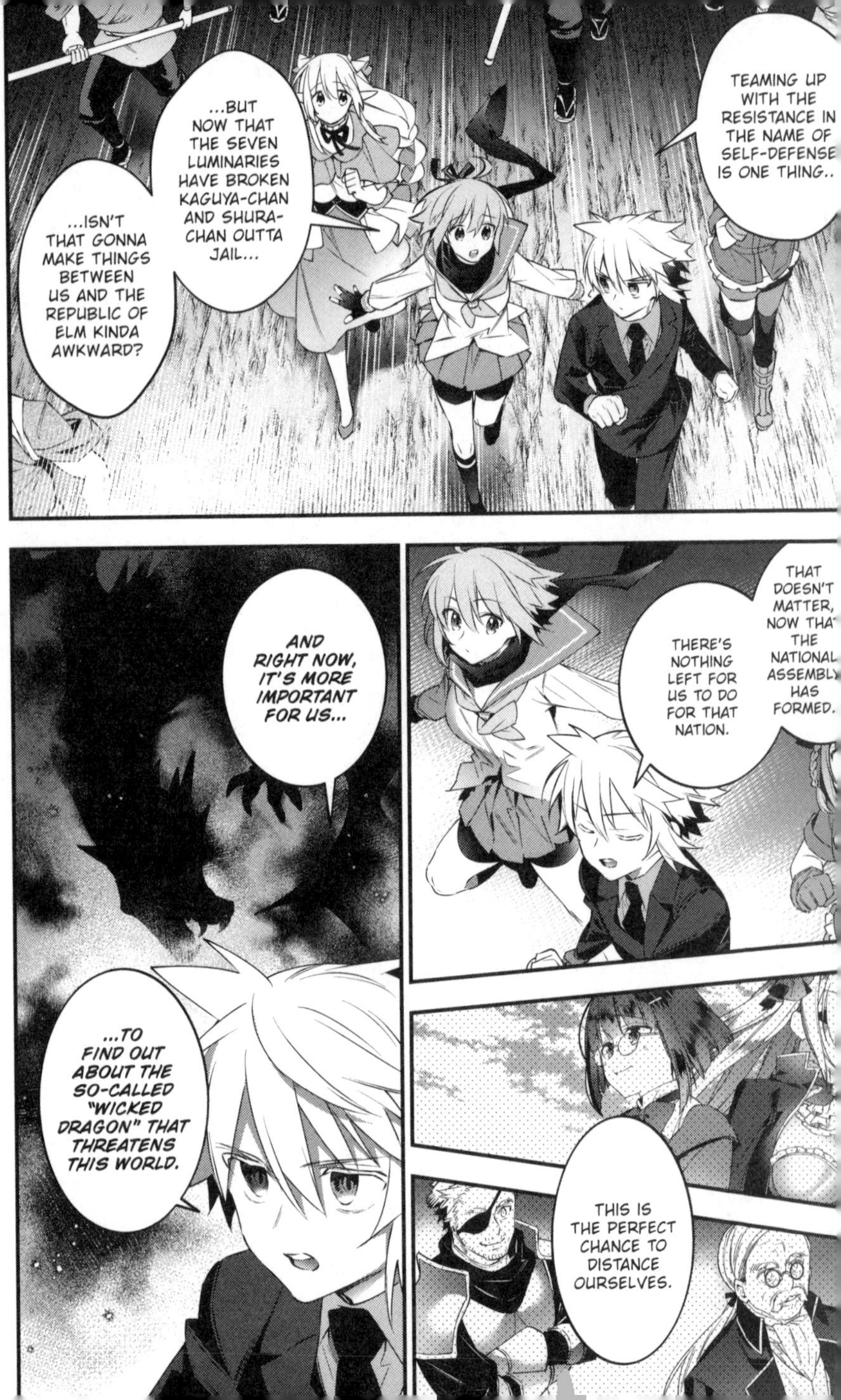
TEAMING UP WITH THE RESISTANCE IN THE NAME OF SELF-DEFENSE IS ONE THING..
...BUT NOW THAT THE SEVEN LUMINARIES HAVE BROKEN KAGUYA-CHAN AND SHURA-CHAN OUTTA JAIL...
...ISN'T THAT GONNA MAKE THINGS BETWEEN US AND THE REPUBLIC OF ELM KINDA AWKWARD?
THAT DOESN'T MATTER, NOW THAT THE NATIONAL ASSEMBLY HAS FORMED.
THERE'S NOTHING LEFT FOR US TO DO FOR THAT NATION.
THIS IS THE PERFECT CHANCE TO DISTANCE OURSELVES.
AND RIGHT NOW, IT'S MORE IMPORTANT FOR US...
...TO FIND OUT ABOUT THE SO-CALLED "WICKED DRAGON" THAT THREATENS THIS WORLD.

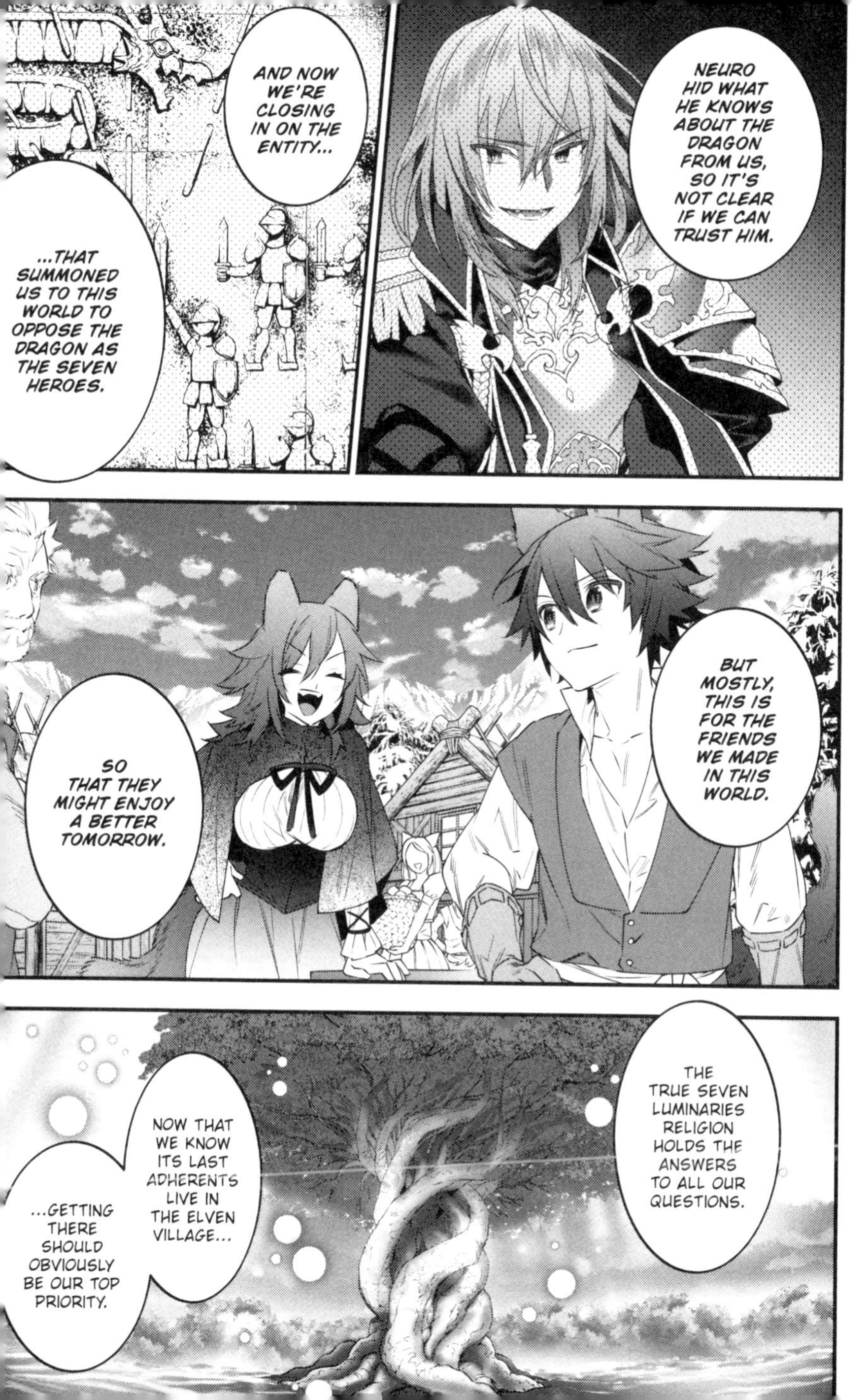
NEURO HID WHAT HE KNOWS ABOUT THE DRAGON FROM US, SO IT'S NOT CLEAR IF WE CAN TRUST HIM.
AND NOW WE'RE CLOSING IN ON THE ENTITY...
...THAT SUMMONED US TO THIS WORLD TO OPPOSE THE DRAGON AS THE SEVEN HEROES.
BUT MOSTLY, THIS IS FOR THE FRIENDS WE MADE IN THIS WORLD.
SO THAT THEY MIGHT ENJOY A BETTER TOMORROW.
THE TRUE SEVEN LUMINARIES RELIGION HOLDS THE ANSWERS TO ALL OUR QUESTIONS.
NOW THAT WE KNOW ITS LAST ADHERENTS LIVE IN THE ELVEN VILLAGE...
...GETTING THERE SHOULD OBVIOUSLY BE OUR TOP PRIORITY.

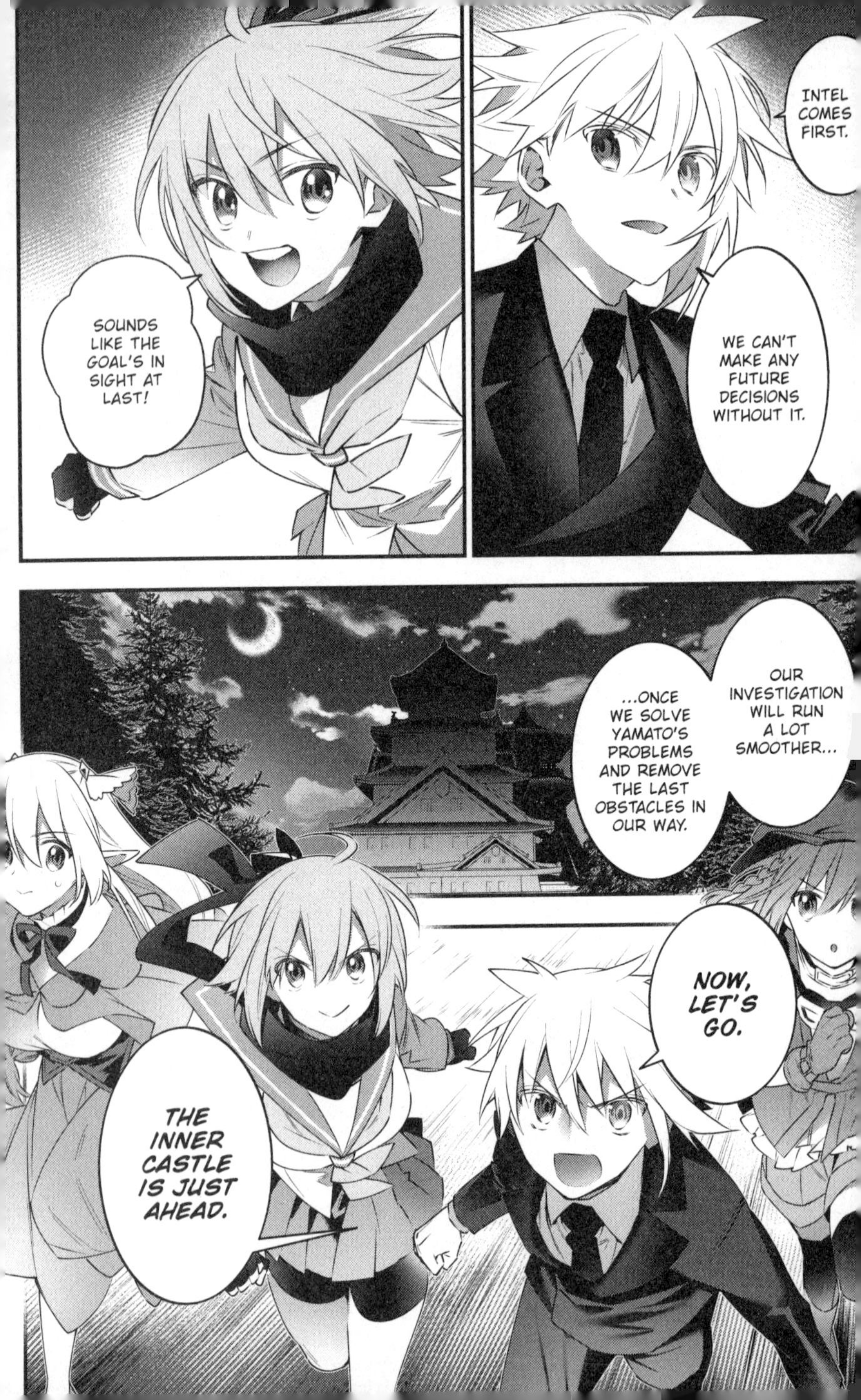
INTEL COMES FIRST.
WE CAN'T MAKE ANY FUTURE DECISIONS WITHOUT IT.
SOUNDS LIKE THE GOAL'S IN SIGHT AT LAST!
OUR INVESTIGATION WILL RUN A LOT SMOOTHER...
...ONCE WE SOLVE YAMATO'S PROBLEMS AND REMOVE THE LAST OBSTACLES IN OUR WAY.
NOW, LET'S GO.
THE INNER CASTLE IS JUST AHEAD.

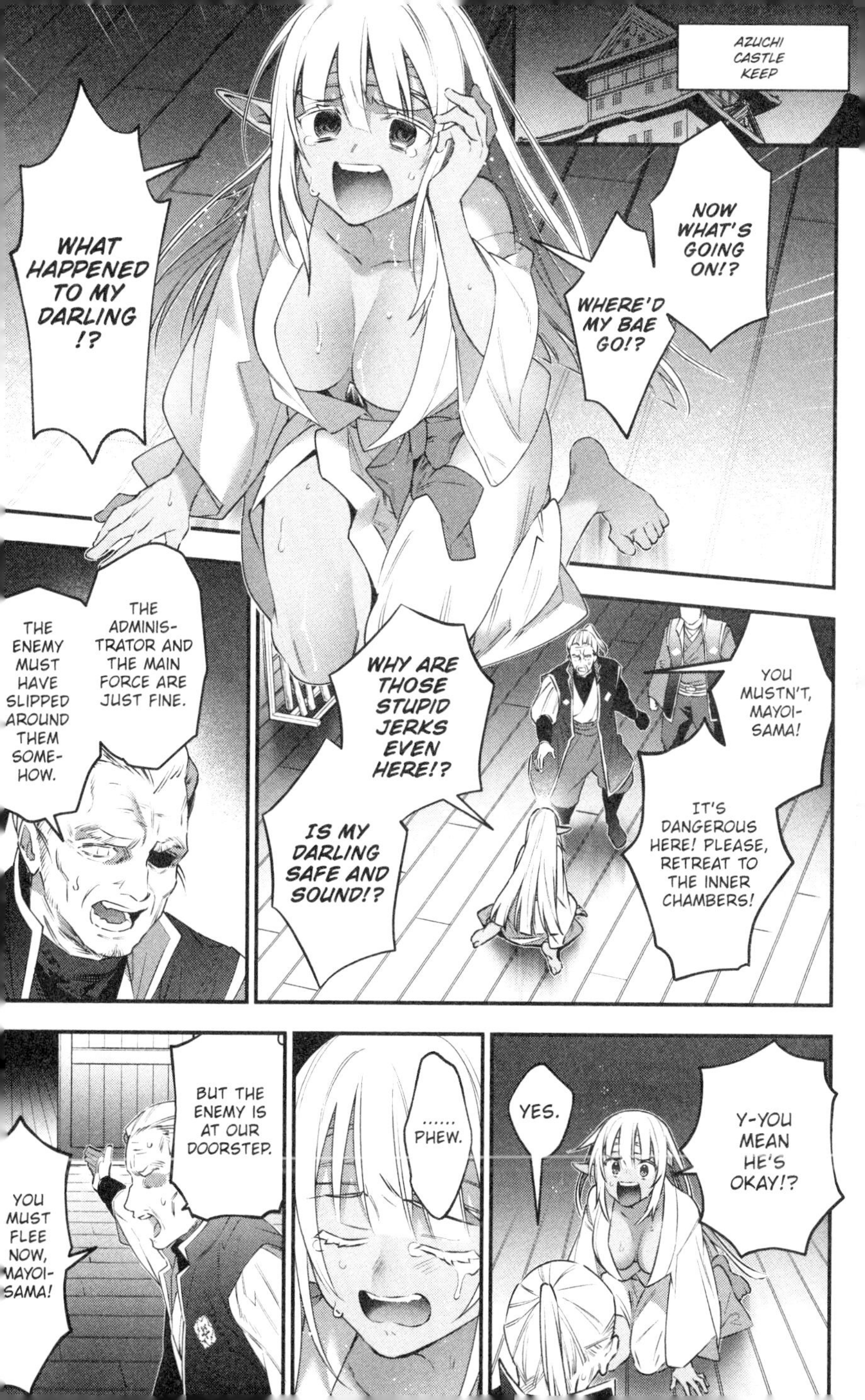
AZUCHI CASTLE KEEP
NOW WHAT'S GOING ON!?
WHERE'D MY BAE GO!?
WHAT HAPPENED TO MY DARLING!?
YOU MUSTN'T, MAYOI-SAMA!
IT'S DANGEROUS HERE! PLEASE, RETREAT TO THE INNER CHAMBERS!
WHY ARE THOSE STUPID JERKS EVEN HERE!?
IS MY DARLING SAFE AND SOUND!?
THE ADMINISTRATOR AND THE MAIN FORCE ARE JUST FINE.
THE ENEMY MUST HAVE SLIPPED AROUND THEM SOMEHOW.
Y-YOU MEAN HE'S OKAY!?
YES.
......PHEW.
BUT THE ENEMY IS AT OUR DOORSTEP.
YOU MUST FLEE NOW, MAYOI-SAMA!

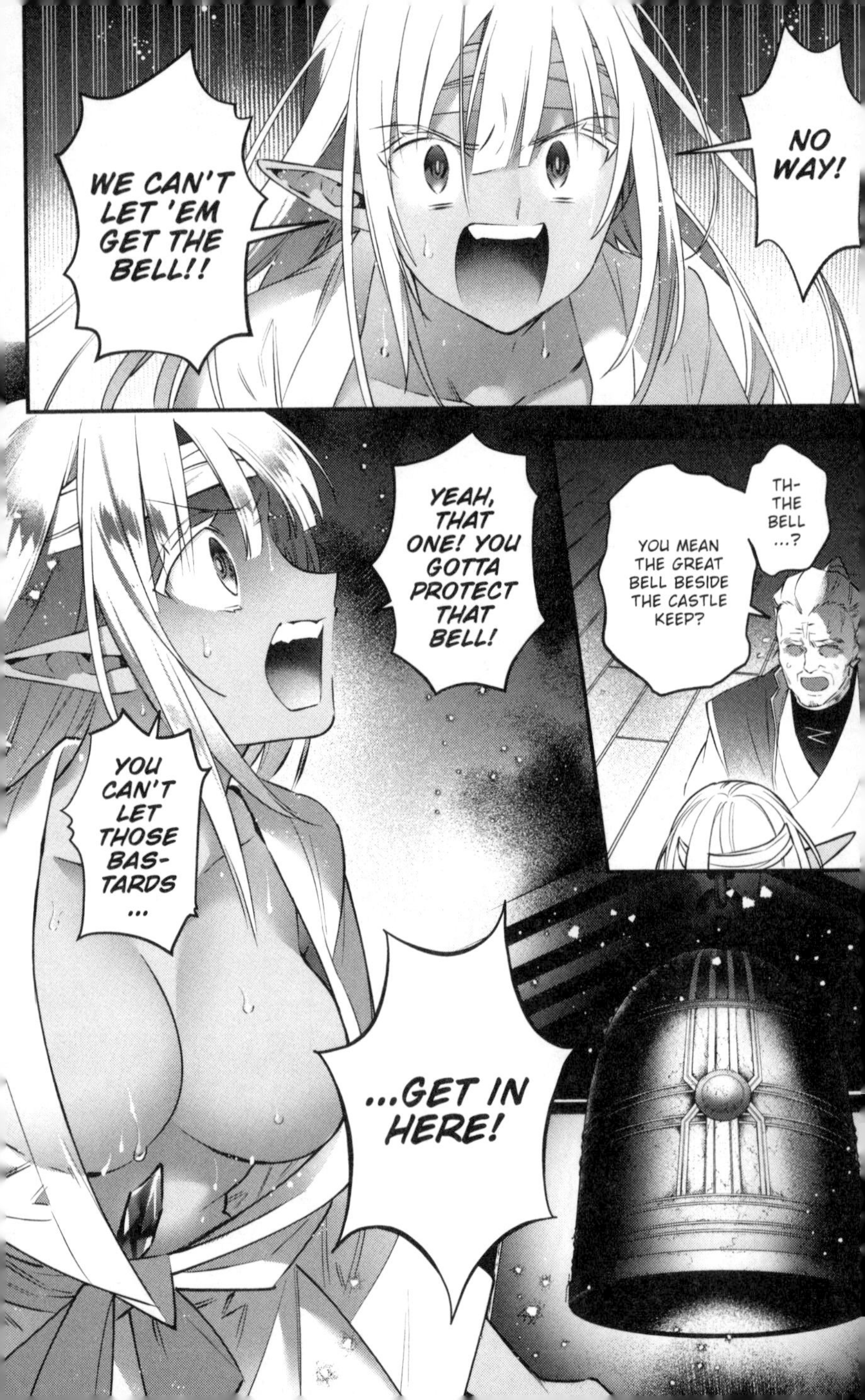
NO WAY!
WE CAN'T LET 'EM GET THE BELL!!
TH-THE BELL ...?
YOU MEAN THE GREAT BELL BESIDE THE CASTLE KEEP?
YEAH, THAT ONE! YOU GOTTA PROTECT THAT BELL!
YOU CAN'T LET THOSE BAS-TARDS ...
...GET IN HERE!

TRANSLATION NOTES

COMMON HONORIFICS

no honorific: Indicates familiarity or closeness; if used without permission or reason, addressing someone in this manner would constitute an insult.

-san: The Japanese equivalent of Mr./Mrs./Miss. If a situation calls for politeness, this is the fail-safe honorific.

-sama: Conveys great respect; may also indicate that the social status of the speaker is lower than the addressee's.

-kun: Used most often when referring to boys, this indicates affection or familiarity. Occasionally used by older men among their peers, but it may also be used by anyone referring to a person of lower standing.

-sensei: A respectful term for teachers, artists, or high-level professionals.

-dono: A respectful term typically equated with "lord" or "master," this honorific has an archaic spin to it when used in colloquial parlance.

Page 128
In Japanese, kanji are sometimes accompanied with text in small print off to the side known as *furigana*, which usually functions as a pronunciation guide for uncommon characters but can also be used to lend an alternative meaning to a term. In this case, the *furigana* for *kesshitai* ("**suicide squad**") reads *suteishi*, meaning "sacrificial stones." In a game of Go, these are pieces that a player allows their opponent to capture in order to gain an even greater number in exchange, similar to "sacrifice pawns" in chess. Interestingly, when members of the Freyjagard Empire later refer to them as "pawns" on pages 133 and 138, they use the actual Japanese term for "sacrifice pawns" in chess, *sutegoma*. While that term is also used in *shogi*, a Japanese game quite similar to chess, there does seem to be some subtext when Yamato, a clear analogue for Japan, uses a Go term while the Western-inspired Freyjagard Empire favors a chess term instead.

Page 157
The **next line of defenses** is referred to in the original Japanese as the *ni no maru* (the "second ring"), while the terms "inner wall" and "inner castle" on pages 163 and 166 are the *honmaru*, or "core"; the more technical translations for these terms are the "outer citadel" and "inner citadel." Japanese castles are typically divided into multiple sections, either through concentric walls or by building in a way that takes advantage of terrain so that invaders have no choice but to proceed through a particular route. This forces the enemy to break through multiple defensive barriers and allows the more important people and valuable resources within the *honmaru* to remain protected even if some of the outer sections are breached.

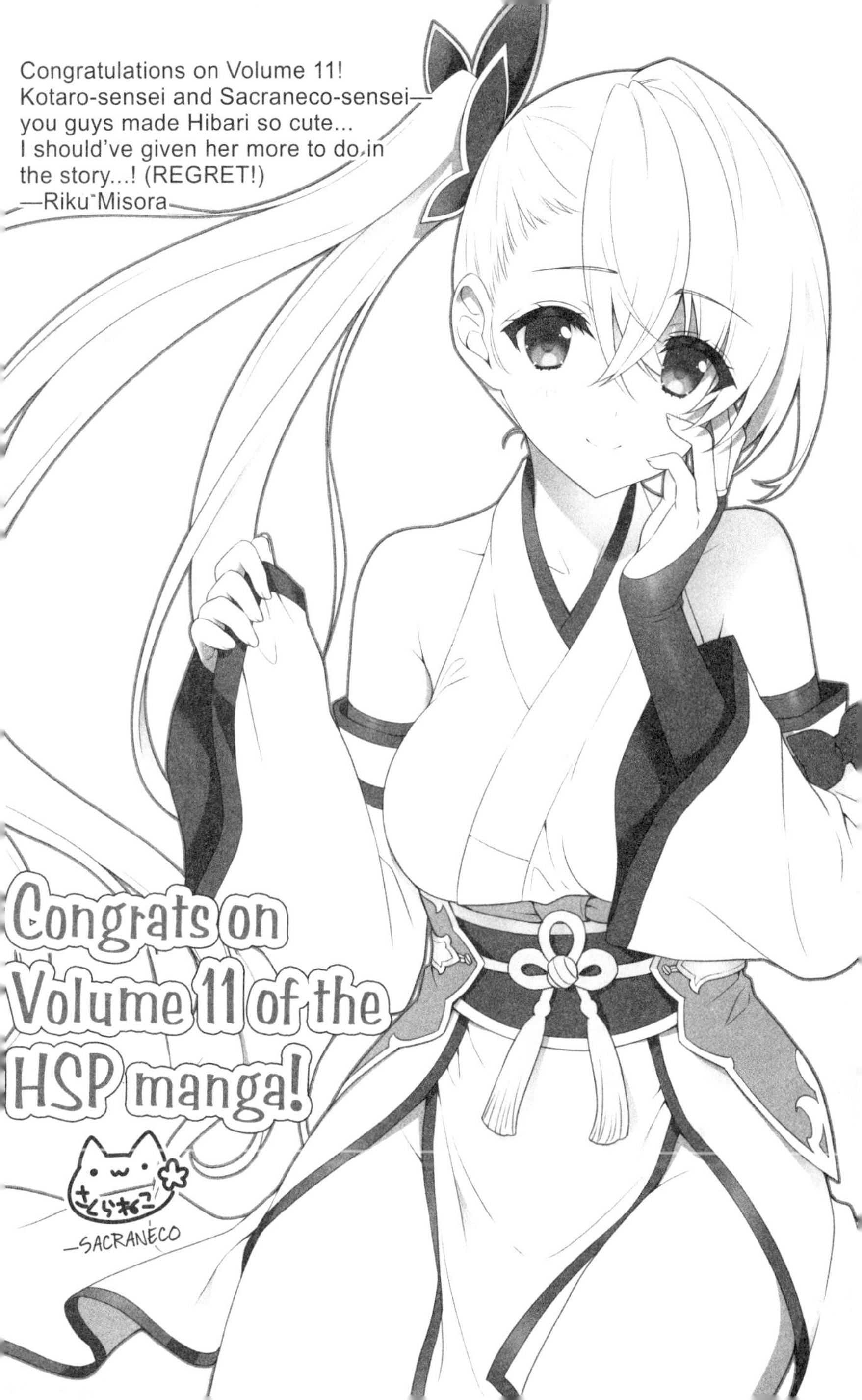
Congratulations on Volume 11!
Kotaro-sensei and Sacraneco-sensei—
you guys made Hibari so cute...
I should've given her more to do in
the story...! (REGRET!)
—Riku Misora
Congrats on Volume 11 of the HSP manga!
—SACRANECO

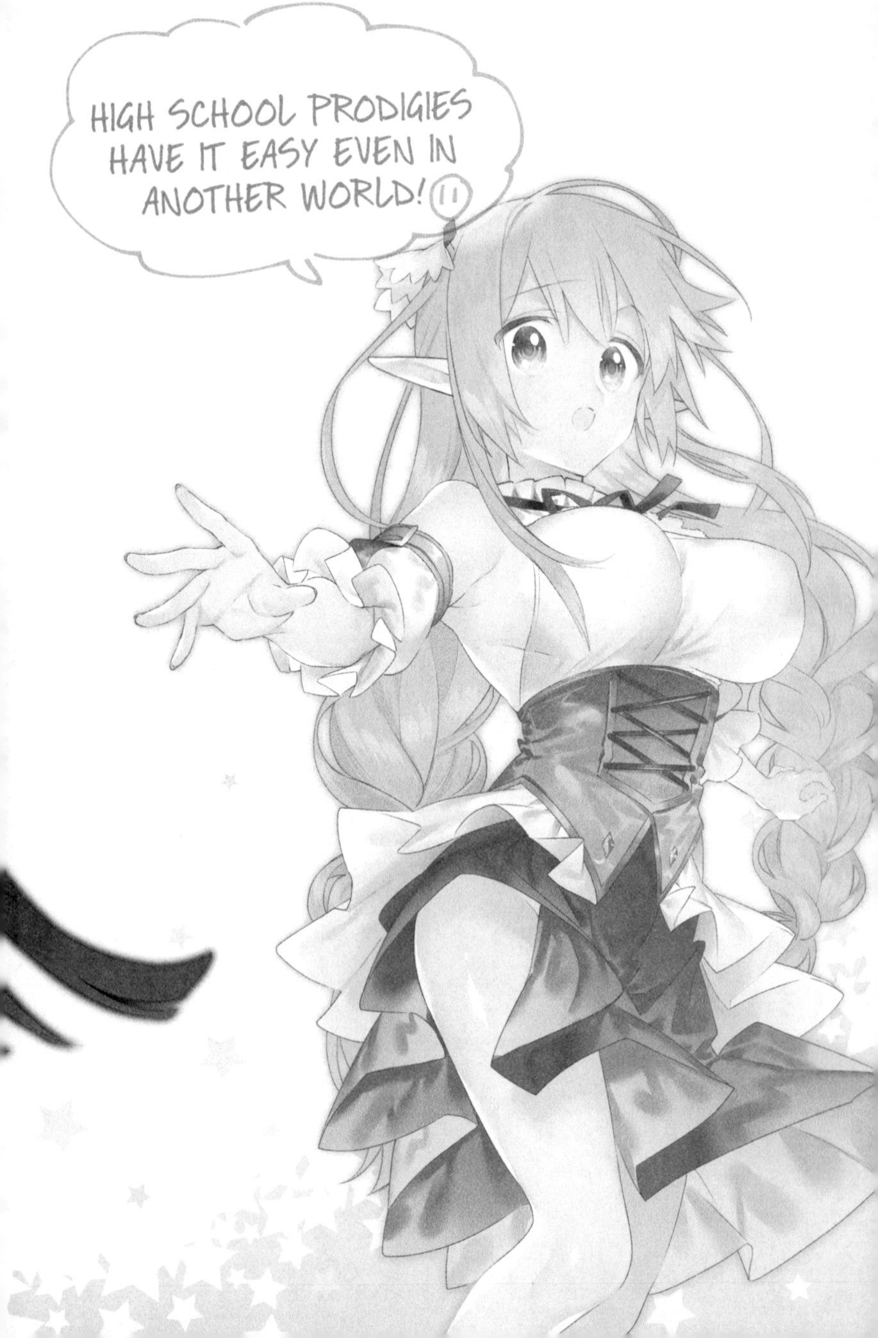
HIGH SCHOOL PRODIGIES HAVE IT EASY EVEN IN ANOTHER WORLD! 11

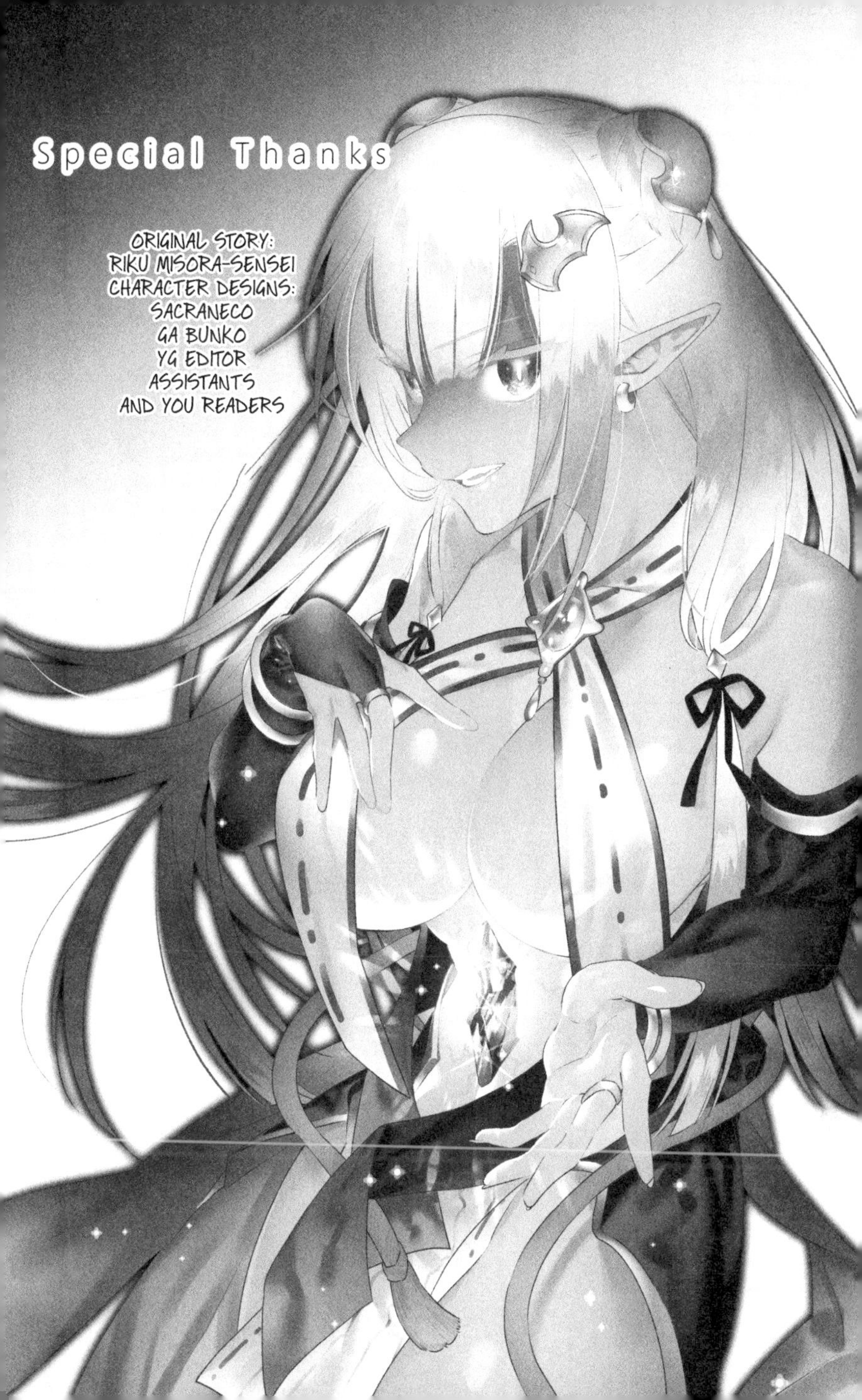
Special Thanks
ORIGINAL STORY:
RIKU MISORA-SENSEI
CHARACTER DESIGNS:
SACRANECO
GA BUNKO
YG EDITOR
ASSISTANTS
AND YOU READERS

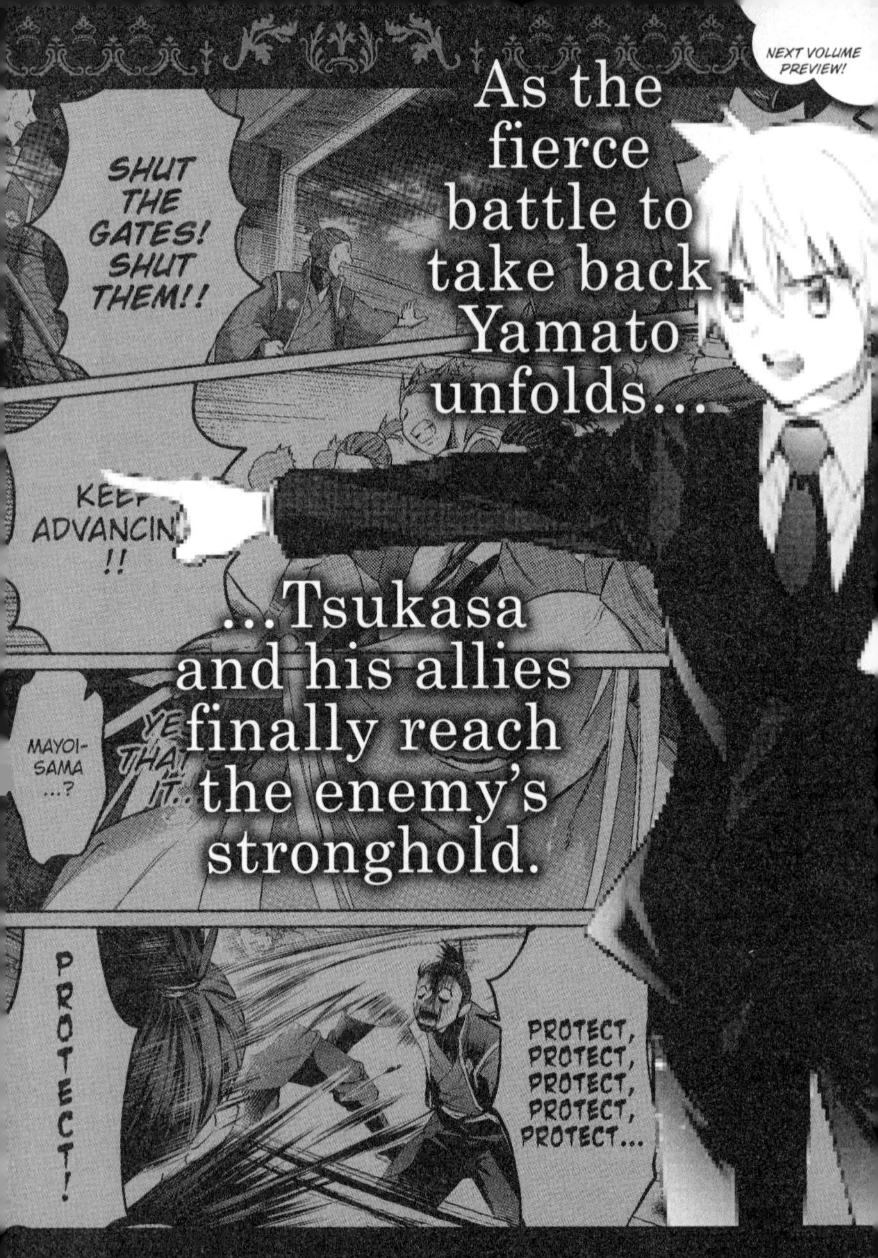
NEXT VOLUME PREVIEW!
As the fierce battle to take back Yamato unfolds...
SHUT THE GATES! SHUT THEM!!
KEEP ADVANCIN'!!
...Tsukasa and his allies finally reach the enemy's stronghold.
MAYOI-SAMA ...?
PROTECT, PROTECT, PROTECT, PROTECT, PROTECT...
PROTECT!

Volume 12 on sale in 2022!

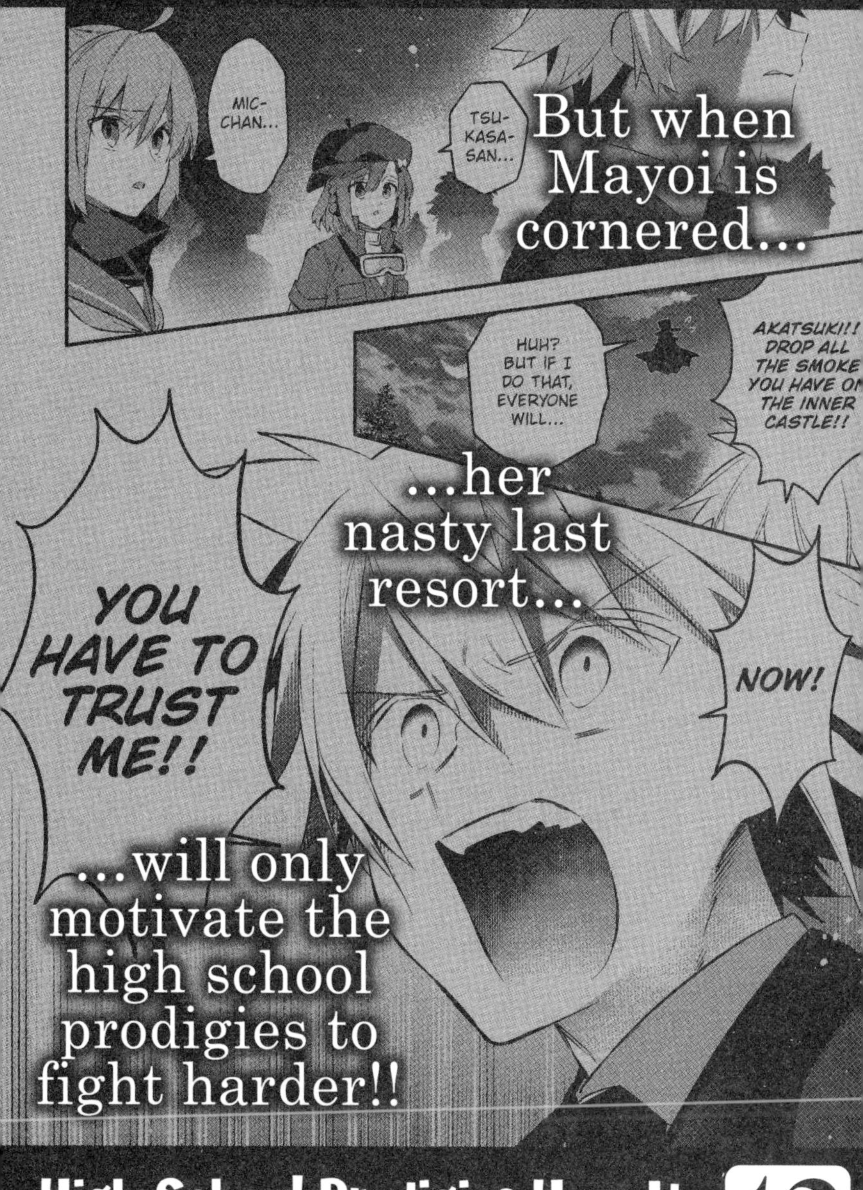
But when Mayoi is cornered...
TSU-KASA-SAN...
MIC-CHAN...
AKATSUKI!! DROP ALL THE SMOKE YOU HAVE ON THE INNER CASTLE!!
HUH? BUT IF I DO THAT, EVERYONE WILL...
...her nasty last resort...
NOW!
YOU HAVE TO TRUST ME!!
...will only motivate the high school prodigies to fight harder!!

High School Prodigies Have It Easy Even in Another World! 12

HE DOES NOT LET ANYONE ROLL THE DICE.

A young Priestess joins her first adventuring party, but blind to the dangers, they almost immediately find themselves in trouble. It's Goblin Slayer who comes to their rescue—a man who has dedicated his life to the extermination of all goblins by any means necessary. A dangerous, dirty, and thankless job, but he does it better than anyone. And when rumors of his feats begin to circulate, there's no telling who might come calling next...

Light Novel V. 1-12 Available Now!

Check out the simul-pub manga chapters every month!